# .hack 2

## //LEGEND OF THE TWILIGHT

MANGA: REI IZUMI



ORIGINAL CONCEPTS: TATSUYA HAMAZAK

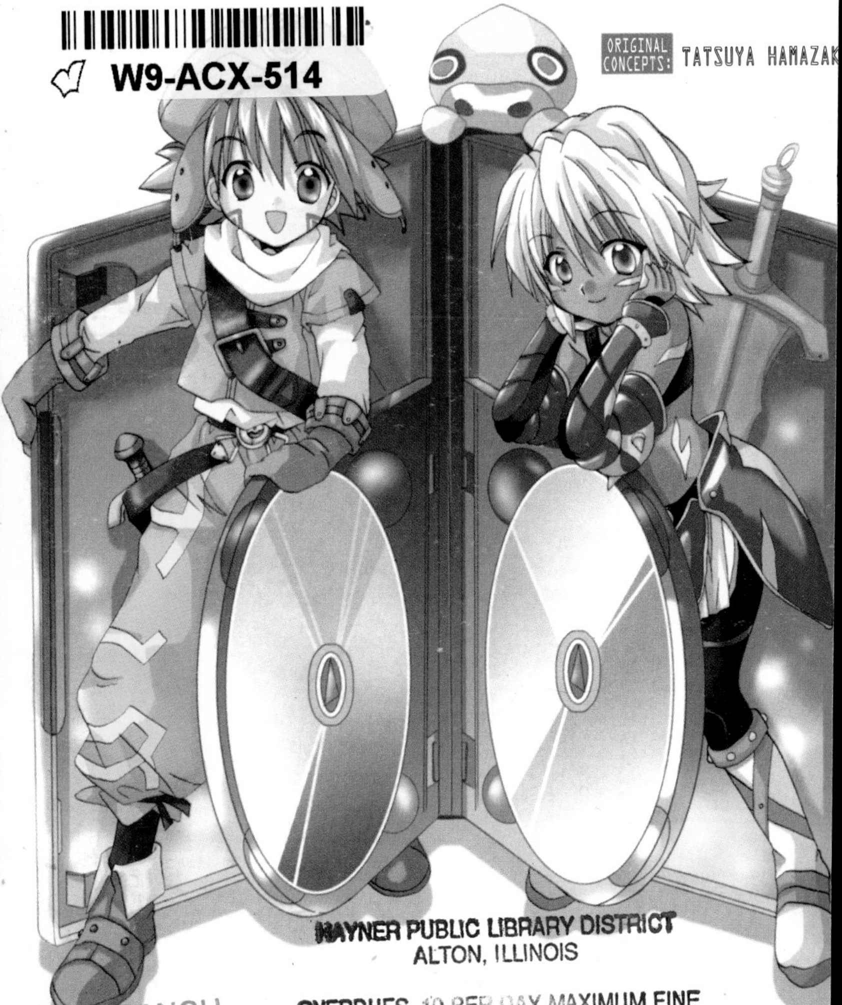

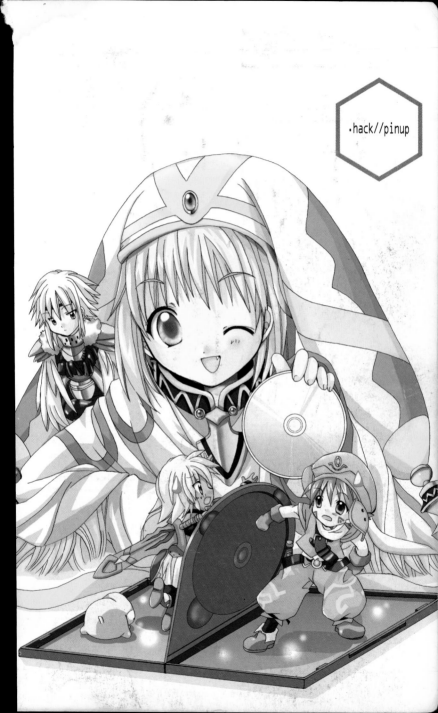

.hack//pinup

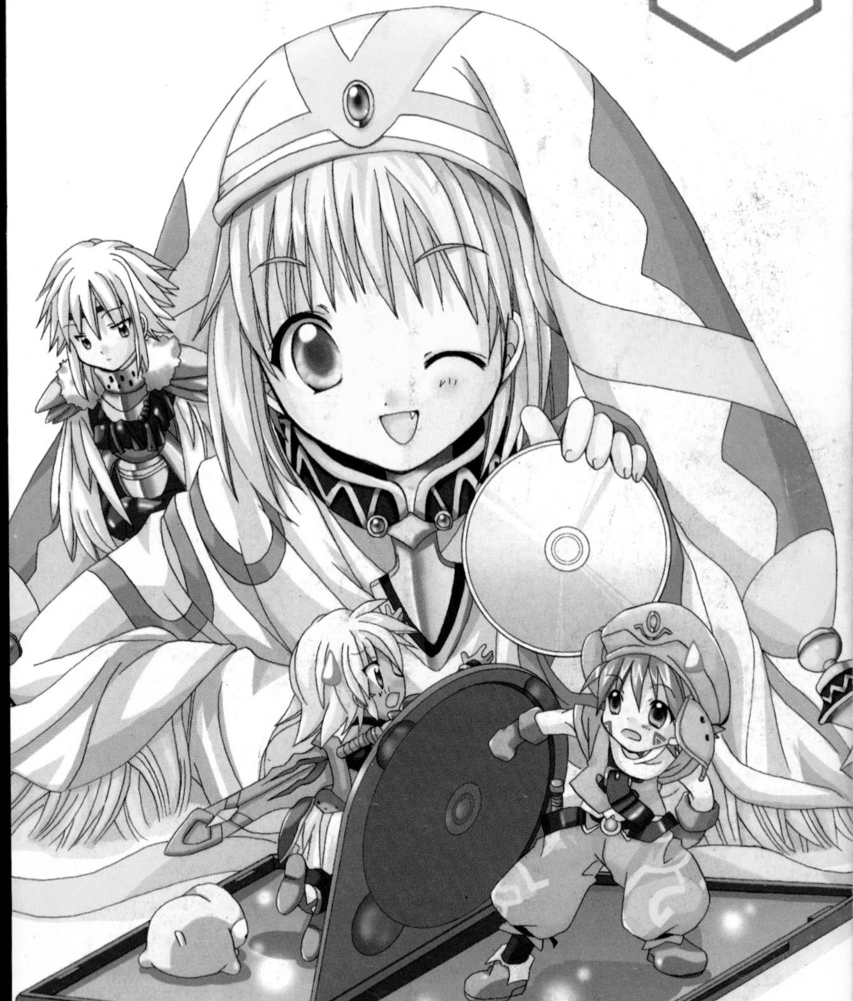

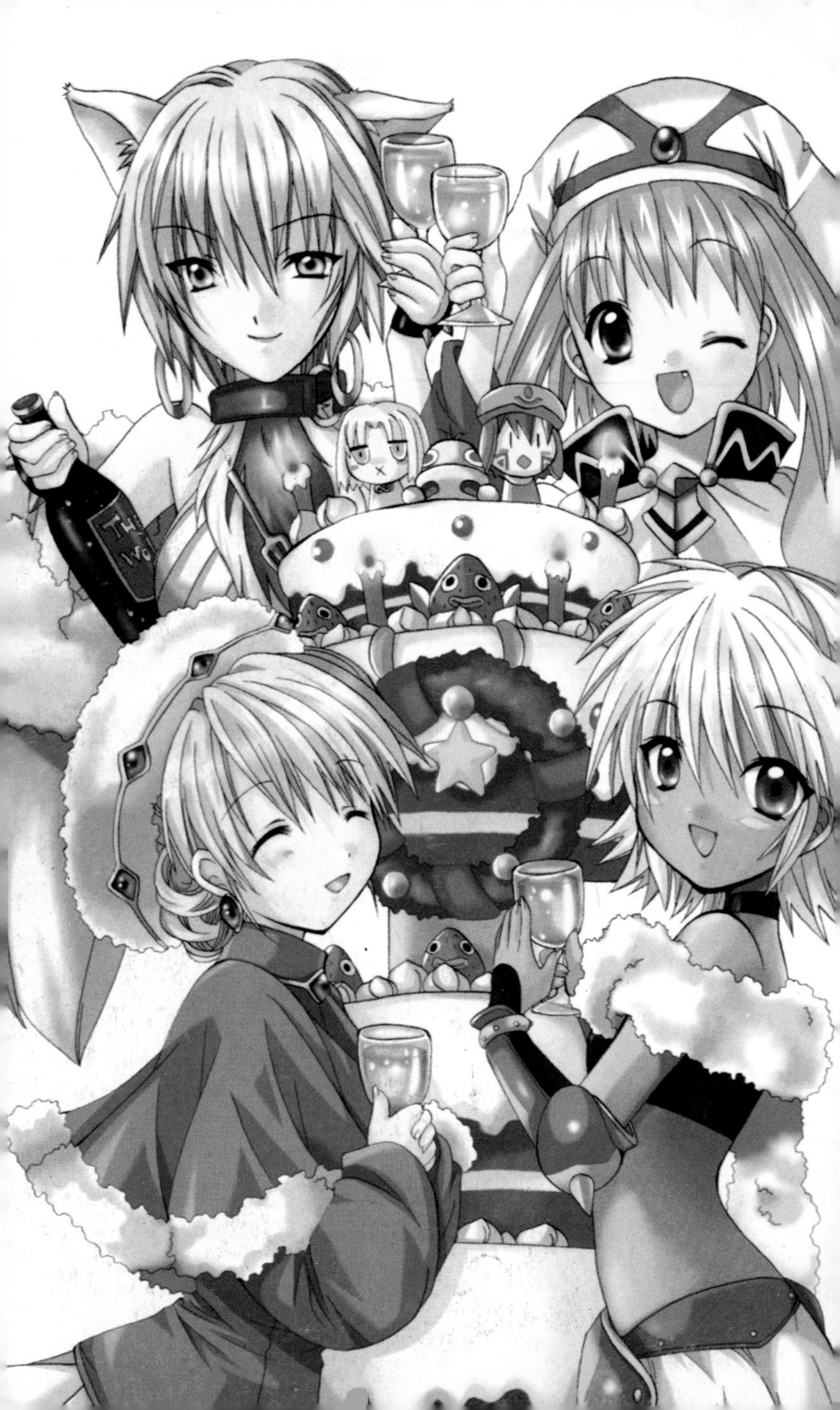

# .hack //TABLE OF CONTENTS

# .hack

## // LEGEND OF THE TWILIGHT

Art by Rei Izumi
Story by Tatsuya Hamazaki

Volume 2

Los Angeles • Tokyo • London

GN
F
I2U

6162319ZZ

Translator - Ben Dunn
Copy Editor - Carol Fox
Retouch & Lettering - Jose Macasocol, Jr.
Cover Layout - Aaron Suhr

Editor - Jake Forbes
Managing Editor - Jill Freshney
Production Coordinator - Antonio DePietro
Production Manager - Jennifer Miller
Art Director - Matt Alford
Editorial Director - Jeremy Ross
VP of Production - Ron Klamert
President & C.O.O. - John Parker
Publisher & C.E.O. - Stuart Levy

Email: editor@TOKYOPOP.com
Come visit us online at www.TOKYOPOP.com

A  TOKYOPOP® Manga

TOKYOPOP Inc.
5900 Wilshire Blvd. Suite 2000
Los Angeles, CA 90036

.hack//Legend of the Twilight Vol. 2 © Project .hack 2003.
First published in Japan in 2003 by KADOKAWA SHOTEN PUBLISHING CO.,
LTD., Tokyo. English translation rights arranged with KADOKAWA SHOTEN
PUBLISHING CO., LTD., Tokyo through TUTTLE-MORI AGENCY, INC., Tokyo.

English text copyright ©2003 TOKYOPOP Inc.

ISBN: 1-59182-415-X

First TOKYOPOP® printing: December 2003

10 9 8 7 6 5 4 3 2 1
Printed in the USA

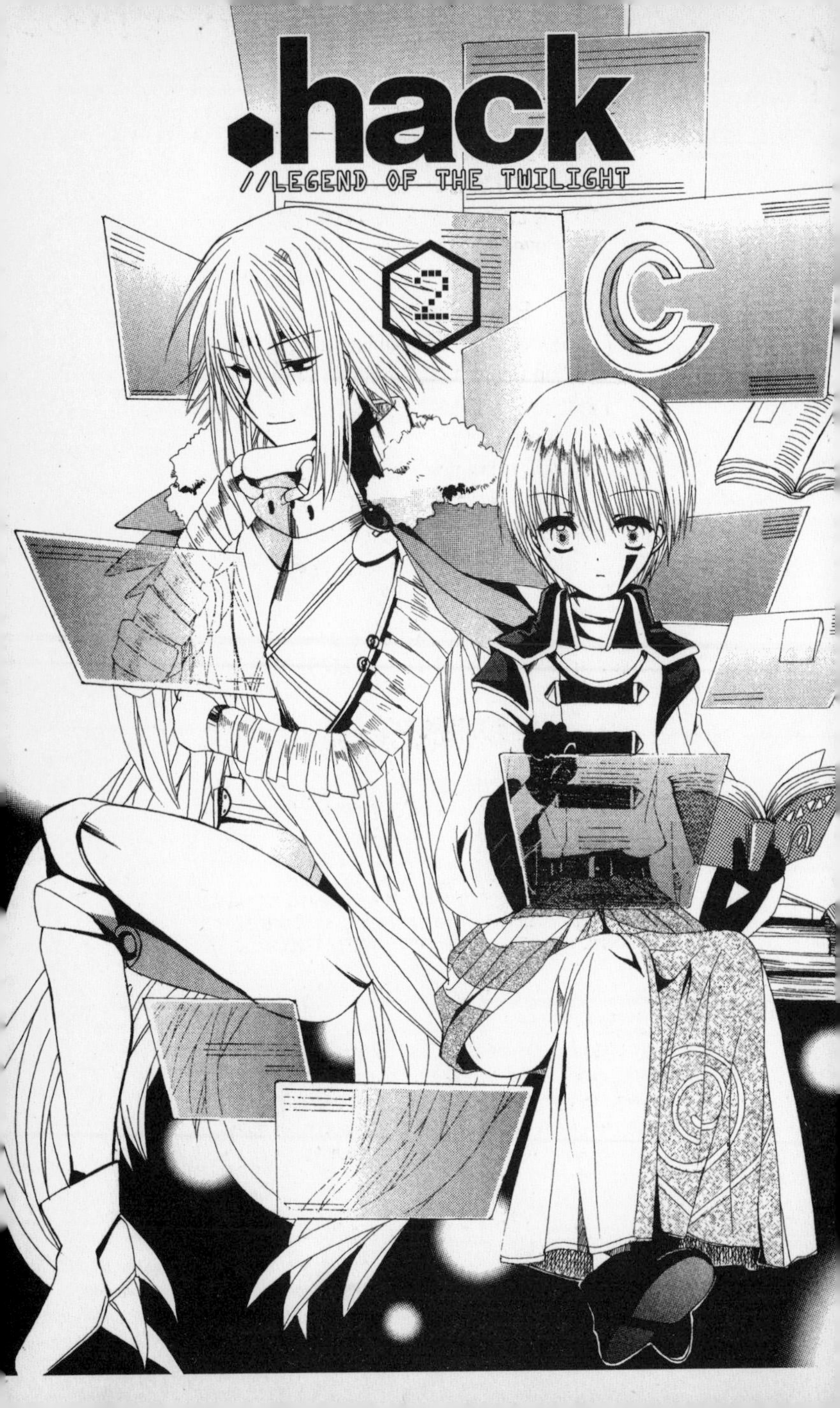
.hack
//LEGEND OF THE TWILIGHT
2

# キャラクター紹介

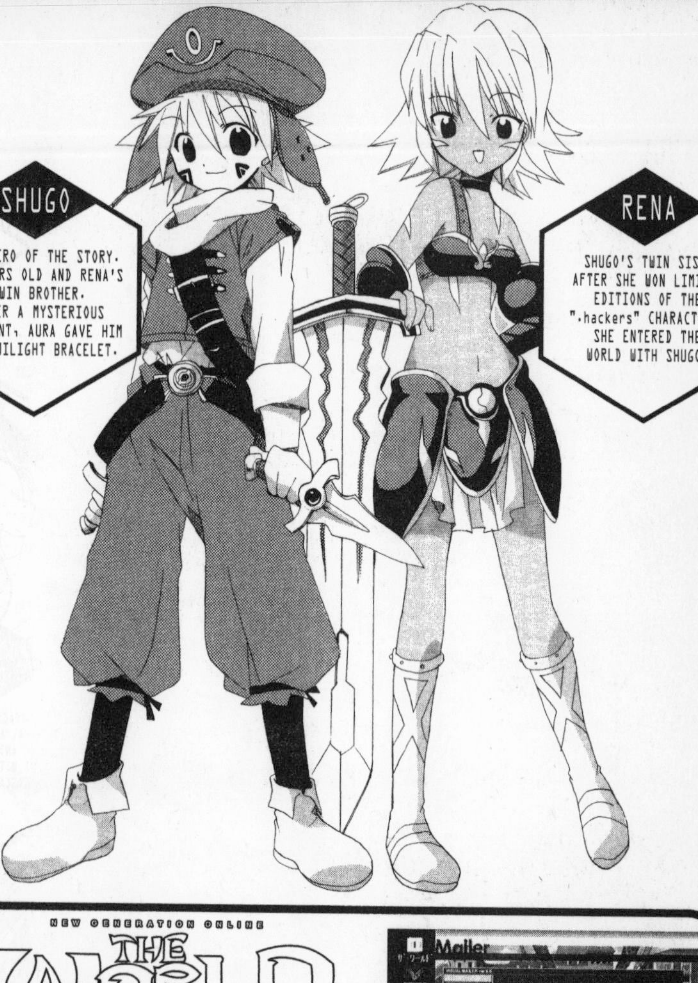

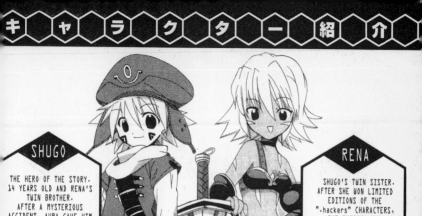

## SHUGO

THE HERO OF THE STORY. 14 YEARS OLD AND RENA'S TWIN BROTHER. AFTER A MYSTERIOUS ACCIDENT, AURA GAVE HIM THE TWILIGHT BRACELET.

## RENA

SHUGO'S TWIN SISTER. AFTER SHE WON LIMITED EDITIONS OF THE ".hackers" CHARACTERS, SHE ENTERED THE WORLD WITH SHUGO.

NEW GENERATION ONLINE

## THE WORLD

What is THE WORLD? It's the largest online game in the world, played by 20 million people. Using head-mounted displays, gamers can freely move inside a totally realistic world. There have been problems with the game in the past, but recently it's been trouble-free. More people are joining each day.

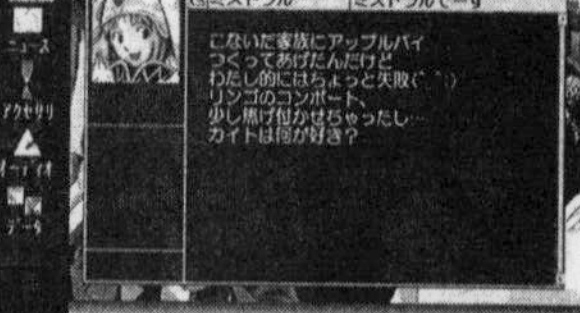
Mailer
ザ・ワールド
メーラー
ニュース
アクセサリ
オーディオ
データ
ミストラル
ミストラルでーす
こないだ家族にアップルパイ
つくってあげたんだけど
わたし的にはちょっと失敗(^^;)
リンゴのコンポート、
少し焦げ付かせちゃったし…
カイトは何が好き？

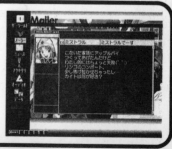

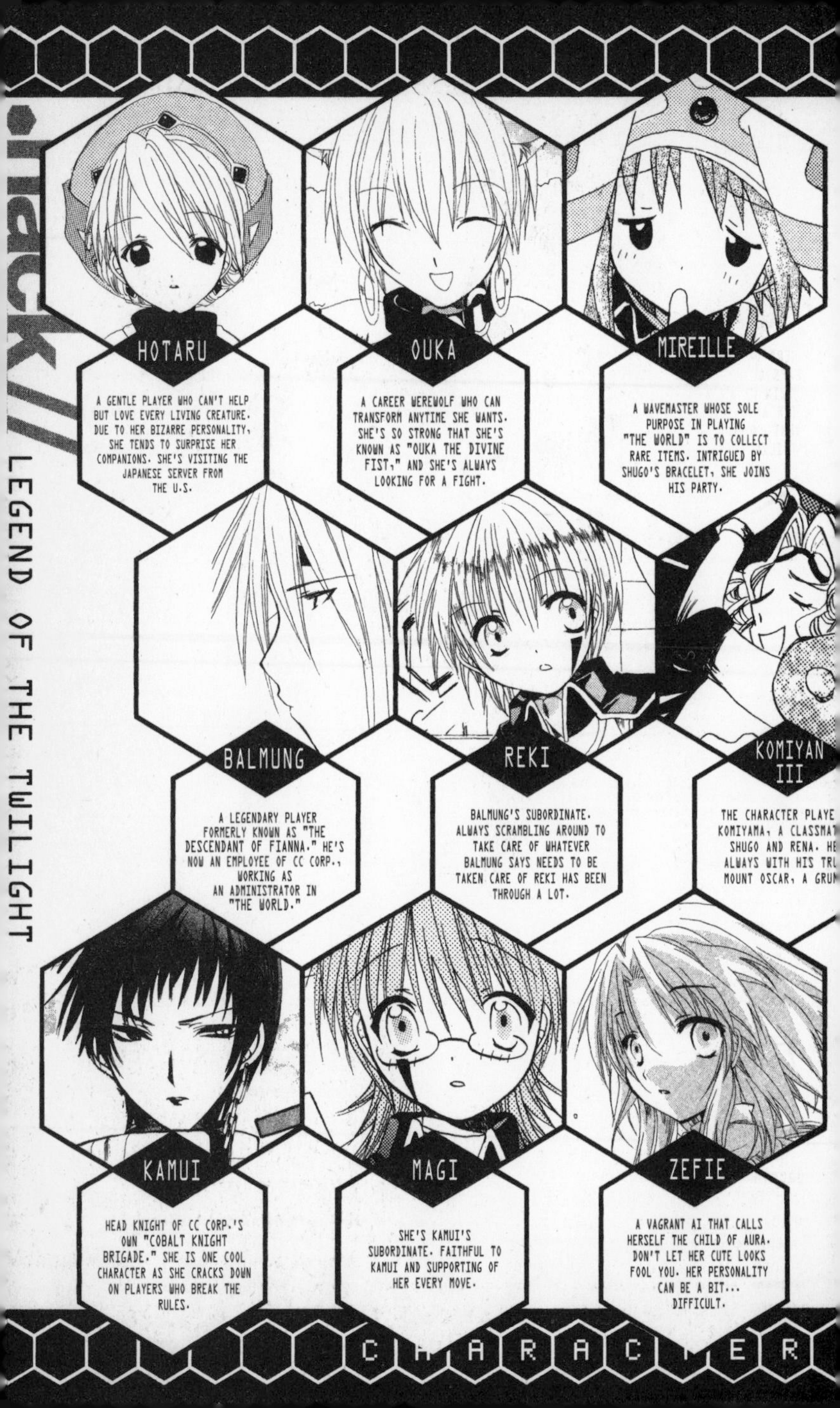

.hack// LEGEND OF THE TWILIGHT
HOTARU
A GENTLE PLAYER WHO CAN'T HELP BUT LOVE EVERY LIVING CREATURE. DUE TO HER BIZARRE PERSONALITY, SHE TENDS TO SURPRISE HER COMPANIONS. SHE'S VISITING THE JAPANESE SERVER FROM THE U.S.
OUKA
A CAREER WEREWOLF WHO CAN TRANSFORM ANYTIME SHE WANTS. SHE'S SO STRONG THAT SHE'S KNOWN AS "OUKA THE DIVINE FIST," AND SHE'S ALWAYS LOOKING FOR A FIGHT.
MIREILLE
A WAVEMASTER WHOSE SOLE PURPOSE IN PLAYING "THE WORLD" IS TO COLLECT RARE ITEMS. INTRIGUED BY SHUGO'S BRACELET, SHE JOINS HIS PARTY.
BALMUNG
A LEGENDARY PLAYER FORMERLY KNOWN AS "THE DESCENDANT OF FIANNA." HE'S NOW AN EMPLOYEE OF CC CORP., WORKING AS AN ADMINISTRATOR IN "THE WORLD."
REKI
BALMUNG'S SUBORDINATE. ALWAYS SCRAMBLING AROUND TO TAKE CARE OF WHATEVER BALMUNG SAYS NEEDS TO BE TAKEN CARE OF REKI HAS BEEN THROUGH A LOT.
KOMIYAN III
THE CHARACTER PLAYE KOMIYAMA, A CLASSMA SHUGO AND RENA. HE ALWAYS WITH HIS TRU MOUNT OSCAR, A GRU
KAMUI
HEAD KNIGHT OF CC CORP.'S OWN "COBALT KNIGHT BRIGADE." SHE IS ONE COOL CHARACTER AS SHE CRACKS DOWN ON PLAYERS WHO BREAK THE RULES.
MAGI
SHE'S KAMUI'S SUBORDINATE. FAITHFUL TO KAMUI AND SUPPORTING OF HER EVERY MOVE.
ZEFIE
A VAGRANT AI THAT CALLS HERSELF THE CHILD OF AURA. DON'T LET HER CUTE LOOKS FOOL YOU. HER PERSONALITY CAN BE A BIT... DIFFICULT.
CHARACTER

NEW GENERATION ONLINE
THE WORLD
TM

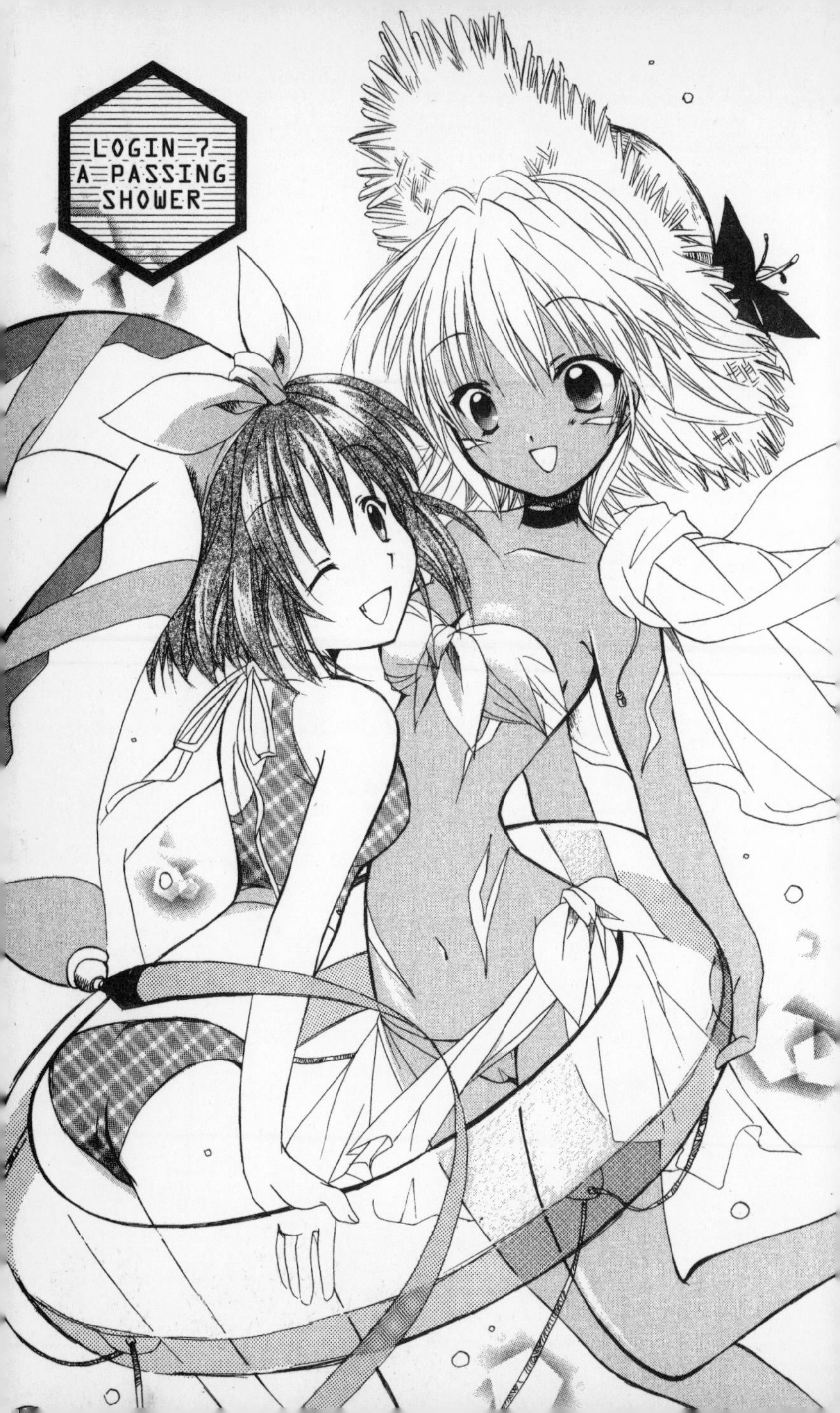
LOGIN 7
A PASSING SHOWER

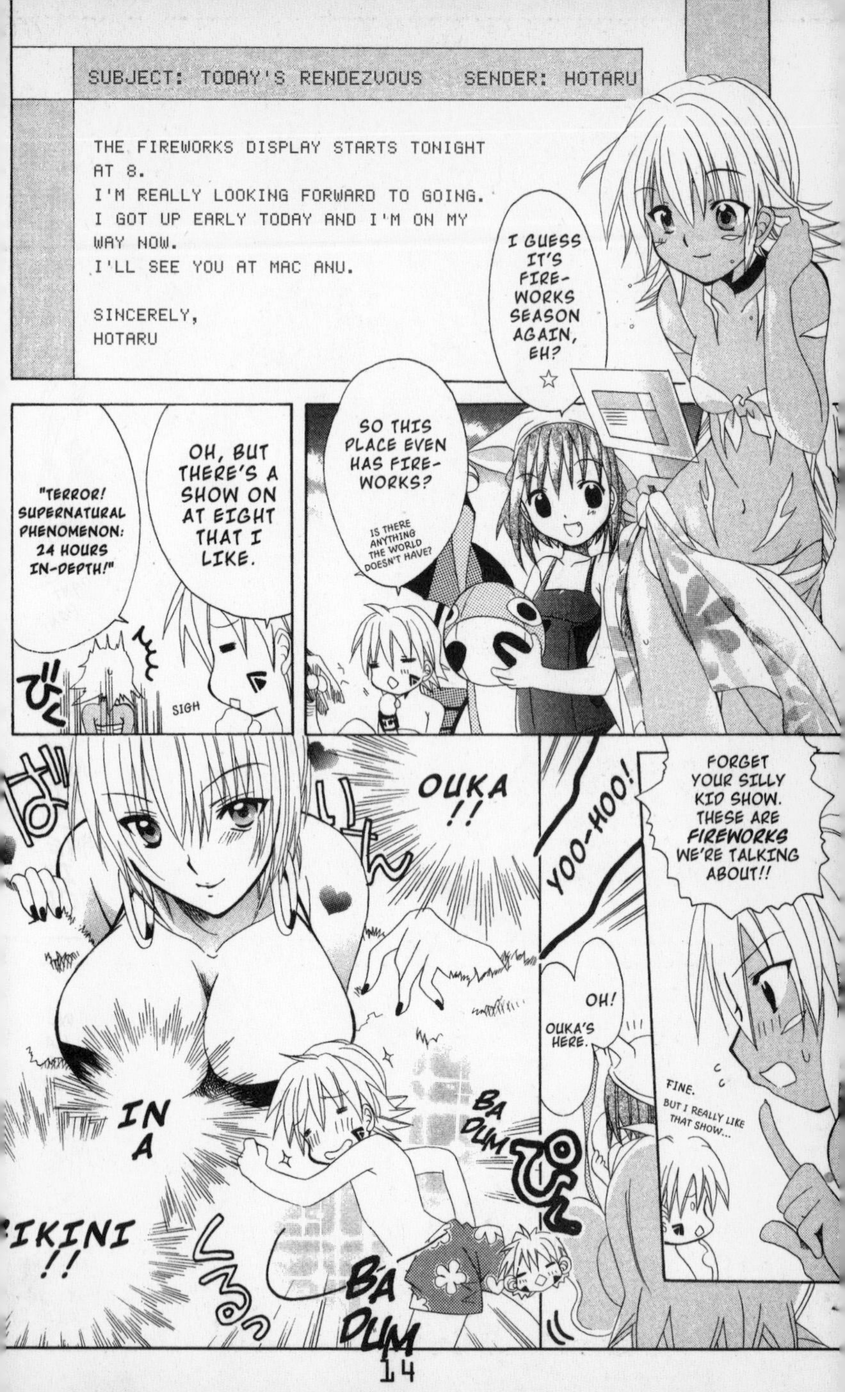
SUBJECT: TODAY'S RENDEZVOUS SENDER: HOTARU
THE FIREWORKS DISPLAY STARTS TONIGHT AT 8.
I'M REALLY LOOKING FORWARD TO GOING.
I GOT UP EARLY TODAY AND I'M ON MY WAY NOW.
I'LL SEE YOU AT MAC ANU.
SINCERELY,
HOTARU
I GUESS IT'S FIRE-WORKS SEASON AGAIN, EH? ☆
SO THIS PLACE EVEN HAS FIRE-WORKS?
IS THERE ANYTHING THE WORLD DOESN'T HAVE?
OH, BUT THERE'S A SHOW ON AT EIGHT THAT I LIKE.
"TERROR! SUPERNATURAL PHENOMENON: 24 HOURS IN-DEPTH!"
SIGH
FORGET YOUR SILLY KID SHOW. THESE ARE FIREWORKS WE'RE TALKING ABOUT!!
FINE.
BUT I REALLY LIKE THAT SHOW...
YOO-HOO!
OH!
OUKA'S HERE.
OUKA !!
IN A
IKINI !!
BA DUM
BA DUM

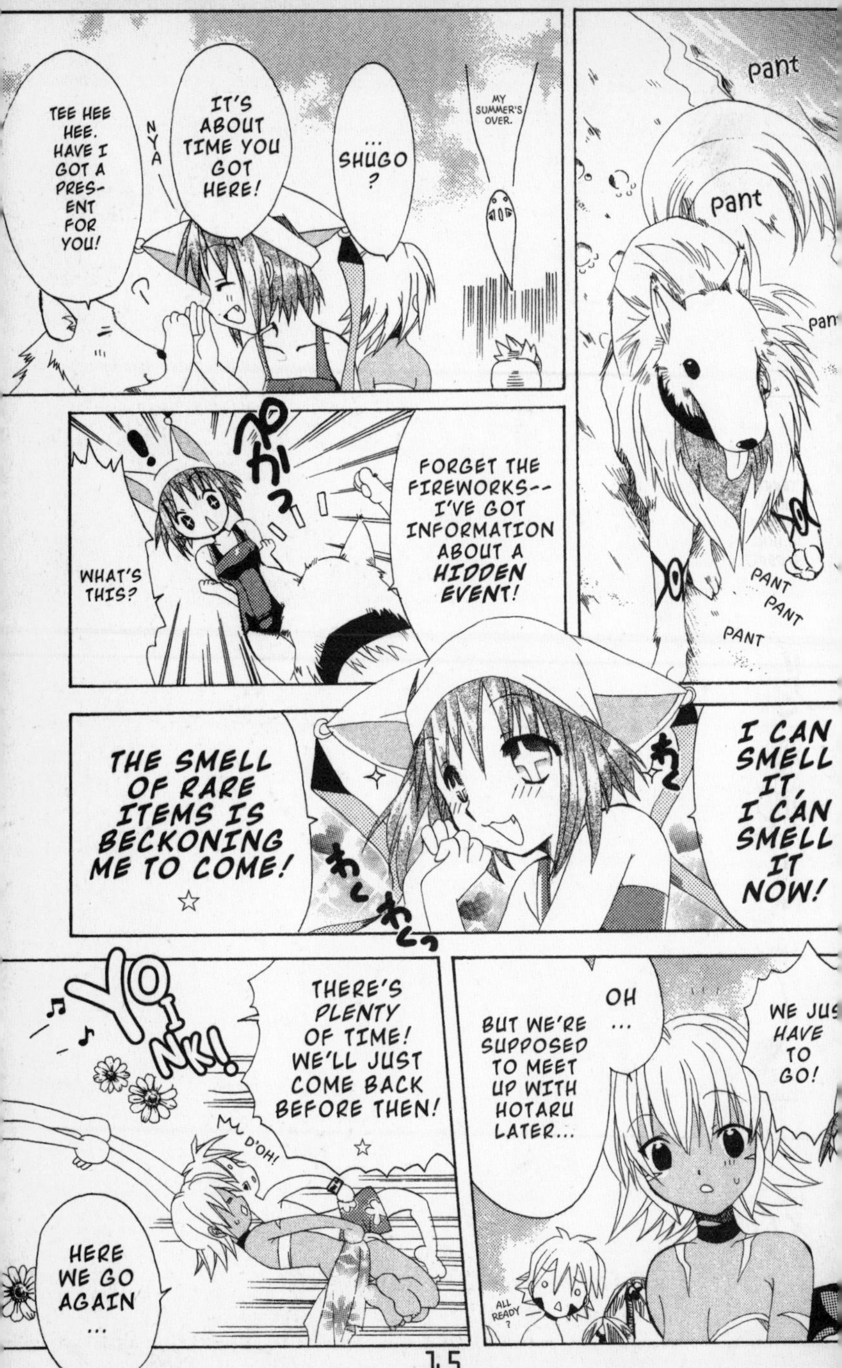
pant
pant
pant
PANT
PANT
PANT
MY SUMMER'S OVER.
... SHUGO ?
IT'S ABOUT TIME YOU GOT HERE!
NYA
TEE HEE HEE. HAVE I GOT A PRES-ENT FOR YOU!
FORGET THE FIREWORKS-- I'VE GOT INFORMATION ABOUT A HIDDEN EVENT!
!
WHAT'S THIS?
I CAN SMELL IT, I CAN SMELL IT NOW!
THE SMELL OF RARE ITEMS IS BECKONING ME TO COME! ☆
WE JUS HAVE TO GO!
OH ...
BUT WE'RE SUPPOSED TO MEET UP WITH HOTARU LATER...
ALL READY ?
THERE'S PLENTY OF TIME! WE'LL JUST COME BACK BEFORE THEN! ☆
YOINK!
D'OH!
HERE WE GO AGAIN ...

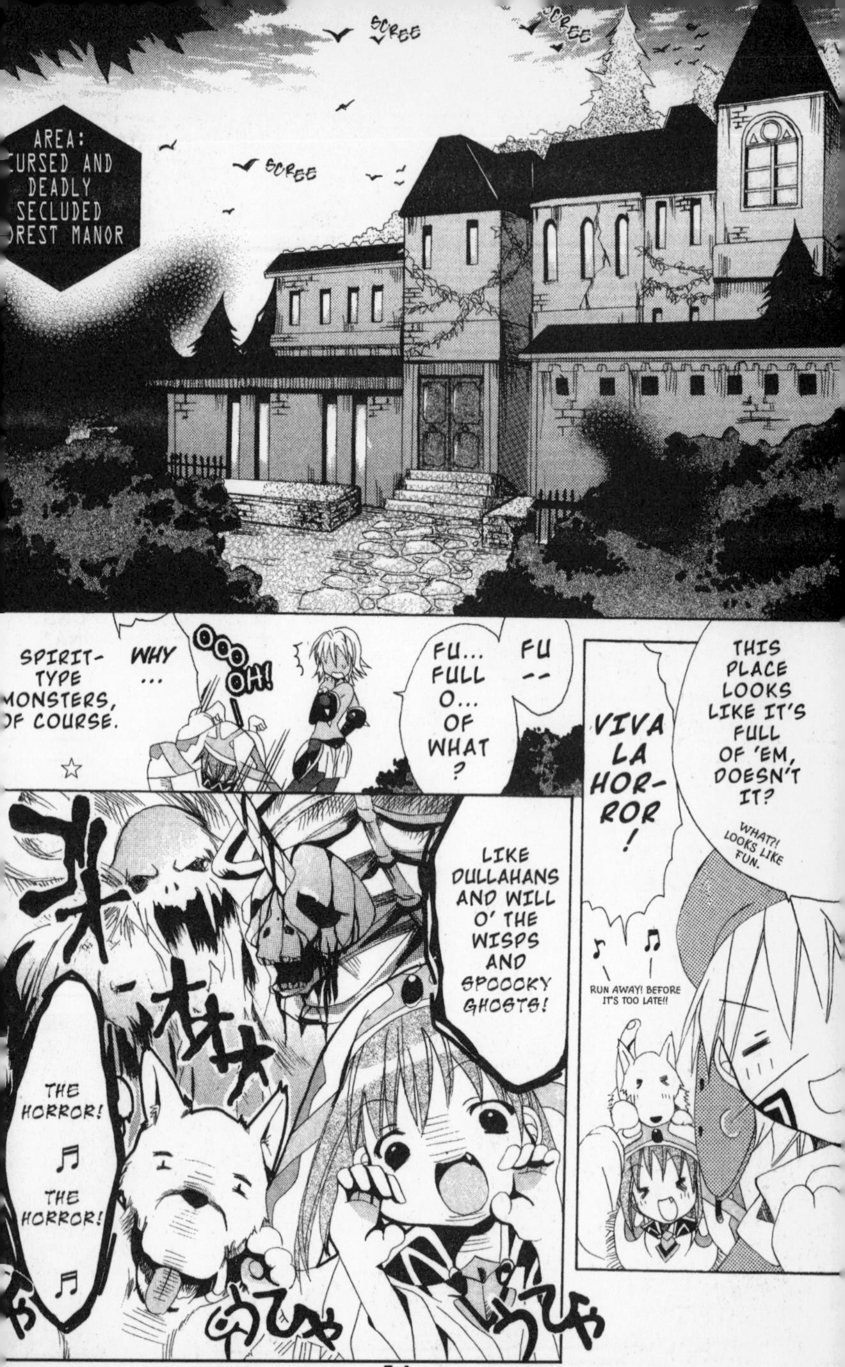

AREA: CURSED AND DEADLY SECLUDED FOREST MANOR
SCREE
SCREE
SCREE
THIS PLACE LOOKS LIKE IT'S FULL OF 'EM, DOESN'T IT?
WHAT?! LOOKS LIKE FUN.
VIVA LA HOR-ROR!
RUN AWAY! BEFORE IT'S TOO LATE!!
FU--
FU... FULL O... OF WHAT?
OOO OH!
WHY...
SPIRIT-TYPE MONSTERS, OF COURSE. ☆
LIKE DULLAHANS AND WILL O' THE WISPS AND SPOOOKY GHOSTS!
THE HORROR! ♫ THE HORROR! ♫

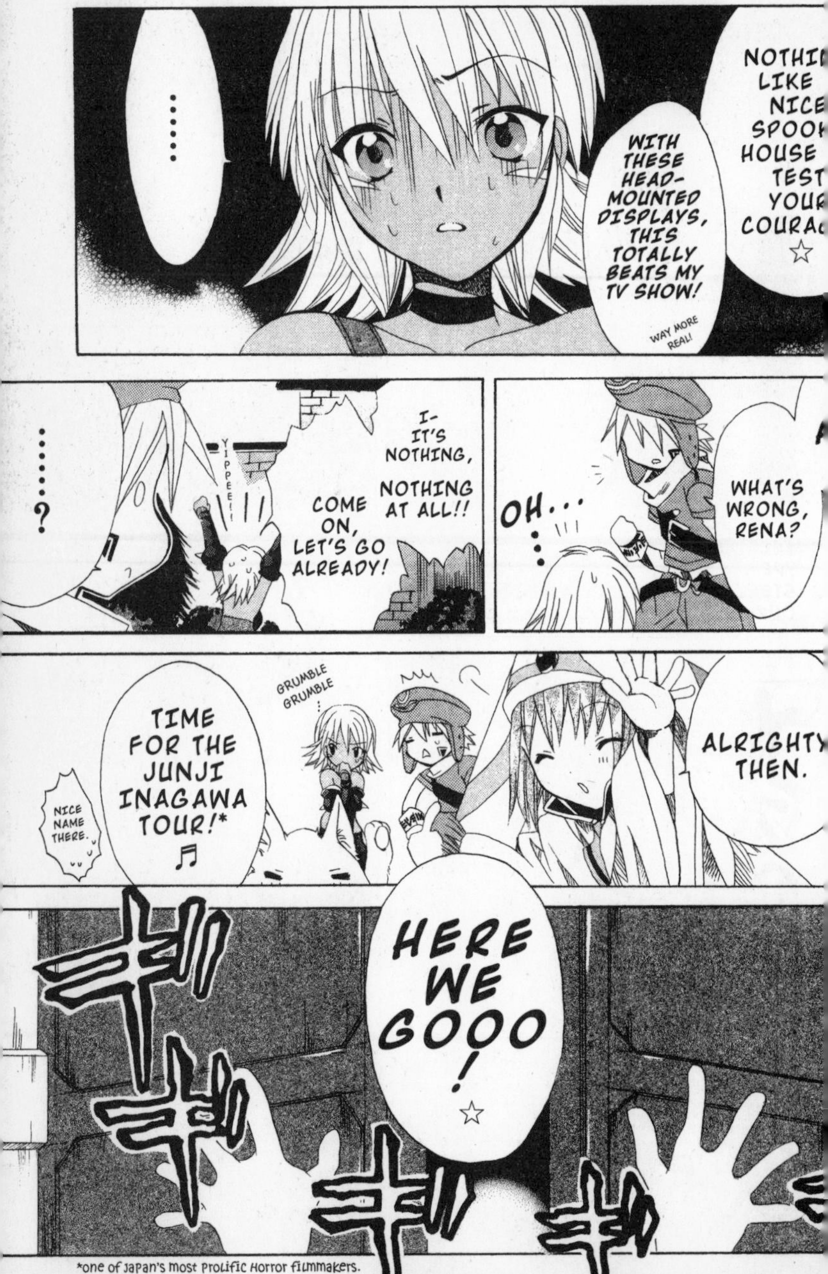
NOTHI LIKE NICE SPOOK HOUSE TEST YOUR COURA ☆
WITH THESE HEAD-MOUNTED DISPLAYS, THIS TOTALLY BEATS MY TV SHOW!
WAY MORE REAL!
......
WHAT'S WRONG, RENA?
OH... ...
I- IT'S NOTHING, NOTHING AT ALL!!
COME ON, LET'S GO ALREADY!
YIPPEE!!
......?
ALRIGHTY THEN.
GRUMBLE GRUMBLE
TIME FOR THE JUNJI INAGAWA TOUR!* ♬
NICE NAME THERE.
HERE WE GOOO! ☆

*one of Japan's most prolific horror filmmakers.

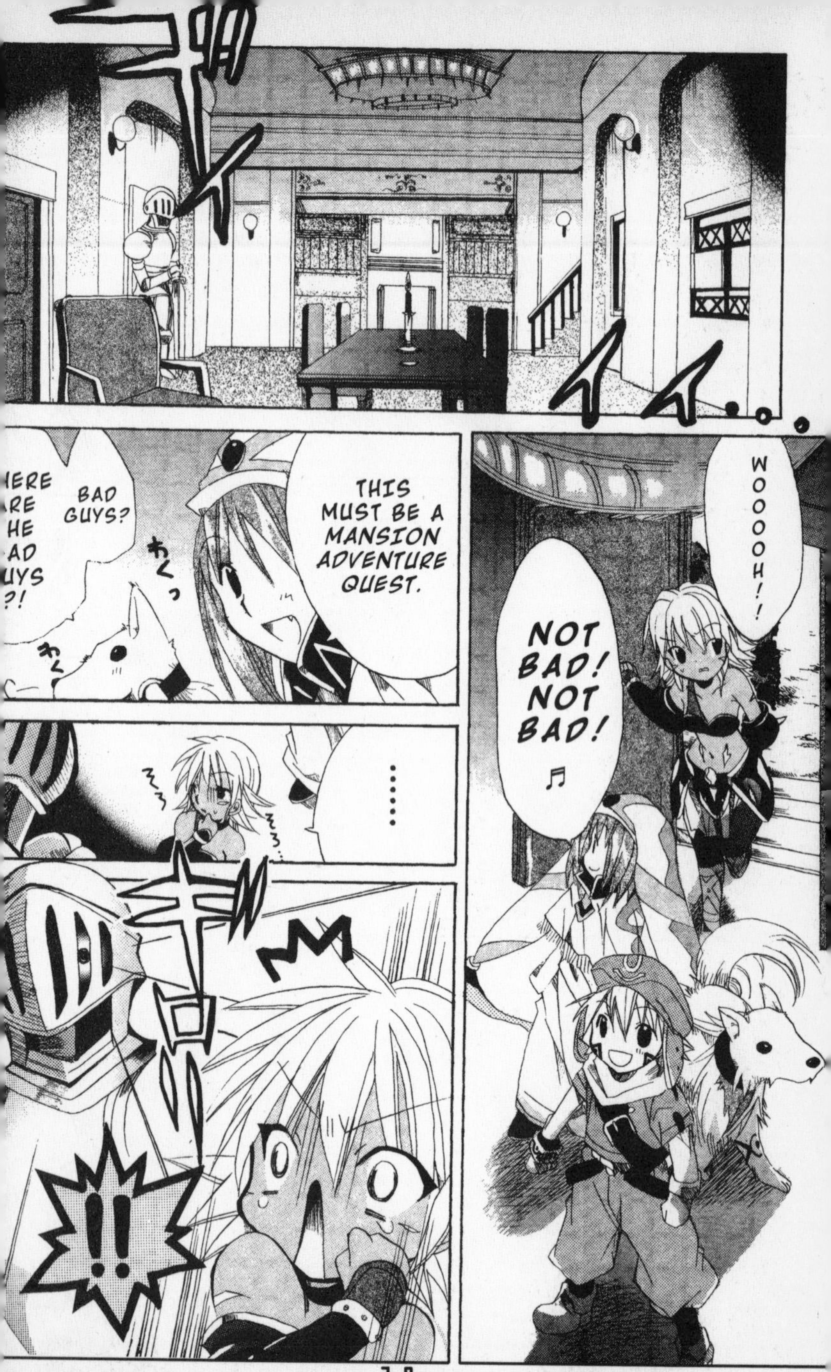
WOOOOOH!!
NOT BAD! NOT BAD! ♫
THIS MUST BE A MANSION ADVENTURE QUEST.
BAD GUYS?
HERE RE HE AD UYS ?!
......
!!

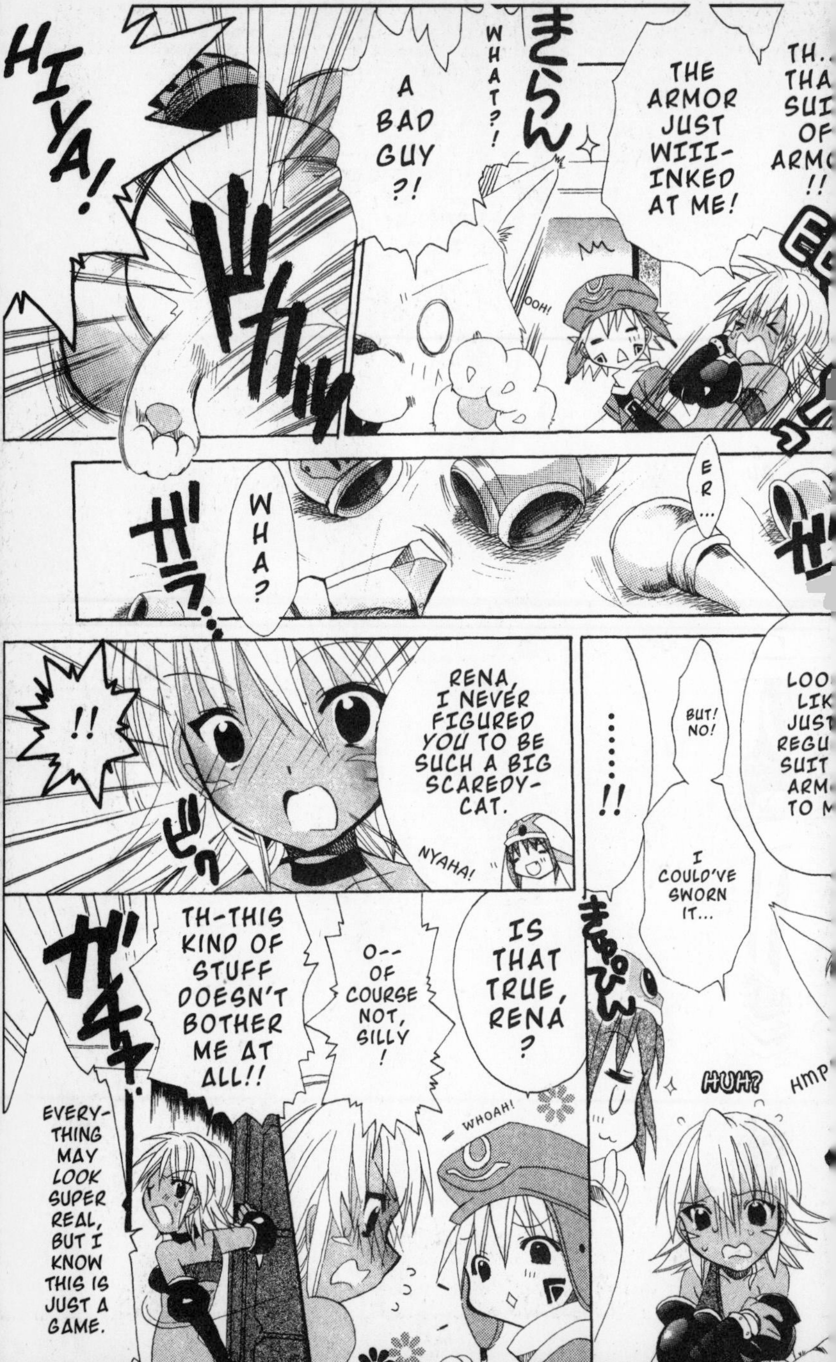
TH... THA SUI OF ARMO !!
THE ARMOR JUST WIIII-INKED AT ME!
EE
OOH!
きらん
WHAT?!
A BAD GUY?!
ドカッ
HIYA!
ER...
WHA?
ガラ...
LOO LIK JUST REGU SUIT ARM TO M
BUT! NO!
......!!
I COULD'VE SWORN IT...
きゅぴん
HUH?
HMP
RENA, I NEVER FIGURED YOU TO BE SUCH A BIG SCAREDY-CAT.
NYAHA!
!!
IS THAT TRUE, RENA?
O-- OF COURSE NOT, SILLY!
TH-THIS KIND OF STUFF DOESN'T BOTHER ME AT ALL!!
WHOAH!
ガチャ
EVERY-THING MAY LOOK SUPER REAL, BUT I KNOW THIS IS JUST A GAME.

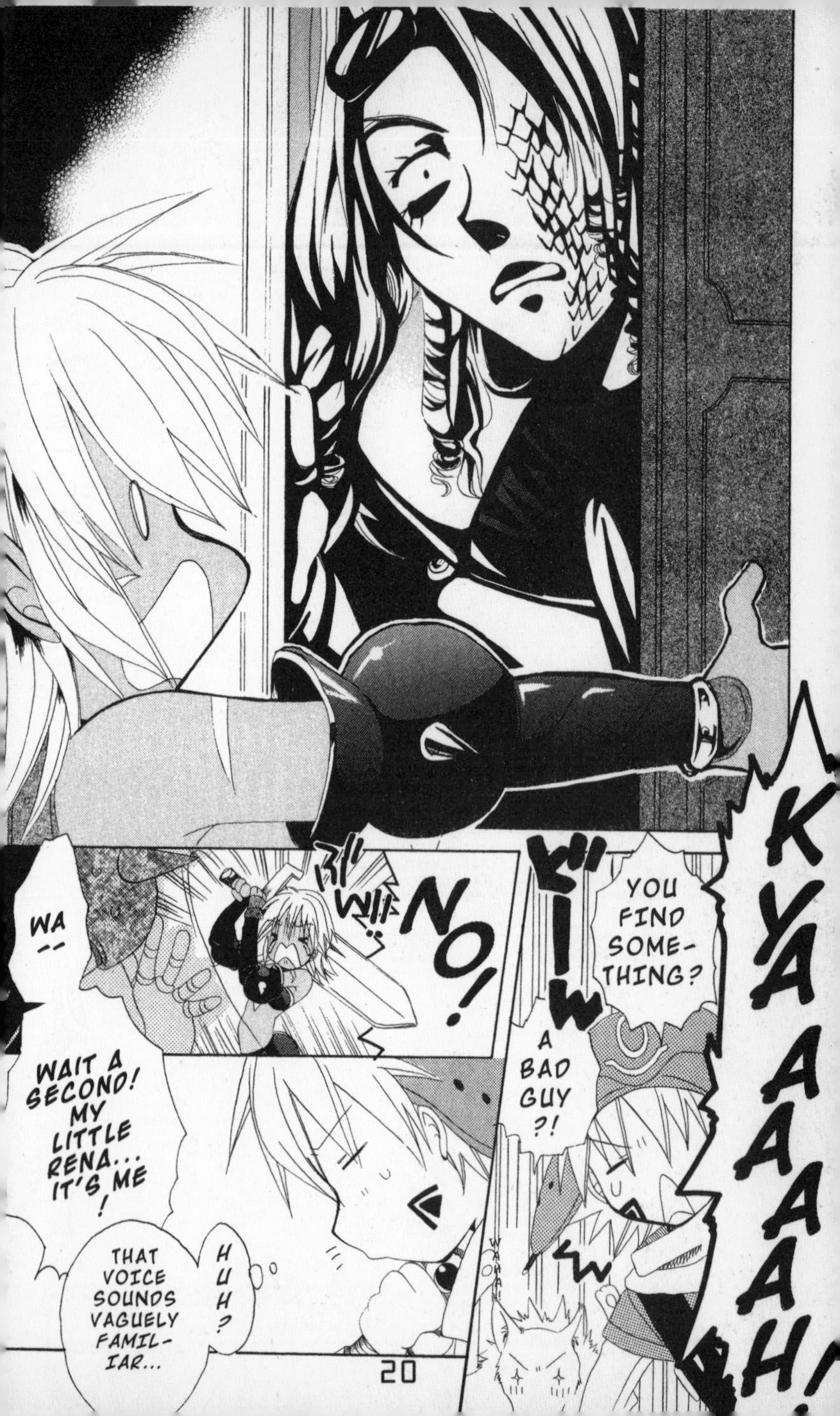
KYAAAAAH!
YOU FIND SOMETHING?
A BAD GUY?!
WAHA!
NO!
WA--
WAIT A SECOND! MY LITTLE RENA... IT'S ME!
HUH?
THAT VOICE SOUNDS VAGUELY FAMILIAR...

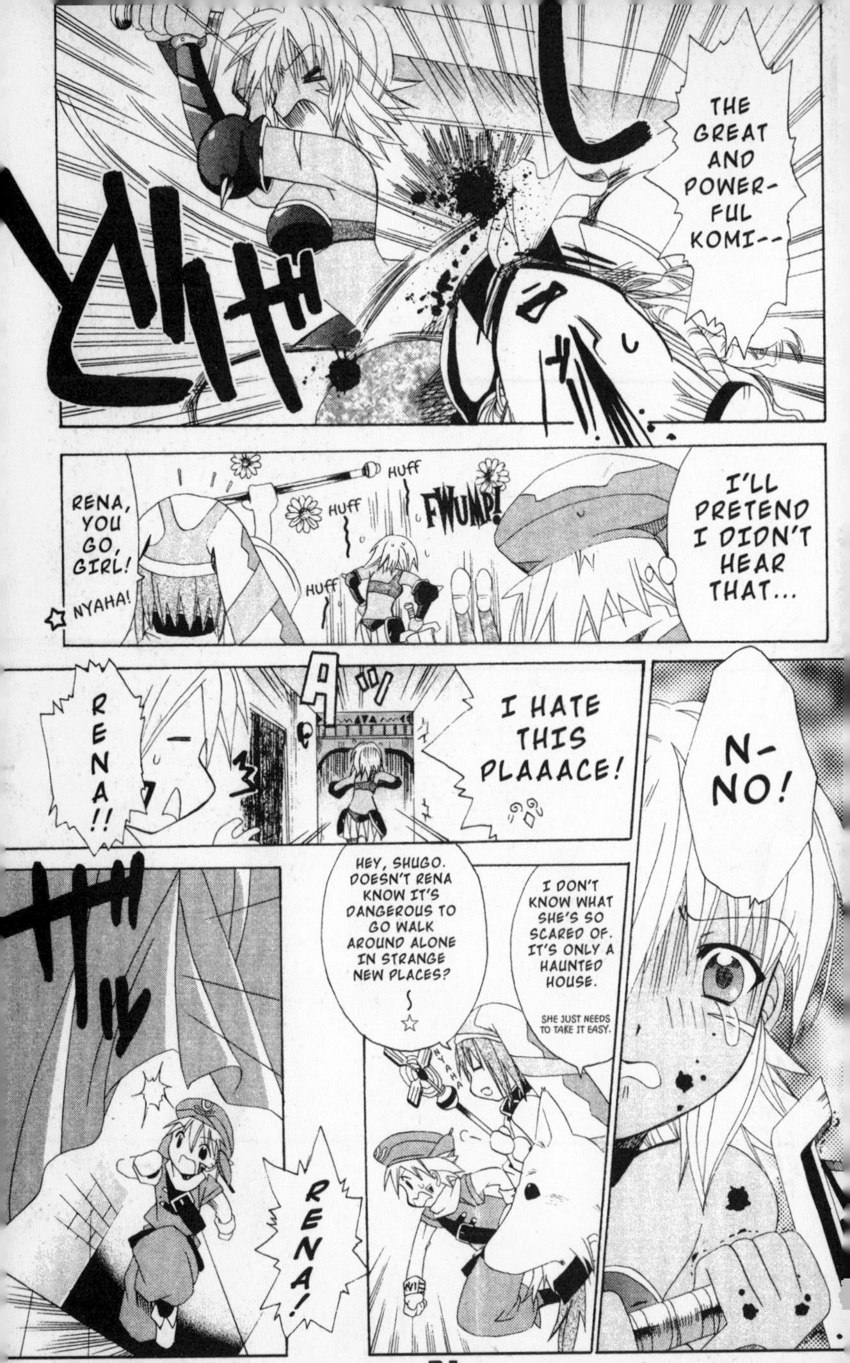
THE GREAT AND POWER-FUL KOMI--
I'LL PRETEND I DIDN'T HEAR THAT...
FWUMP!
HUFF
HUFF
HUFF
RENA, YOU GO, GIRL!
NYAHA!
N-NO!
I HATE THIS PLAAACE!
RENA!!
HEY, SHUGO. DOESN'T RENA KNOW IT'S DANGEROUS TO GO WALK AROUND ALONE IN STRANGE NEW PLACES?
I DON'T KNOW WHAT SHE'S SO SCARED OF. IT'S ONLY A HAUNTED HOUSE.
SHE JUST NEEDS TO TAKE IT EASY.
NYAHA
RENA!

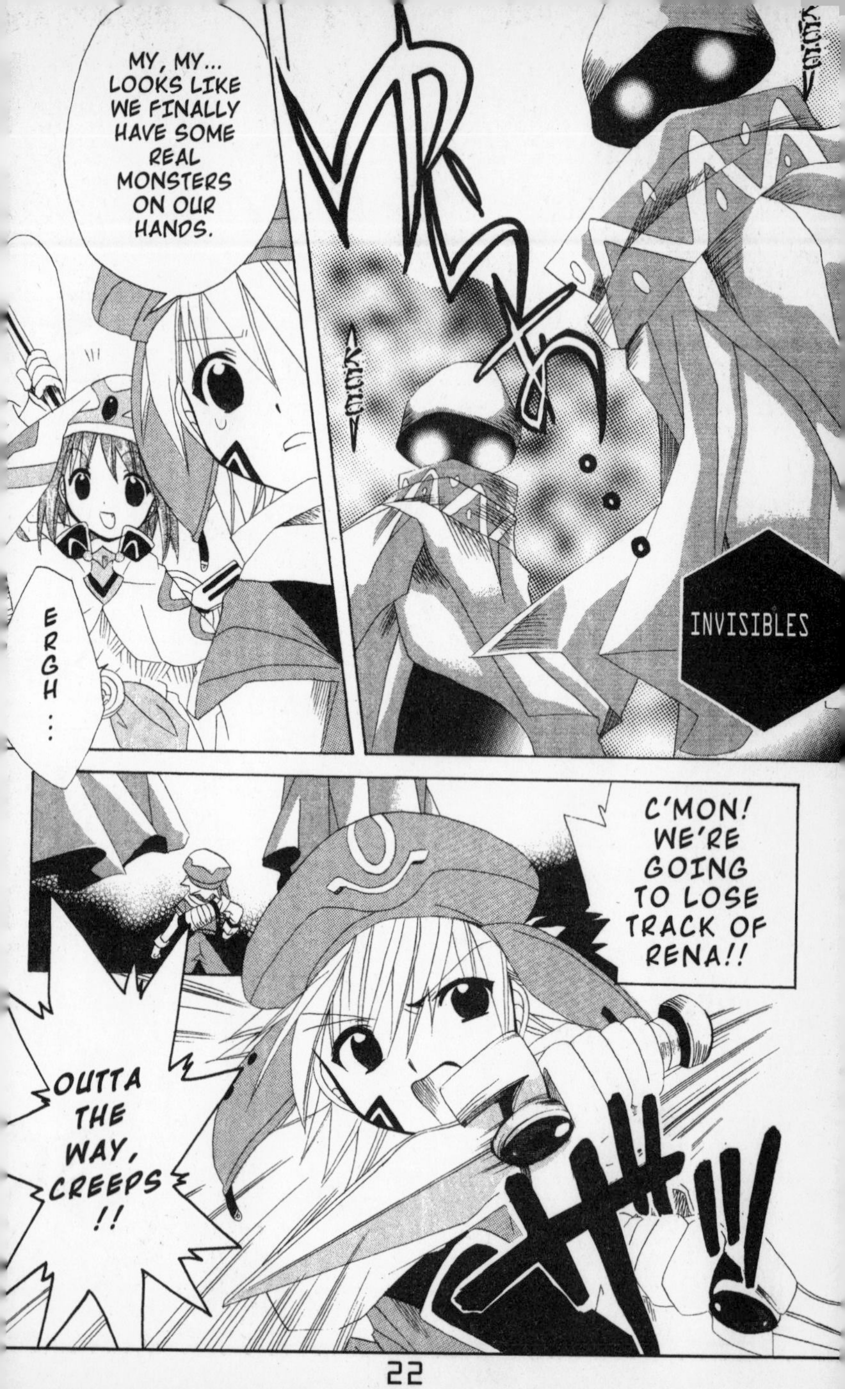

INVISIBLES
MY, MY... LOOKS LIKE WE FINALLY HAVE SOME REAL MONSTERS ON OUR HANDS.
ERGH ...
C'MON! WE'RE GOING TO LOSE TRACK OF RENA!!
OUTTA THE WAY, CREEPS!!

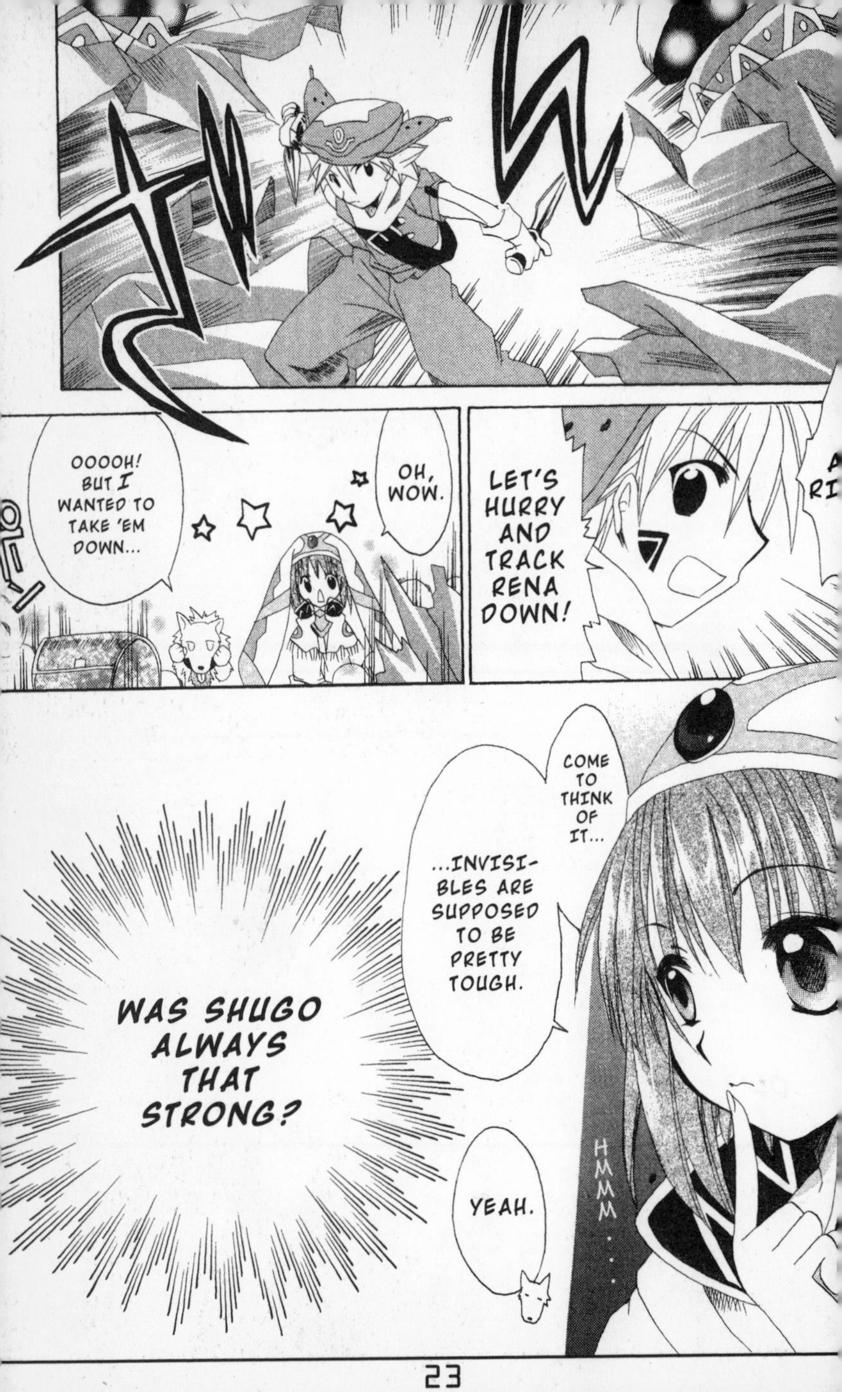
LET'S HURRY AND TRACK RENA DOWN!
OH, WOW.
OOOOH! BUT I WANTED TO TAKE 'EM DOWN...
COME TO THINK OF IT...
...INVISIBLES ARE SUPPOSED TO BE PRETTY TOUGH.
HMMM...
YEAH.
WAS SHUGO ALWAYS THAT STRONG?

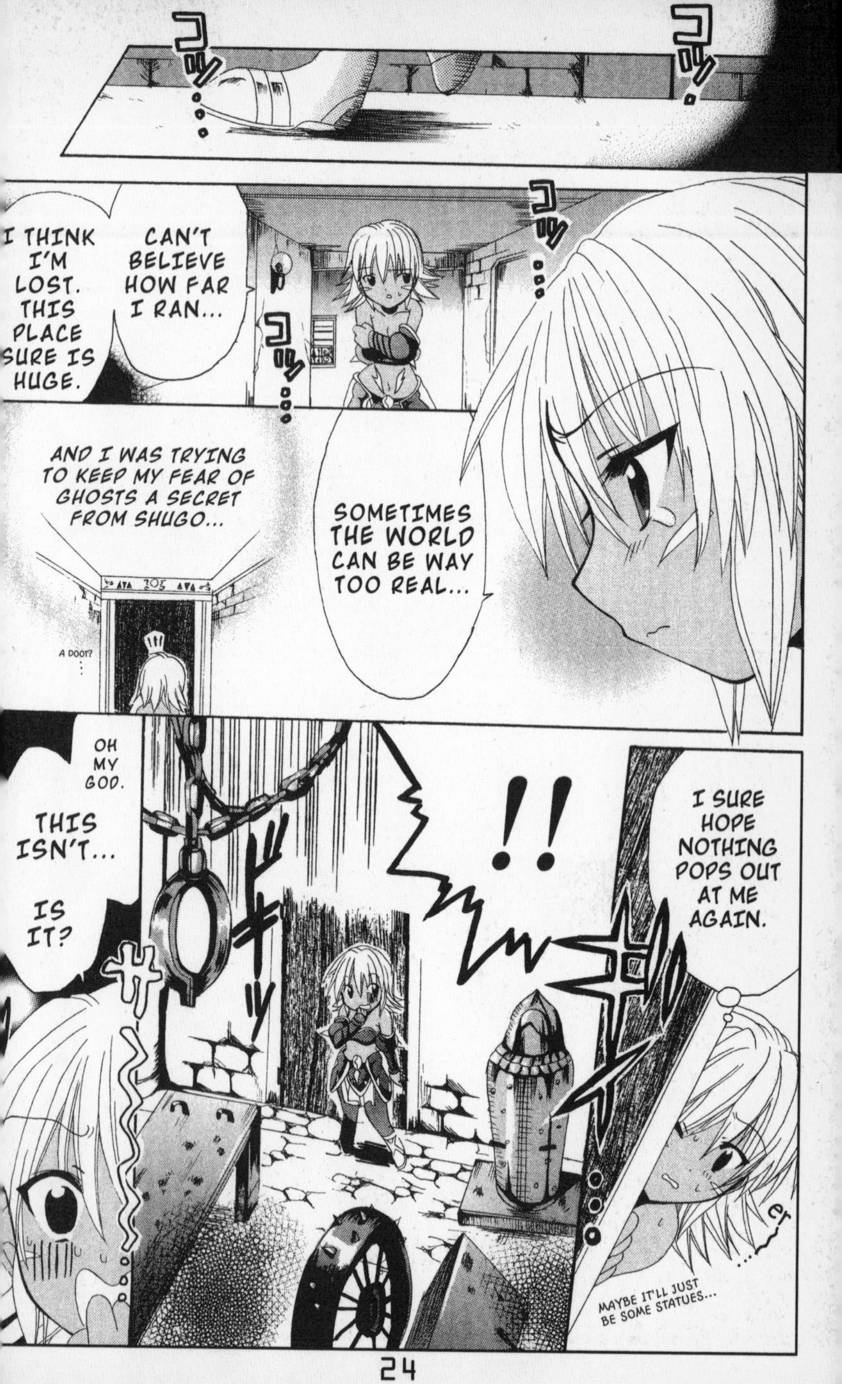
SOMETIMES THE WORLD CAN BE WAY TOO REAL...
CAN'T BELIEVE HOW FAR I RAN...
I THINK I'M LOST. THIS PLACE SURE IS HUGE.
AND I WAS TRYING TO KEEP MY FEAR OF GHOSTS A SECRET FROM SHUGO...
A DOOR? ...
I SURE HOPE NOTHING POPS OUT AT ME AGAIN.
...er~
MAYBE IT'LL JUST BE SOME STATUES...
!!
OH MY GOD.
THIS ISN'T...
IS IT?

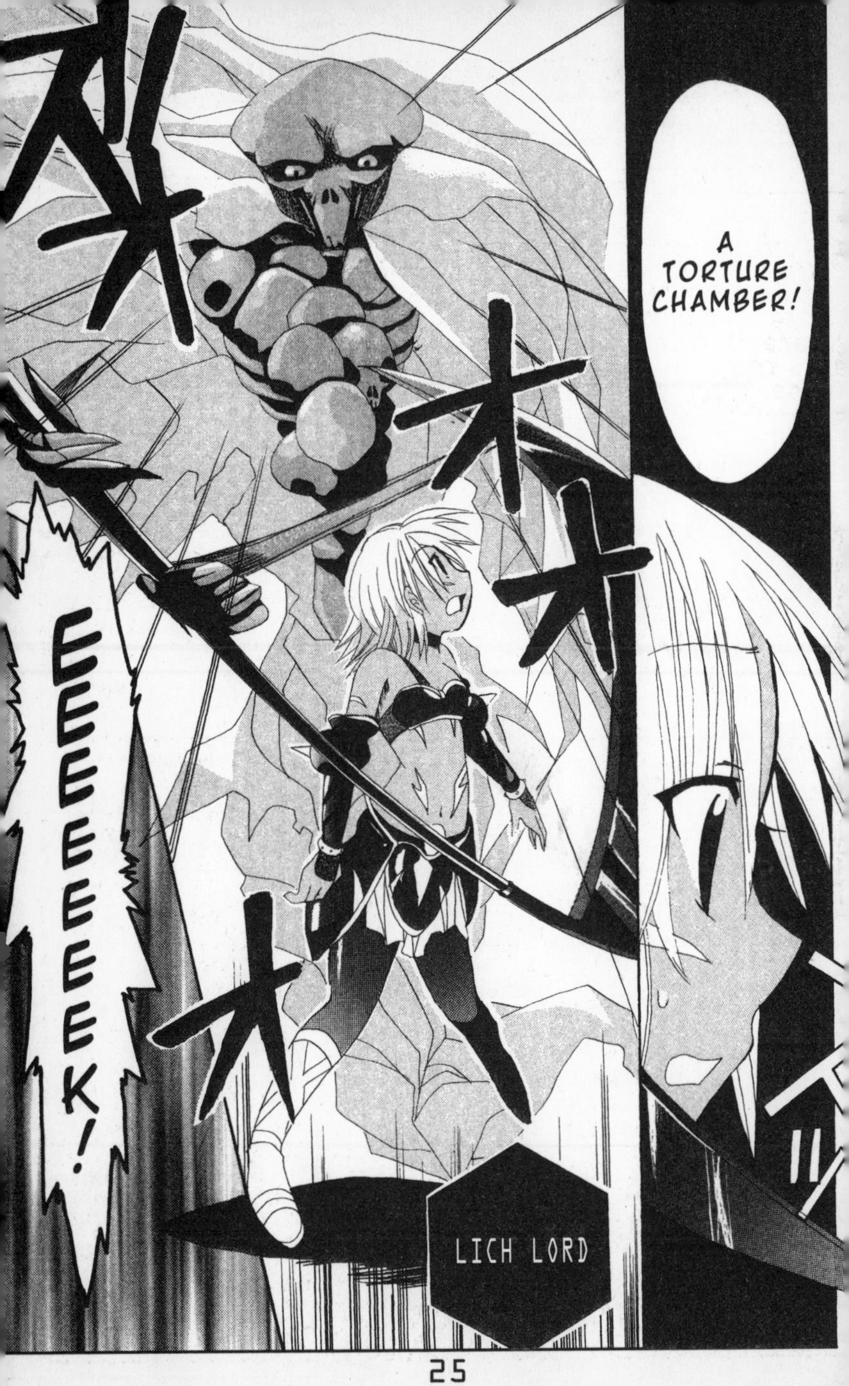
A TORTURE CHAMBER!
EEEEEEEEK!
LICH LORD

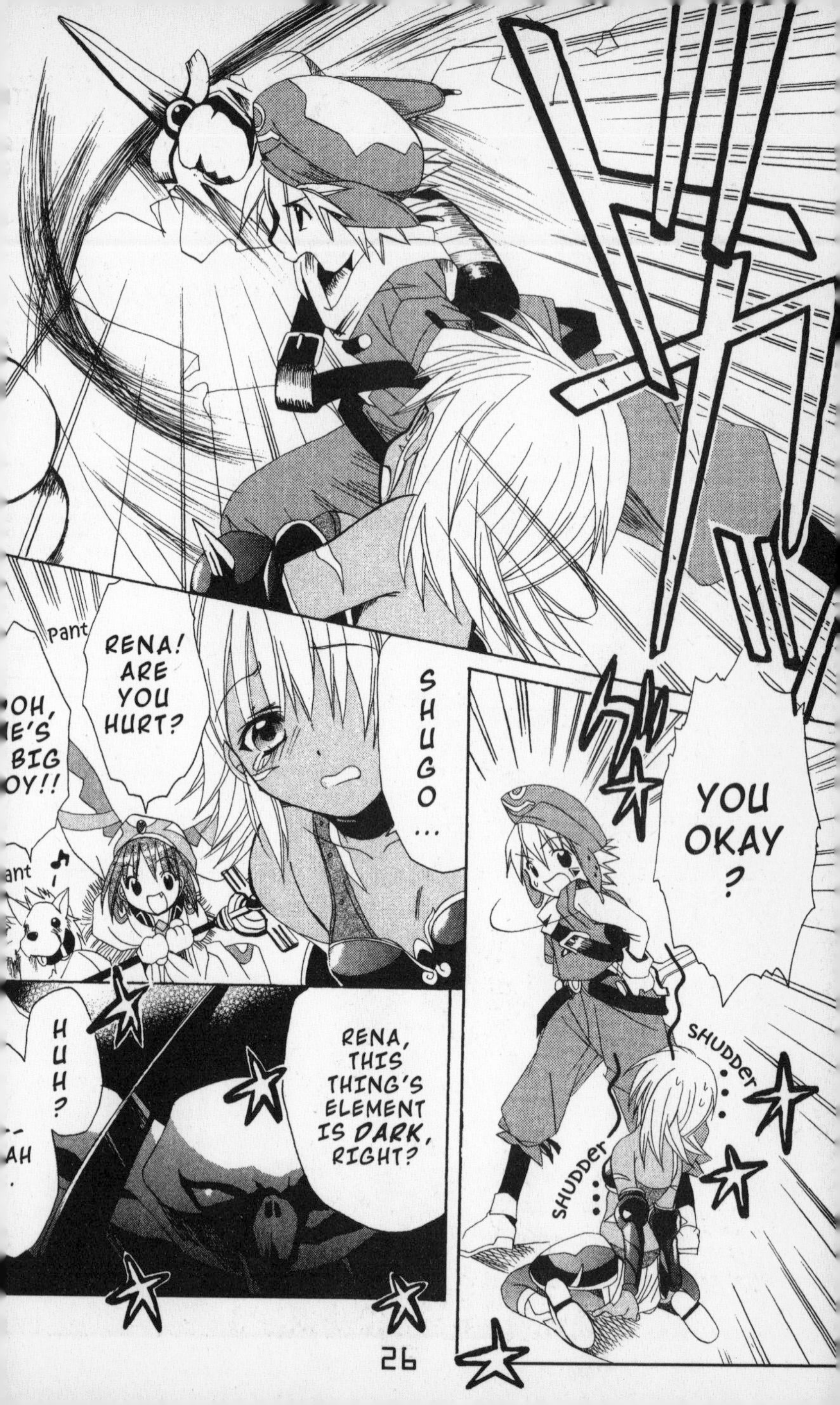
YOU OKAY?
SHUDDER...
SHUDDER...
SHUGO...
RENA! ARE YOU HURT?
Pant
OH, E'S BIG OY!!
ant
RENA, THIS THING'S ELEMENT IS DARK, RIGHT?
HUH?
AH

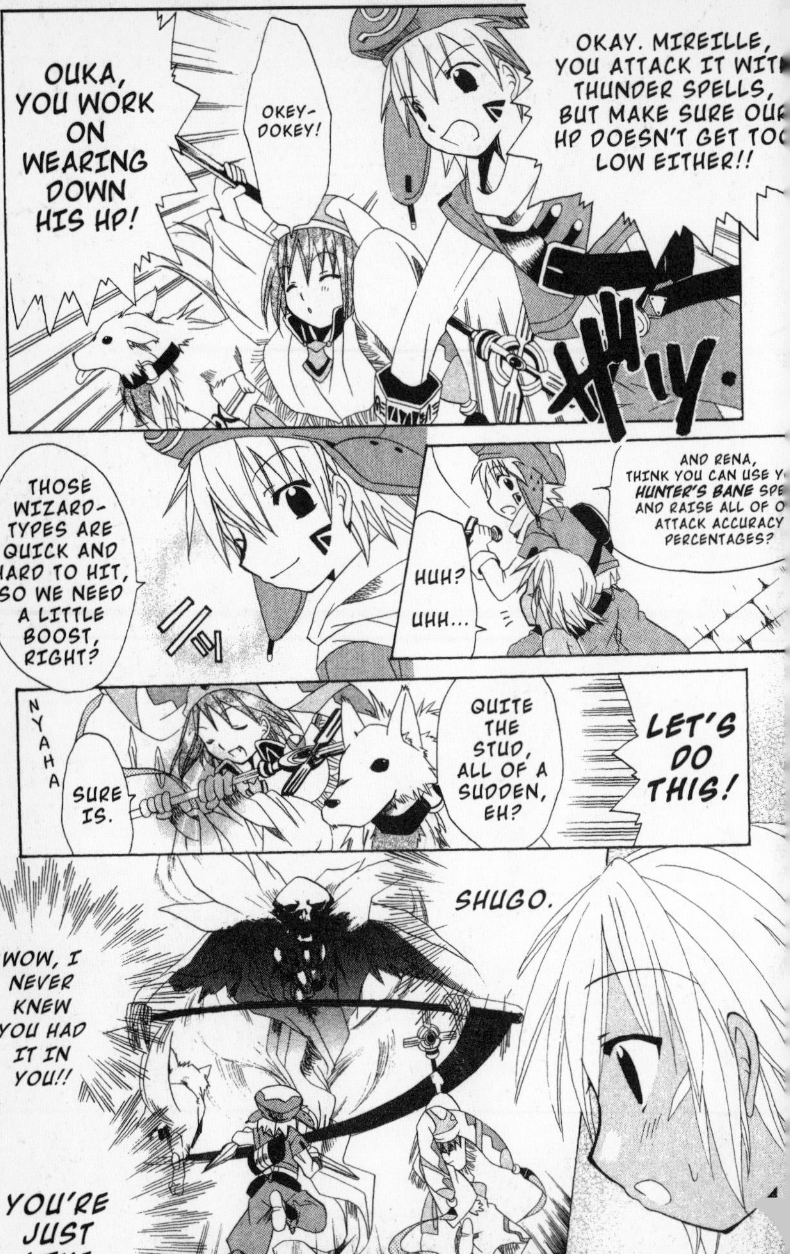
OKAY. MIREILLE, YOU ATTACK IT WITH THUNDER SPELLS, BUT MAKE SURE OUR HP DOESN'T GET TOO LOW EITHER!!
OKEY-DOKEY!
OUKA, YOU WORK ON WEARING DOWN HIS HP!
AND RENA, THINK YOU CAN USE Y HUNTER'S BANE SPE AND RAISE ALL OF O ATTACK ACCURACY PERCENTAGES?
HUH?
UHH...
THOSE WIZARD-TYPES ARE QUICK AND HARD TO HIT, SO WE NEED A LITTLE BOOST, RIGHT?
LET'S DO THIS!
QUITE THE STUD, ALL OF A SUDDEN, EH?
NYAHA
SURE IS.
SHUGO.
WOW, I NEVER KNEW YOU HAD IT IN YOU!!
YOU'RE JUST LIKE ...

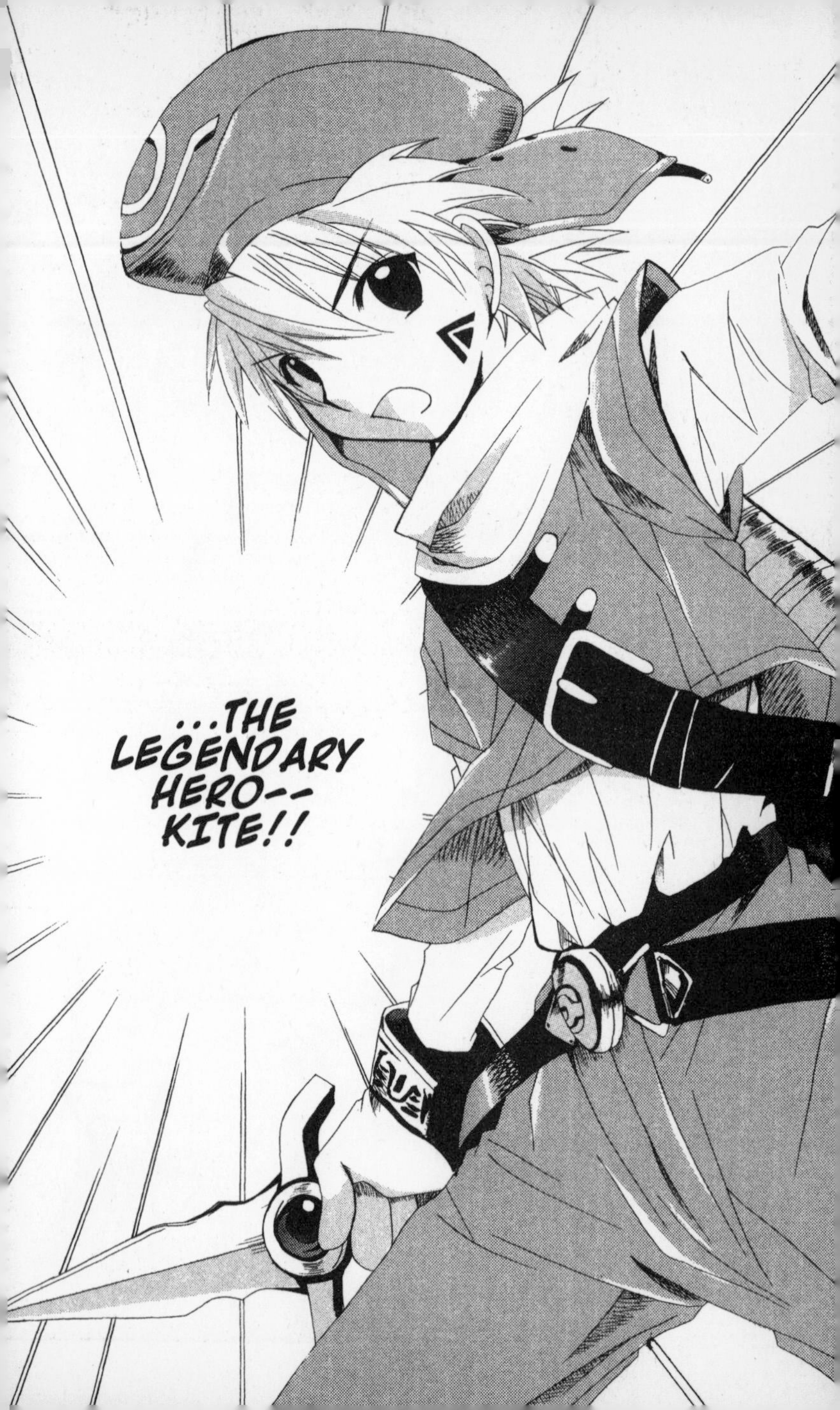
...THE
LEGENDARY
HERO--
KITE!!

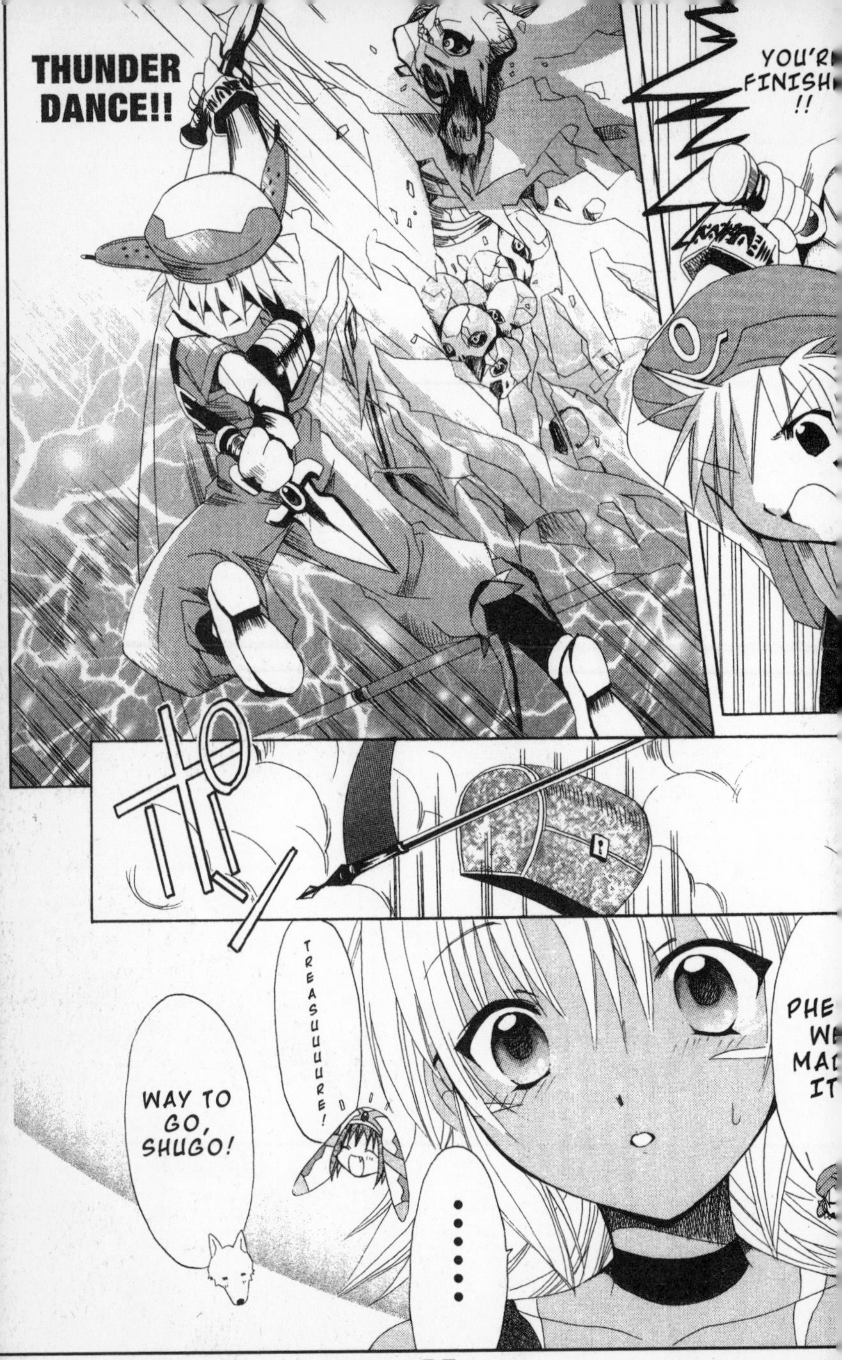
YOU'R FINISH !!
THUNDER DANCE!!
PHE WE MA IT
TREASUUUURE!
......
WAY TO GO, SHUGO!

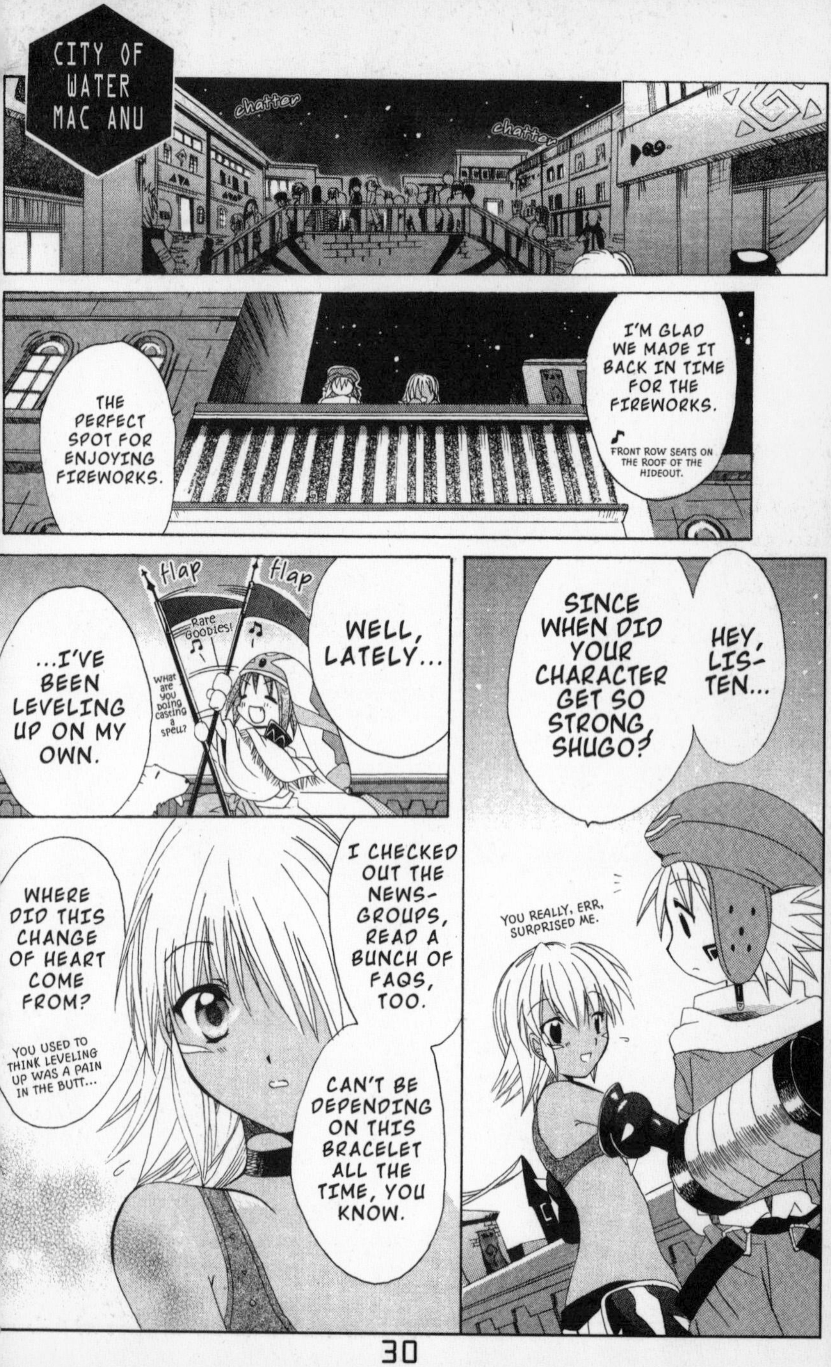
CITY OF WATER MAC ANU
chatter
chatter
I'M GLAD WE MADE IT BACK IN TIME FOR THE FIREWORKS.
FRONT ROW SEATS ON THE ROOF OF THE HIDEOUT.
THE PERFECT SPOT FOR ENJOYING FIREWORKS.
HEY, LIS-TEN...
SINCE WHEN DID YOUR CHARACTER GET SO STRONG, SHUGO?
YOU REALLY, ERR, SURPRISED ME.
flap
flap
WELL, LATELY...
Rare Goodies!
What are you doing casting a spell?
...I'VE BEEN LEVELING UP ON MY OWN.
WHERE DID THIS CHANGE OF HEART COME FROM?
YOU USED TO THINK LEVELING UP WAS A PAIN IN THE BUTT...
I CHECKED OUT THE NEWS-GROUPS, READ A BUNCH OF FAQS, TOO.
CAN'T BE DEPENDING ON THIS BRACELET ALL THE TIME, YOU KNOW.

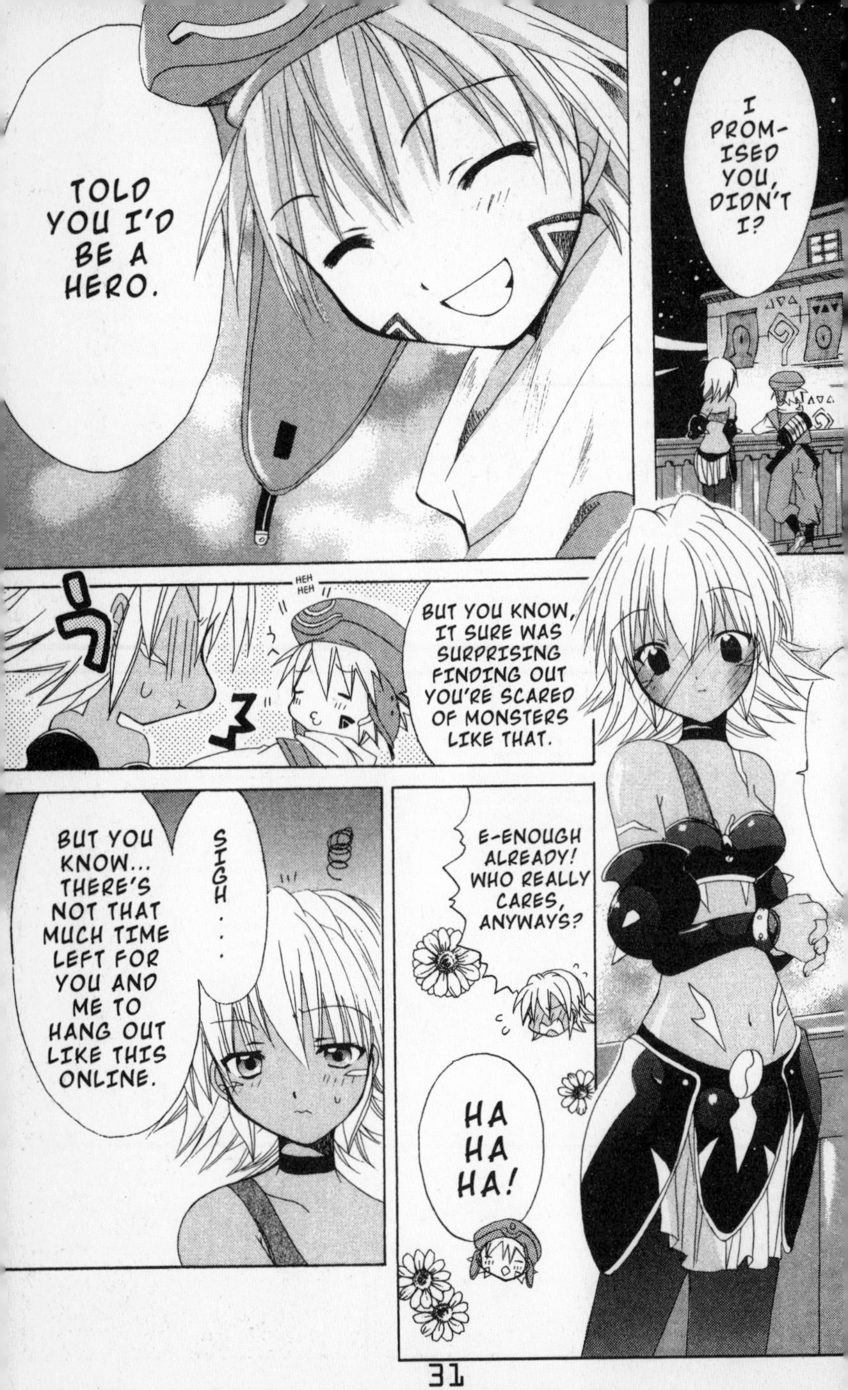
I PROMISED YOU, DIDN'T I?
TOLD YOU I'D BE A HERO.
HEH HEH
う
BUT YOU KNOW, IT SURE WAS SURPRISING FINDING OUT YOU'RE SCARED OF MONSTERS LIKE THAT.
E-ENOUGH ALREADY! WHO REALLY CARES, ANYWAYS?
HA HA HA!
SIGH...
BUT YOU KNOW... THERE'S NOT THAT MUCH TIME LEFT FOR YOU AND ME TO HANG OUT LIKE THIS ONLINE.

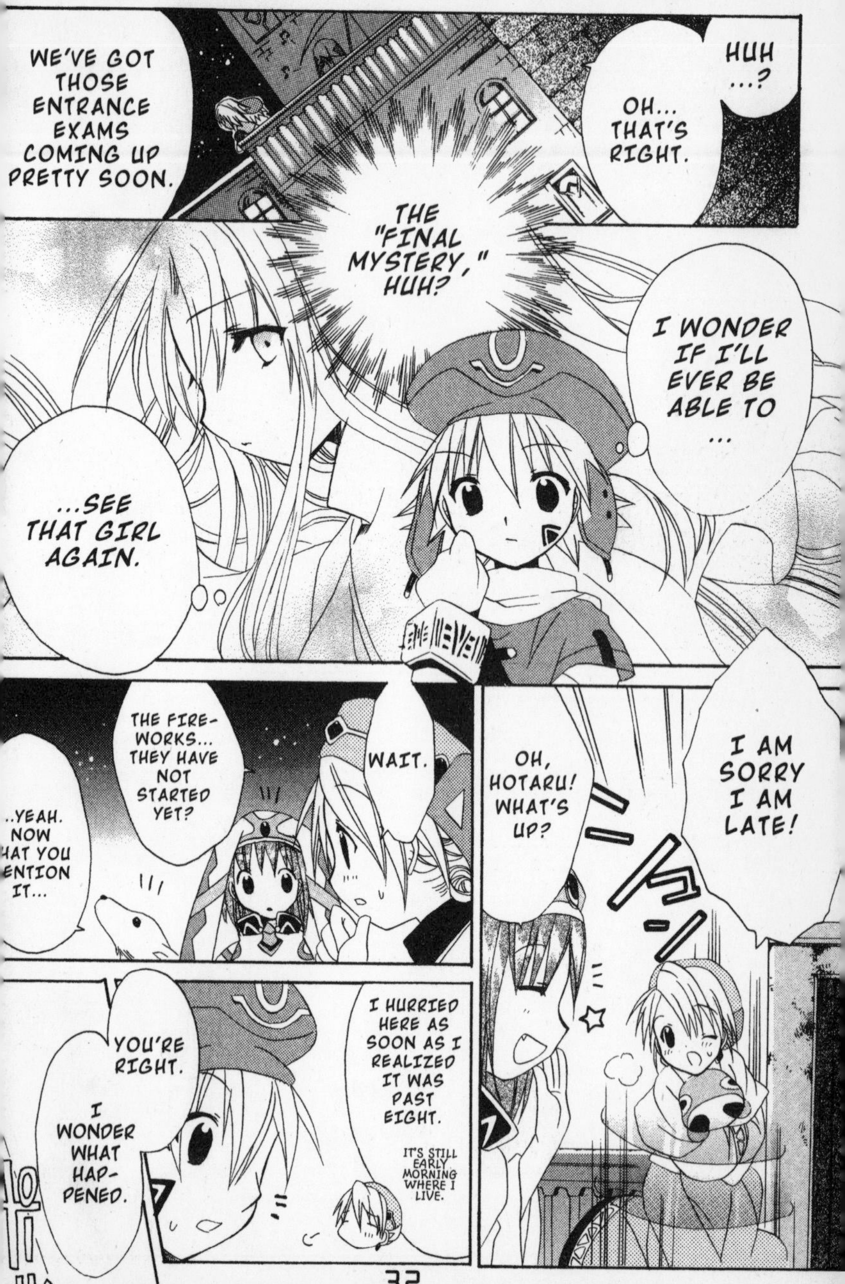
HUH ...?
OH... THAT'S RIGHT.
WE'VE GOT THOSE ENTRANCE EXAMS COMING UP PRETTY SOON.
THE "FINAL MYSTERY," HUH?
I WONDER IF I'LL EVER BE ABLE TO ...
...SEE THAT GIRL AGAIN.
I AM SORRY I AM LATE!
OH, HOTARU! WHAT'S UP?
WAIT.
THE FIRE-WORKS... THEY HAVE NOT STARTED YET?
..YEAH. NOW HAT YOU ENTION IT...
I HURRIED HERE AS SOON AS I REALIZED IT WAS PAST EIGHT.
IT'S STILL EARLY MORNING WHERE I LIVE.
YOU'RE RIGHT.
I WONDER WHAT HAP-PENED.

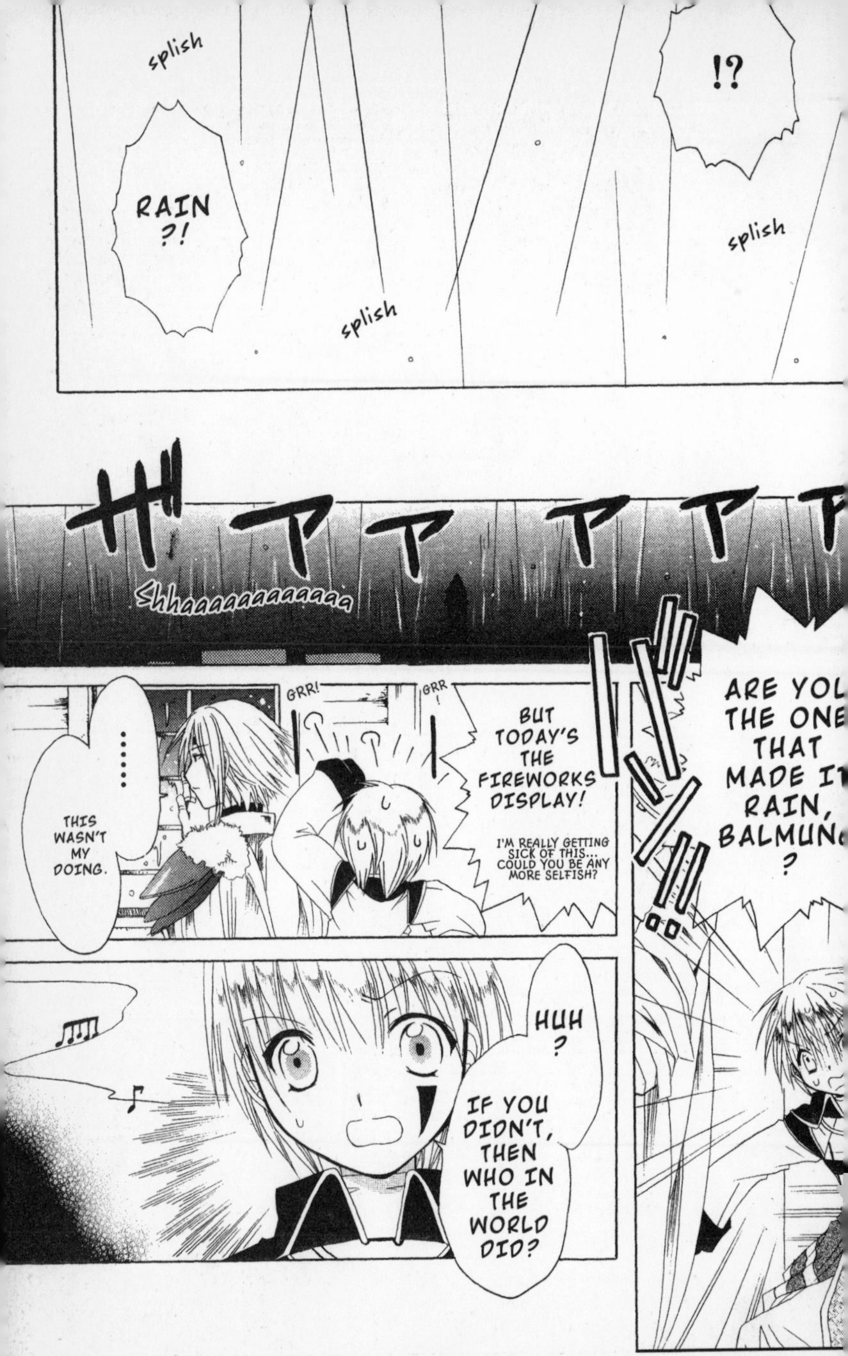
!?
splish
RAIN ?!
splish
splish
ザアアアア
Shhaaaaaaaaaaaa
ARE YOU THE ONE THAT MADE IT RAIN, BALMUNG?
GRR!
GRR!
BUT TODAY'S THE FIREWORKS DISPLAY!
I'M REALLY GETTING SICK OF THIS... COULD YOU BE ANY MORE SELFISH?
......
THIS WASN'T MY DOING.
HUH?
IF YOU DIDN'T, THEN WHO IN THE WORLD DID?

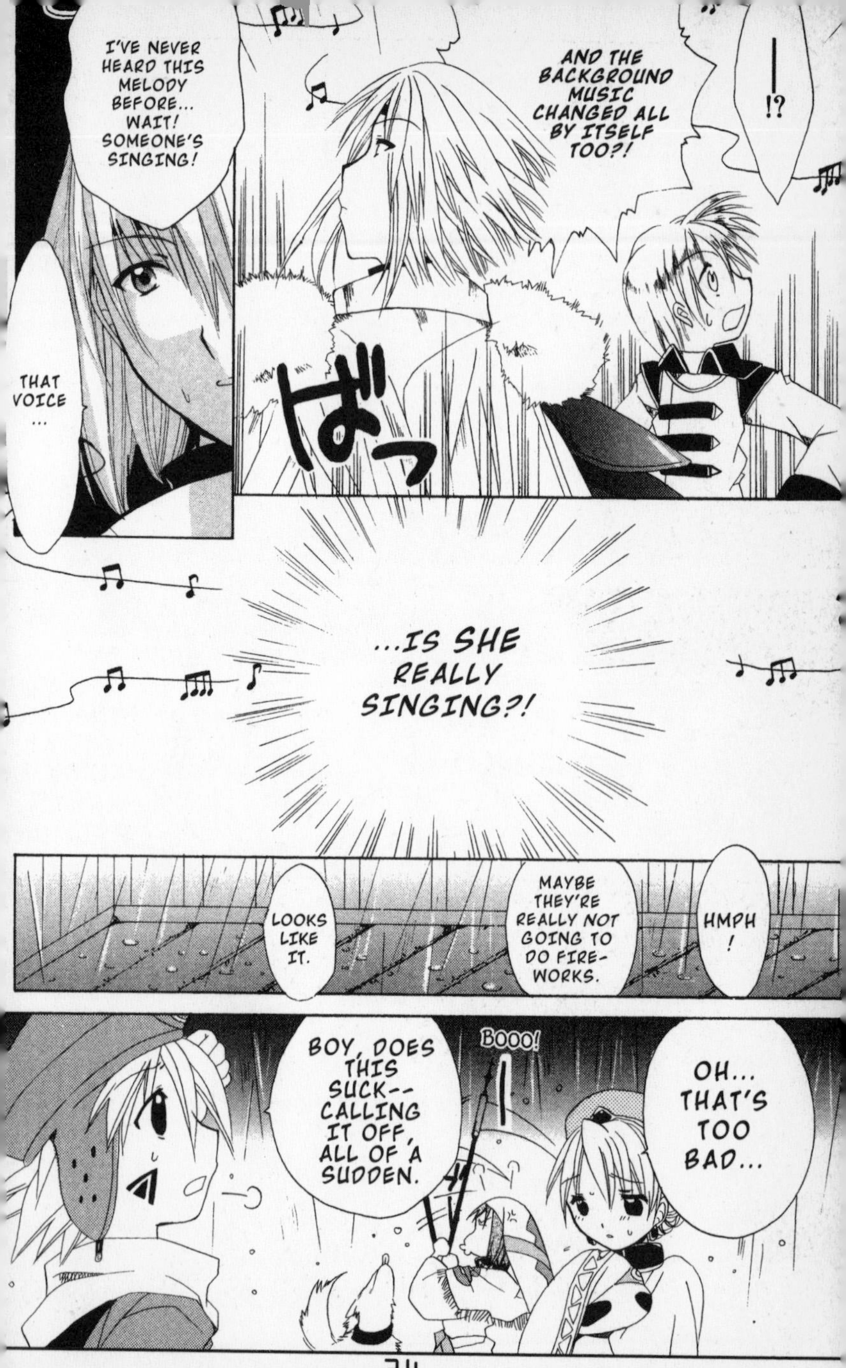
!?
AND THE BACKGROUND MUSIC CHANGED ALL BY ITSELF TOO?!
ぱっ
I'VE NEVER HEARD THIS MELODY BEFORE... WAIT! SOMEONE'S SINGING!
THAT VOICE ...
...IS SHE REALLY SINGING?!
HMPH!
MAYBE THEY'RE REALLY NOT GOING TO DO FIRE-WORKS.
LOOKS LIKE IT.
OH... THAT'S TOO BAD...
BOOO!
BOY, DOES THIS SUCK--CALLING IT OFF, ALL OF A SUDDEN.

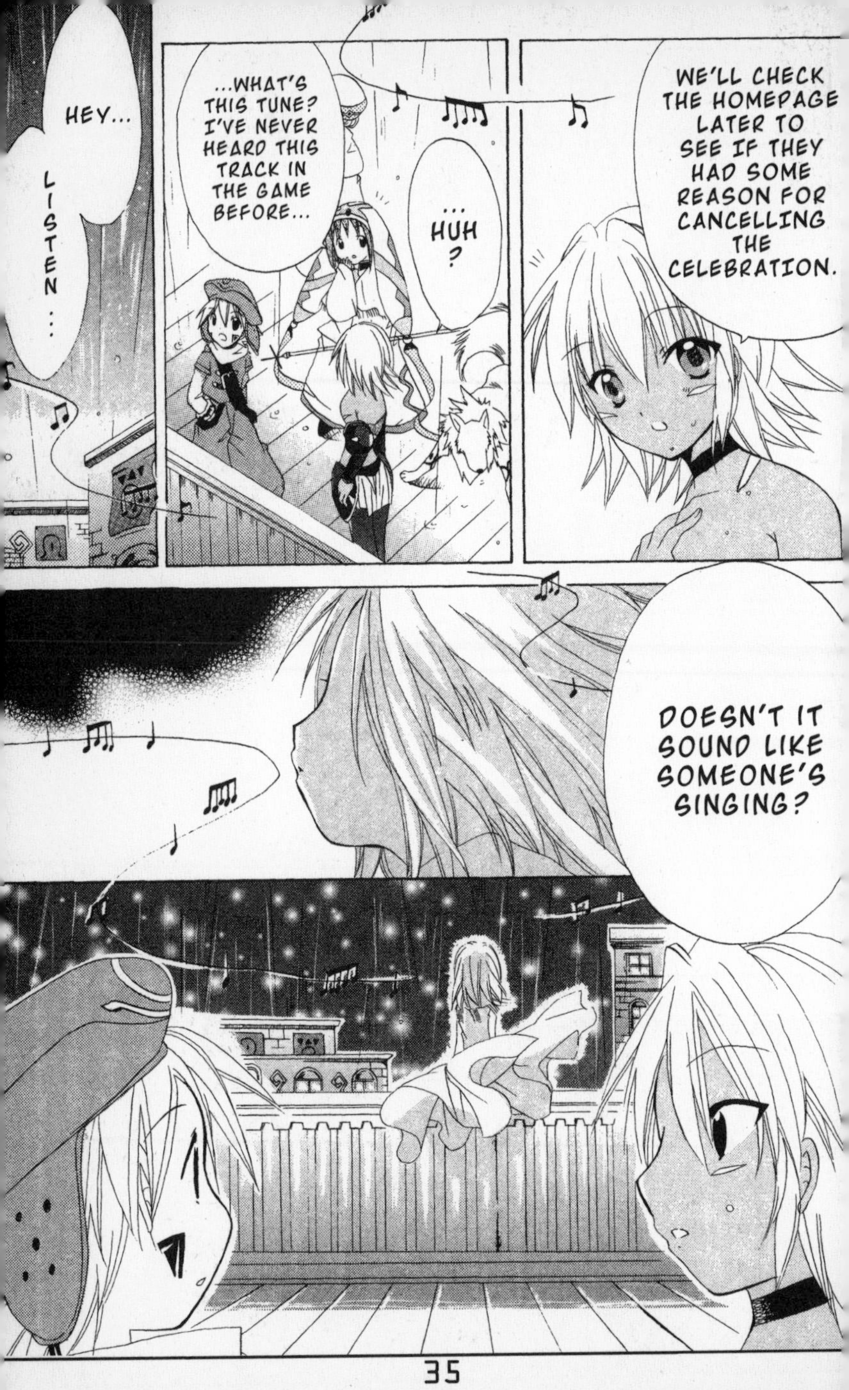
WE'LL CHECK THE HOMEPAGE LATER TO SEE IF THEY HAD SOME REASON FOR CANCELLING THE CELEBRATION.
...HUH?
...WHAT'S THIS TUNE? I'VE NEVER HEARD THIS TRACK IN THE GAME BEFORE...
HEY...
LISTEN...
DOESN'T IT SOUND LIKE SOMEONE'S SINGING?

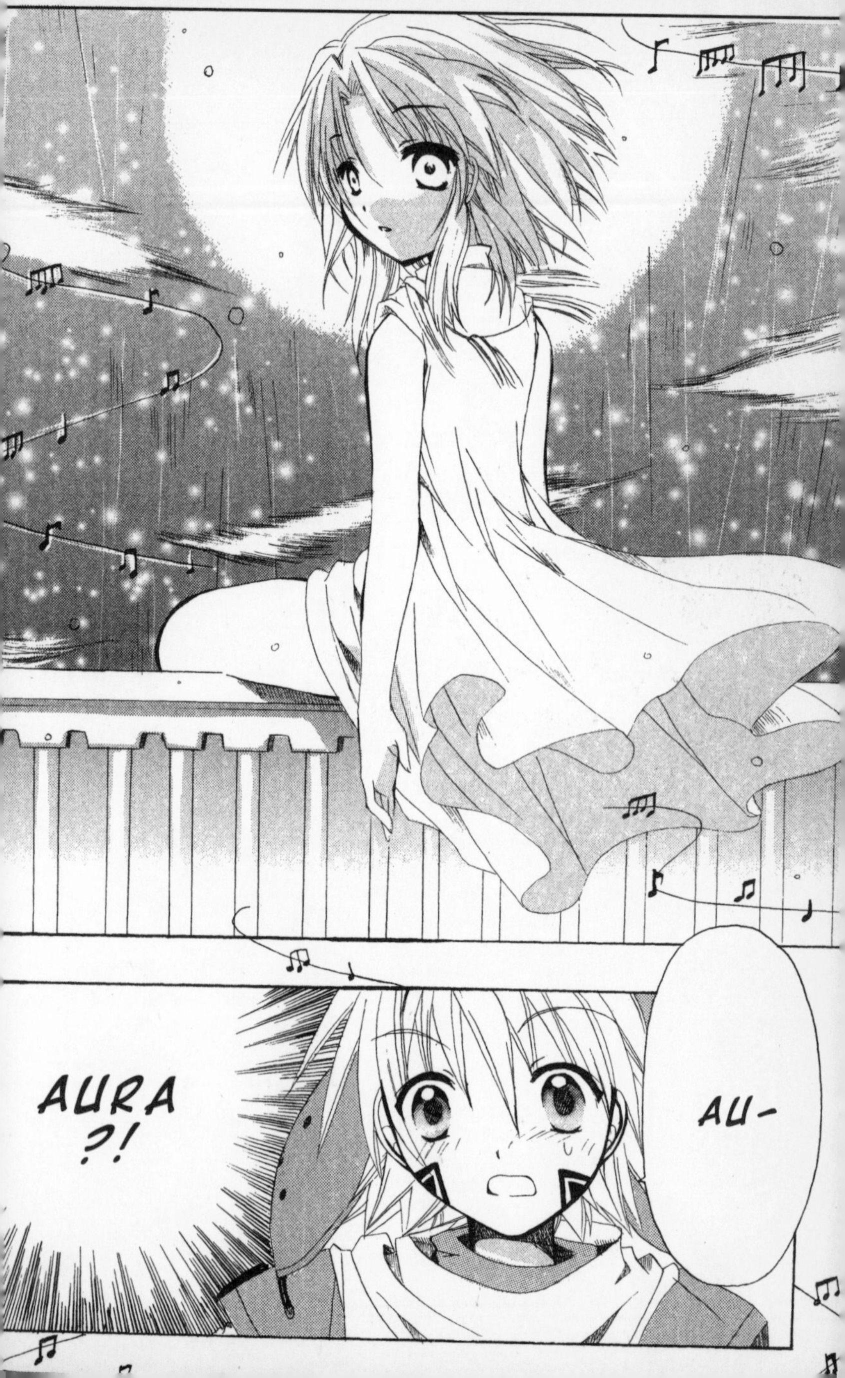
AU-
AURA ?!

NEW GENERATION ONLINE

THE WORLD

| | SUBJECT: THE INVESTIGATION | SENDER: MAGI |

I HAVE ATTACHED A REPORT AND LOGIN HISTORY ON
THE USER SHUGO, AND HIS LIMITED EDITION CHARACTER
MODEL, AS PER YOUR REQUEST.
I KNOW IT MAY NOT BE WHAT YOU ARE LOOKING FOR,
BUT I FEEL THAT TRYING TO OBTAIN MORE DETAILED
DATA ANONYMOUSLY ON THE GM SIDE OF THINGS MAY
PROVE DIFFICULT.

...BY THE WAY, HOW WAS YOUR BUSINESS TRIP TO
SHANGHAI?


CC CORP., DEPT. OF NETWORK GAMES
ADMINISTRATION DIVISION, DEBUG TEAM
SATOU (USERNAME: MAGI)

login_8

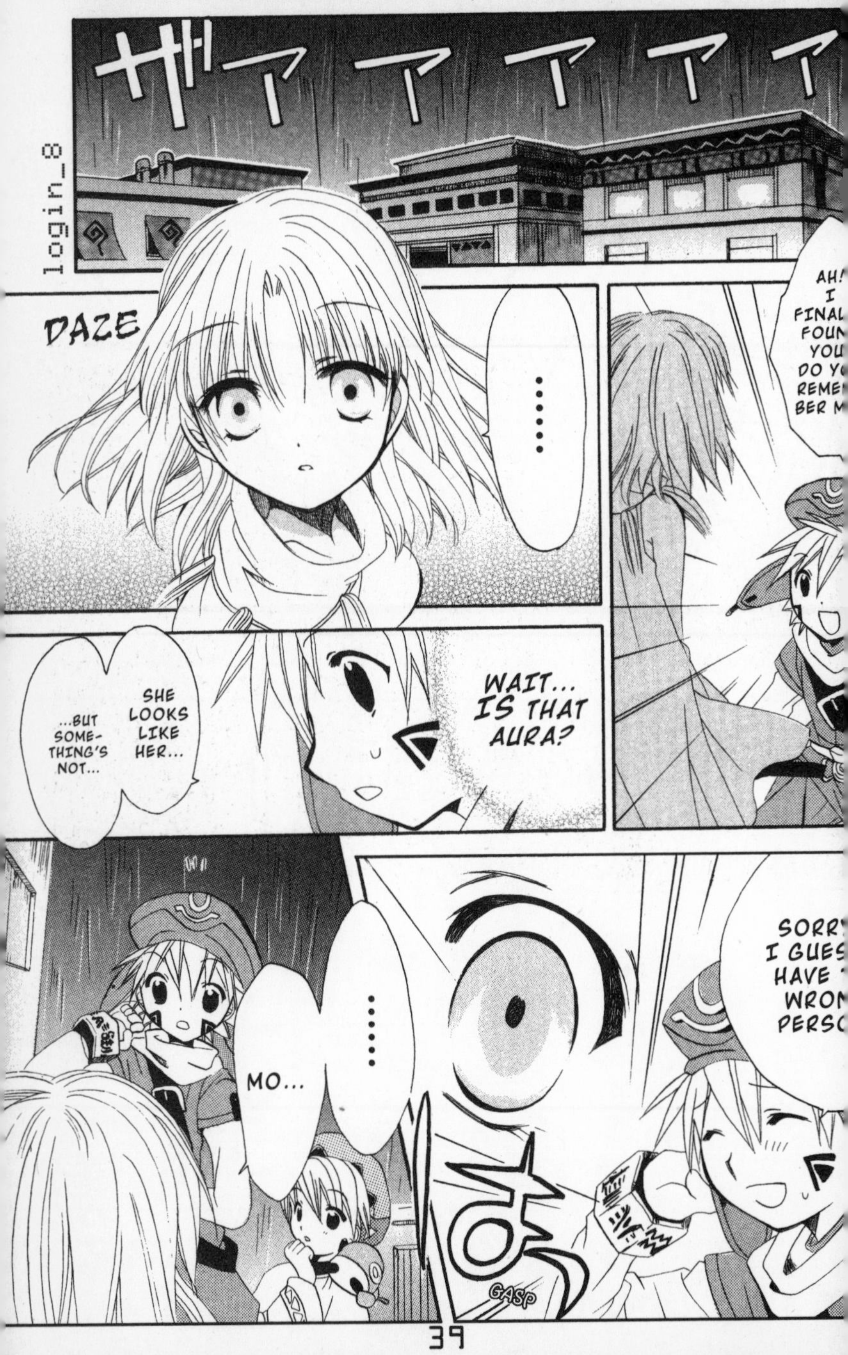

ザアアアア
AH! I FINAL FOUN YOU DO YO REME BER M
DAZE
......
WAIT... IS THAT AURA?
SHE LOOKS LIKE HER...
...BUT SOME-THING'S NOT...
SORR I GUES HAVE WRON PERSO
はっ
GASP
......
MO...

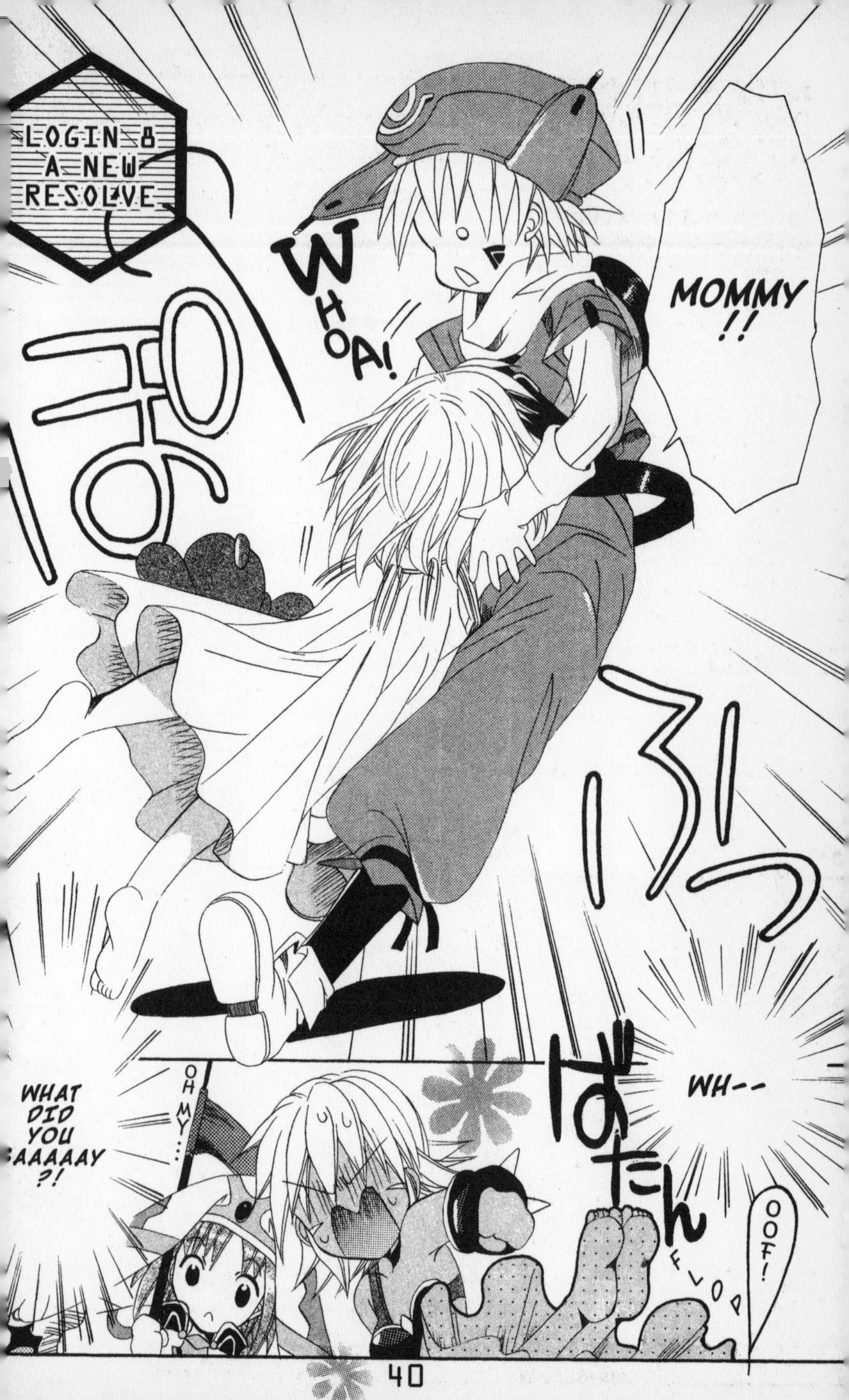
LOGIN 8 A NEW RESOLVE
MOMMY!!
WHOA!
WH--
OOF!
FLOP
OH MY...
WHAT DID YOU SAAAAAY?!

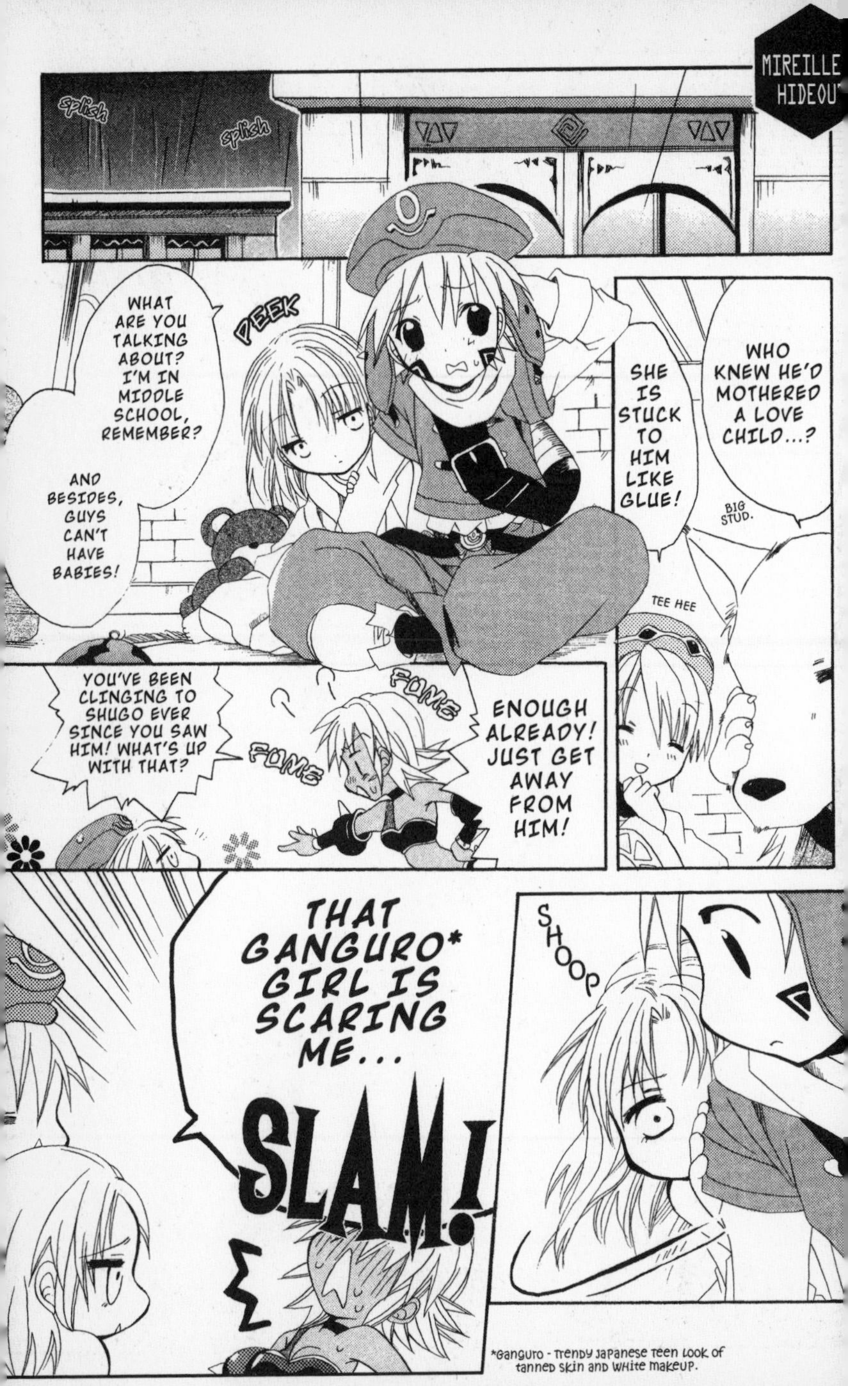
MIREILLE HIDEOUT
splish
splish
WHO KNEW HE'D MOTHERED A LOVE CHILD...?
SHE IS STUCK TO HIM LIKE GLUE!
BIG STUD.
TEE HEE
PEEK
WHAT ARE YOU TALKING ABOUT? I'M IN MIDDLE SCHOOL, REMEMBER?
AND BESIDES, GUYS CAN'T HAVE BABIES!
ENOUGH ALREADY! JUST GET AWAY FROM HIM!
FUME
FUME
YOU'VE BEEN CLINGING TO SHUGO EVER SINCE YOU SAW HIM! WHAT'S UP WITH THAT?
SHOOP
THAT GANGURO* GIRL IS SCARING ME...
SLAM!

*Ganguro - Trendy Japanese teen look of tanned skin and white makeup.

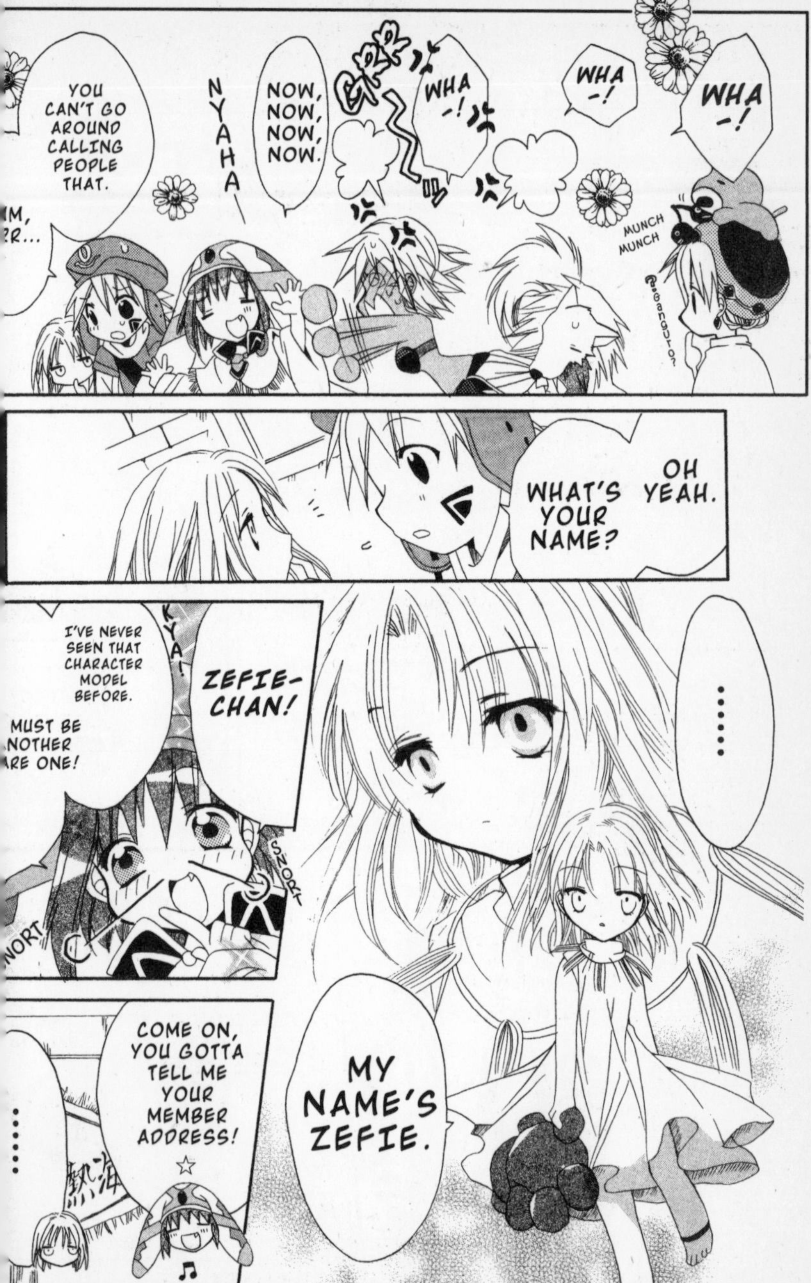
WHA-!
WHA-!
MUNCH MUNCH
?GANGURO?
WHA-!
NOW, NOW, NOW, NOW.
NYAHA
YOU CAN'T GO AROUND CALLING PEOPLE THAT.
OH YEAH.
WHAT'S YOUR NAME?
......
MY NAME'S ZEFIE.
ZEFIE-CHAN!
KYA!
I'VE NEVER SEEN THAT CHARACTER MODEL BEFORE.
SNORT
SNORT
COME ON, YOU GOTTA TELL ME YOUR MEMBER ADDRESS! ☆
♪
......

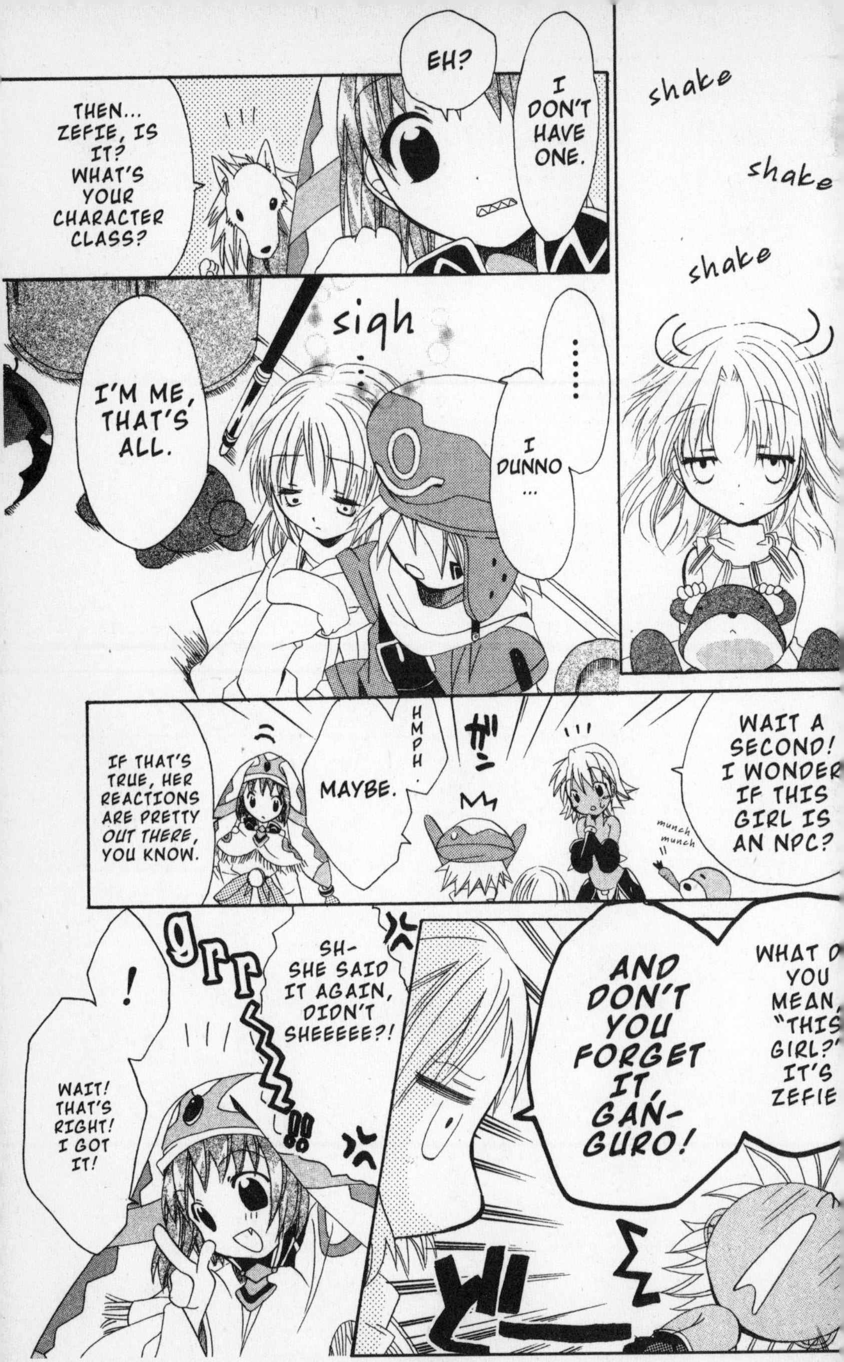
shake
shake
shake
THEN... ZEFIE, IS IT? WHAT'S YOUR CHARACTER CLASS?
EH?
I DON'T HAVE ONE.
......
I DUNNO ...
sigh
I'M ME, THAT'S ALL.
WAIT A SECOND! I WONDER IF THIS GIRL IS AN NPC?
munch munch
HMPH.
MAYBE.
IF THAT'S TRUE, HER REACTIONS ARE PRETTY OUT THERE, YOU KNOW.
WHAT DO YOU MEAN, "THIS GIRL?" IT'S ZEFIE
AND DON'T YOU FORGET IT, GAN-GURO!
SH-SHE SAID IT AGAIN, DIDN'T SHEEEEE?!
grr
!
WAIT! THAT'S RIGHT! I GOT IT!

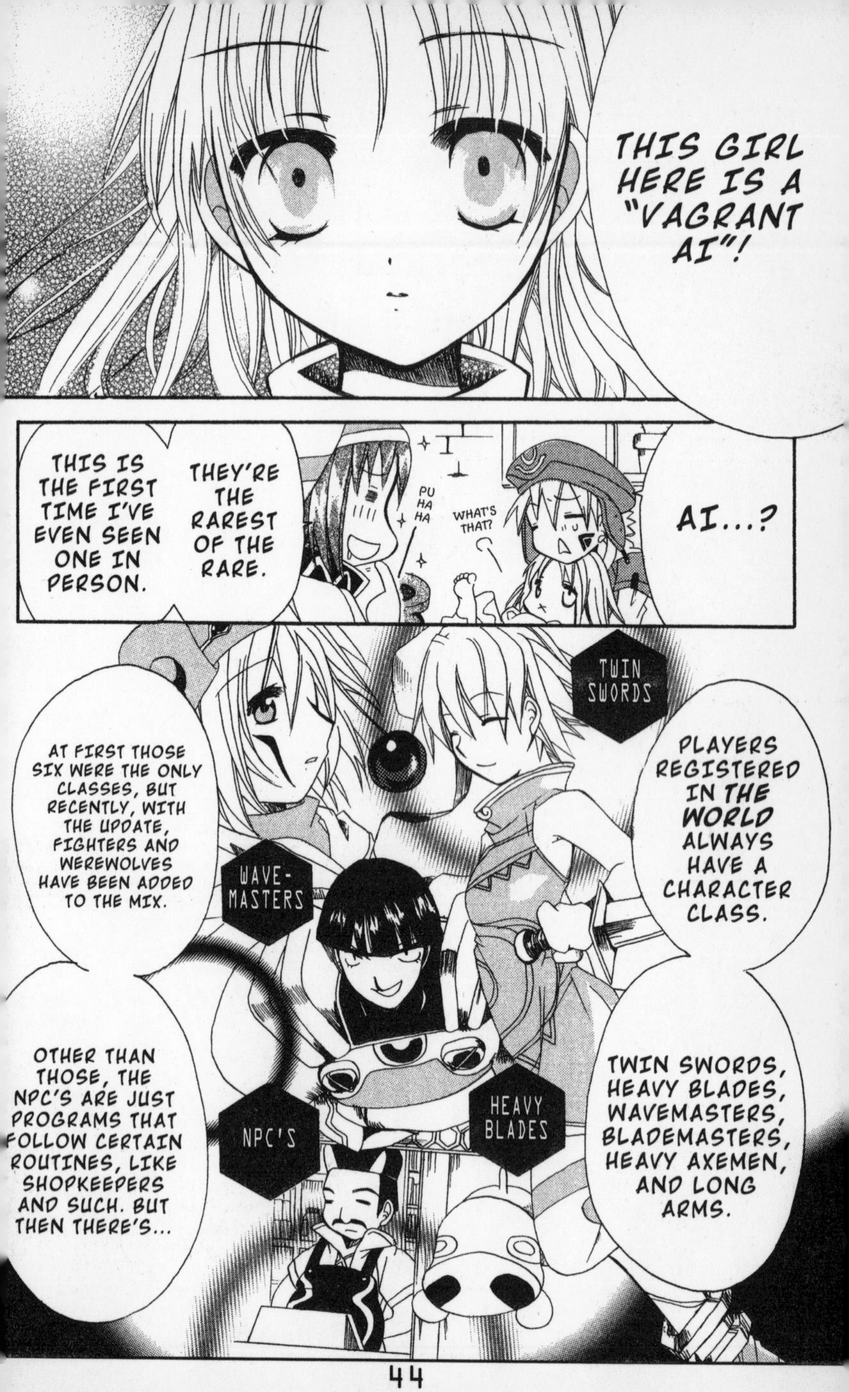

THIS GIRL HERE IS A "VAGRANT AI"!
AI...?
WHAT'S THAT?
PU HA HA
THEY'RE THE RAREST OF THE RARE.
THIS IS THE FIRST TIME I'VE EVEN SEEN ONE IN PERSON.
PLAYERS REGISTERED IN *THE WORLD* ALWAYS HAVE A CHARACTER CLASS.
TWIN SWORDS
TWIN SWORDS, HEAVY BLADES, WAVEMASTERS, BLADEMASTERS, HEAVY AXEMEN, AND LONG ARMS.
AT FIRST THOSE SIX WERE THE ONLY CLASSES, BUT RECENTLY, WITH THE UPDATE, FIGHTERS AND WEREWOLVES HAVE BEEN ADDED TO THE MIX.
WAVE-MASTERS
HEAVY BLADES
NPC'S
OTHER THAN THOSE, THE NPC'S ARE JUST PROGRAMS THAT FOLLOW CERTAIN ROUTINES, LIKE SHOPKEEPERS AND SUCH. BUT THEN THERE'S...

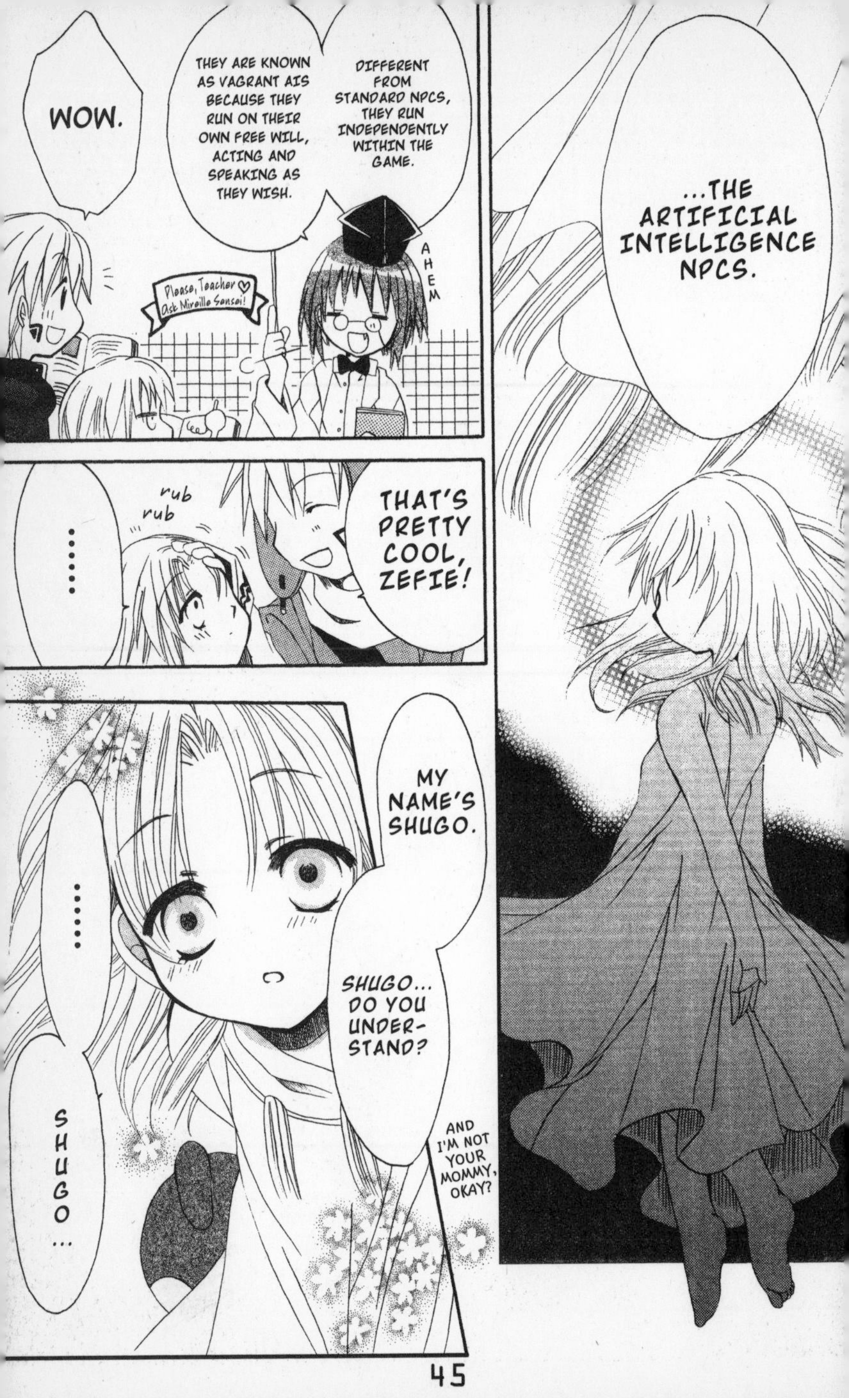

...THE ARTIFICIAL INTELLIGENCE NPCS.
DIFFERENT FROM STANDARD NPCS, THEY RUN INDEPENDENTLY WITHIN THE GAME.
THEY ARE KNOWN AS VAGRANT AIS BECAUSE THEY RUN ON THEIR OWN FREE WILL, ACTING AND SPEAKING AS THEY WISH.
AHEM
Please, Teacher ♡ Ask Mireille Sensei!
WOW.
THAT'S PRETTY COOL, ZEFIE!
rub rub
......
MY NAME'S SHUGO.
SHUGO... DO YOU UNDERSTAND?
AND I'M NOT YOUR MOMMY, OKAY?
......
SHUGO...

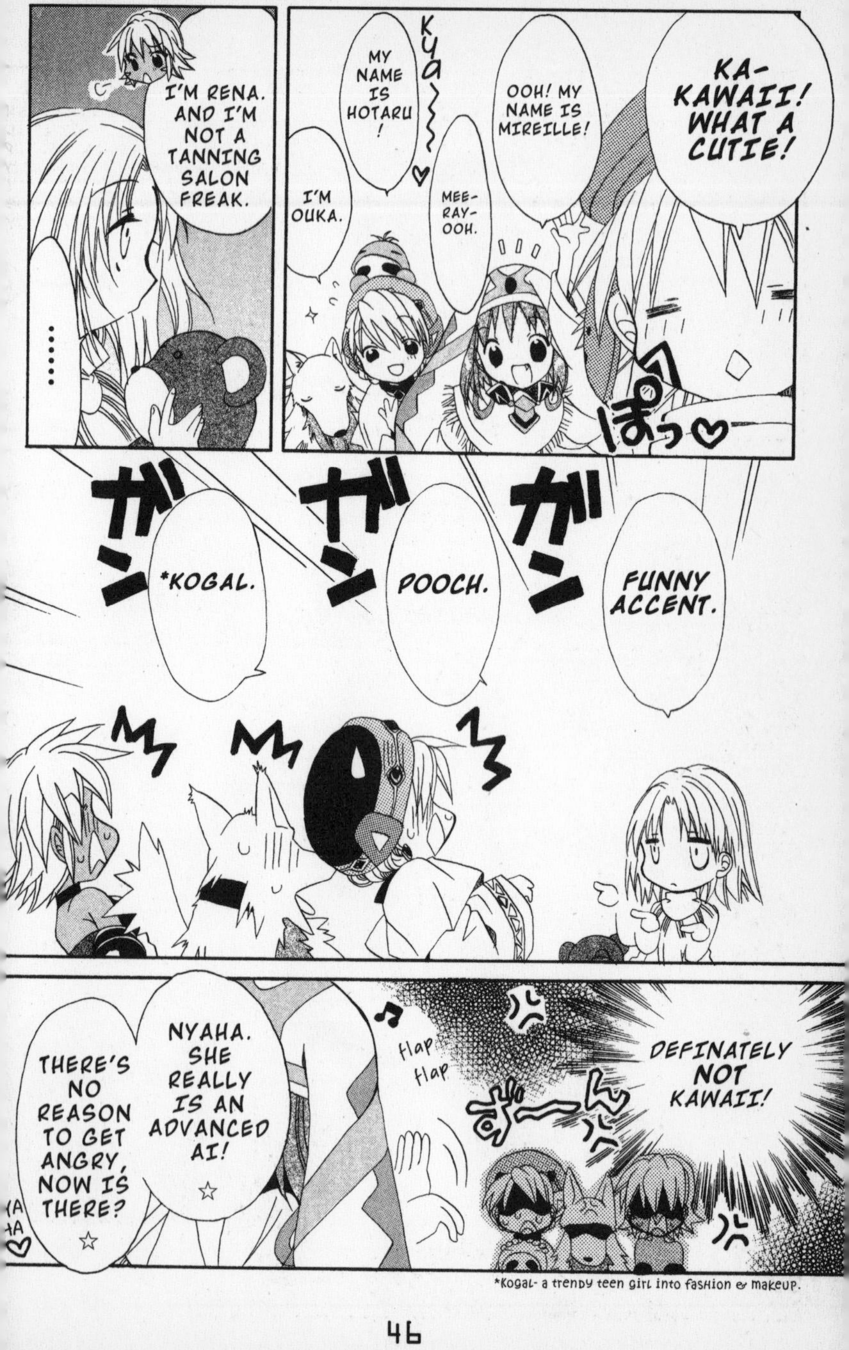
KA-KAWAII! WHAT A CUTIE!
ぽっ♥
OOH! MY NAME IS MIREILLE!
MEE-RAY-OOH.
MY NAME IS HOTARU!
KYA~~~♥
I'M OUKA.
I'M RENA. AND I'M NOT A TANNING SALON FREAK.
......
ガン
FUNNY ACCENT.
ガン
POOCH.
ガン
*KOGAL.
DEFINATELY NOT KAWAII!
ずーん
Flap Flap
NYAHA. SHE REALLY IS AN ADVANCED AI! ☆
THERE'S NO REASON TO GET ANGRY, NOW IS THERE? ☆

*Kogal- a trendy teen girl into fashion & makeup.

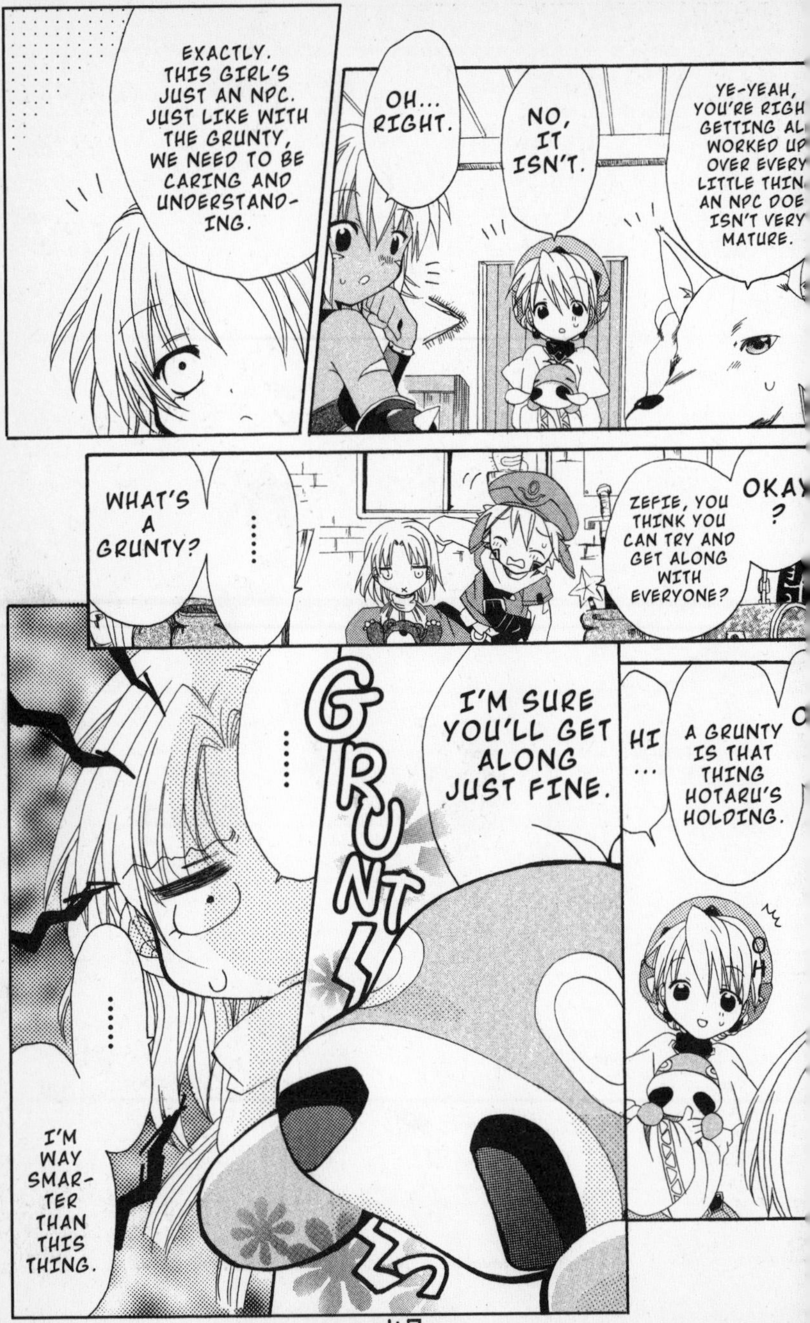
YE-YEAH, YOU'RE RIGH GETTING AL WORKED UP OVER EVERY LITTLE THIN AN NPC DOE ISN'T VERY MATURE.
NO, IT ISN'T.
OH... RIGHT.
EXACTLY. THIS GIRL'S JUST AN NPC. JUST LIKE WITH THE GRUNTY, WE NEED TO BE CARING AND UNDERSTAND-ING.
OKA ?
ZEFIE, YOU THINK YOU CAN TRY AND GET ALONG WITH EVERYONE?
......
WHAT'S A GRUNTY?
A GRUNTY IS THAT THING HOTARU'S HOLDING.
HI ...
I'M SURE YOU'LL GET ALONG JUST FINE.
GRUNT
......
......
I'M WAY SMAR-TER THAN THIS THING.

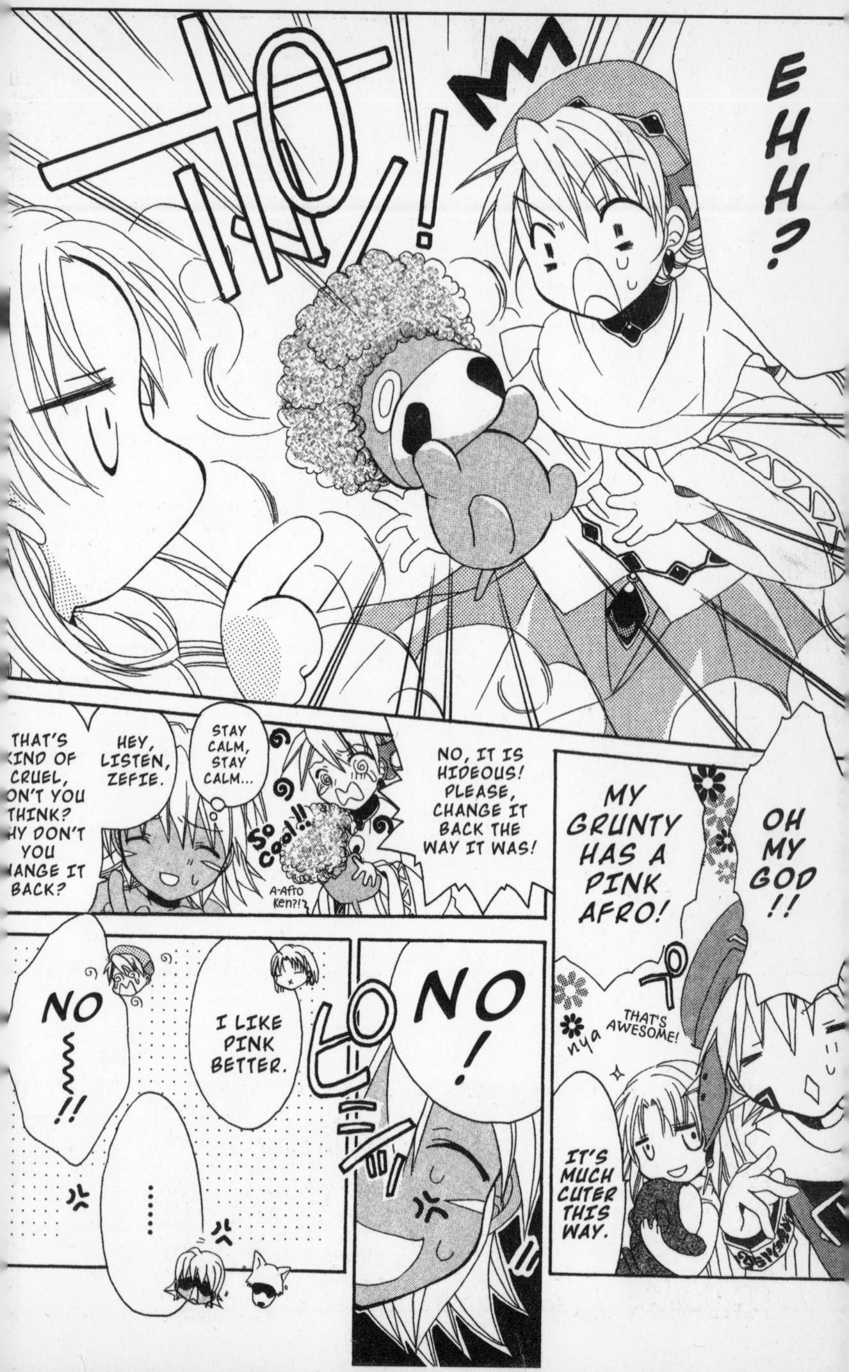
EHHH?
NO!
OH MY GOD!!
MY GRUNTY HAS A PINK AFRO!
NO, IT IS HIDEOUS! PLEASE, CHANGE IT BACK THE WAY IT WAS!
So cool!!
A-Afro Ken?!
STAY CALM, STAY CALM...
HEY, LISTEN, ZEFIE.
THAT'S KIND OF CRUEL, ON'T YOU THINK? HY DON'T YOU HANGE IT BACK?
THAT'S AWESOME!
nya
IT'S MUCH CUTER THIS WAY.
NO!
I LIKE PINK BETTER.
NO~~~!!
......

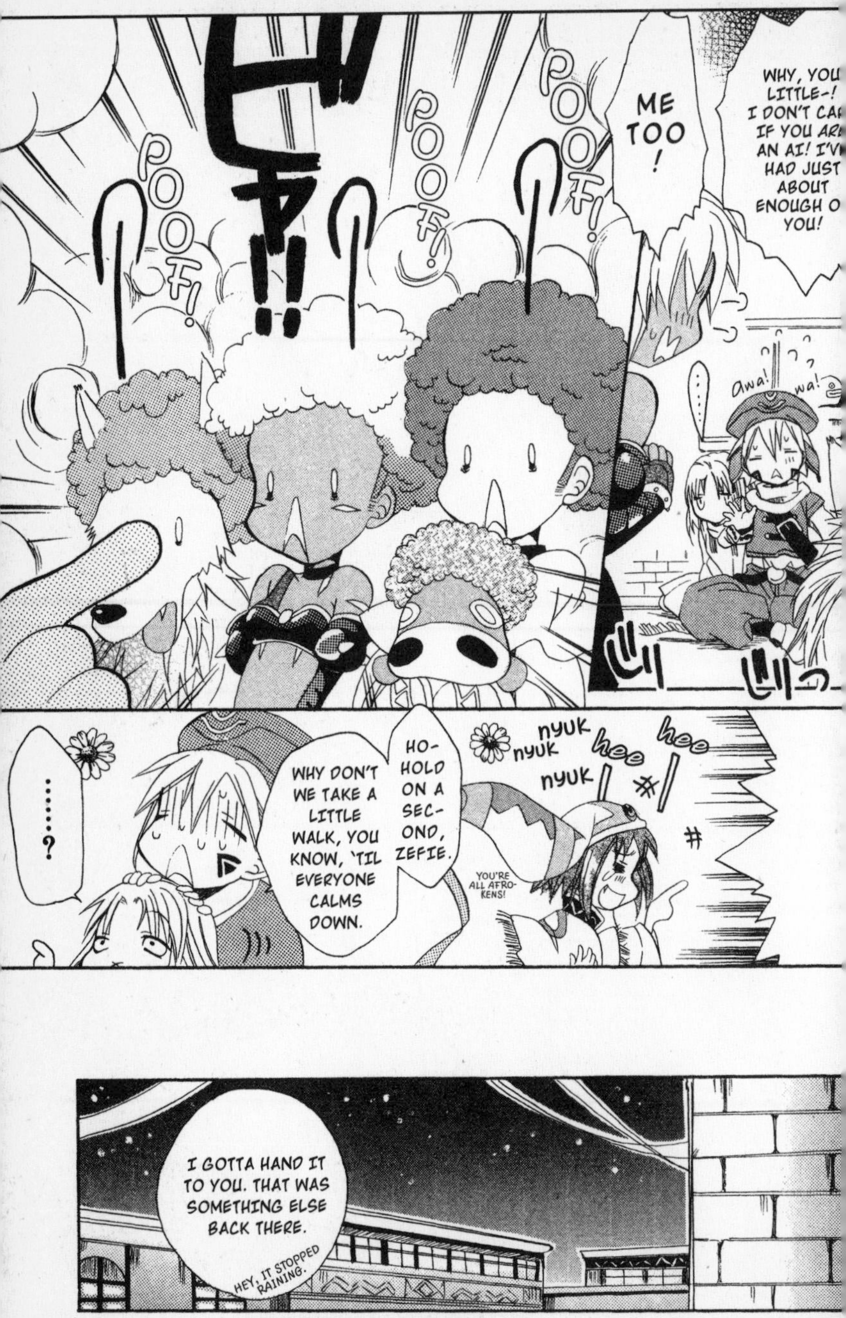
WHY, YOU LITTLE-! I DON'T CAR IF YOU AR AN AI! I'V HAD JUST ABOUT ENOUGH O YOU!
ME TOO!
awa! wa!
POOF!
POOF!
POOF!
nyuk nyuk nyuk
hee hee
YOU'RE ALL AFRO-KENS!
HO-HOLD ON A SEC-OND, ZEFIE.
WHY DON'T WE TAKE A LITTLE WALK, YOU KNOW, 'TIL EVERYONE CALMS DOWN.
......?
I GOTTA HAND IT TO YOU. THAT WAS SOMETHING ELSE BACK THERE.
HEY, IT STOPPED RAINING.

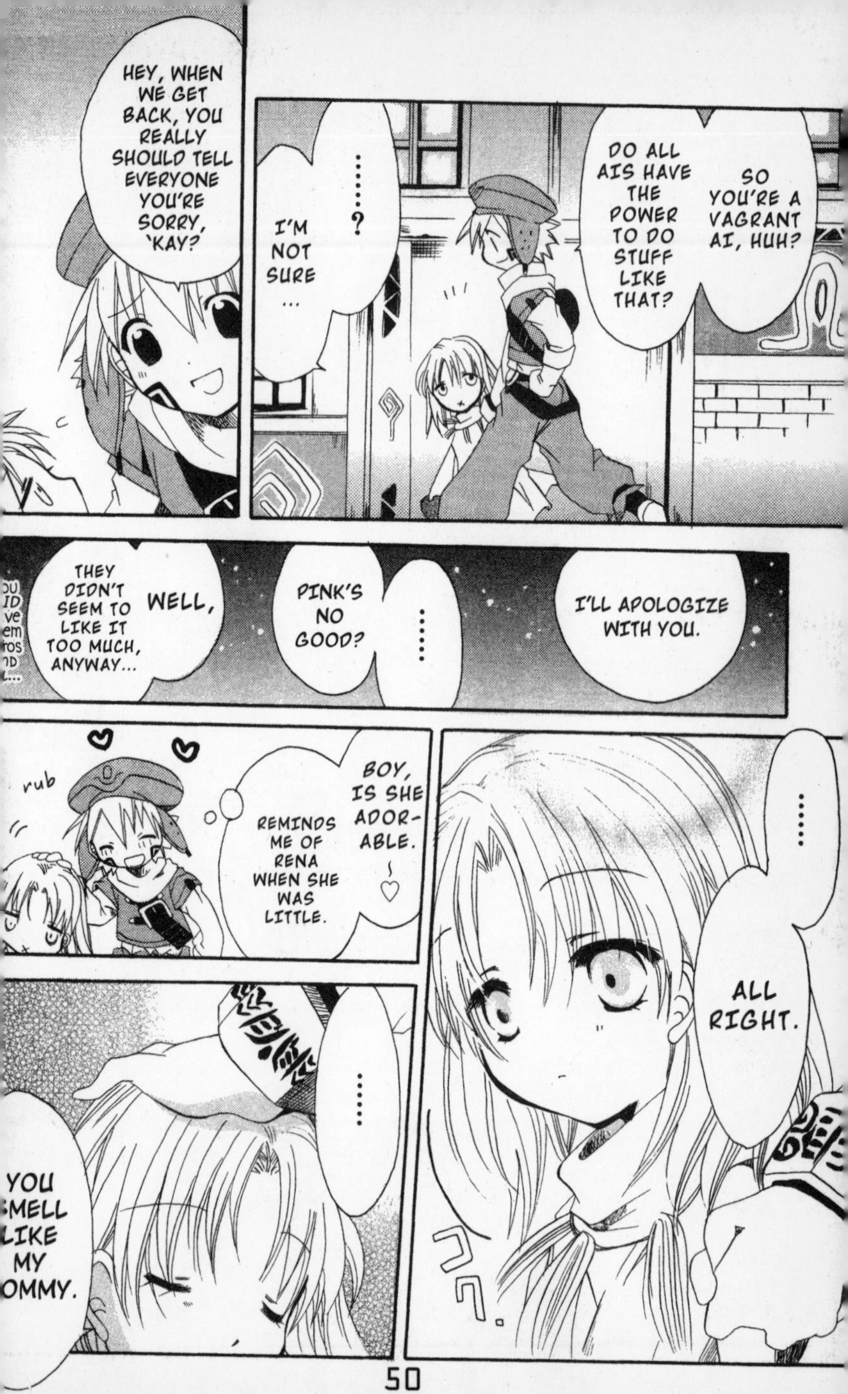

SO YOU'RE A VAGRANT AI, HUH?
DO ALL AIS HAVE THE POWER TO DO STUFF LIKE THAT?
......?
I'M NOT SURE ...
HEY, WHEN WE GET BACK, YOU REALLY SHOULD TELL EVERYONE YOU'RE SORRY, 'KAY?
I'LL APOLOGIZE WITH YOU.
......
PINK'S NO GOOD?
WELL,
THEY DIDN'T SEEM TO LIKE IT TOO MUCH, ANYWAY...
......
ALL RIGHT.
BOY, IS SHE ADORABLE.
REMINDS ME OF RENA WHEN SHE WAS LITTLE.
rub
......
YOU MELL LIKE MY OMMY.

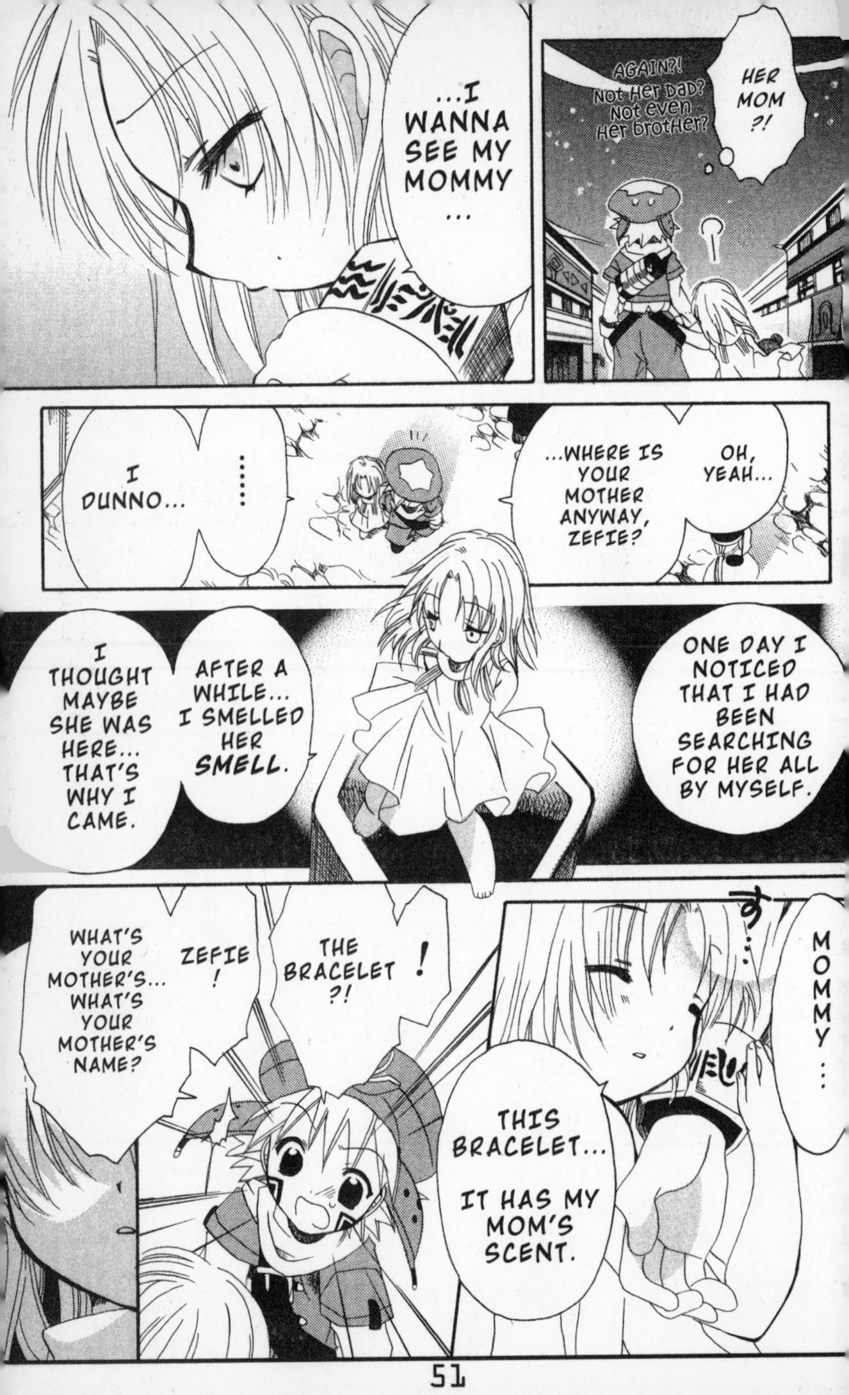
HER MOM ?!
AGAIN?! Not Her Dad? Not even Her brother?
...I WANNA SEE MY MOMMY ...
OH, YEAH...
...WHERE IS YOUR MOTHER ANYWAY, ZEFIE?
......
I DUNNO...
ONE DAY I NOTICED THAT I HAD BEEN SEARCHING FOR HER ALL BY MYSELF.
AFTER A WHILE... I SMELLED HER **SMELL**.
I THOUGHT MAYBE SHE WAS HERE... THAT'S WHY I CAME.
す...
MOMMY ...
THIS BRACELET... IT HAS MY MOM'S SCENT.
!
THE BRACELET ?!
ZEFIE !
WHAT'S YOUR MOTHER'S... WHAT'S YOUR MOTHER'S NAME?

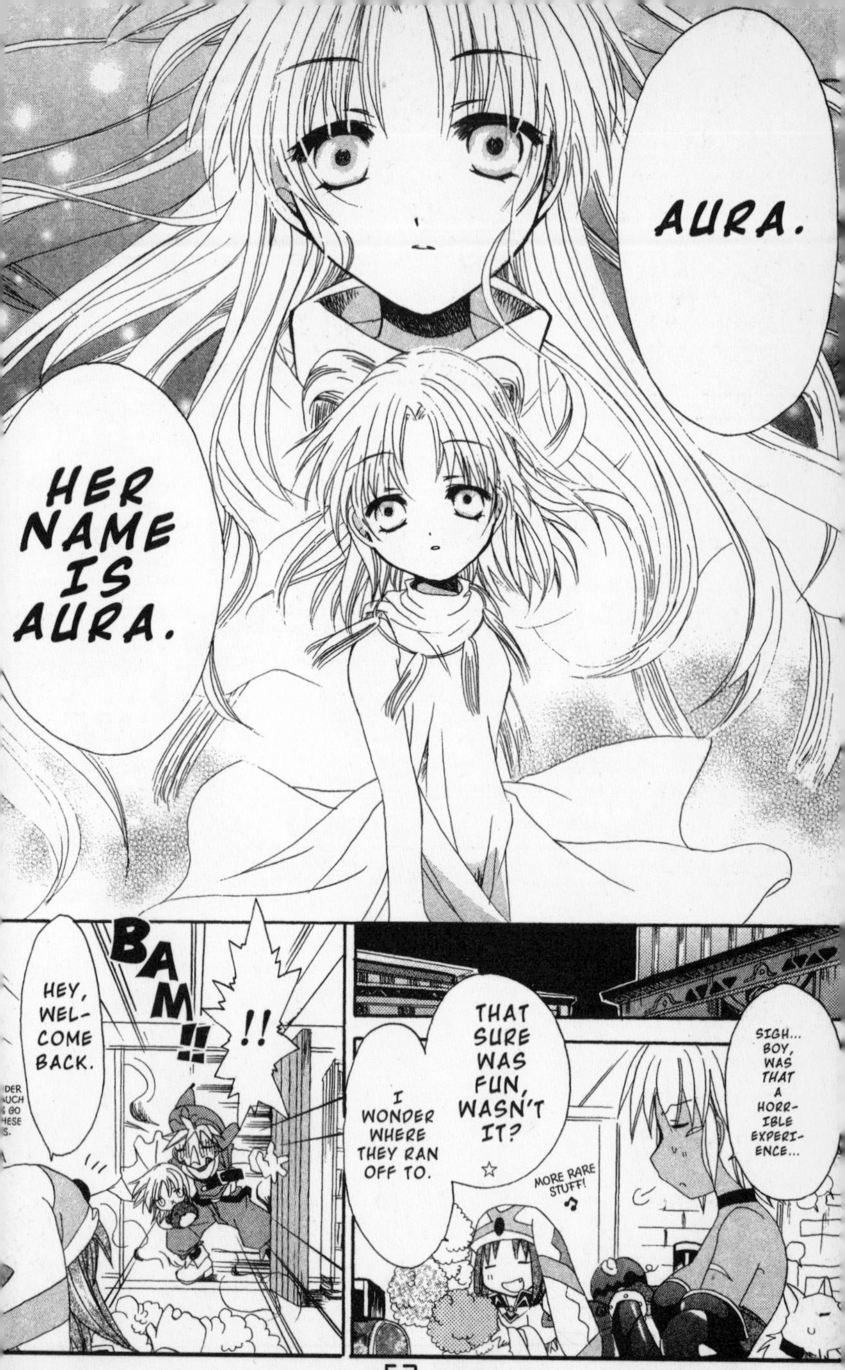
AURA.
HER NAME IS AURA.
SIGH... BOY, WAS THAT A HORRIBLE EXPERIENCE...
THAT SURE WAS FUN, WASN'T IT? ☆
I WONDER WHERE THEY RAN OFF TO.
MORE RARE STUFF! ♪
BAM!!
!!
HEY, WELCOME BACK.

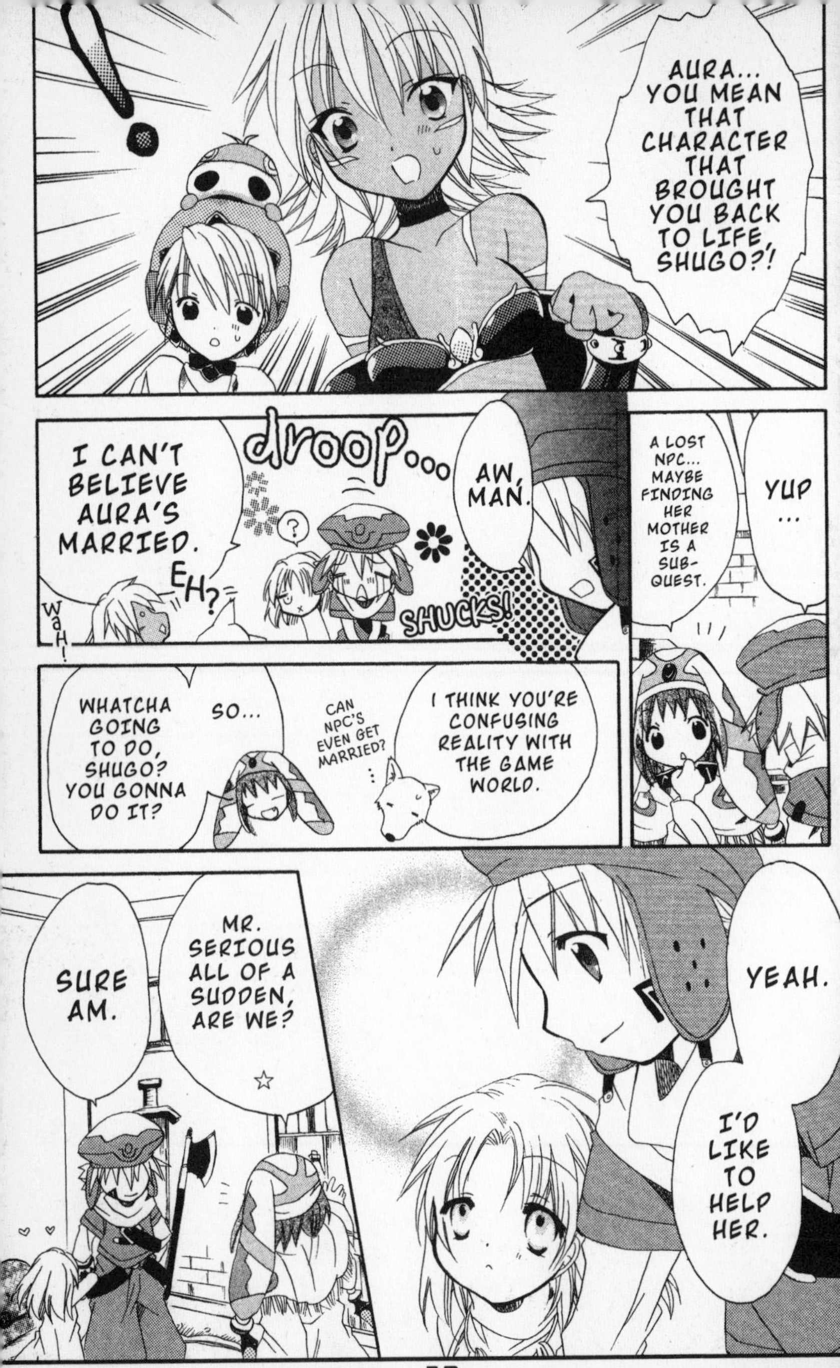
!
AURA... YOU MEAN THAT CHARACTER THAT BROUGHT YOU BACK TO LIFE, SHUGO?!
YUP ...
A LOST NPC... MAYBE FINDING HER MOTHER IS A SUB-QUEST.
AW, MAN.
droop...
SHUCKS!
?
I CAN'T BELIEVE AURA'S MARRIED.
EH?
WaH!
I THINK YOU'RE CONFUSING REALITY WITH THE GAME WORLD.
CAN NPC'S EVEN GET MARRIED?
SO...
WHATCHA GOING TO DO, SHUGO? YOU GONNA DO IT?
YEAH.
I'D LIKE TO HELP HER.
MR. SERIOUS ALL OF A SUDDEN, ARE WE?
SURE AM.

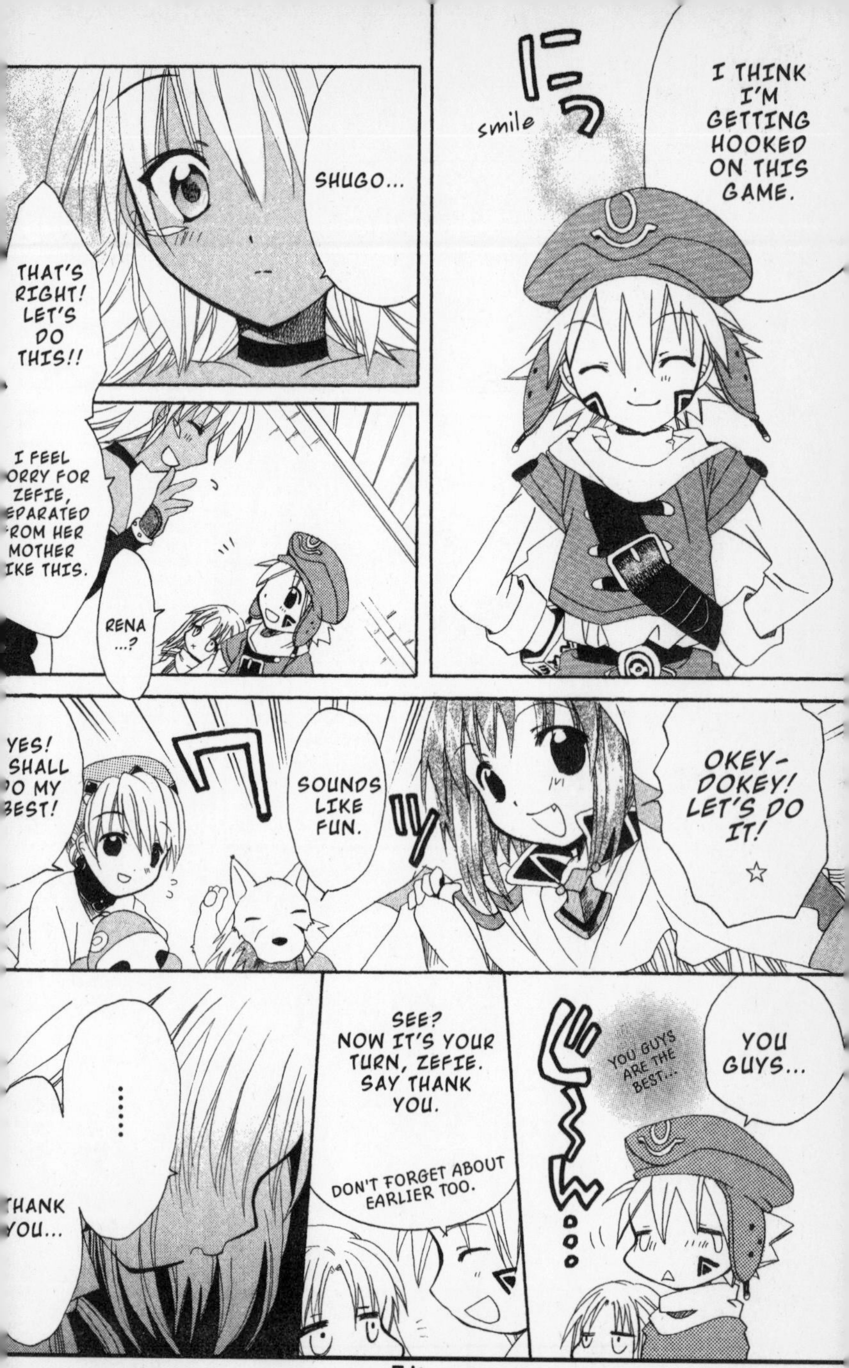
I THINK I'M GETTING HOOKED ON THIS GAME.
smile
SHUGO...
THAT'S RIGHT! LET'S DO THIS!!
I FEEL SORRY FOR ZEFIE, SEPARATED FROM HER MOTHER LIKE THIS.
RENA ...?
OKEY-DOKEY! LET'S DO IT! ☆
SOUNDS LIKE FUN.
YES! I SHALL DO MY BEST!
YOU GUYS...
YOU GUYS ARE THE BEST...
SEE? NOW IT'S YOUR TURN, ZEFIE. SAY THANK YOU.
DON'T FORGET ABOUT EARLIER TOO.
......
THANK YOU...

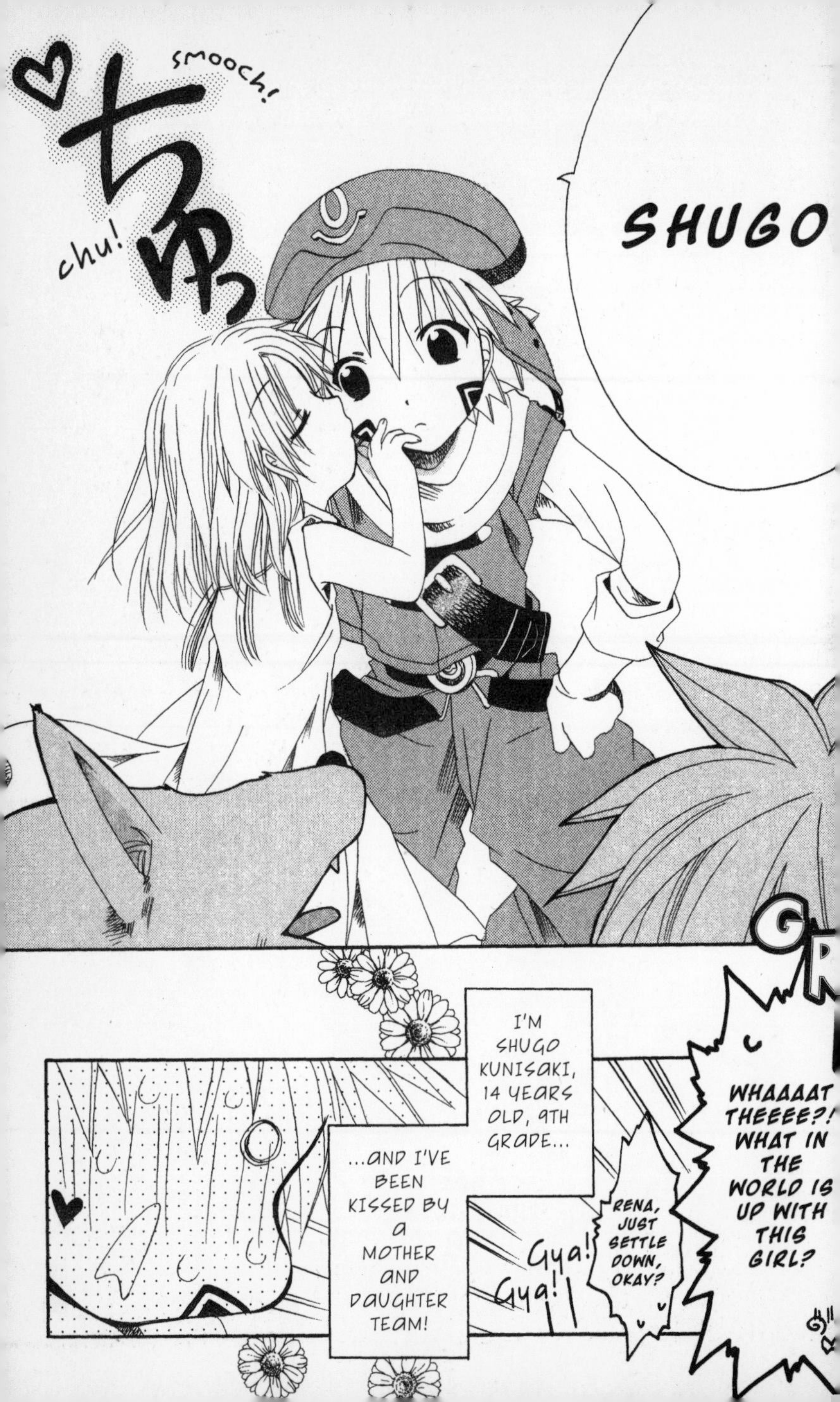

SHUGO
ちゅっ
chu!
smooch!
WHAAAAT THEEEE?! WHAT IN THE WORLD IS UP WITH THIS GIRL?
RENA, JUST SETTLE DOWN, OKAY?
Gya! Gya!
I'M SHUGO KUNISAKI, 14 YEARS OLD, 9TH GRADE...
...and I'VE BEEN KISSED BY a MOTHER and DAUGHTER TEAM!

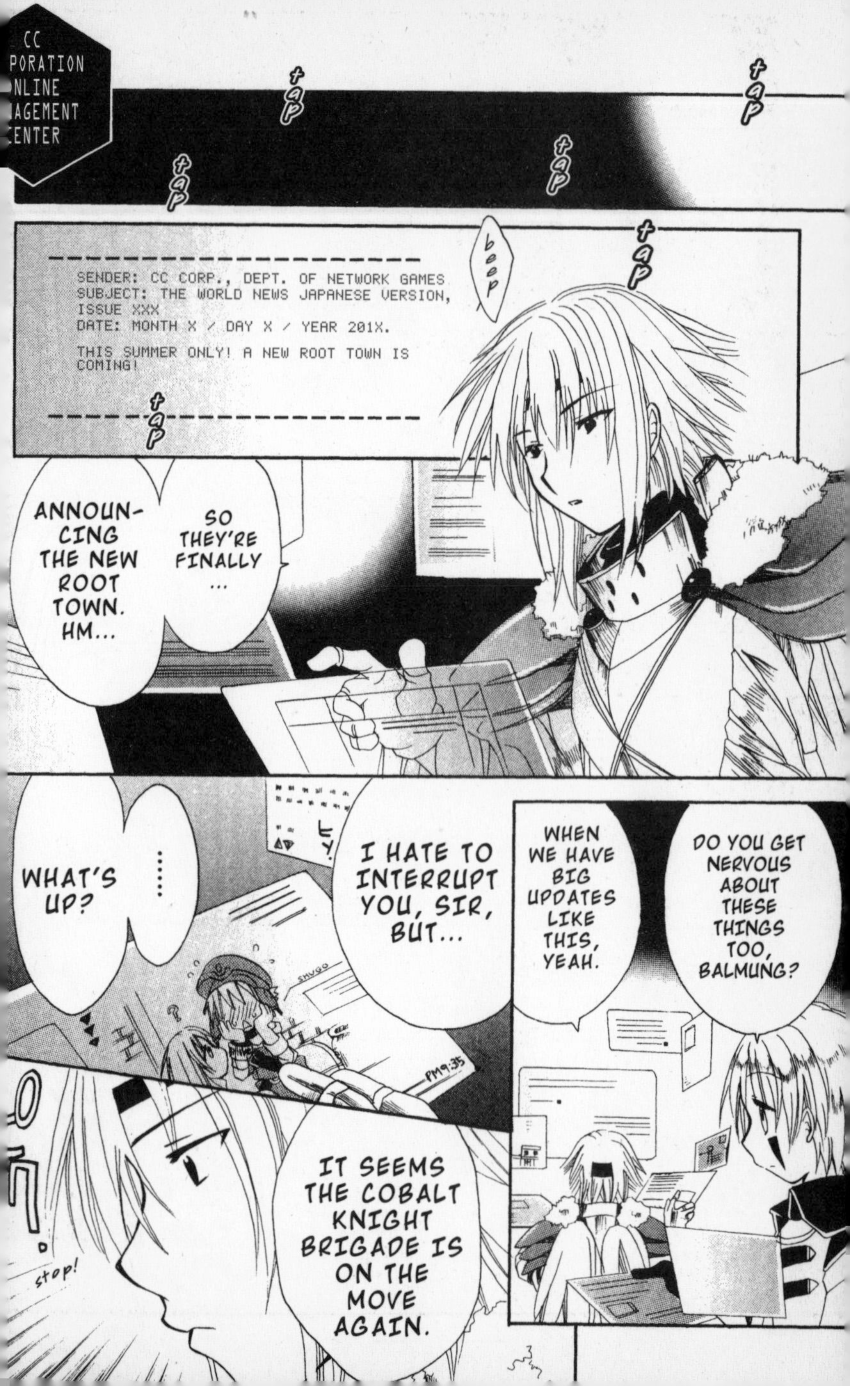

CC
PORATION
NLINE
AGEMENT
ENTER
tap
tap
tap
tap
tap
beep
SENDER: CC CORP., DEPT. OF NETWORK GAMES
SUBJECT: THE WORLD NEWS JAPANESE VERSION, ISSUE XXX
DATE: MONTH X / DAY X / YEAR 201X.
THIS SUMMER ONLY! A NEW ROOT TOWN IS COMING!
tap
SO THEY'RE FINALLY ...
ANNOUNCING THE NEW ROOT TOWN. HM...
DO YOU GET NERVOUS ABOUT THESE THINGS TOO, BALMUNG?
WHEN WE HAVE BIG UPDATES LIKE THIS, YEAH.
I HATE TO INTERRUPT YOU, SIR, BUT...
......
WHAT'S UP?
SHUGO
PM9:35
IT SEEMS THE COBALT KNIGHT BRIGADE IS ON THE MOVE AGAIN.
stop!

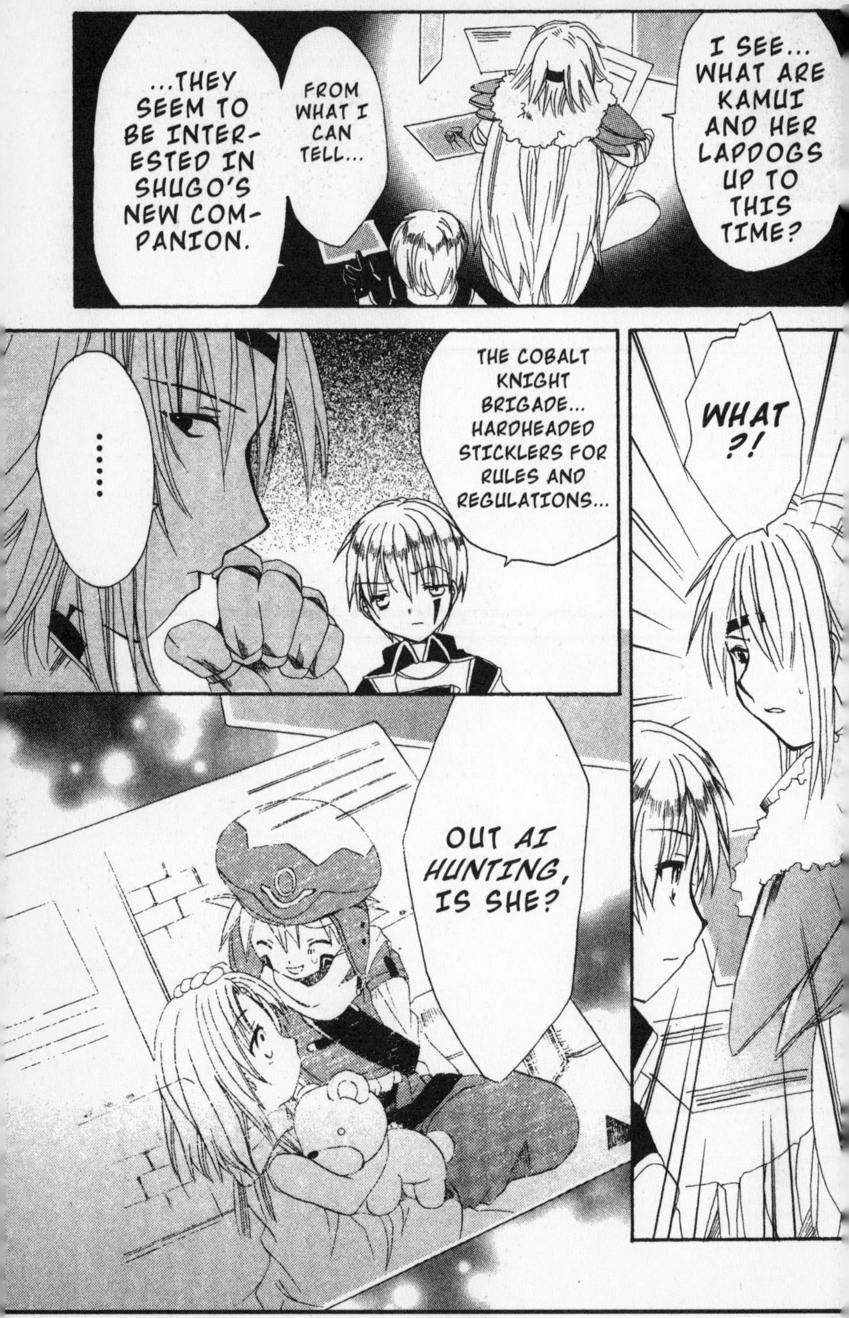
I SEE... WHAT ARE KAMUI AND HER LAPDOGS UP TO THIS TIME?
FROM WHAT I CAN TELL...
...THEY SEEM TO BE INTER-ESTED IN SHUGO'S NEW COM-PANION.
WHAT?!
THE COBALT KNIGHT BRIGADE... HARDHEADED STICKLERS FOR RULES AND REGULATIONS...
......
OUT *AI HUNTING*, IS SHE?

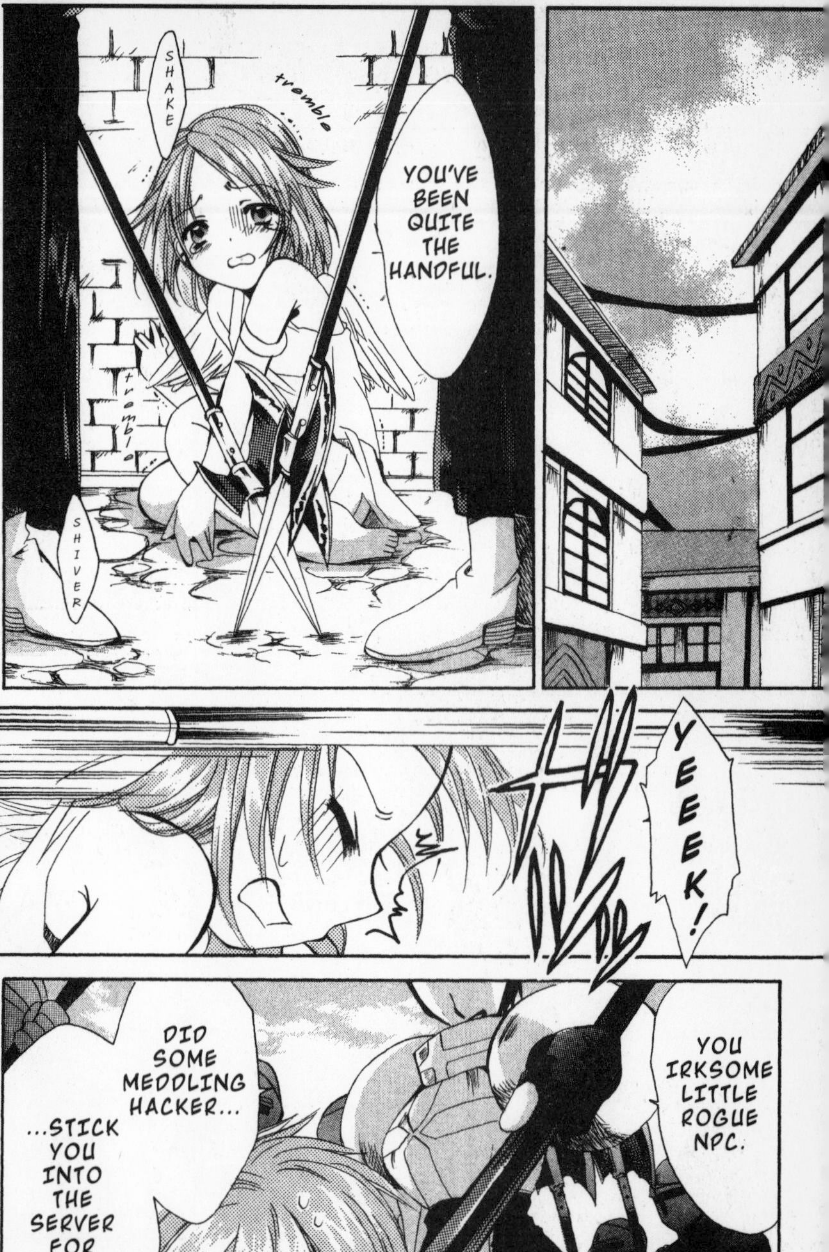
YOU'VE BEEN QUITE THE HANDFUL.
tremble...
SHAKE
tremble...
SHIVER
YEEEK!
YOU IRKSOME LITTLE ROGUE NPC.
DID SOME MEDDLING HACKER...
...STICK YOU INTO THE SERVER FOR KICKS?

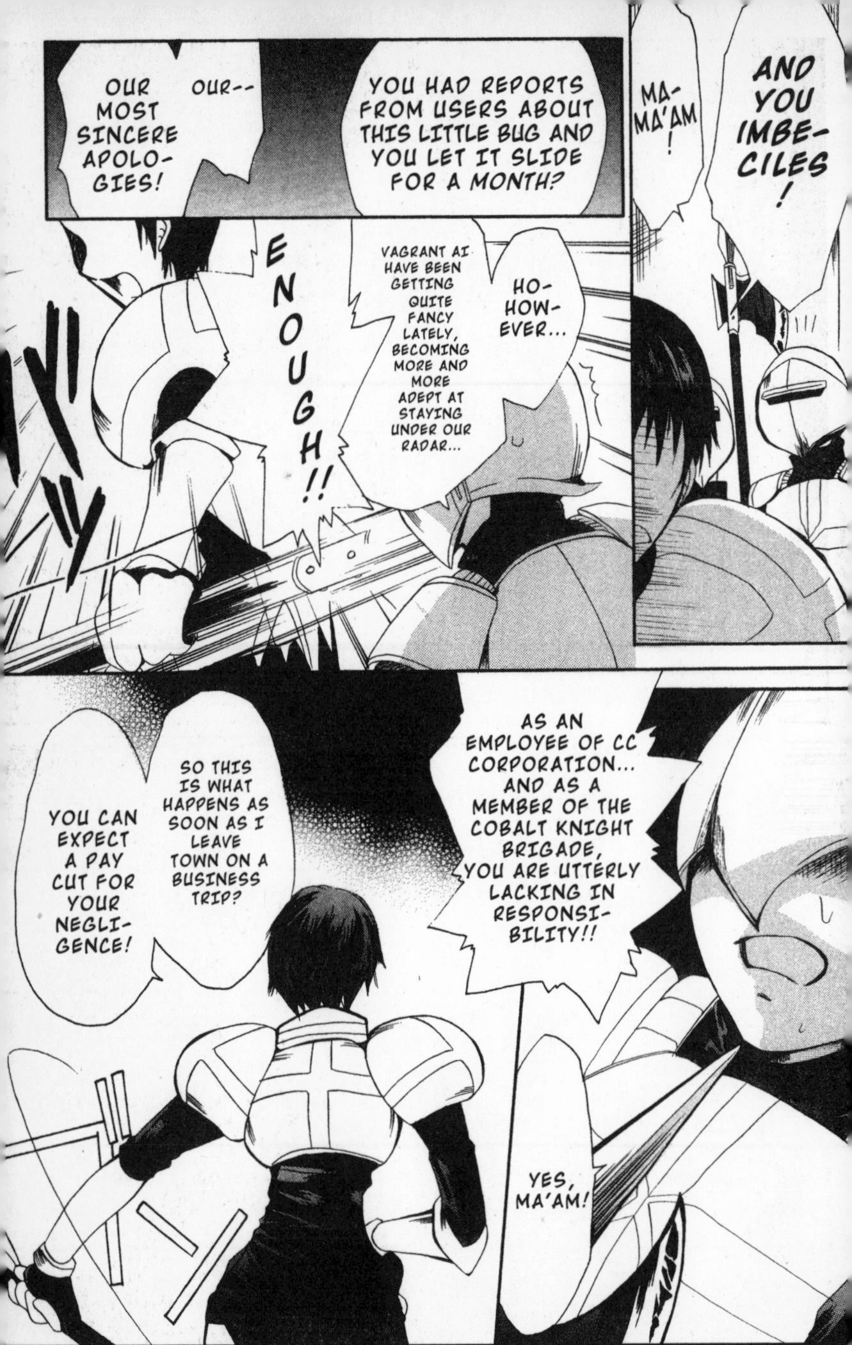
AND YOU IMBE-CILES!
MA-MA'AM!
YOU HAD REPORTS FROM USERS ABOUT THIS LITTLE BUG AND YOU LET IT SLIDE FOR A MONTH?
OUR-- OUR MOST SINCERE APOLOGIES!
HO-HOW-EVER...
VAGRANT AI HAVE BEEN GETTING QUITE FANCY LATELY, BECOMING MORE AND MORE ADEPT AT STAYING UNDER OUR RADAR...
ENOUGH!!
AS AN EMPLOYEE OF CC CORPORATION... AND AS A MEMBER OF THE COBALT KNIGHT BRIGADE, YOU ARE UTTERLY LACKING IN RESPONSI-BILITY!!
YES, MA'AM!
SO THIS IS WHAT HAPPENS AS SOON AS I LEAVE TOWN ON A BUSINESS TRIP?
YOU CAN EXPECT A PAY CUT FOR YOUR NEGLI-GENCE!

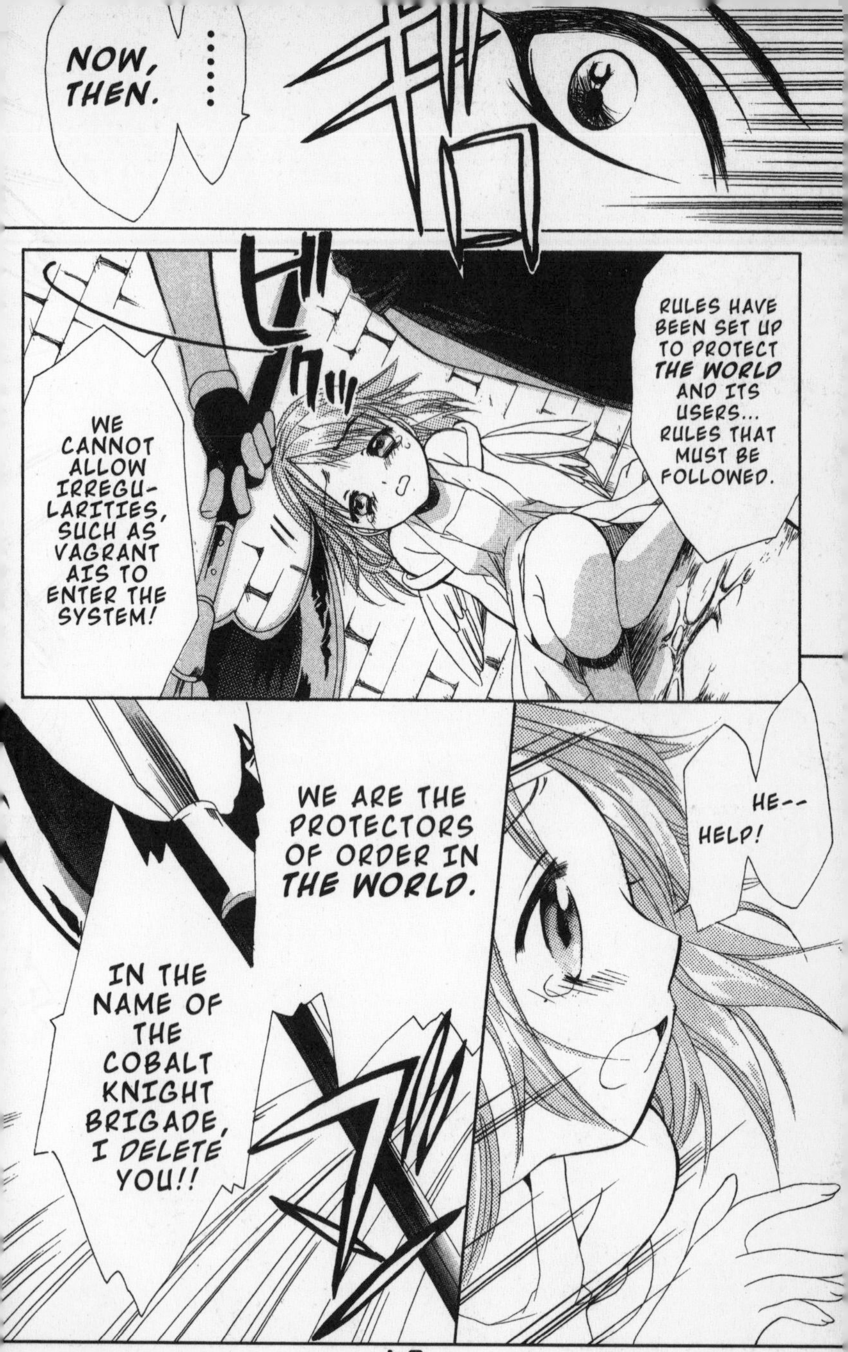

NOW, THEN. .....
RULES HAVE BEEN SET UP TO PROTECT THE WORLD AND ITS USERS... RULES THAT MUST BE FOLLOWED.
WE CANNOT ALLOW IRREGU-LARITIES, SUCH AS VAGRANT AIS TO ENTER THE SYSTEM!
HE-- HELP!
WE ARE THE PROTECTORS OF ORDER IN THE WORLD.
IN THE NAME OF THE COBALT KNIGHT BRIGADE, I DELETE YOU!!

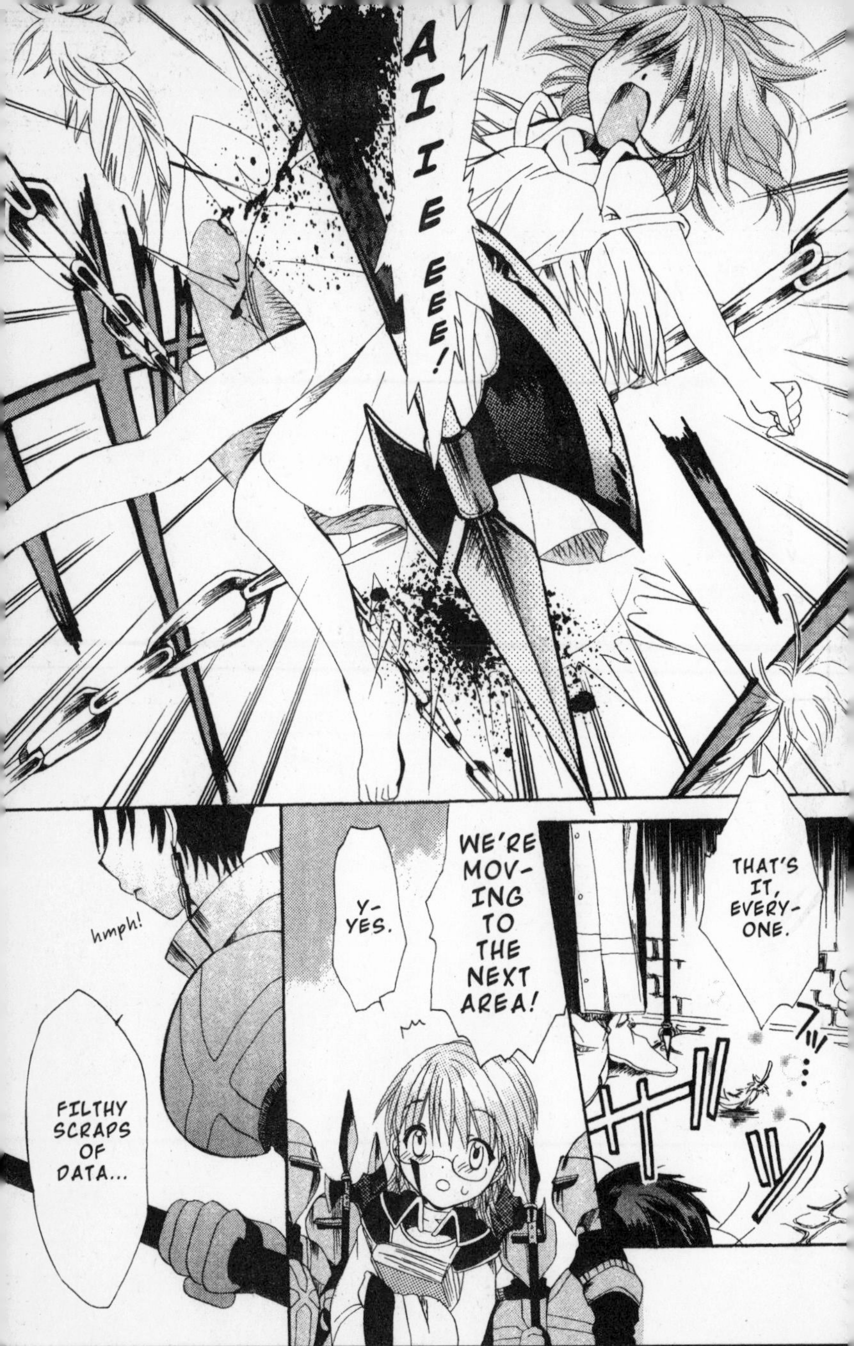
AIIEEEE!
THAT'S IT, EVERY-ONE.
WE'RE MOV-ING TO THE NEXT AREA!
Y-YES.
hmph!
FILTHY SCRAPS OF DATA...

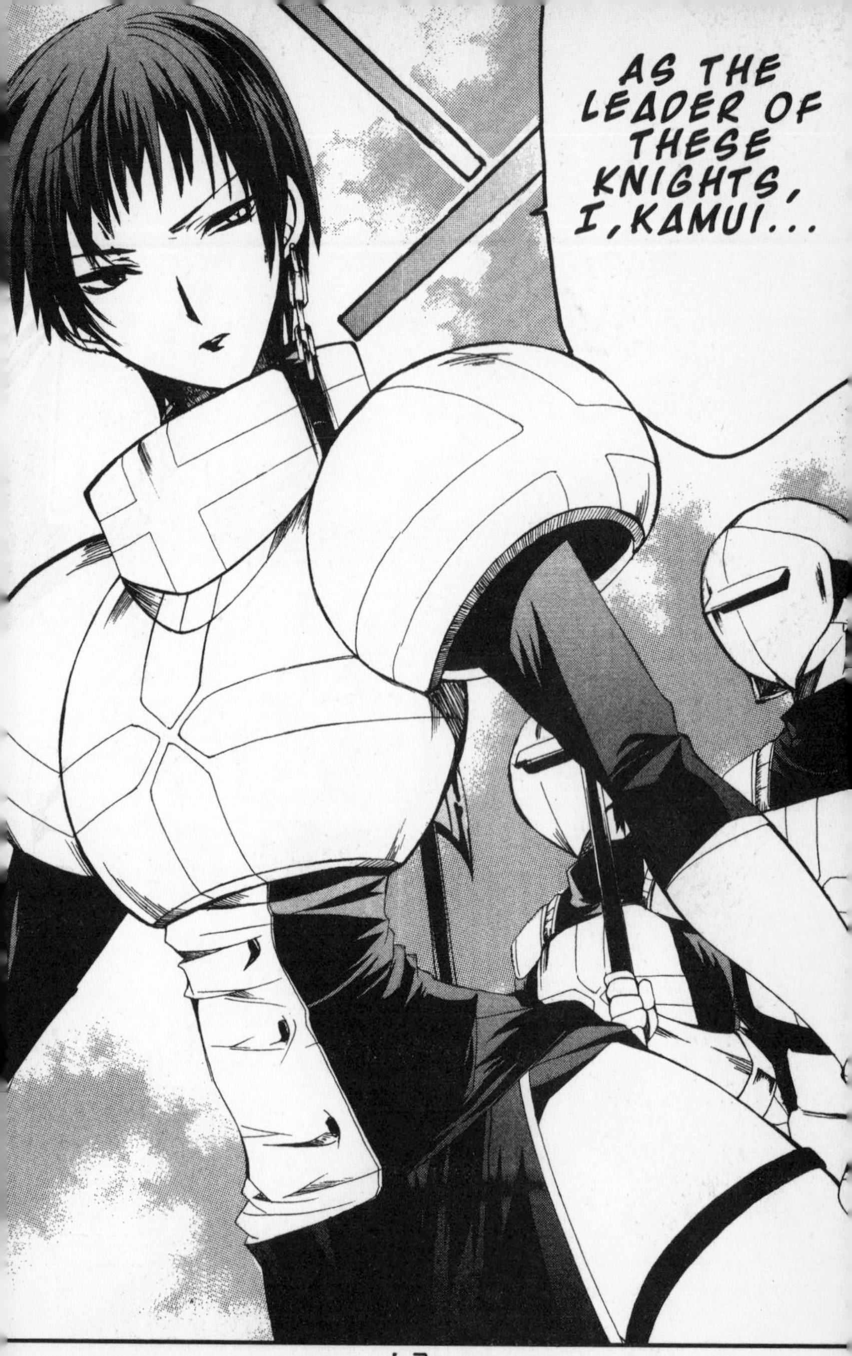
AS THE LEADER OF THESE KNIGHTS, I, KAMUI...

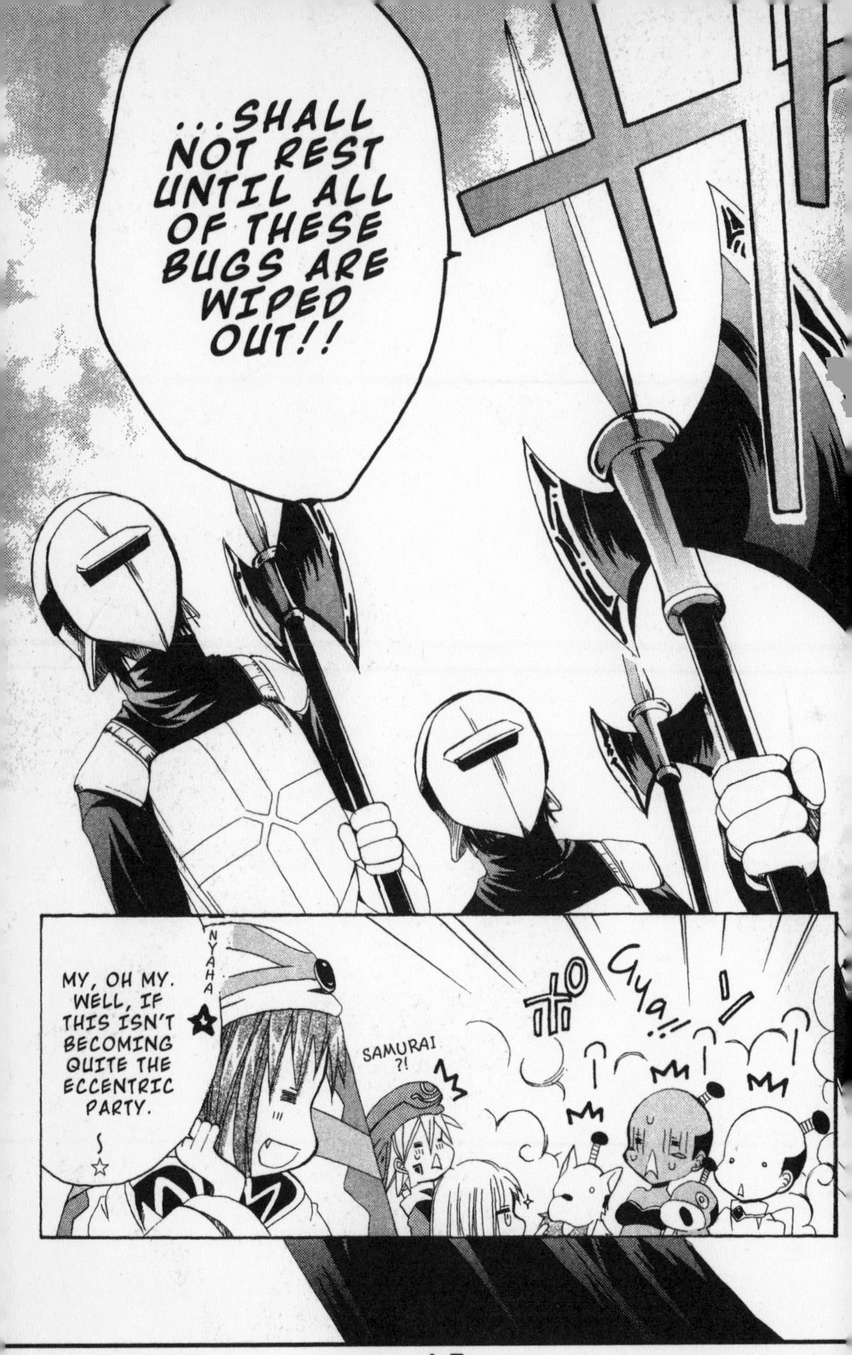
...SHALL NOT REST UNTIL ALL OF THESE BUGS ARE WIPED OUT!!
Gya!!
Ho
SAMURAI ?!
NYAHA
MY, OH MY. WELL, IF THIS ISN'T BECOMING QUITE THE ECCENTRIC PARTY.

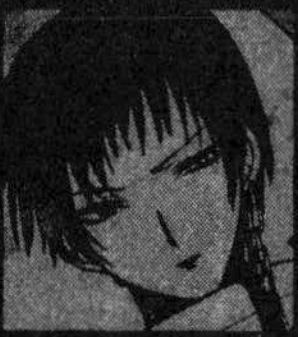

SUBJECT: RE: THE INVESTIGATION SENDER: KAMUI

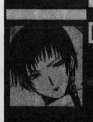

BOY, WHAT A BORING TRIP.
AT LEAST THE SHANGHAI CRAB WAS GOOD.

REGARDING THE REPORT, IT WILL BE NECESSARY TO OBTAIN MORE SUBSTANTIAL EVIDENCE AFTER ALL.

REMEMBER TO PREPARE ADEQUATELY FOR THE OPENING OF THE NEW ROOT TOWN.
WE OF THE COBALT KNIGHT BRIGADE ARE THE ONES PROTECTING THE WORLD AND ITS SYSTEM.
BE AWARE. ANY SLACK IN DISCIPLINE CREATES HOLES FOR BUGS TO CREEP IN.

CC CORP., DEPT. OF NETWORK GAMES
ADMINISTRATION DIVISION, DEBUG TEAM
SHIBAYAMA (USERNAME: KAMUI)

login_9

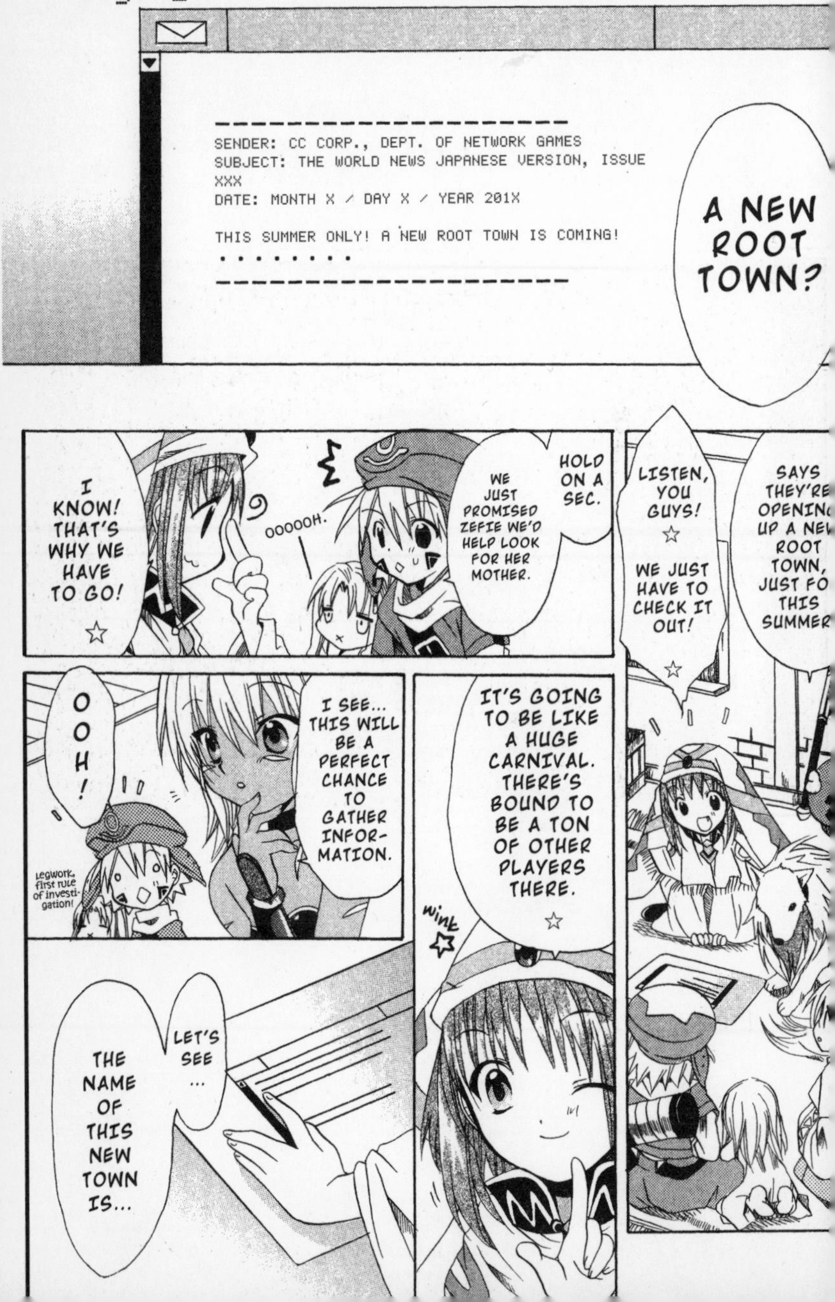
SENDER: CC CORP., DEPT. OF NETWORK GAMES
SUBJECT: THE WORLD NEWS JAPANESE VERSION, ISSUE XXX
DATE: MONTH X / DAY X / YEAR 201X
THIS SUMMER ONLY! A NEW ROOT TOWN IS COMING!
A NEW ROOT TOWN?
SAYS THEY'RE OPENIN UP A NE ROOT TOWN, JUST FO THIS SUMMER
LISTEN, YOU GUYS! ☆ WE JUST HAVE TO CHECK IT OUT! ☆
HOLD ON A SEC.
WE JUST PROMISED ZEFIE WE'D HELP LOOK FOR HER MOTHER.
OOOOOH.
I KNOW! THAT'S WHY WE HAVE TO GO! ☆
IT'S GOING TO BE LIKE A HUGE CARNIVAL. THERE'S BOUND TO BE A TON OF OTHER PLAYERS THERE. ☆
wink
I SEE... THIS WILL BE A PERFECT CHANCE TO GATHER INFORMATION.
OOH!
Legwork, first rule of investigation!
LET'S SEE ...
THE NAME OF THIS NEW TOWN IS...

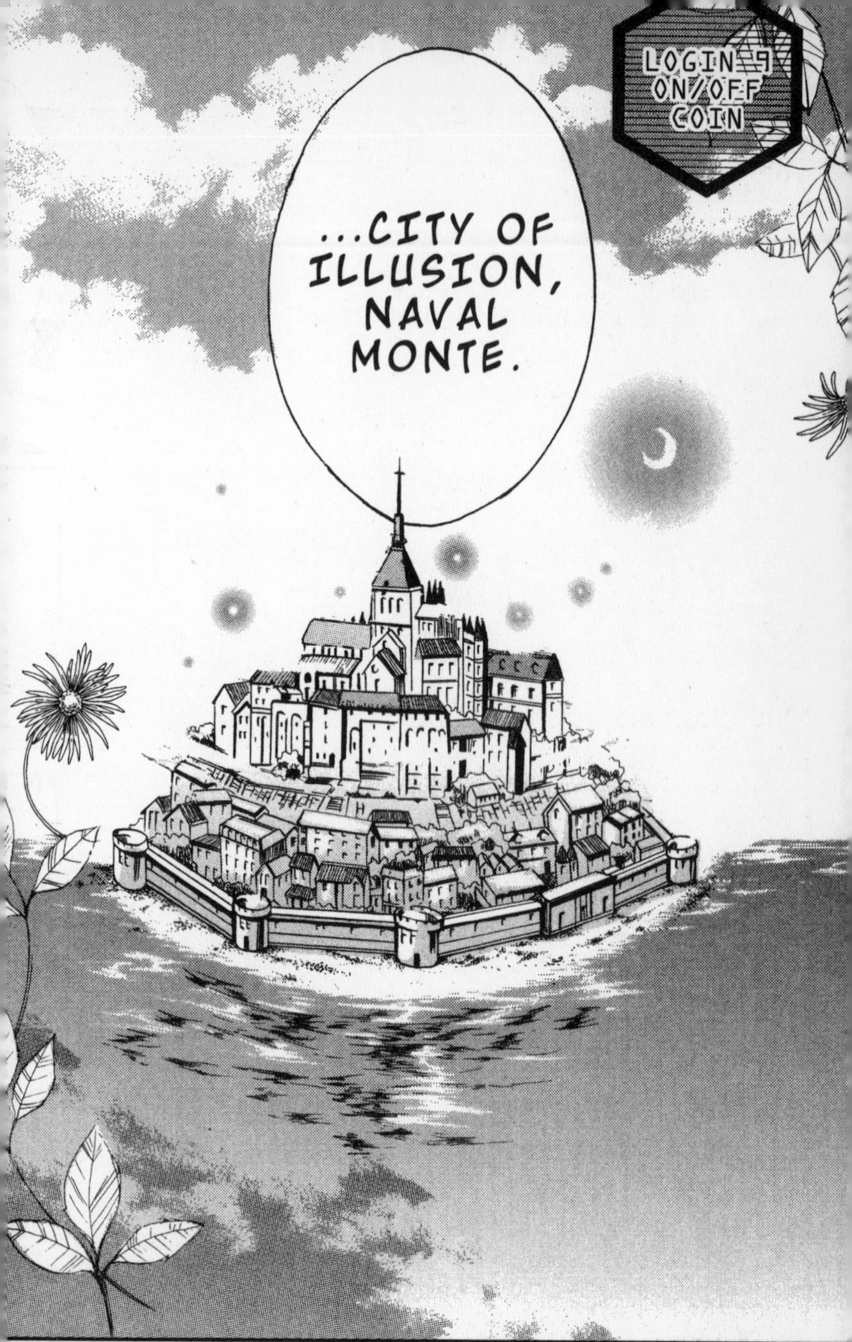
LOGIN 9 ON/OFF COIN
...CITY OF ILLUSION, NAVAL MONTE.

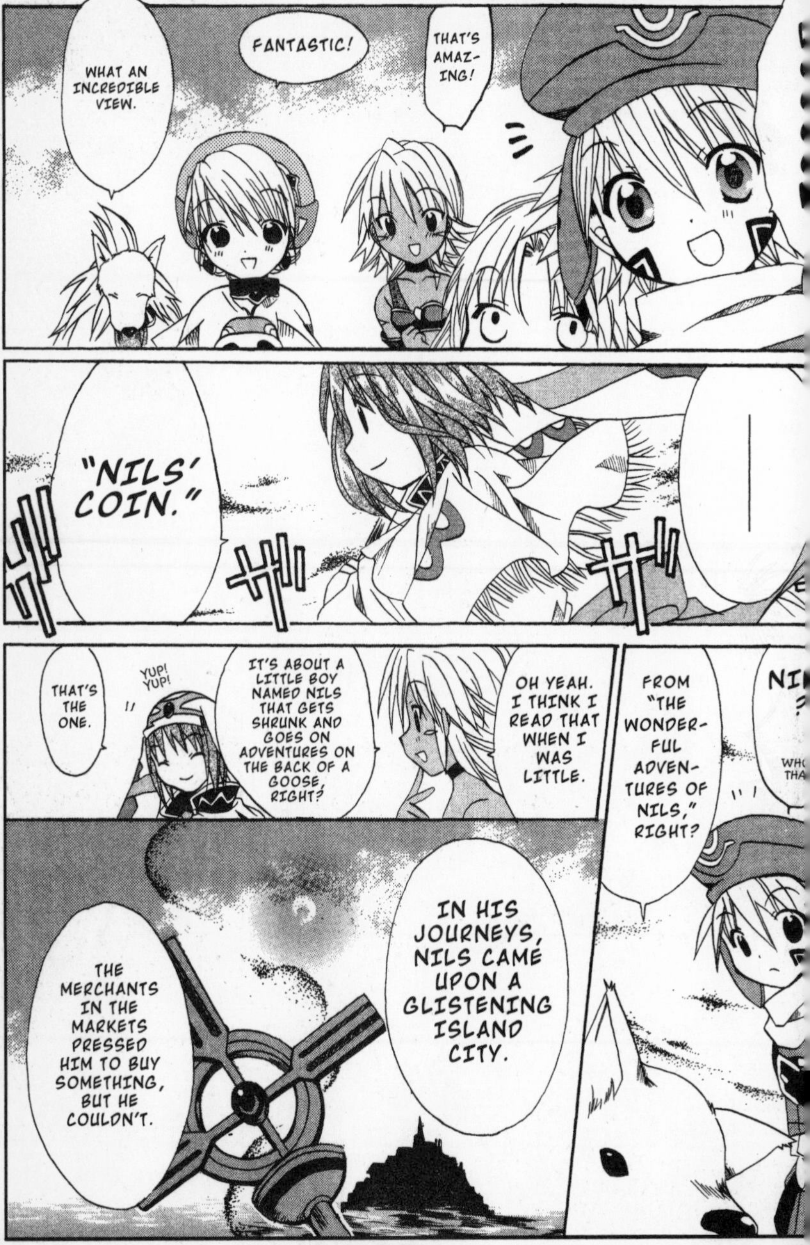
THAT'S AMAZ-ING!
FANTASTIC!
WHAT AN INCREDIBLE VIEW.
"NILS' COIN."
FROM "THE WONDER-FUL ADVEN-TURES OF NILS," RIGHT?
OH YEAH. I THINK I READ THAT WHEN I WAS LITTLE.
IT'S ABOUT A LITTLE BOY NAMED NILS THAT GETS SHRUNK AND GOES ON ADVENTURES ON THE BACK OF A GOOSE, RIGHT?
YUP! YUP!
THAT'S THE ONE.
IN HIS JOURNEYS, NILS CAME UPON A GLISTENING ISLAND CITY.
THE MERCHANTS IN THE MARKETS PRESSED HIM TO BUY SOMETHING, BUT HE COULDN'T.

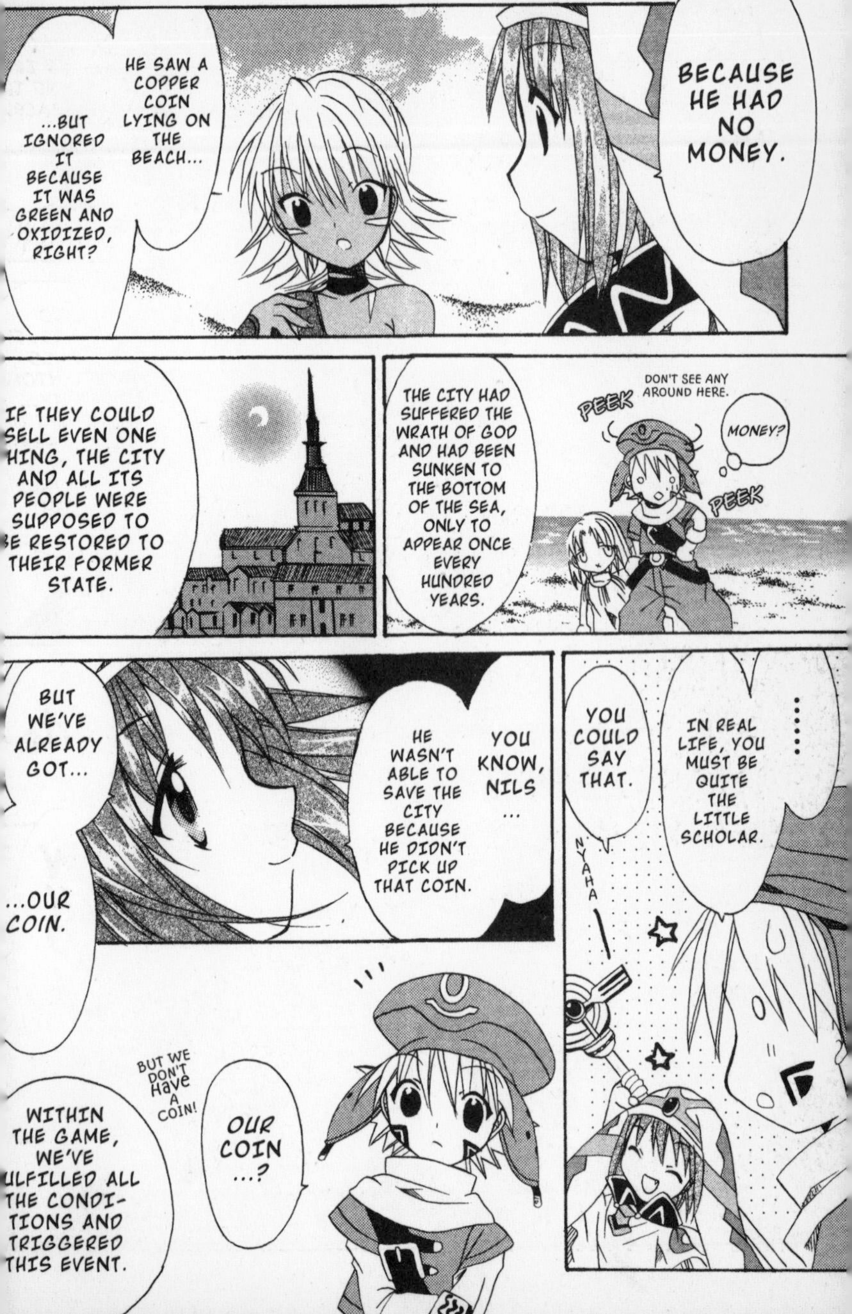
BECAUSE HE HAD NO MONEY.
HE SAW A COPPER COIN LYING ON THE BEACH...
...BUT IGNORED IT BECAUSE IT WAS GREEN AND OXIDIZED, RIGHT?
DON'T SEE ANY AROUND HERE.
PEEK
MONEY?
PEEK
THE CITY HAD SUFFERED THE WRATH OF GOD AND HAD BEEN SUNKEN TO THE BOTTOM OF THE SEA, ONLY TO APPEAR ONCE EVERY HUNDRED YEARS.
IF THEY COULD SELL EVEN ONE HING, THE CITY AND ALL ITS PEOPLE WERE SUPPOSED TO E RESTORED TO THEIR FORMER STATE.
......
IN REAL LIFE, YOU MUST BE QUITE THE LITTLE SCHOLAR.
YOU COULD SAY THAT.
NYAHA
YOU KNOW, NILS...
HE WASN'T ABLE TO SAVE THE CITY BECAUSE HE DIDN'T PICK UP THAT COIN.
BUT WE'VE ALREADY GOT...
...OUR COIN.
OUR COIN...?
BUT WE DON'T HAVE A COIN!
WITHIN THE GAME, WE'VE ULFILLED ALL THE CONDITIONS AND TRIGGERED THIS EVENT.

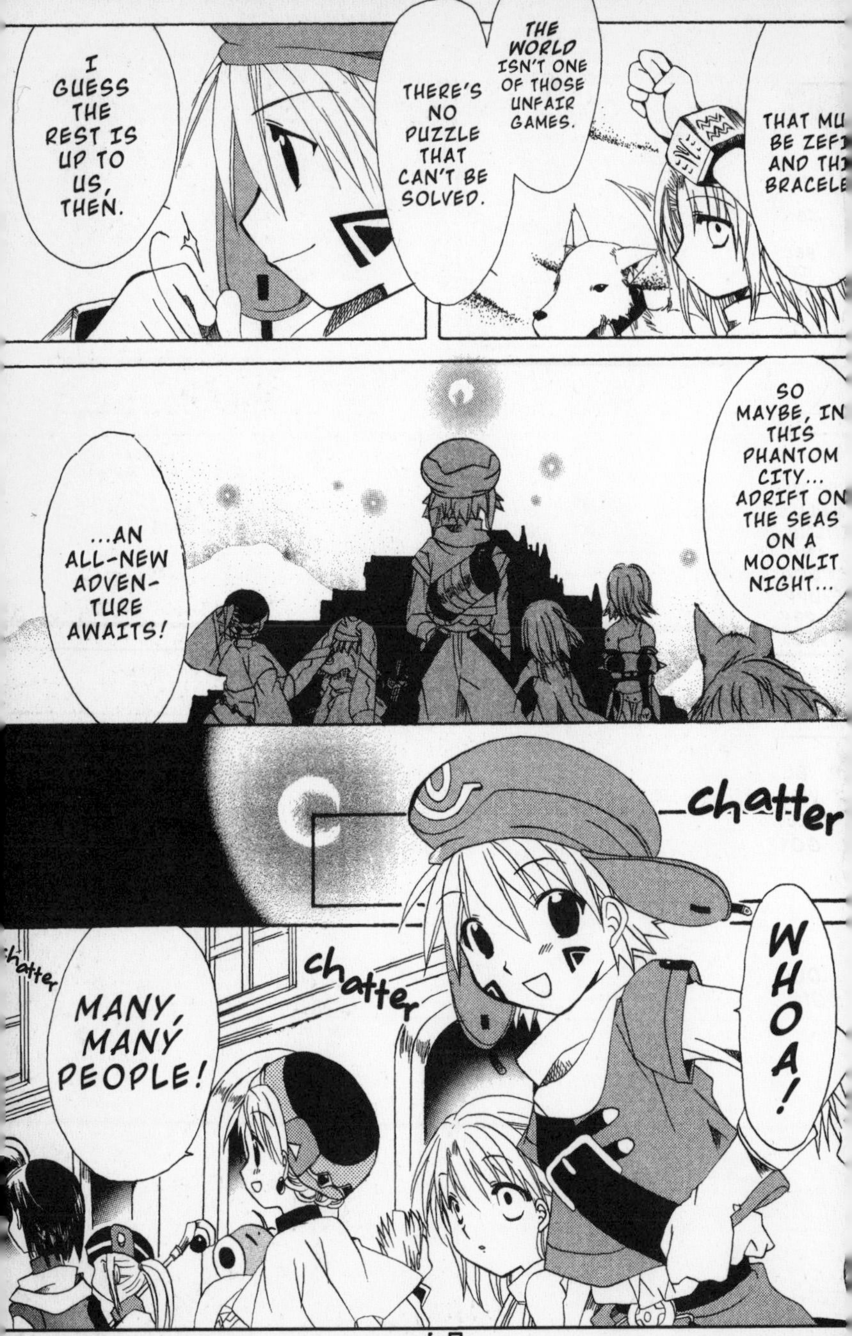
THAT MU
BE ZEFI
AND THI
BRACELE
THE WORLD ISN'T ONE OF THOSE UNFAIR GAMES.
THERE'S NO PUZZLE THAT CAN'T BE SOLVED.
I GUESS THE REST IS UP TO US, THEN.
SO MAYBE, IN THIS PHANTOM CITY... ADRIFT ON THE SEAS ON A MOONLIT NIGHT...
...AN ALL-NEW ADVEN-TURE AWAITS!
chatter
WHOA!
chatter
chatter
MANY, MANY PEOPLE!

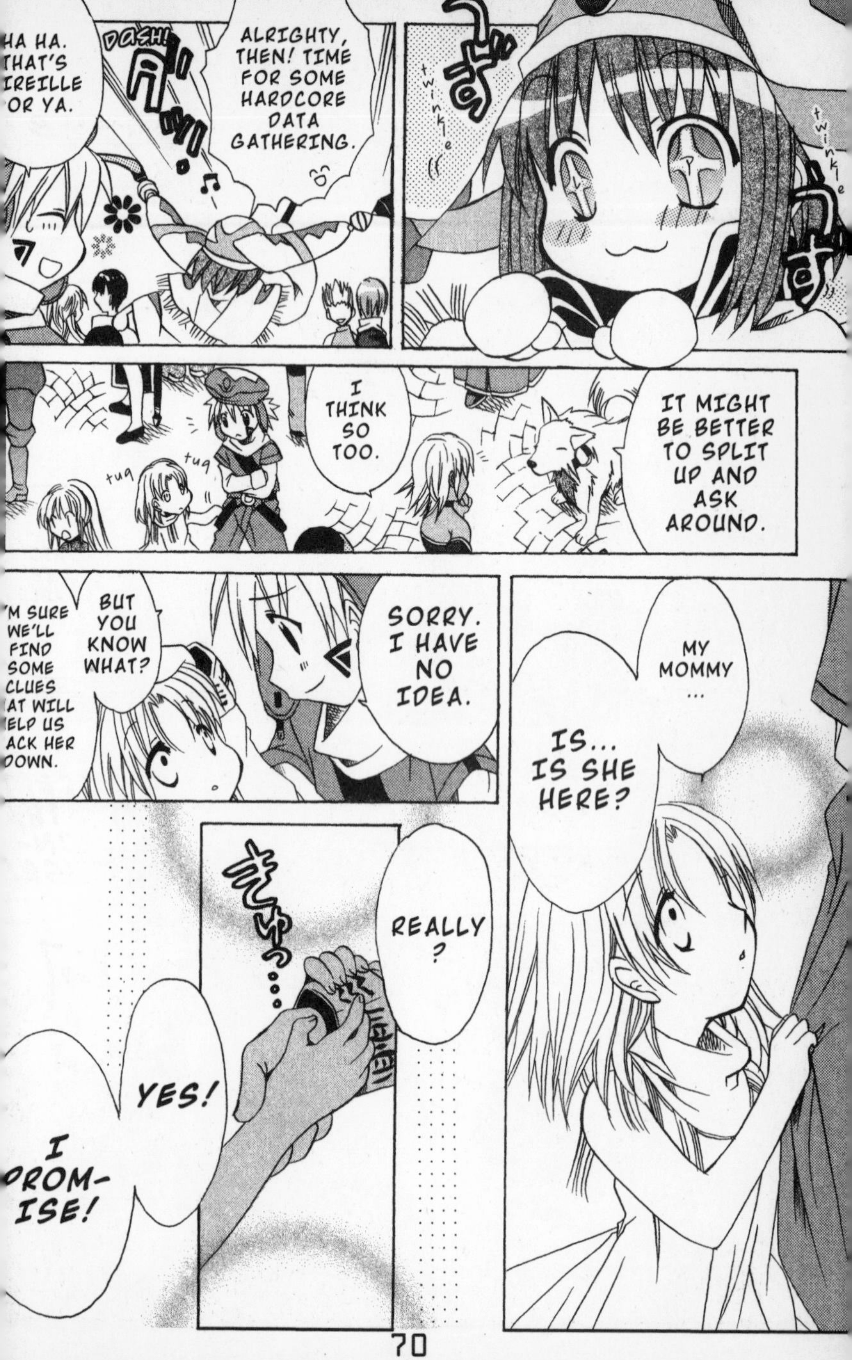
twinkle
twinkle
ALRIGHTY, THEN! TIME FOR SOME HARDCORE DATA GATHERING.
DASH!
HA HA. THAT'S
IREILLE
OR YA.
IT MIGHT BE BETTER TO SPLIT UP AND ASK AROUND.
I THINK SO TOO.
tug
tug
MY MOMMY...
IS... IS SHE HERE?
SORRY. I HAVE NO IDEA.
BUT YOU KNOW WHAT?
'M SURE WE'LL FIND SOME CLUES
AT WILL
ELP US
ACK HER
OWN.
REALLY?
YES!
I
ROM-
ISE!

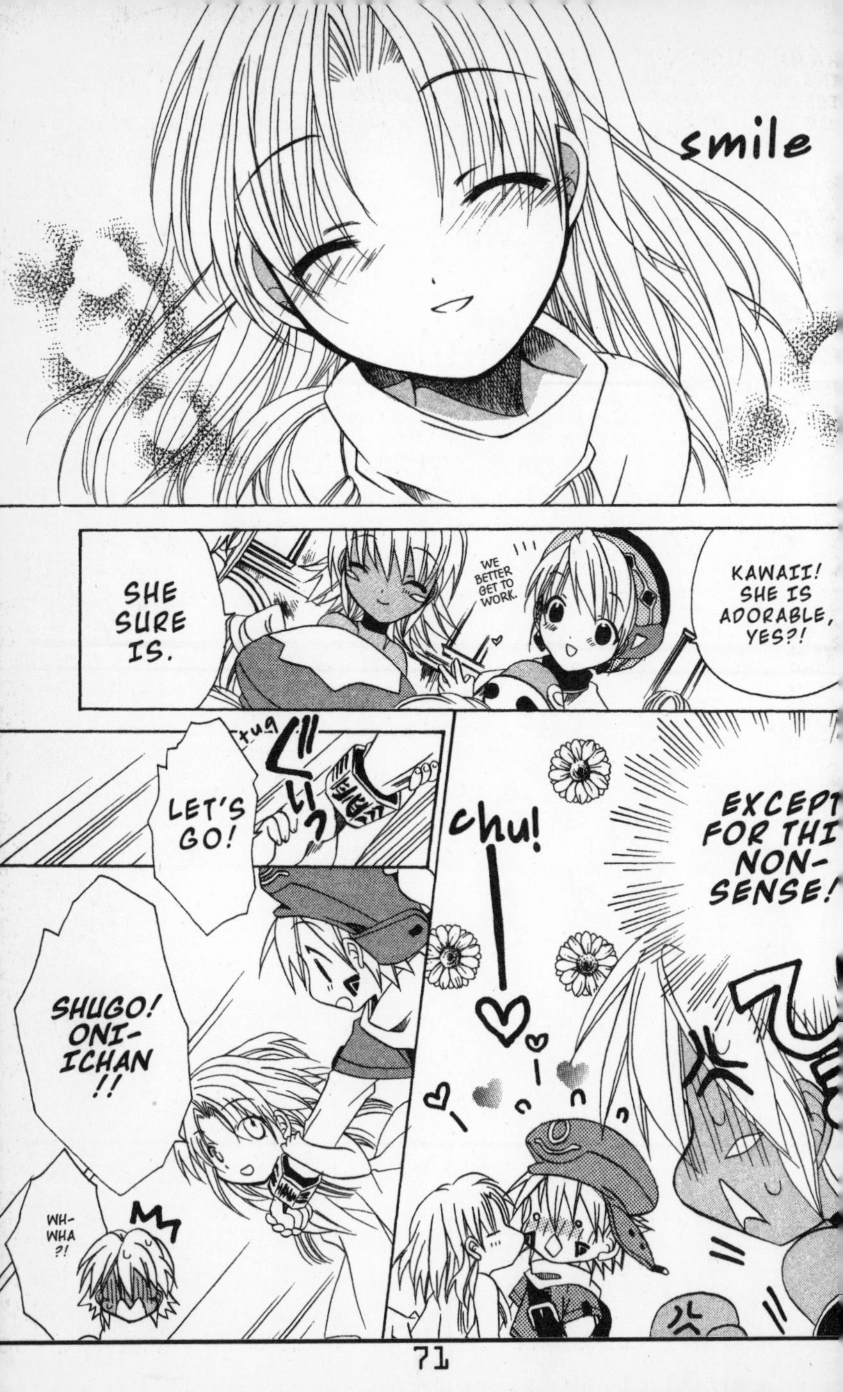

smile
KAWAII! SHE IS ADORABLE, YES?!
WE BETTER GET TO WORK.
SHE SURE IS.
EXCEPT FOR THI NON-SENSE!
chu!
tug
LET'S GO!
SHUGO! ONI-ICHAN!!
WH-WHA?!

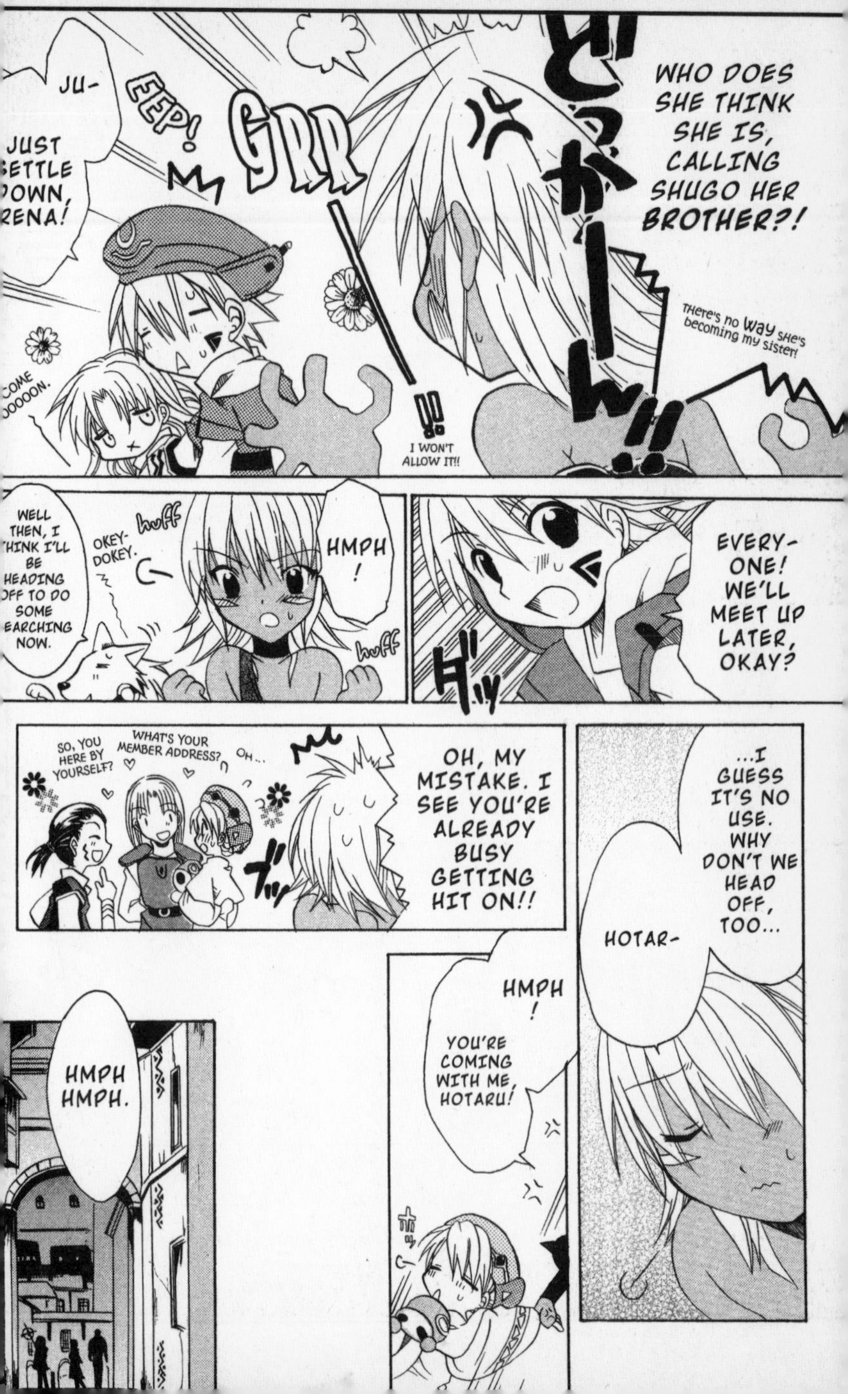
WHO DOES SHE THINK SHE IS, CALLING SHUGO HER BROTHER?!
There's no way she's becoming my sister!
I WON'T ALLOW IT!!
GRR
EEP!
JU-
JUST ETTLE OWN, RENA!
COME OOOOON.
EVERY-ONE! WE'LL MEET UP LATER, OKAY?
HMPH!
huff
huff
OKEY-DOKEY.
WELL THEN, I HINK I'LL BE HEADING FF TO DO SOME EARCHING NOW.
...I GUESS IT'S NO USE. WHY DON'T WE HEAD OFF, TOO...
HOTAR-
OH, MY MISTAKE. I SEE YOU'RE ALREADY BUSY GETTING HIT ON!!
WHAT'S YOUR MEMBER ADDRESS?
OH...
SO, YOU HERE BY YOURSELF?
HMPH!
YOU'RE COMING WITH ME, HOTARU!
HMPH HMPH.

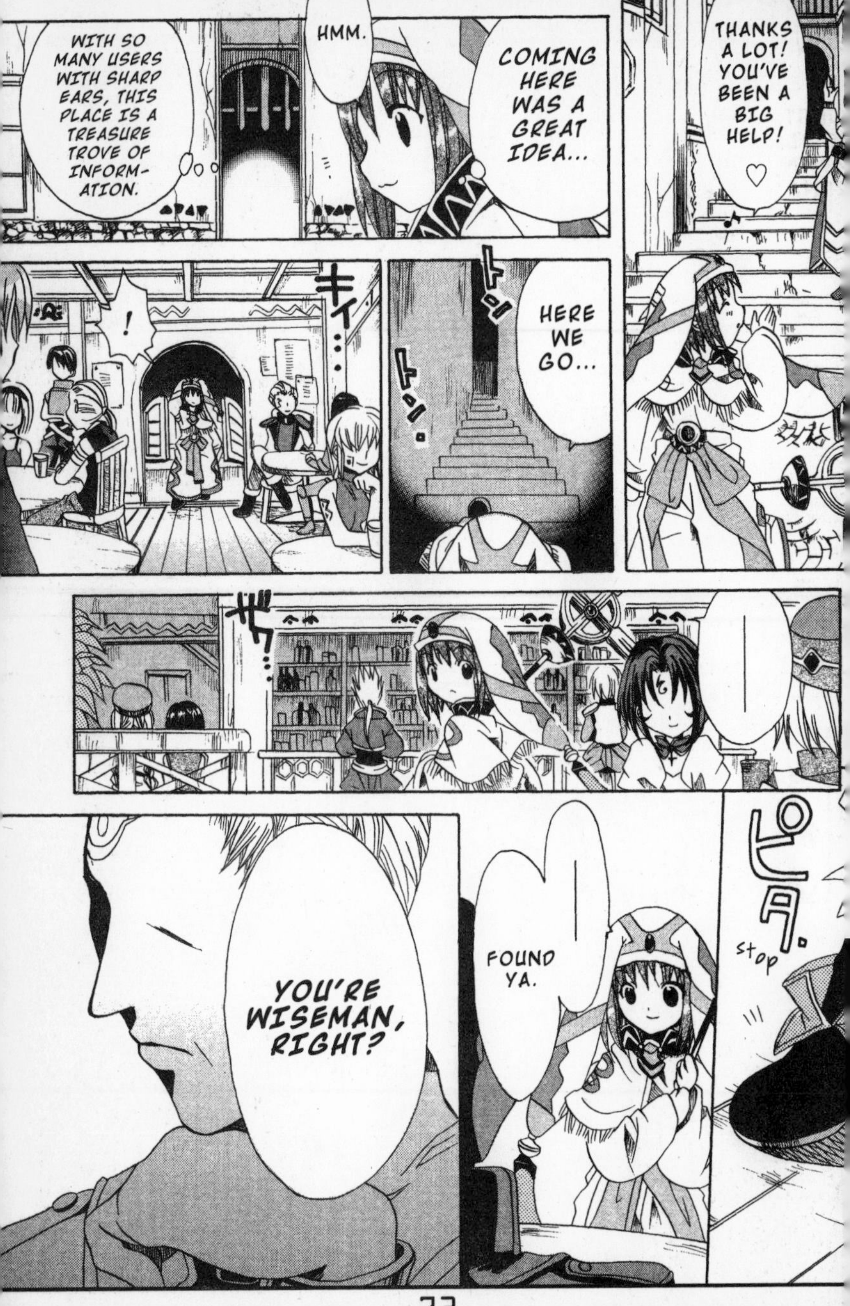
THANKS A LOT! YOU'VE BEEN A BIG HELP! ♡
HMM.
COMING HERE WAS A GREAT IDEA...
WITH SO MANY USERS WITH SHARP EARS, THIS PLACE IS A TREASURE TROVE OF INFORMATION.
トッ
トッ。
HERE WE GO...
キイ…
!
ザワ…
ピタ。
stop
FOUND YA.
YOU'RE WISEMAN, RIGHT?

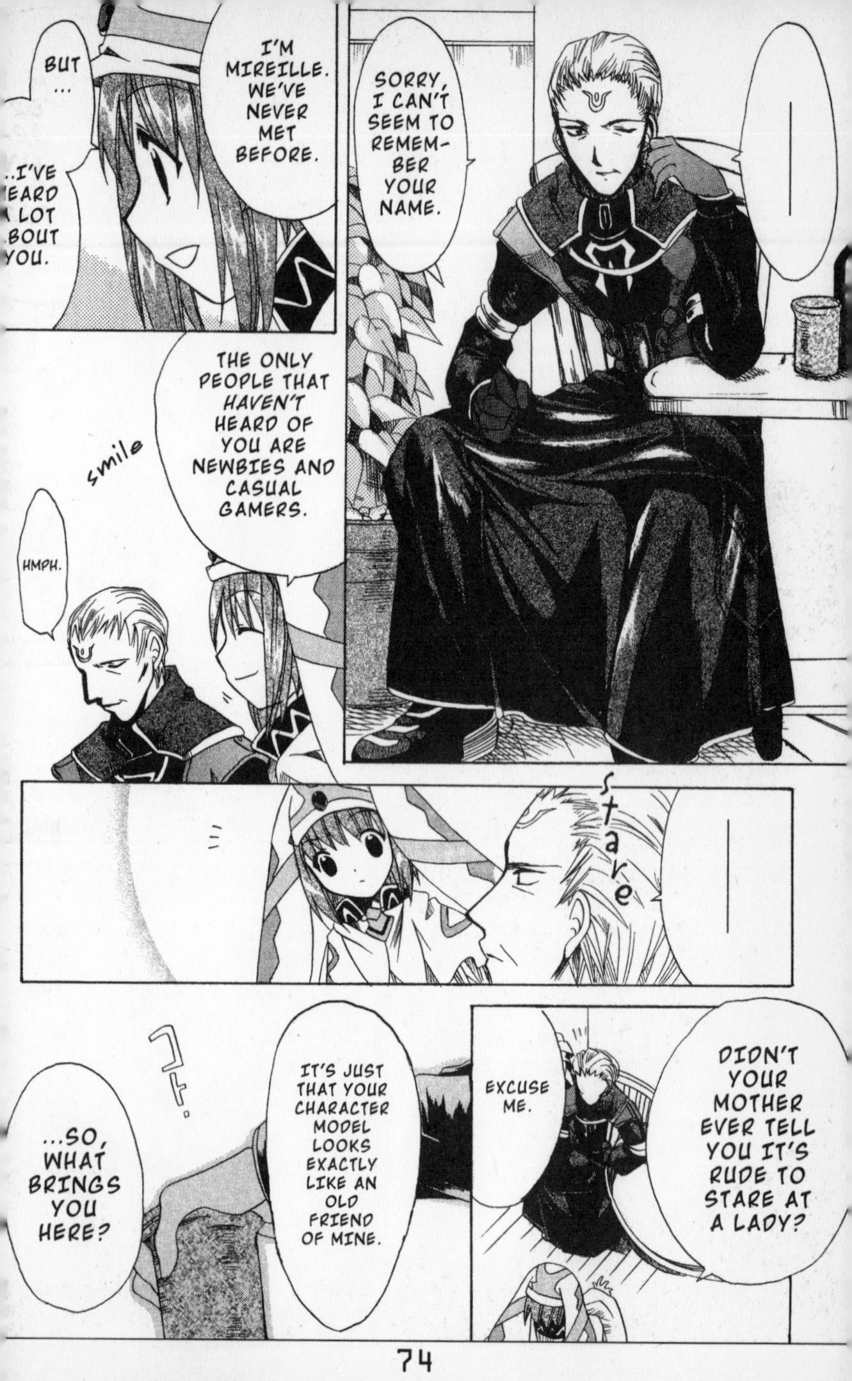

SORRY, I CAN'T SEEM TO REMEMBER YOUR NAME.
I'M MIREILLE. WE'VE NEVER MET BEFORE.
BUT ...
..I'VE EARD LOT BOUT YOU.
THE ONLY PEOPLE THAT HAVEN'T HEARD OF YOU ARE NEWBIES AND CASUAL GAMERS.
smile
HMPH.
stare
DIDN'T YOUR MOTHER EVER TELL YOU IT'S RUDE TO STARE AT A LADY?
EXCUSE ME.
IT'S JUST THAT YOUR CHARACTER MODEL LOOKS EXACTLY LIKE AN OLD FRIEND OF MINE.
コト.
...SO, WHAT BRINGS YOU HERE?

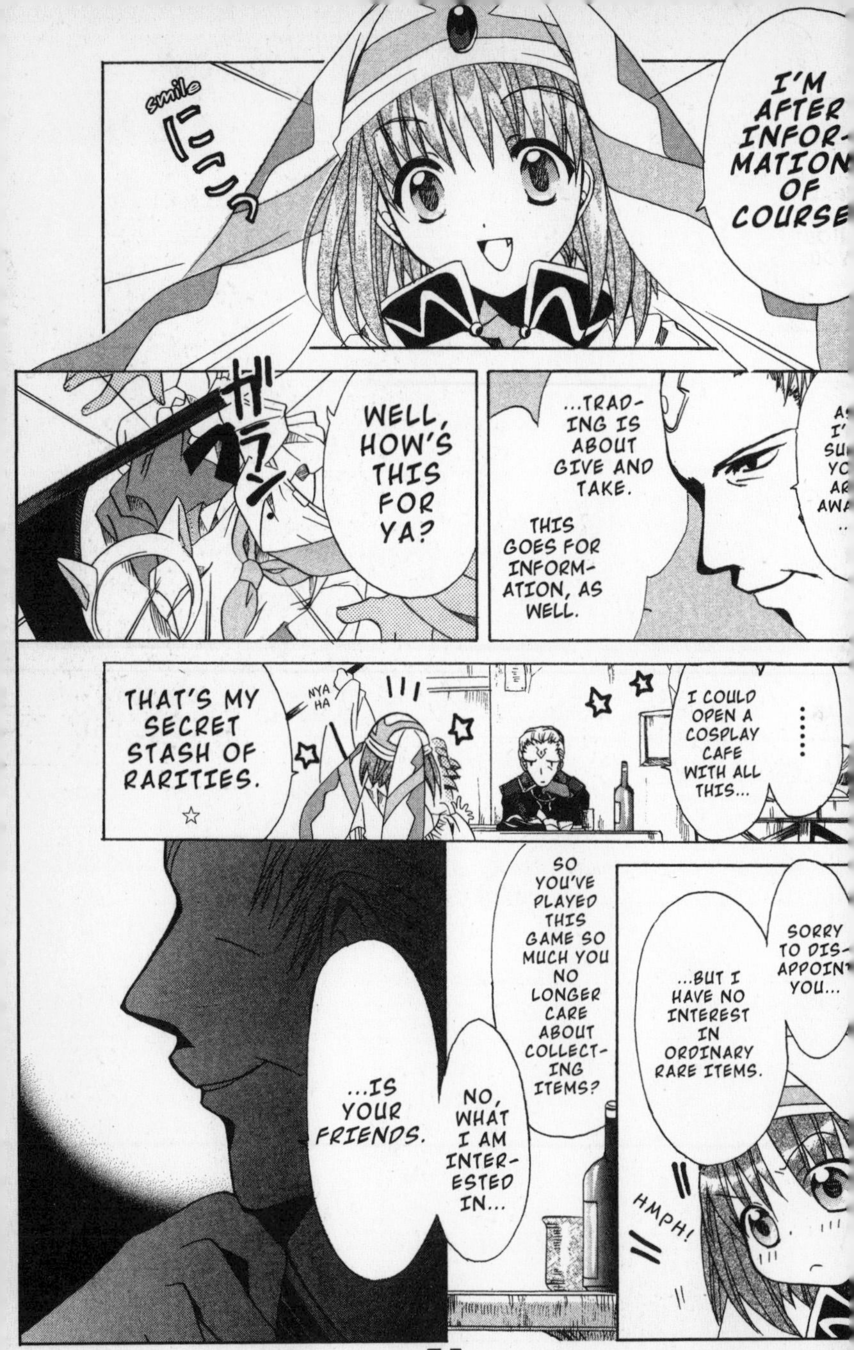
I'M AFTER INFORMATION OF COURSE
smile
にこっ
...TRADING IS ABOUT GIVE AND TAKE.
THIS GOES FOR INFORMATION, AS WELL.
WELL, HOW'S THIS FOR YA?
ガラン
......
I COULD OPEN A COSPLAY CAFE WITH ALL THIS...
NYA HA
THAT'S MY SECRET STASH OF RARITIES. ☆
SORRY TO DISAPPOINT YOU...
...BUT I HAVE NO INTEREST IN ORDINARY RARE ITEMS.
HMPH!
SO YOU'VE PLAYED THIS GAME SO MUCH YOU NO LONGER CARE ABOUT COLLECTING ITEMS?
NO, WHAT I AM INTERESTED IN...
...IS YOUR FRIENDS.

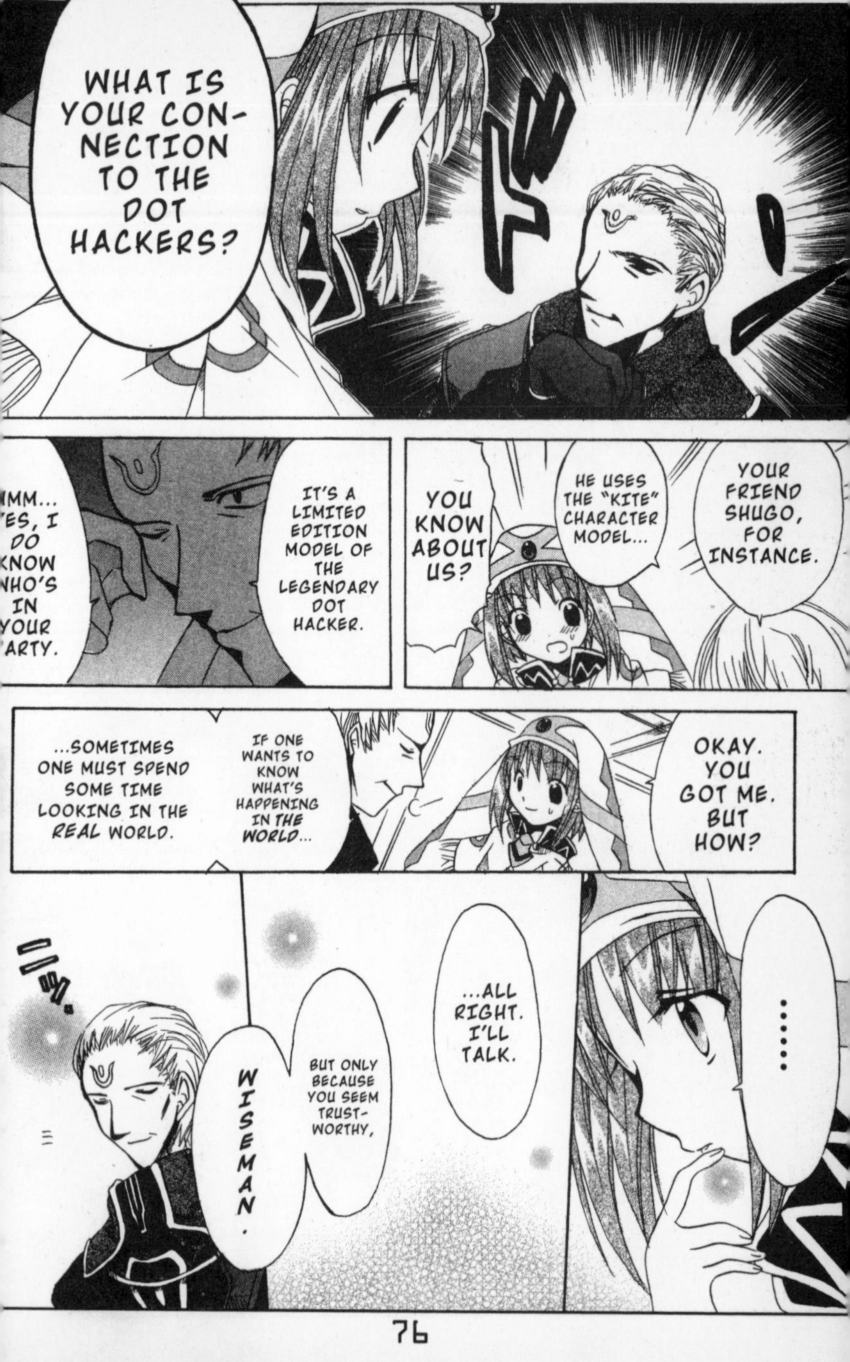
WHAT IS YOUR CONNECTION TO THE DOT HACKERS?
YOUR FRIEND SHUGO, FOR INSTANCE.
HE USES THE "KITE" CHARACTER MODEL...
YOU KNOW ABOUT US?
IT'S A LIMITED EDITION MODEL OF THE LEGENDARY DOT HACKER.
MM... ES, I DO KNOW HO'S IN YOUR ARTY.
OKAY. YOU GOT ME. BUT HOW?
IF ONE WANTS TO KNOW WHAT'S HAPPENING IN *THE WORLD*...
...SOMETIMES ONE MUST SPEND SOME TIME LOOKING IN THE *REAL* WORLD.
......
...ALL RIGHT. I'LL TALK.
BUT ONLY BECAUSE YOU SEEM TRUST-WORTHY,
WISEMAN.

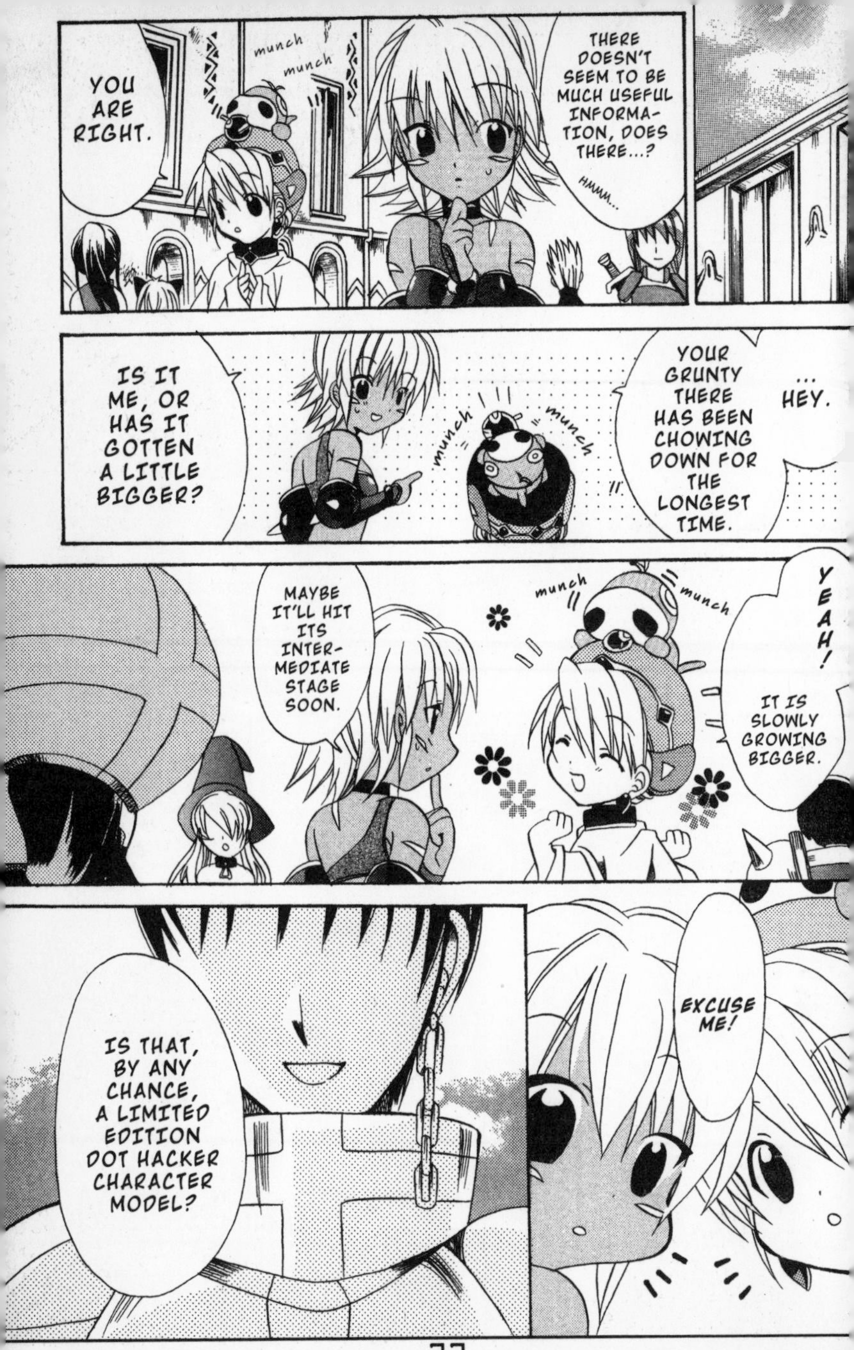

THERE DOESN'T SEEM TO BE MUCH USEFUL INFORMATION, DOES THERE...?
HMMM...
munch munch
YOU ARE RIGHT.
...HEY.
YOUR GRUNTY THERE HAS BEEN CHOWING DOWN FOR THE LONGEST TIME.
munch munch
IS IT ME, OR HAS IT GOTTEN A LITTLE BIGGER?
YEAH!
IT IS SLOWLY GROWING BIGGER.
munch munch
MAYBE IT'LL HIT ITS INTERMEDIATE STAGE SOON.
EXCUSE ME!
IS THAT, BY ANY CHANCE, A LIMITED EDITION DOT HACKER CHARACTER MODEL?

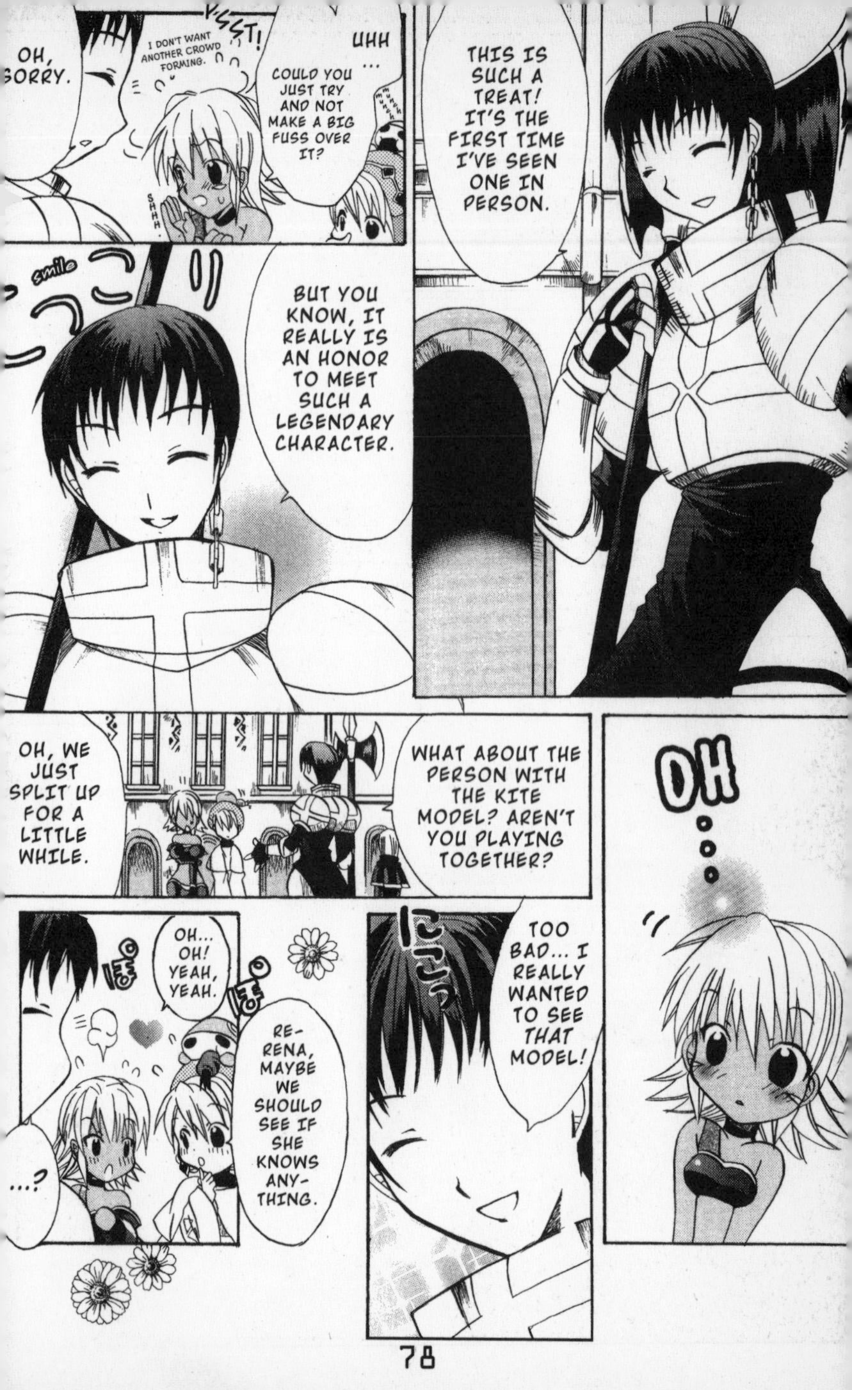
THIS IS SUCH A TREAT! IT'S THE FIRST TIME I'VE SEEN ONE IN PERSON.
V-SSST!
UHH ...
COULD YOU JUST TRY AND NOT MAKE A BIG FUSS OVER IT?
I DON'T WANT ANOTHER CROWD FORMING.
SHHH
OH, SORRY.
BUT YOU KNOW, IT REALLY IS AN HONOR TO MEET SUCH A LEGENDARY CHARACTER.
smile
OH...
WHAT ABOUT THE PERSON WITH THE KITE MODEL? AREN'T YOU PLAYING TOGETHER?
OH, WE JUST SPLIT UP FOR A LITTLE WHILE.
TOO BAD... I REALLY WANTED TO SEE THAT MODEL!
OH... OH! YEAH, YEAH.
RE-RENA, MAYBE WE SHOULD SEE IF SHE KNOWS ANYTHING.
...?

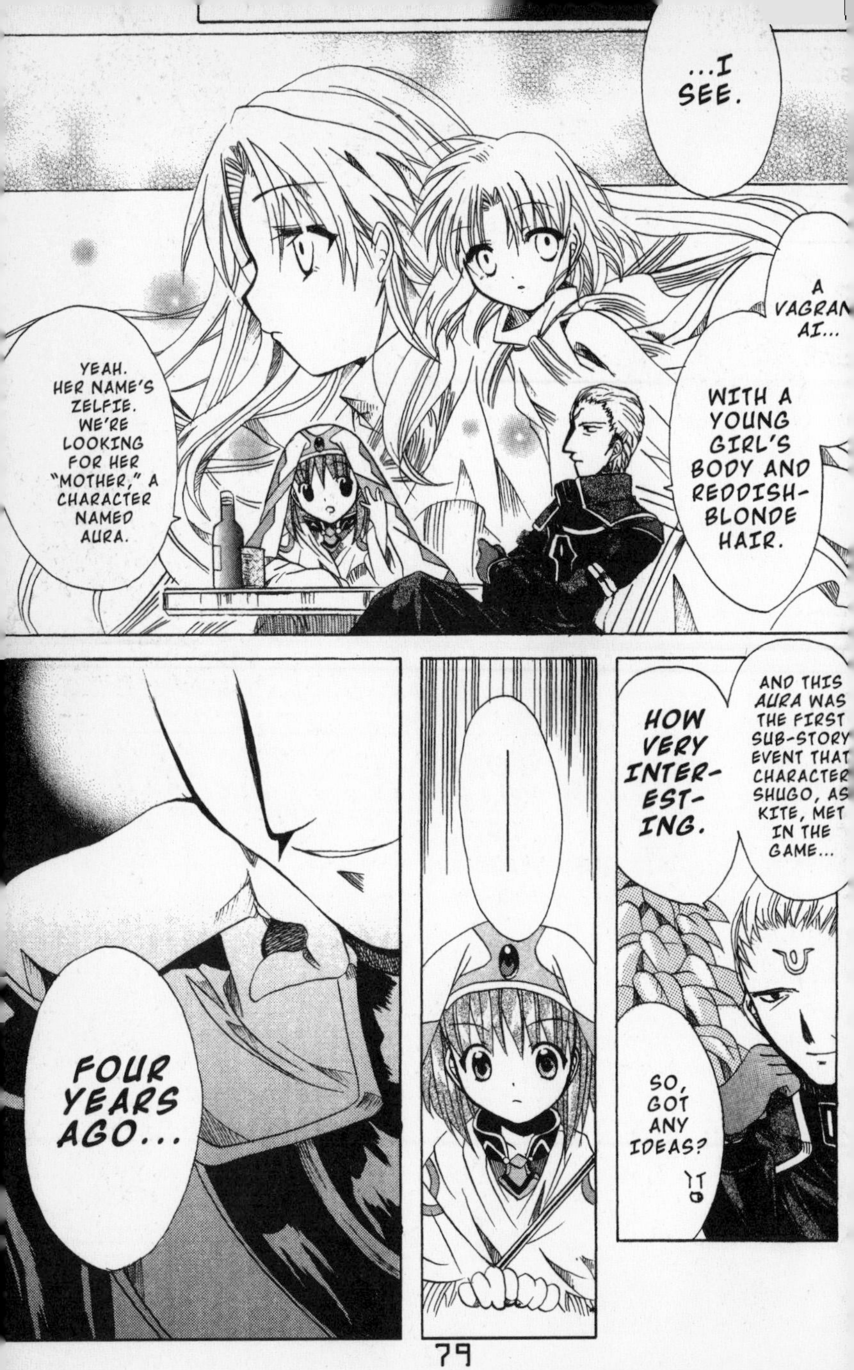
...I SEE.
A VAGRAN
AI...
WITH A YOUNG GIRL'S BODY AND REDDISH-BLONDE HAIR.
YEAH. HER NAME'S ZELFIE. WE'RE LOOKING FOR HER "MOTHER," A CHARACTER NAMED AURA.
AND THIS AURA WAS THE FIRST SUB-STORY EVENT THAT CHARACTER SHUGO, AS KITE, MET IN THE GAME...
HOW VERY INTER-EST-ING.
SO, GOT ANY IDEAS?
FOUR YEARS AGO...

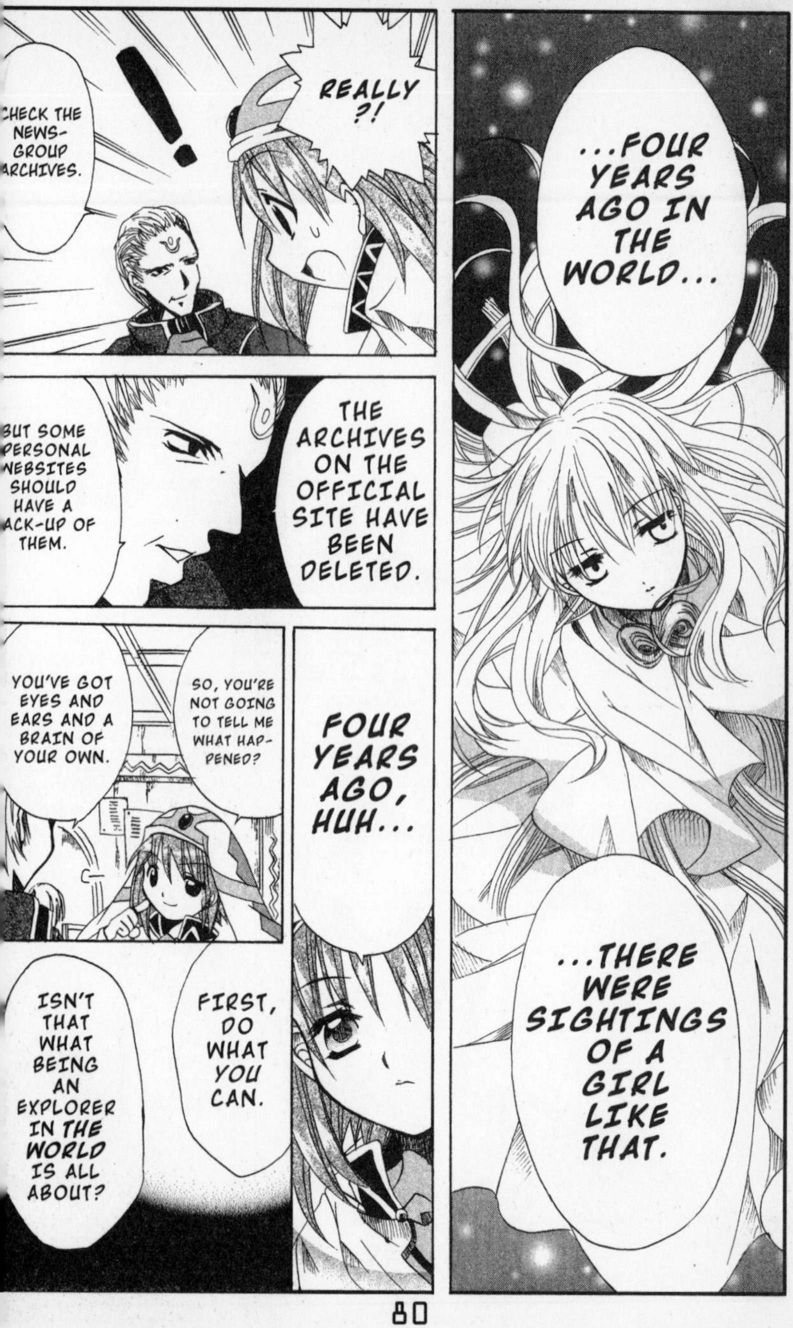
...FOUR YEARS AGO IN THE WORLD...
...THERE WERE SIGHTINGS OF A GIRL LIKE THAT.
REALLY ?!
CHECK THE NEWS-GROUP ARCHIVES.
THE ARCHIVES ON THE OFFICIAL SITE HAVE BEEN DELETED.
BUT SOME PERSONAL WEBSITES SHOULD HAVE A BACK-UP OF THEM.
FOUR YEARS AGO, HUH...
SO, YOU'RE NOT GOING TO TELL ME WHAT HAP-PENED?
YOU'VE GOT EYES AND EARS AND A BRAIN OF YOUR OWN.
FIRST, DO WHAT *YOU* CAN.
ISN'T THAT WHAT BEING AN EXPLORER IN *THE WORLD* IS ALL ABOUT?

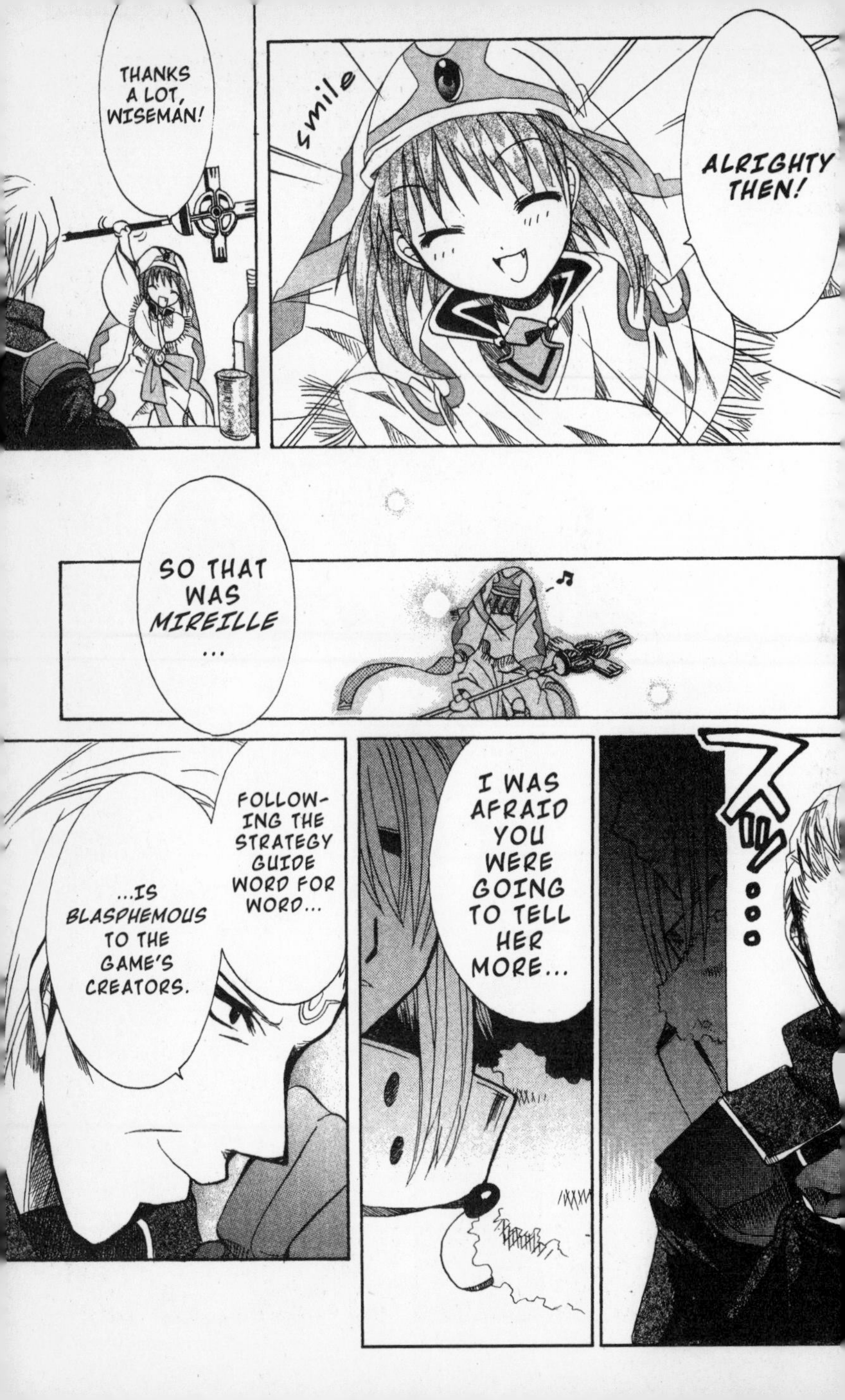
ALRIGHTY THEN!
smile
THANKS A LOT, WISEMAN!
SO THAT WAS MIREILLE...
I WAS AFRAID YOU WERE GOING TO TELL HER MORE...
FOLLOWING THE STRATEGY GUIDE WORD FOR WORD...
...IS BLASPHEMOUS TO THE GAME'S CREATORS.

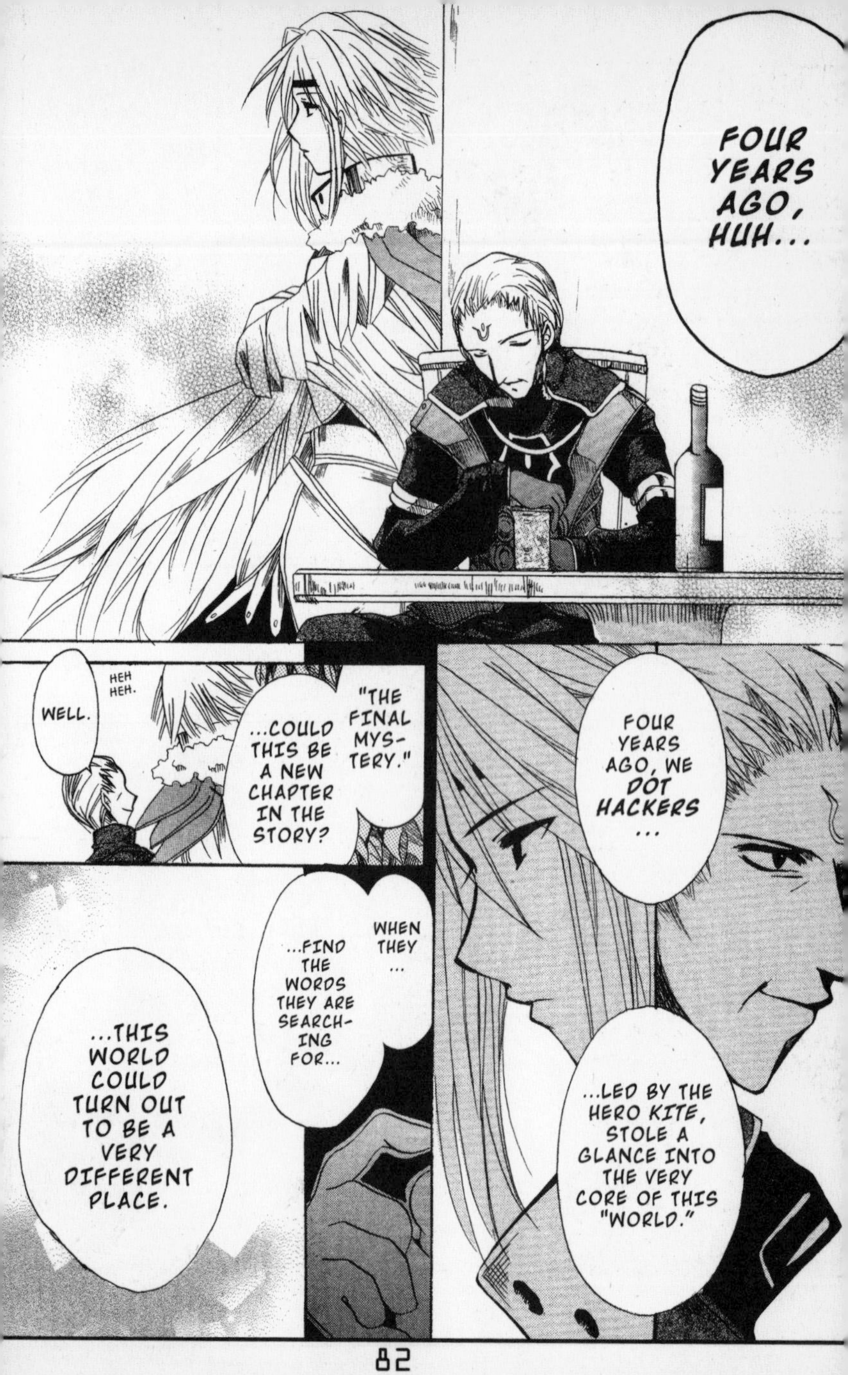
FOUR YEARS AGO, HUH...
FOUR YEARS AGO, WE DOT HACKERS...
...LED BY THE HERO KITE, STOLE A GLANCE INTO THE VERY CORE OF THIS "WORLD."
"THE FINAL MYSTERY."
...COULD THIS BE A NEW CHAPTER IN THE STORY?
HEH HEH.
WELL.
WHEN THEY...
...FIND THE WORDS THEY ARE SEARCHING FOR...
...THIS WORLD COULD TURN OUT TO BE A VERY DIFFERENT PLACE.

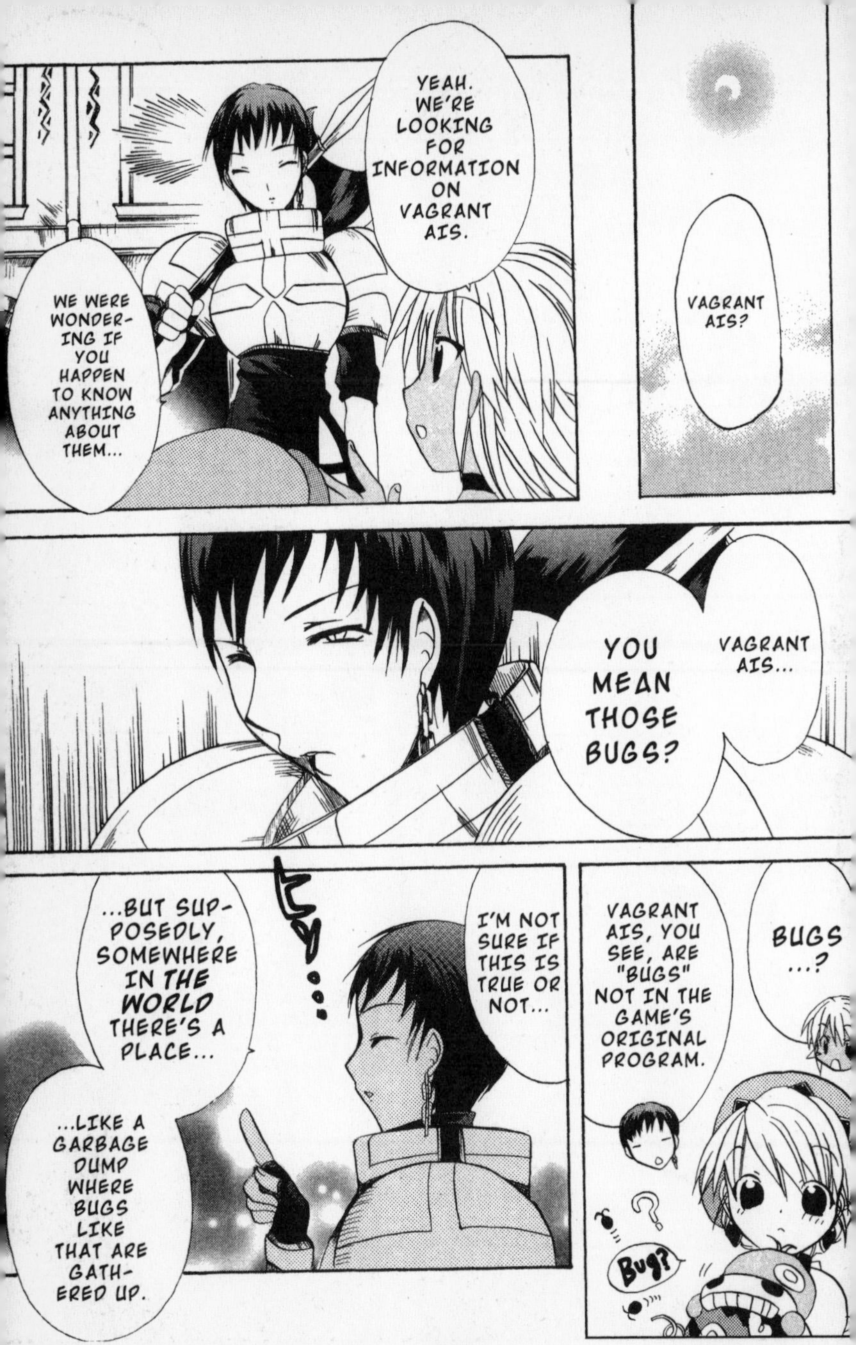
VAGRANT AIS?
YEAH. WE'RE LOOKING FOR INFORMATION ON VAGRANT AIS.
WE WERE WONDERING IF YOU HAPPEN TO KNOW ANYTHING ABOUT THEM...
VAGRANT AIS...
YOU MEAN THOSE BUGS?
BUGS ...?
VAGRANT AIS, YOU SEE, ARE "BUGS" NOT IN THE GAME'S ORIGINAL PROGRAM.
Bug?
I'M NOT SURE IF THIS IS TRUE OR NOT...
...BUT SUPPOSEDLY, SOMEWHERE IN *THE WORLD* THERE'S A PLACE...
...LIKE A GARBAGE DUMP WHERE BUGS LIKE THAT ARE GATHERED UP.

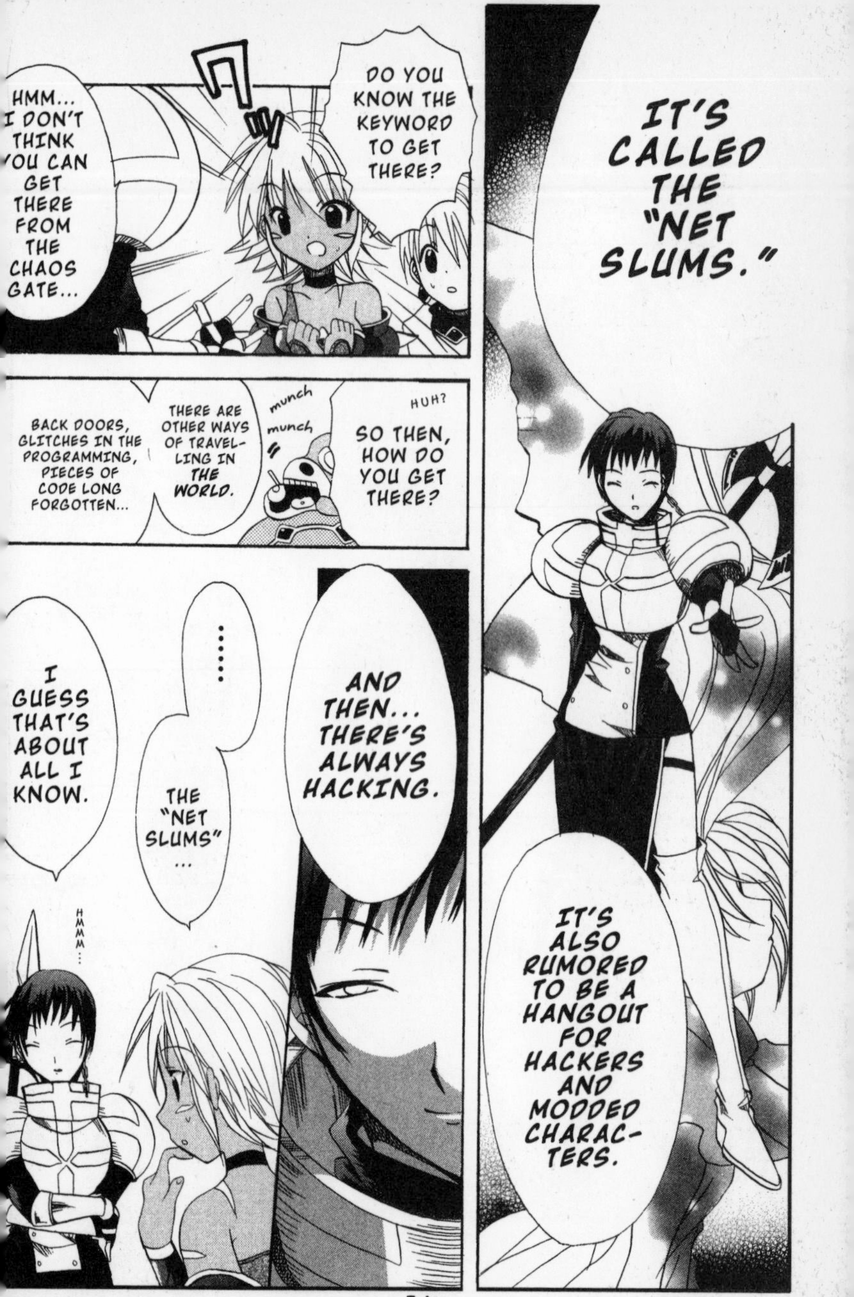
IT'S CALLED THE "NET SLUMS."
IT'S ALSO RUMORED TO BE A HANGOUT FOR HACKERS AND MODDED CHARACTERS.
DO YOU KNOW THE KEYWORD TO GET THERE?
HMM... I DON'T THINK 'OU CAN GET THERE FROM THE CHAOS GATE...
HUH?
SO THEN, HOW DO YOU GET THERE?
munch munch
THERE ARE OTHER WAYS OF TRAVEL-LING IN THE WORLD.
BACK DOORS, GLITCHES IN THE PROGRAMMING, PIECES OF CODE LONG FORGOTTEN...
AND THEN... THERE'S ALWAYS HACKING.
......
THE "NET SLUMS" ...
I GUESS THAT'S ABOUT ALL I KNOW.
HMMM...

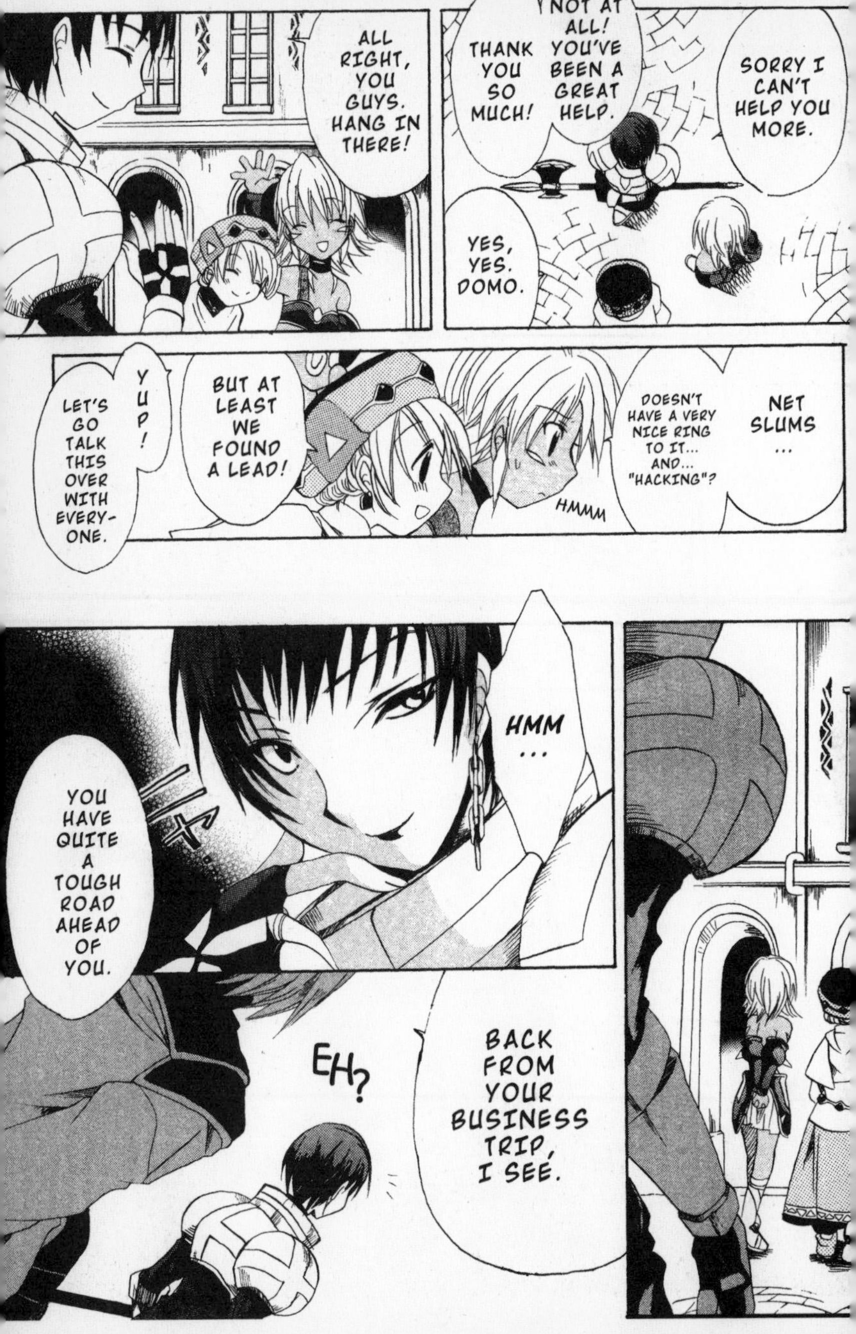
SORRY I CAN'T HELP YOU MORE.
NOT AT ALL! YOU'VE BEEN A GREAT HELP.
THANK YOU SO MUCH!
YES, YES. DOMO.
ALL RIGHT, YOU GUYS. HANG IN THERE!
NET SLUMS ...
DOESN'T HAVE A VERY NICE RING TO IT... AND... "HACKING"?
HMMM
BUT AT LEAST WE FOUND A LEAD!
YUP!
LET'S GO TALK THIS OVER WITH EVERY-ONE.
HMM ...
YOU HAVE QUITE A TOUGH ROAD AHEAD OF YOU.
EH?
BACK FROM YOUR BUSINESS TRIP, I SEE.

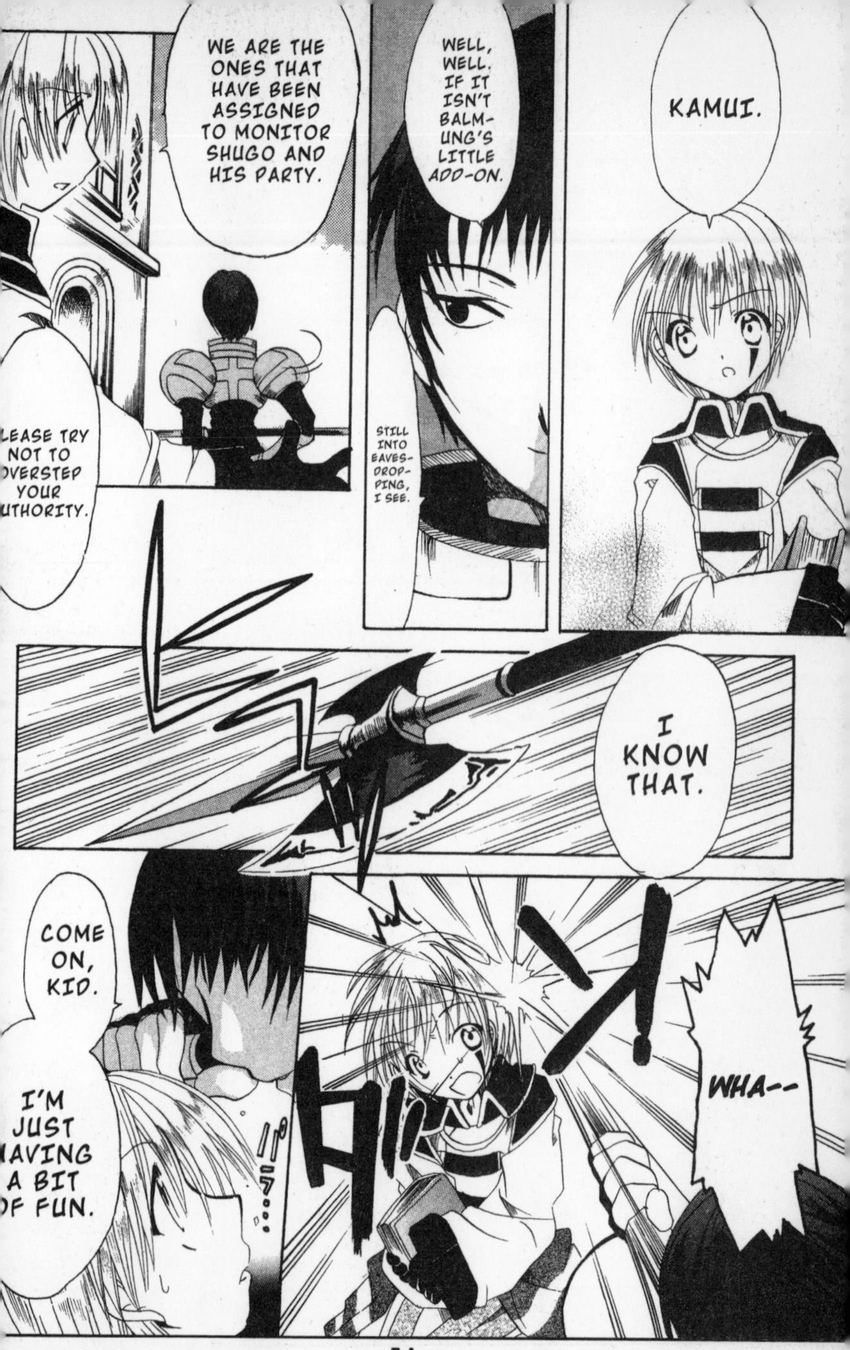
KAMUI.
WELL, WELL. IF IT ISN'T BALMUNG'S LITTLE ADD-ON.
STILL INTO EAVES-DROPPING, I SEE.
WE ARE THE ONES THAT HAVE BEEN ASSIGNED TO MONITOR SHUGO AND HIS PARTY.
LEASE TRY NOT TO OVERSTEP YOUR UTHORITY.
I KNOW THAT.
WHA--
COME ON, KID.
I'M JUST AVING A BIT OF FUN.

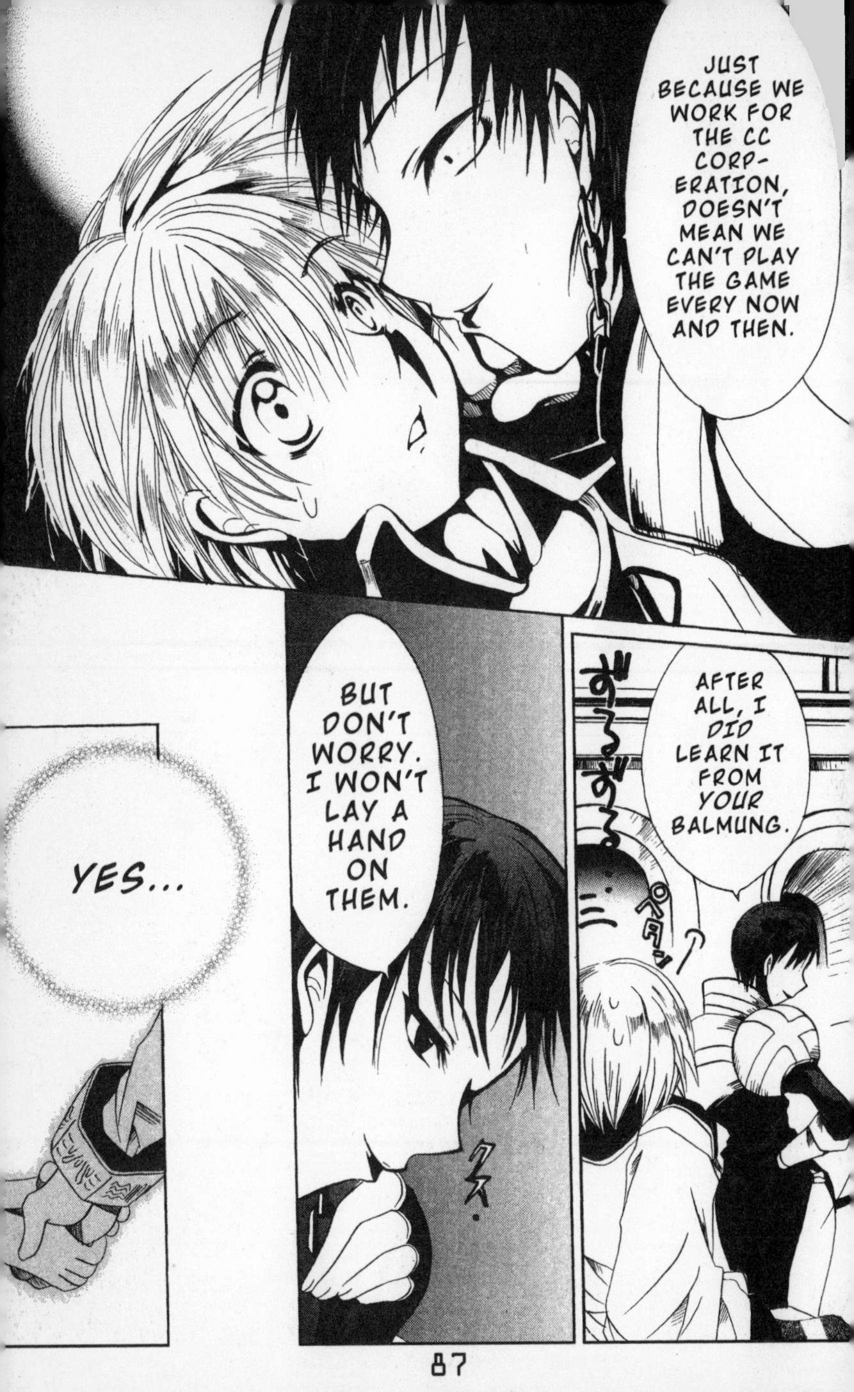
JUST BECAUSE WE WORK FOR THE CC CORP-ERATION, DOESN'T MEAN WE CAN'T PLAY THE GAME EVERY NOW AND THEN.
AFTER ALL, I *DID* LEARN IT FROM *YOUR* BALMUNG.
BUT DON'T WORRY. I WON'T LAY A HAND ON THEM.
*YES...*

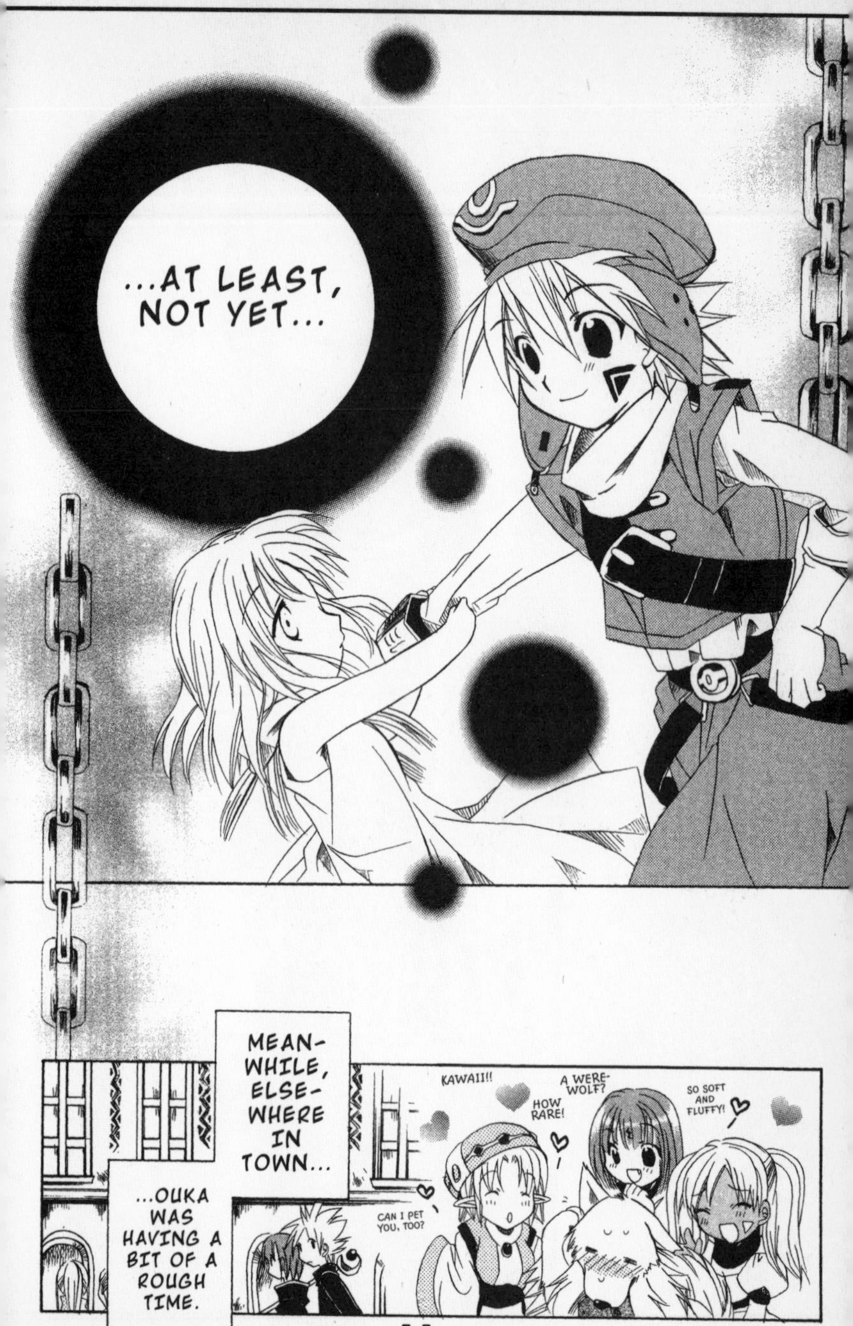
...AT LEAST, NOT YET...
MEAN-WHILE, ELSE-WHERE IN TOWN...
...OUKA WAS HAVING A BIT OF A ROUGH TIME.
SO SOFT AND FLUFFY!
A WERE-WOLF?
HOW RARE!
KAWAII!!
CAN I PET YOU, TOO?

NEW GENERATION ONLINE
THE WORLD

**SUBJECT: BALMUNG!**  **SENDER: REKI**

KAMUI FROM THE DEBUG TEAM IS BACK FROM
SHANGHAI ALREADY!

I JUST RAN INTO HER IN NAVAL MONTE. SHE
CALLED ME "BALMUNG'S LITTLE ADD-ON."

THIS IS ALL YOUR FAULT! (T_T)

REKI

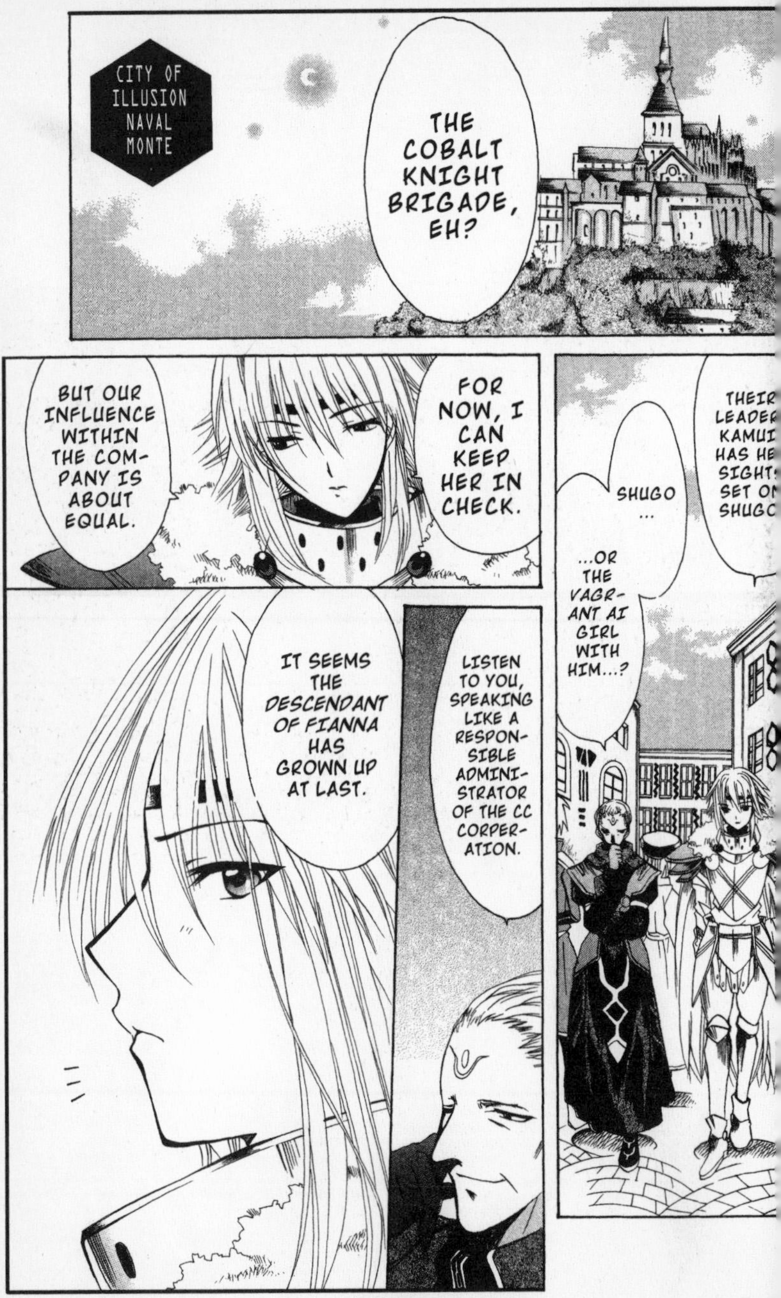
CITY OF ILLUSION NAVAL MONTE
THE COBALT KNIGHT BRIGADE, EH?
THEIR LEADER KAMUI HAS HE SIGHT SET O SHUG
SHUGO ...
...OR THE VAGRANT AI GIRL WITH HIM...?
FOR NOW, I CAN KEEP HER IN CHECK.
BUT OUR INFLUENCE WITHIN THE COMPANY IS ABOUT EQUAL.
LISTEN TO YOU, SPEAKING LIKE A RESPONSIBLE ADMINISTRATOR OF THE CC CORPERATION.
IT SEEMS THE DESCENDANT OF FIANNA HAS GROWN UP AT LAST.

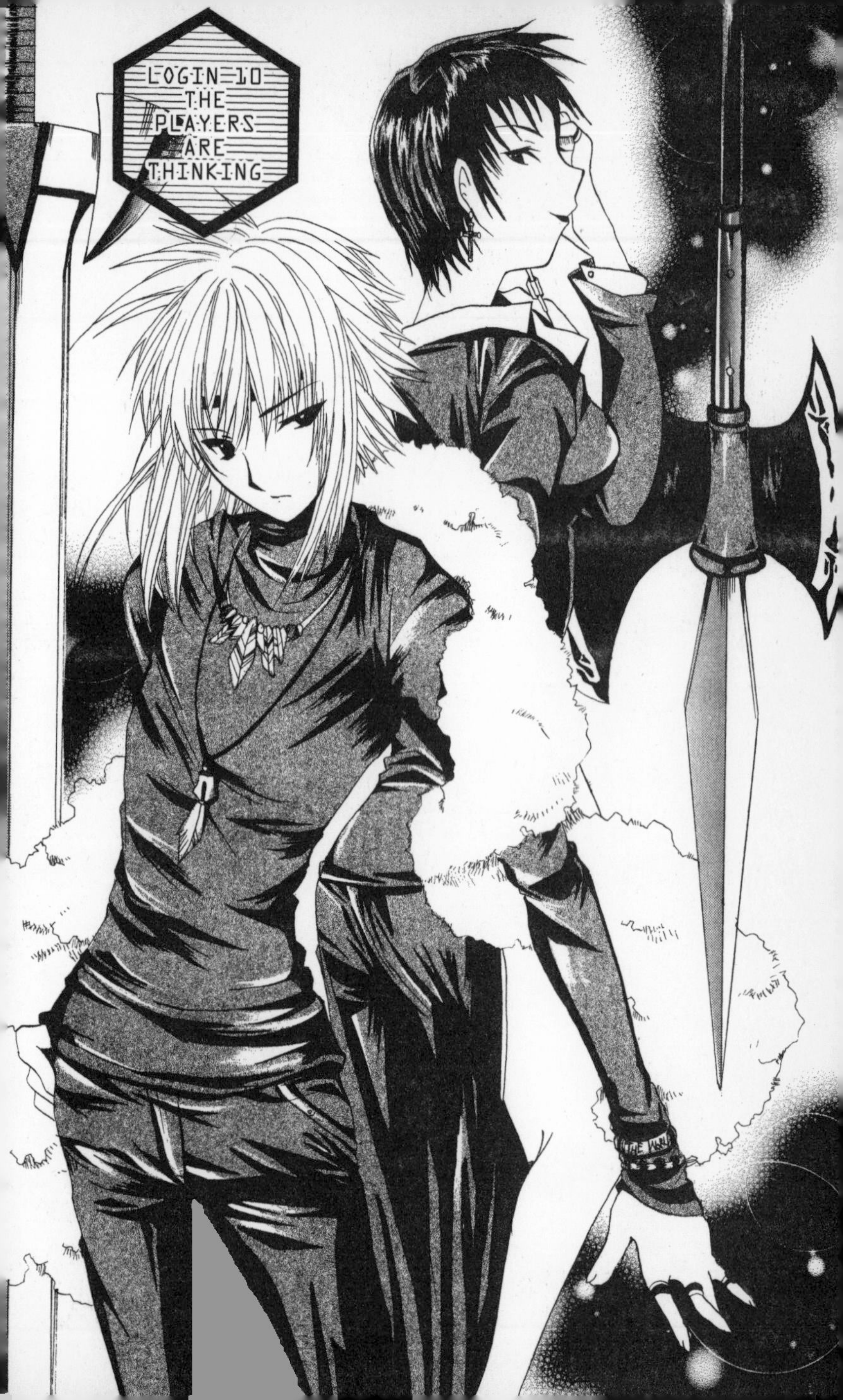
LOGIN 10
THE PLAYERS ARE THINKING

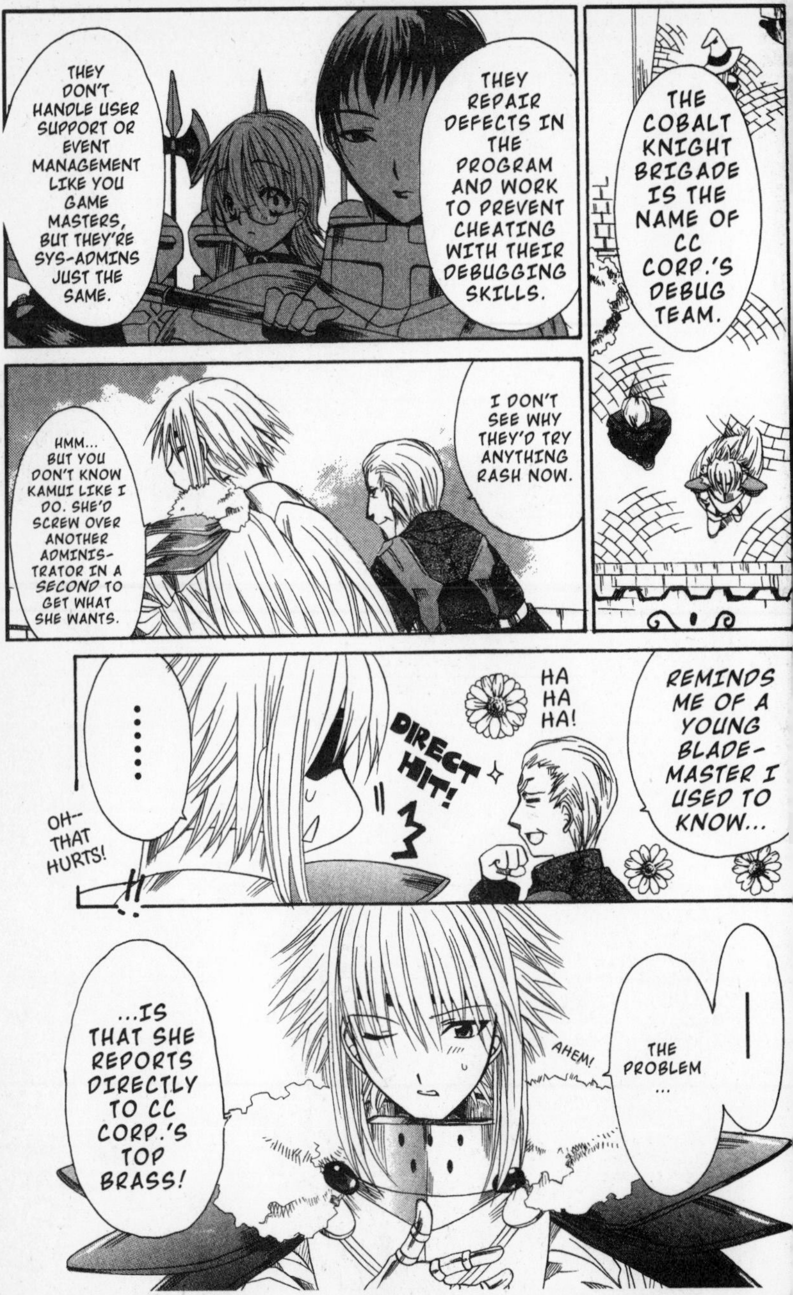
THE COBALT KNIGHT BRIGADE IS THE NAME OF CC CORP.'S DEBUG TEAM.
THEY REPAIR DEFECTS IN THE PROGRAM AND WORK TO PREVENT CHEATING WITH THEIR DEBUGGING SKILLS.
THEY DON'T HANDLE USER SUPPORT OR EVENT MANAGEMENT LIKE YOU GAME MASTERS, BUT THEY'RE SYS-ADMINS JUST THE SAME.
I DON'T SEE WHY THEY'D TRY ANYTHING RASH NOW.
HMM... BUT YOU DON'T KNOW KAMUI LIKE I DO. SHE'D SCREW OVER ANOTHER ADMINISTRATOR IN A *SECOND* TO GET WHAT SHE WANTS.
REMINDS ME OF A YOUNG BLADE-MASTER I USED TO KNOW...
HA HA HA!
DIRECT HIT!
......
OH--THAT HURTS!
THE PROBLEM ...
AHEM!
...IS THAT SHE REPORTS DIRECTLY TO CC CORP.'S TOP BRASS!

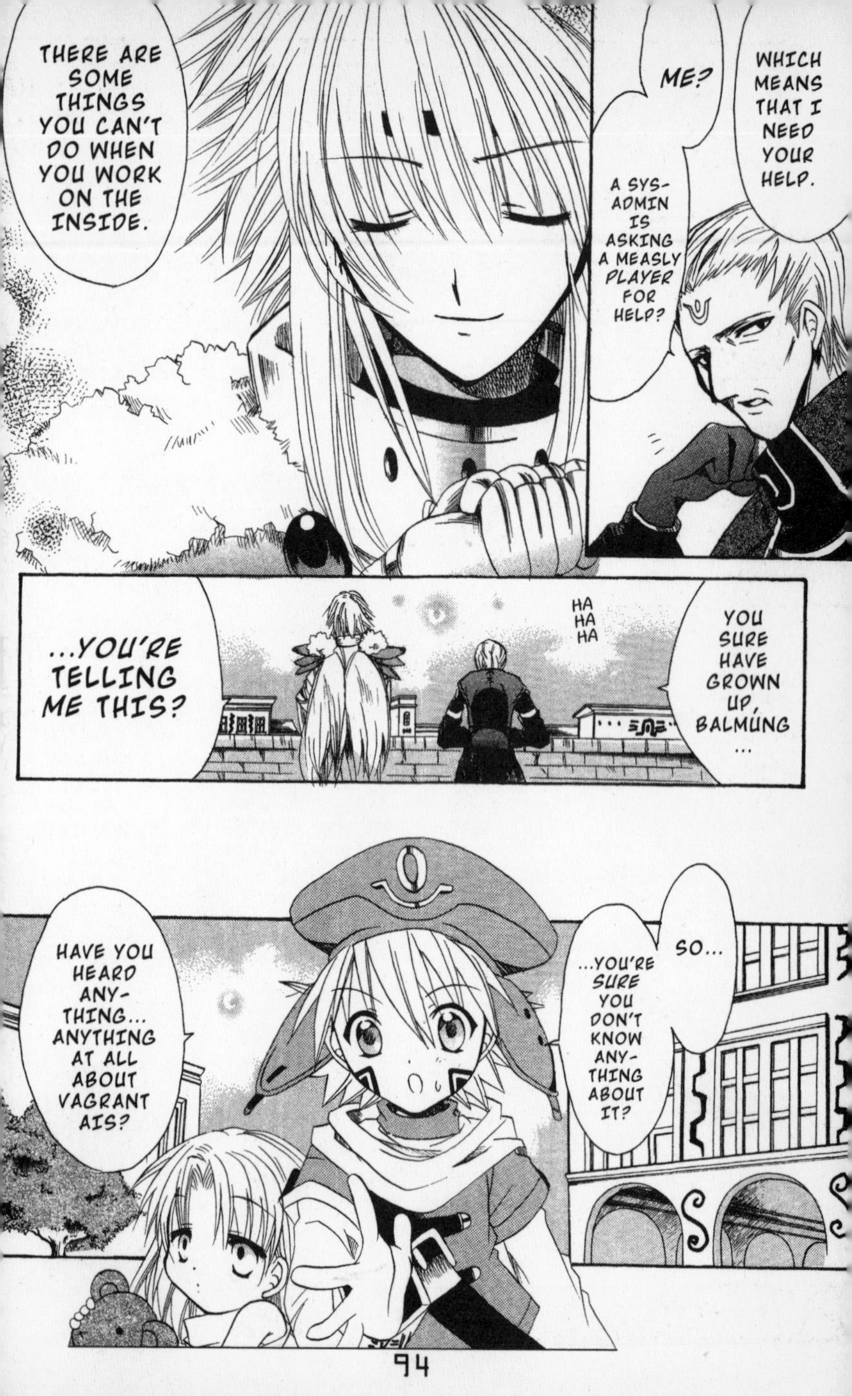

WHICH MEANS THAT I NEED YOUR HELP.
ME?
A SYS-ADMIN IS ASKING A MEASLY PLAYER FOR HELP?
THERE ARE SOME THINGS YOU CAN'T DO WHEN YOU WORK ON THE INSIDE.
YOU SURE HAVE GROWN UP, BALMUNG...
HA HA HA
...YOU'RE TELLING ME THIS?
SO...
...YOU'RE SURE YOU DON'T KNOW ANYTHING ABOUT IT?
HAVE YOU HEARD ANYTHING... ANYTHING AT ALL ABOUT VAGRANT AIS?

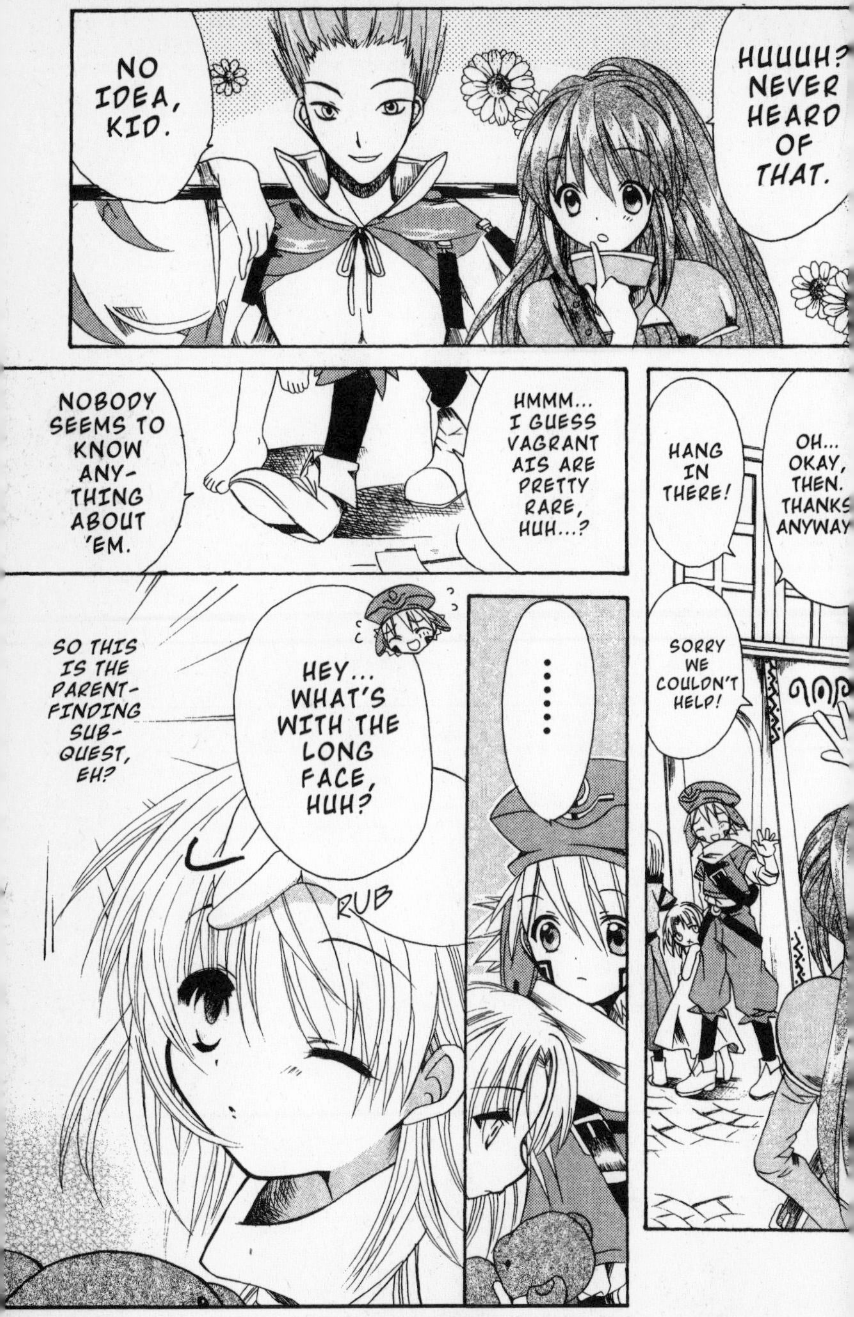
HUUUH? NEVER HEARD OF THAT.
NO IDEA, KID.
OH... OKAY, THEN. THANKS ANYWAY
HANG IN THERE!
SORRY WE COULDN'T HELP!
HMMM... I GUESS VAGRANT AIS ARE PRETTY RARE, HUH...?
NOBODY SEEMS TO KNOW ANY-THING ABOUT 'EM.
......
HEY... WHAT'S WITH THE LONG FACE, HUH?
SO THIS IS THE PARENT-FINDING SUB-QUEST, EH?
RUB

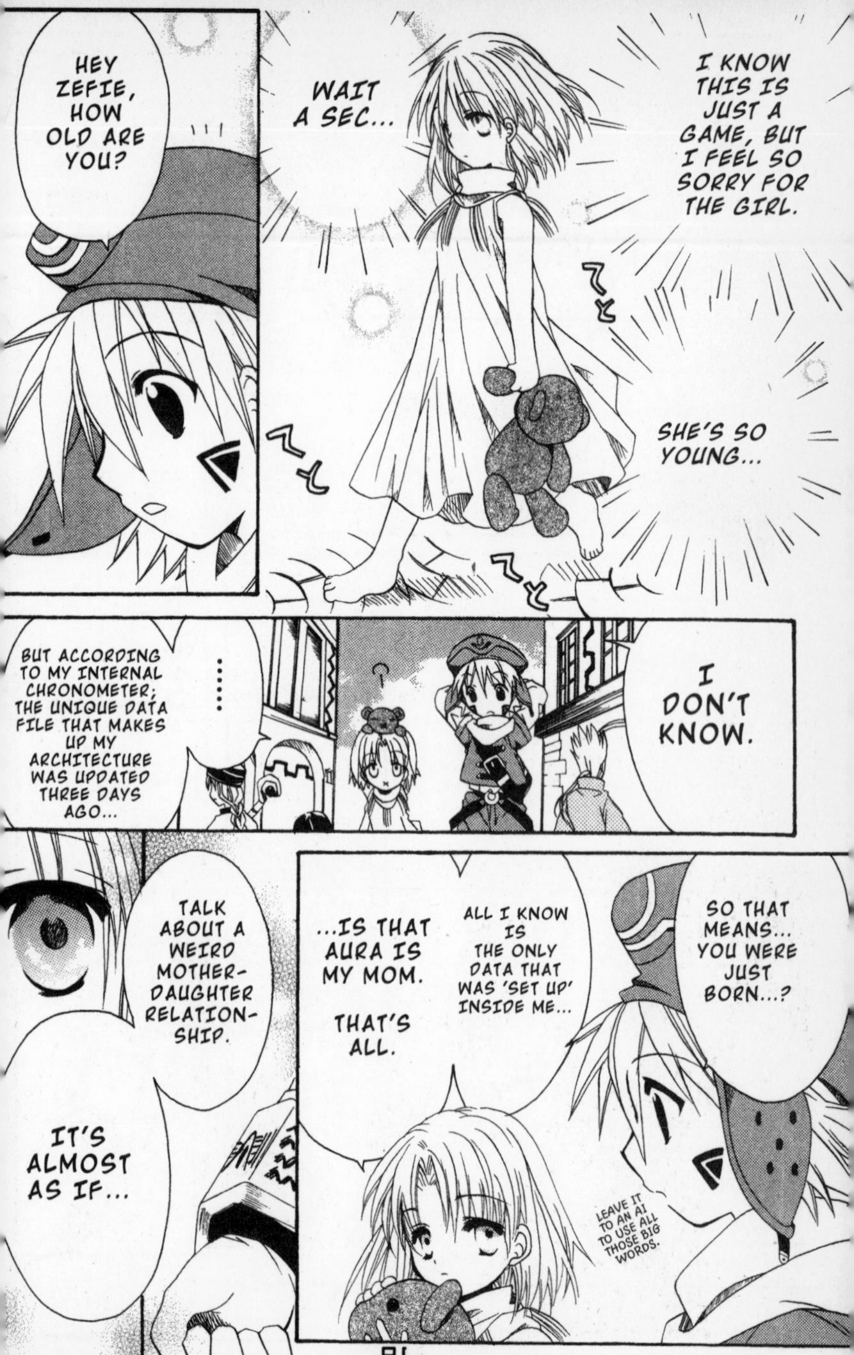
I KNOW THIS IS JUST A GAME, BUT I FEEL SO SORRY FOR THE GIRL.
WAIT A SEC...
SHE'S SO YOUNG...
HEY ZEFIE, HOW OLD ARE YOU?
I DON'T KNOW.
......
BUT ACCORDING TO MY INTERNAL CHRONOMETER; THE UNIQUE DATA FILE THAT MAKES UP MY ARCHITECTURE WAS UPDATED THREE DAYS AGO...
SO THAT MEANS... YOU WERE JUST BORN...?
ALL I KNOW IS THE ONLY DATA THAT WAS 'SET UP' INSIDE ME...
...IS THAT AURA IS MY MOM.
THAT'S ALL.
LEAVE IT TO AN AI TO USE ALL THOSE BIG WORDS.
TALK ABOUT A WEIRD MOTHER-DAUGHTER RELATIONSHIP.
IT'S ALMOST AS IF...

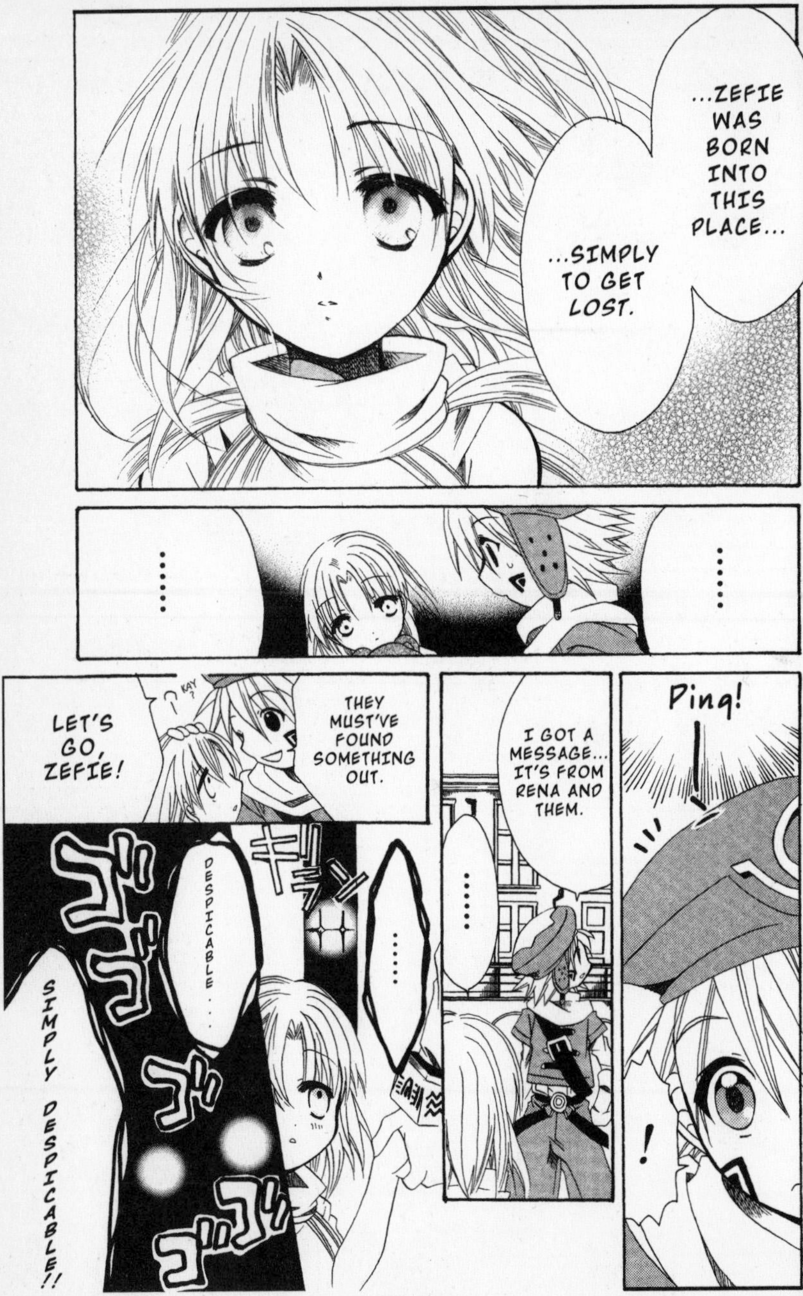
...ZEFIE WAS BORN INTO THIS PLACE...
...SIMPLY TO GET LOST.
......
......
Ping!
!
!
I GOT A MESSAGE... IT'S FROM RENA AND THEM.
......
THEY MUST'VE FOUND SOMETHING OUT.
KAY?
LET'S GO, ZEFIE!
......
DESPICABLE...
SIMPLY DESPICABLE!!

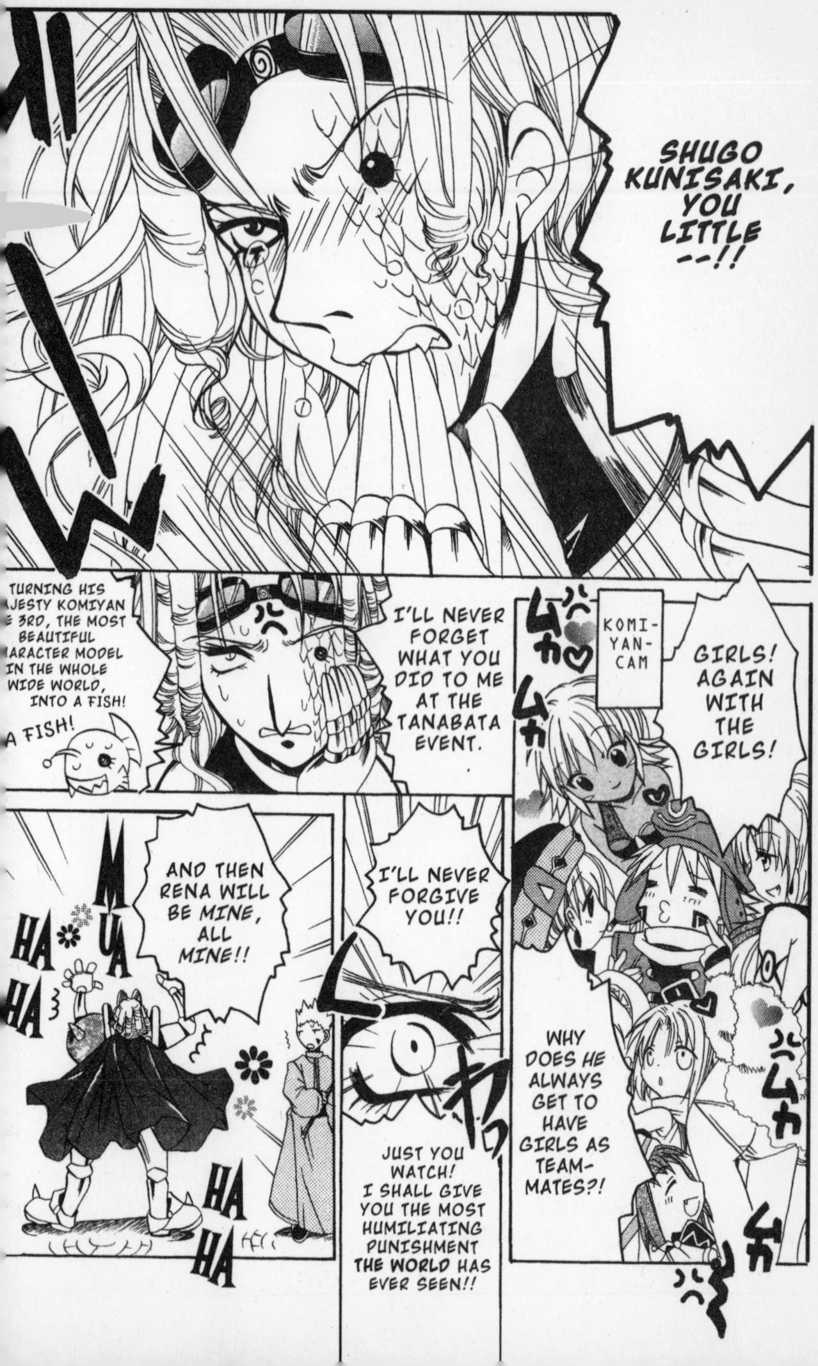

SHUGO KUNISAKI, YOU LITTLE--!!
KOMI-YAN-CAM
GIRLS! AGAIN WITH THE GIRLS!
WHY DOES HE ALWAYS GET TO HAVE GIRLS AS TEAM-MATES?!
I'LL NEVER FORGET WHAT YOU DID TO ME AT THE TANABATA EVENT.
TURNING HIS
AJESTY KOMIYAN
E 3RD, THE MOST
BEAUTIFUL
ARACTER MODEL
IN THE WHOLE
WIDE WORLD,
INTO A FISH!
A FISH!
I'LL NEVER FORGIVE YOU!!
JUST YOU WATCH! I SHALL GIVE YOU THE MOST HUMILIATING PUNISHMENT THE WORLD HAS EVER SEEN!!
AND THEN RENA WILL BE MINE, ALL MINE!!
MUA HA HA HA HA

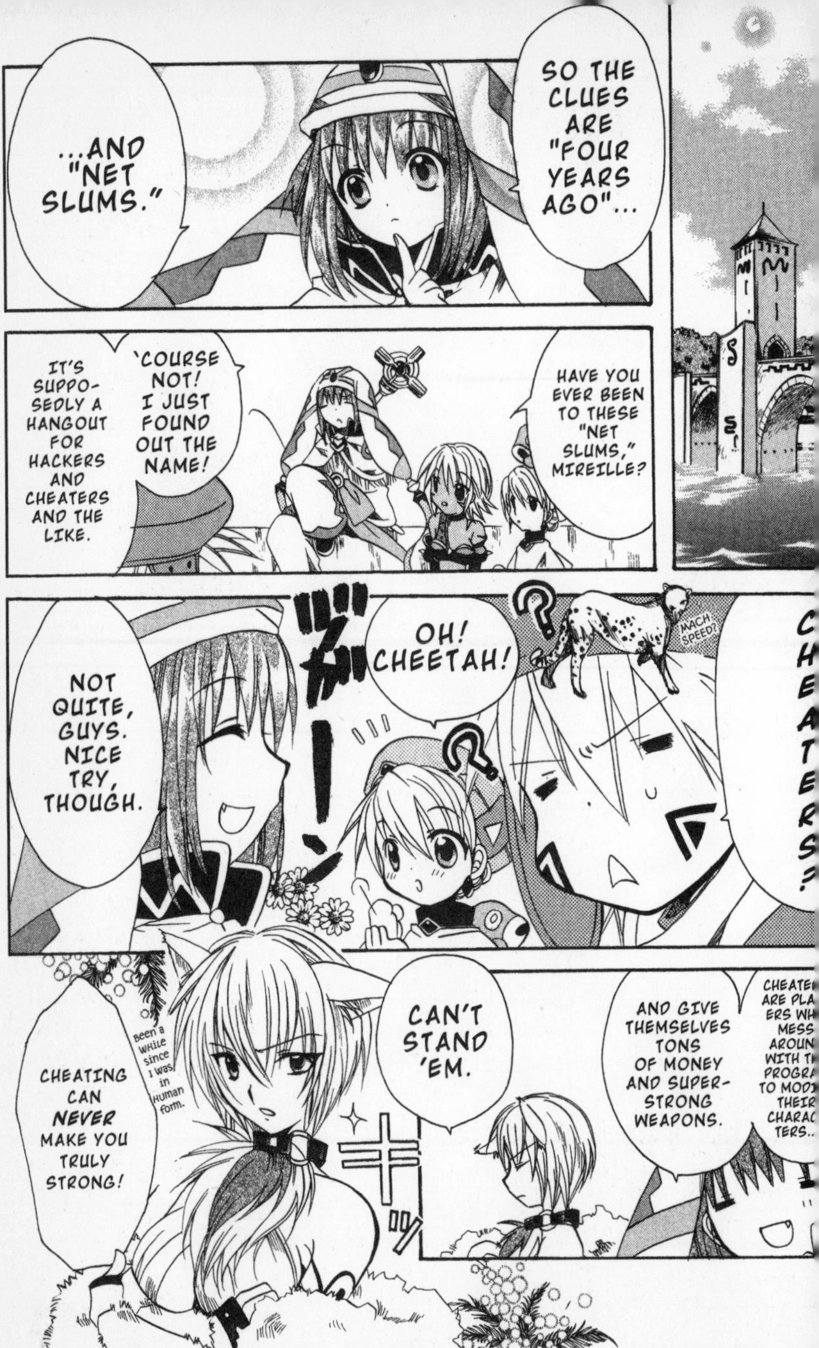
SO THE CLUES ARE "FOUR YEARS AGO"...
...AND "NET SLUMS."
HAVE YOU EVER BEEN TO THESE "NET SLUMS," MIREILLE?
'COURSE NOT! I JUST FOUND OUT THE NAME!
IT'S SUPPOSEDLY A HANGOUT FOR HACKERS AND CHEATERS AND THE LIKE.
CHEATERS?
MACH SPEED?
OH! CHEETAH!
NOT QUITE, GUYS. NICE TRY, THOUGH.
CHEATE ARE PLA ERS WH MESS AROUN WITH TH PROGRA TO MODI THEIR CHARAC TERS..
AND GIVE THEMSELVES TONS OF MONEY AND SUPER-STRONG WEAPONS.
CAN'T STAND 'EM.
Been a While since I Was in Human form.
CHEATING CAN *NEVER* MAKE YOU TRULY STRONG!

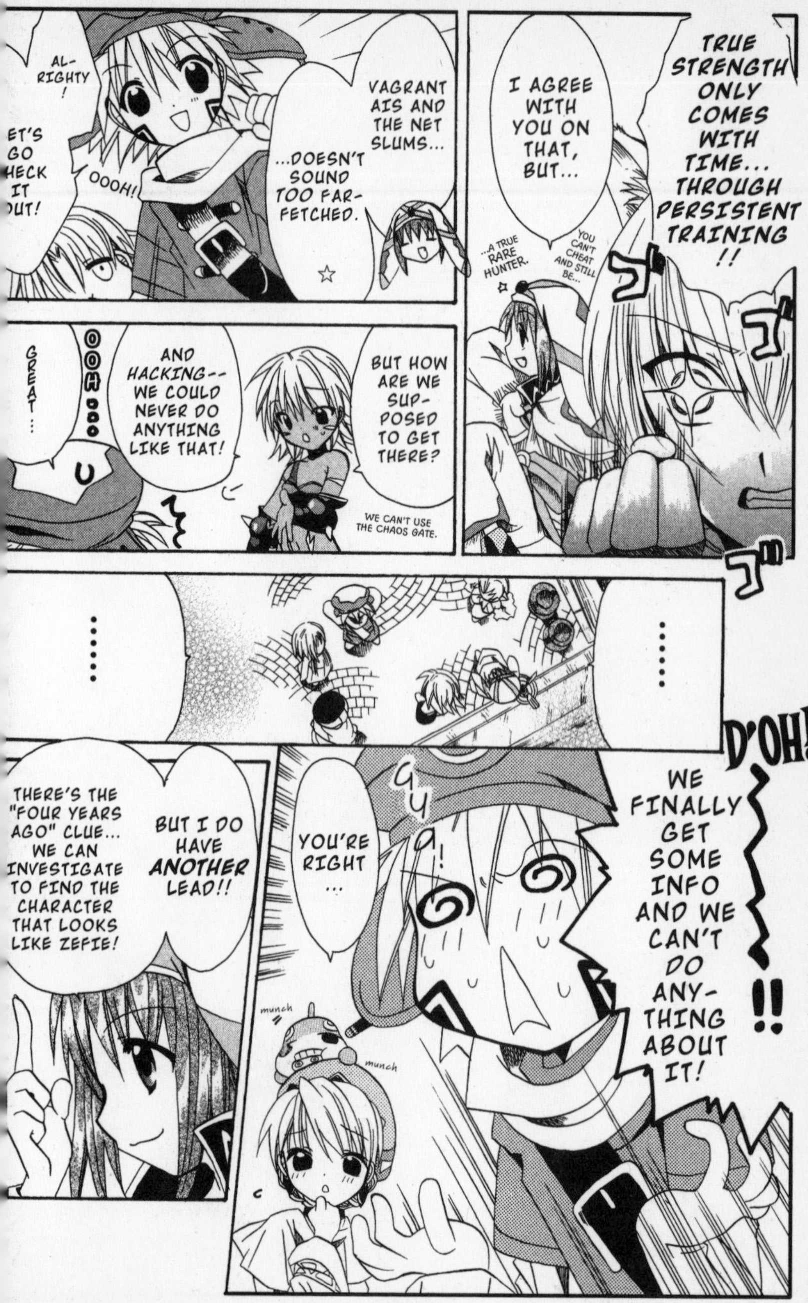
TRUE STRENGTH ONLY COMES WITH TIME... THROUGH PERSISTENT TRAINING!!
I AGREE WITH YOU ON THAT, BUT...
YOU CAN'T CHEAT AND STILL BE...
...A TRUE RARE HUNTER.
VAGRANT AIS AND THE NET SLUMS...
...DOESN'T SOUND TOO FAR-FETCHED.
AL-RIGHTY!
OOOH!
ET'S GO HECK IT UT!
BUT HOW ARE WE SUPPOSED TO GET THERE?
WE CAN'T USE THE CHAOS GATE.
AND HACKING-- WE COULD NEVER DO ANYTHING LIKE THAT!
OOH...
GREAT...
......
......
D'OH!
WE FINALLY GET SOME INFO AND WE CAN'T DO ANYTHING ABOUT IT!!
GYA!
YOU'RE RIGHT...
munch
munch
BUT I DO HAVE ANOTHER LEAD!!
THERE'S THE "FOUR YEARS AGO" CLUE... WE CAN INVESTIGATE TO FIND THE CHARACTER THAT LOOKS LIKE ZEFIE!

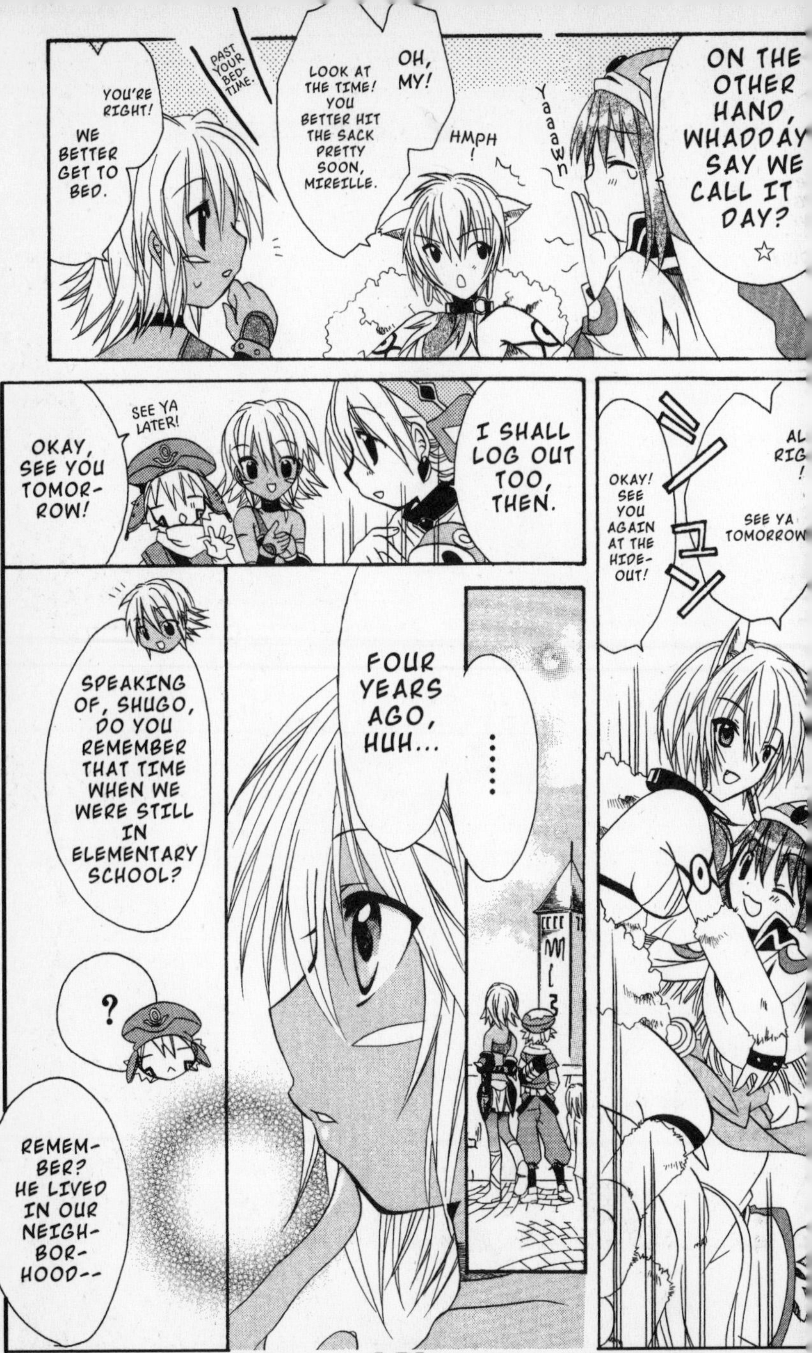
ON THE OTHER HAND, WHADDAY SAY WE CALL IT DAY? ☆
Yaaawn
HMPH!
OH, MY!
LOOK AT THE TIME! YOU BETTER HIT THE SACK PRETTY SOON, MIREILLE.
PAST YOUR BED-TIME.
YOU'RE RIGHT!
WE BETTER GET TO BED.
AL RIG!
SEE YA TOMORROW
OKAY! SEE YOU AGAIN AT THE HIDE-OUT!
I SHALL LOG OUT TOO, THEN.
SEE YA LATER!
OKAY, SEE YOU TOMOR-ROW!
FOUR YEARS AGO, HUH...
......
SPEAKING OF, SHUGO, DO YOU REMEMBER THAT TIME WHEN WE WERE STILL IN ELEMENTARY SCHOOL?
?
REMEM-BER? HE LIVED IN OUR NEIGH-BOR-HOOD--

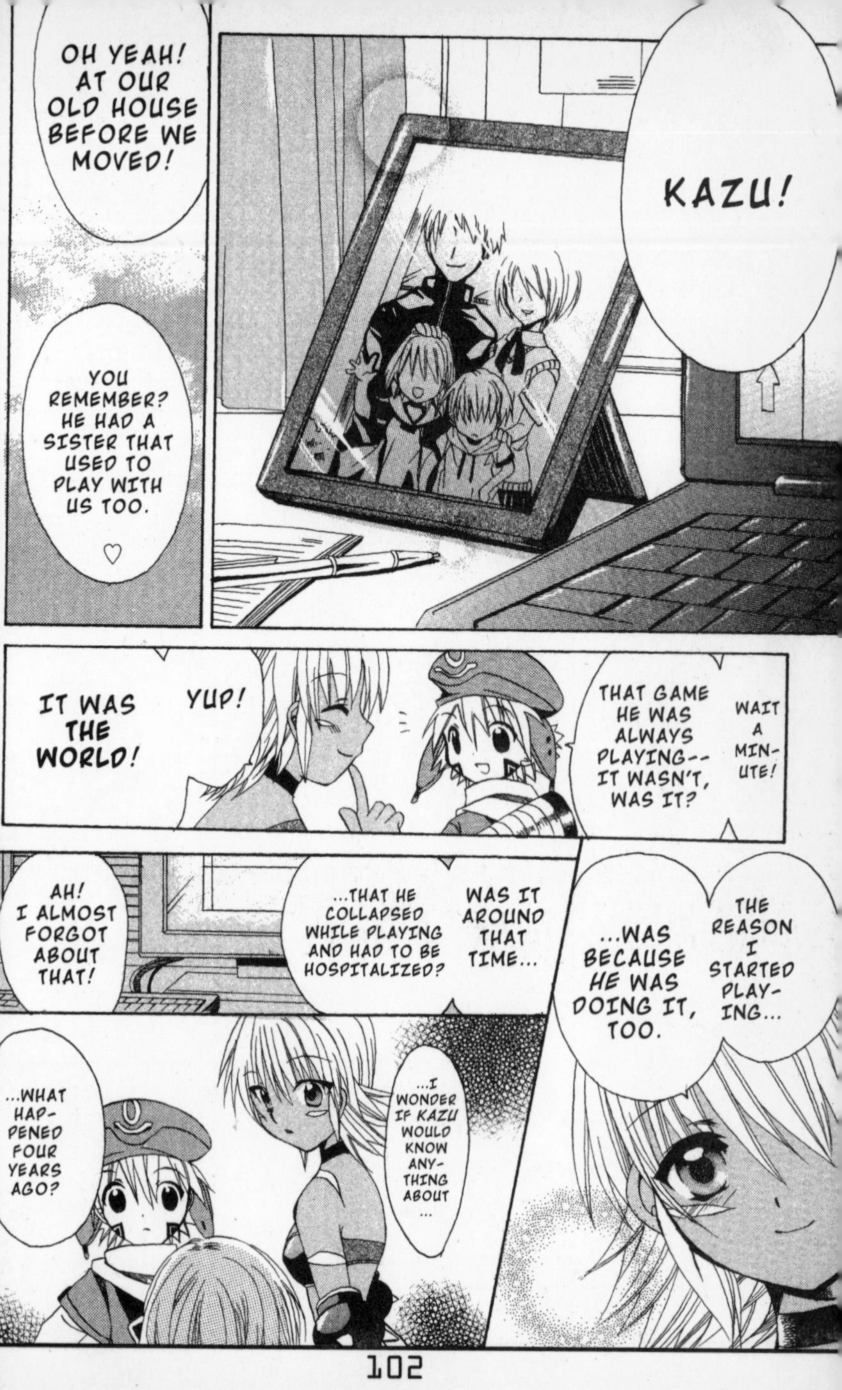
KAZU!
OH YEAH! AT OUR OLD HOUSE BEFORE WE MOVED!
YOU REMEMBER? HE HAD A SISTER THAT USED TO PLAY WITH US TOO. ♡
WAIT A MIN-UTE!
THAT GAME HE WAS ALWAYS PLAYING-- IT WASN'T, WAS IT?
YUP!
IT WAS THE WORLD!
THE REASON I STARTED PLAY-ING...
...WAS BECAUSE HE WAS DOING IT, TOO.
WAS IT AROUND THAT TIME...
...THAT HE COLLAPSED WHILE PLAYING AND HAD TO BE HOSPITALIZED?
AH! I ALMOST FORGOT ABOUT THAT!
...I WONDER IF KAZU WOULD KNOW ANY-THING ABOUT ...
...WHAT HAP-PENED FOUR YEARS AGO?

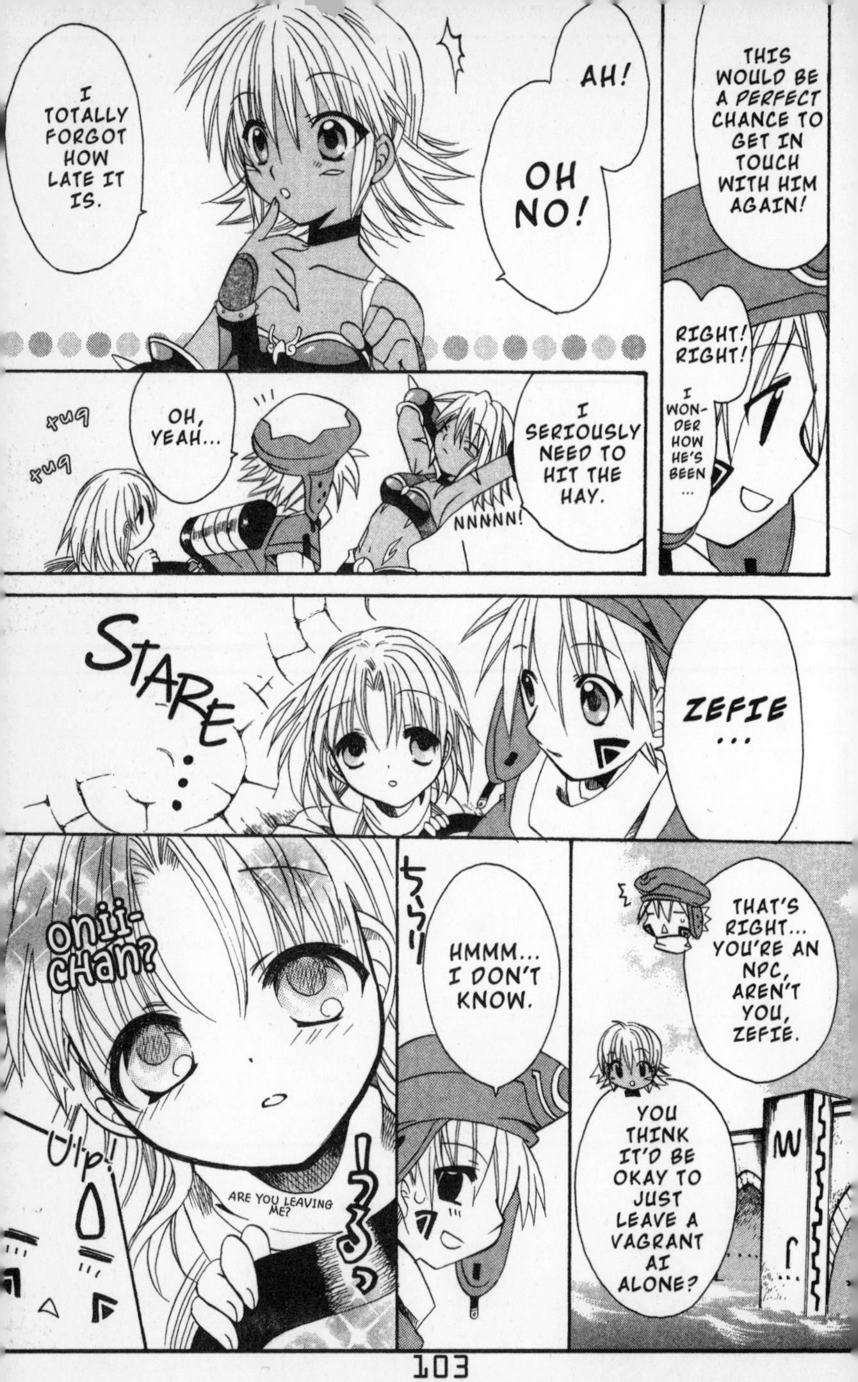
THIS WOULD BE A PERFECT CHANCE TO GET IN TOUCH WITH HIM AGAIN!
RIGHT! RIGHT!
I WONDER HOW HE'S BEEN...
AH!
OH NO!
I TOTALLY FORGOT HOW LATE IT IS.
I SERIOUSLY NEED TO HIT THE HAY.
NNNNN!
OH, YEAH...
ZEFIE...
STARE
THAT'S RIGHT... YOU'RE AN NPC, AREN'T YOU, ZEFIE.
YOU THINK IT'D BE OKAY TO JUST LEAVE A VAGRANT AI ALONE?
HMMM... I DON'T KNOW.
onii-chan?
Ulp!
ARE YOU LEAVING ME?

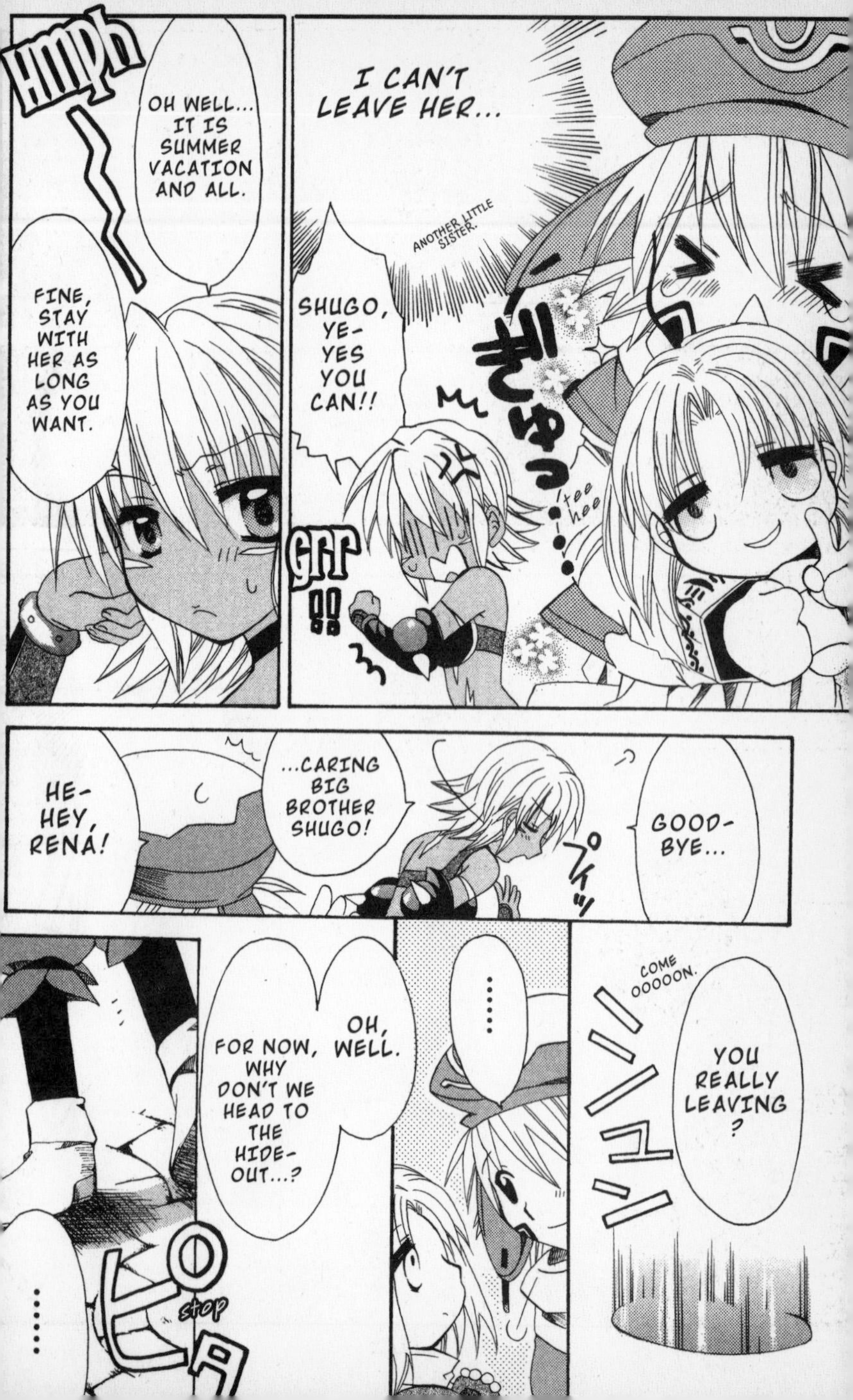
I CAN'T LEAVE HER...
ANOTHER LITTLE SISTER.
ぎゅっ
tee hee
SHUGO, YE- YES YOU CAN!!
GRR!!
HMPH
OH WELL... IT IS SUMMER VACATION AND ALL.
FINE, STAY WITH HER AS LONG AS YOU WANT.
GOOD-BYE...
...CARING BIG BROTHER SHUGO!
HE- HEY, RENA!
COME OOOOON.
YOU REALLY LEAVING?
......
OH, WELL.
FOR NOW, WHY DON'T WE HEAD TO THE HIDE-OUT...?
......
stop

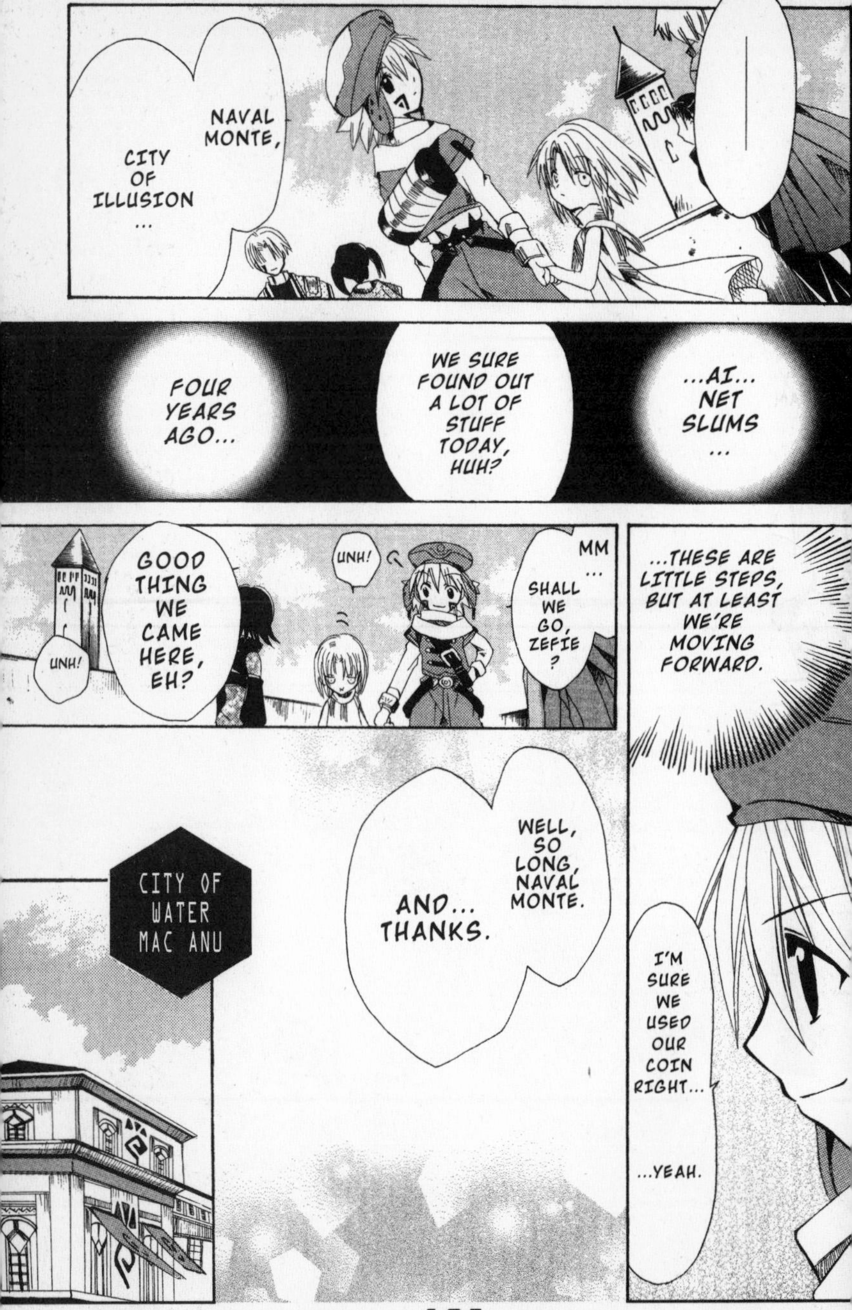
NAVAL MONTE,
CITY OF ILLUSION ...
...AI... NET SLUMS ...
WE SURE FOUND OUT A LOT OF STUFF TODAY, HUH?
FOUR YEARS AGO...
...THESE ARE LITTLE STEPS, BUT AT LEAST WE'RE MOVING FORWARD.
I'M SURE WE USED OUR COIN RIGHT...
...YEAH.
MM ... SHALL WE GO, ZEFIE ?
UNH!
GOOD THING WE CAME HERE, EH?
UNH!
WELL, SO LONG, NAVAL MONTE.
AND... THANKS.
CITY OF WATER MAC ANU

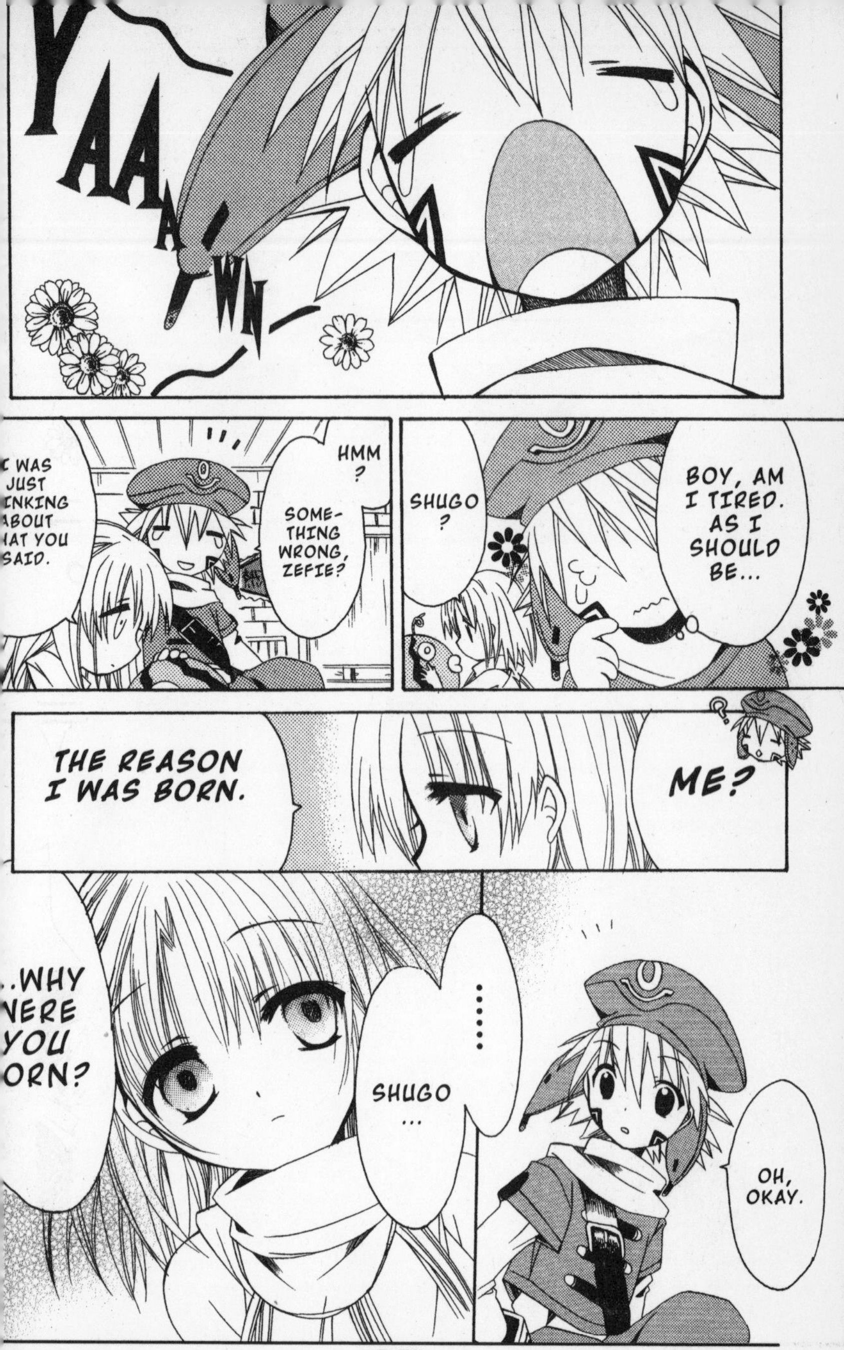
YAAAAWN
BOY, AM I TIRED. AS I SHOULD BE...
SHUGO?
HMM? SOMETHING WRONG, ZEFIE?
WAS JUST INKING ABOUT AT YOU SAID.
ME?
THE REASON I WAS BORN.
OH, OKAY.
......
SHUGO...
..WHY ERE YOU ORN?

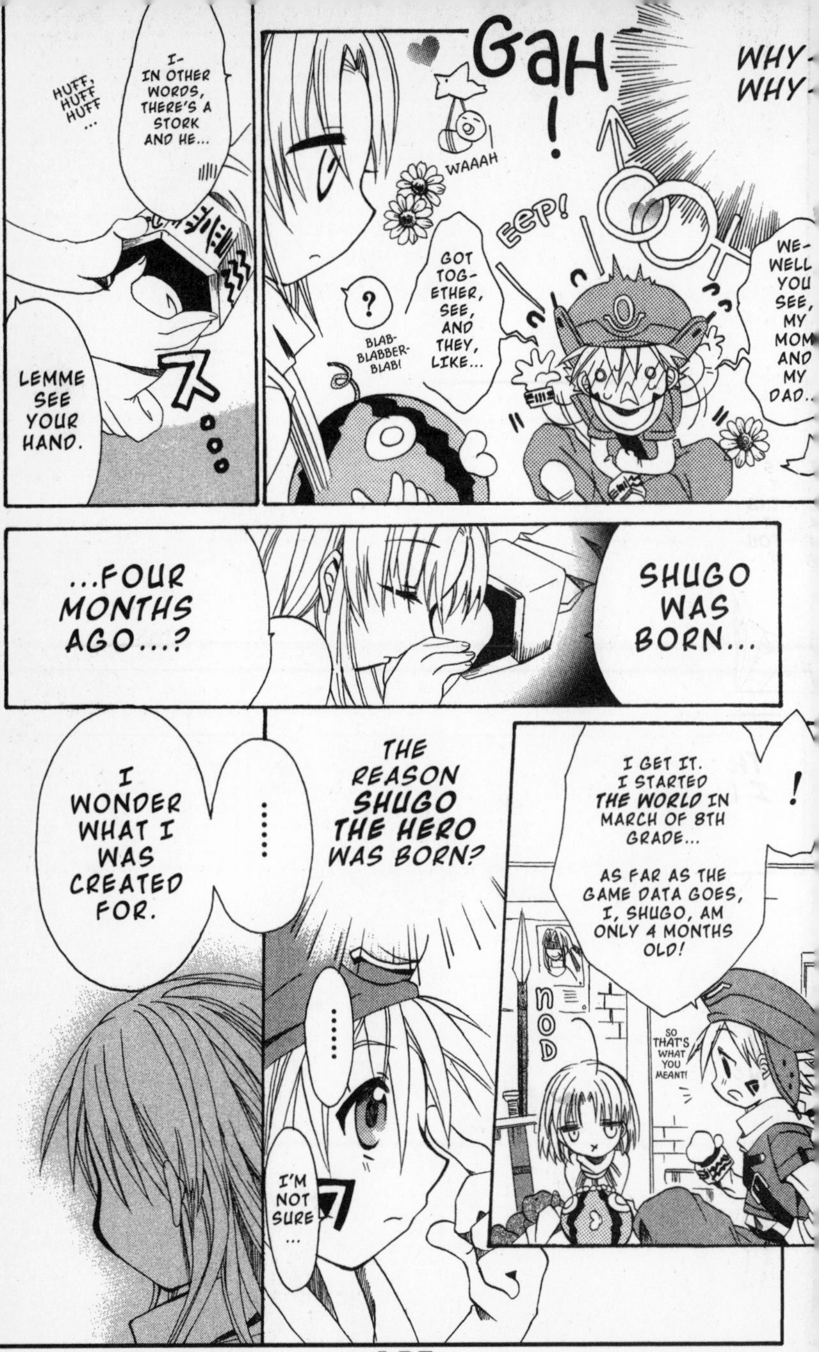
GAH!
WHY-WHY-
WE-WELL YOU SEE, MY MOM AND MY DAD...
EEP!
WAAAH
GOT TOGETHER, SEE, AND THEY, LIKE...
?
BLAB-BLABBER-BLAB!
I- IN OTHER WORDS, THERE'S A STORK AND HE...
HUFF, HUFF HUFF...
LEMME SEE YOUR HAND.
SHUGO WAS BORN...
...FOUR MONTHS AGO...?
!
I GET IT. I STARTED THE WORLD IN MARCH OF 8TH GRADE...
AS FAR AS THE GAME DATA GOES, I, SHUGO, AM ONLY 4 MONTHS OLD!
SO THAT'S WHAT YOU MEANT!
NOD
THE REASON SHUGO THE HERO WAS BORN?
......
I'M NOT SURE...
......
I WONDER WHAT I WAS CREATED FOR.

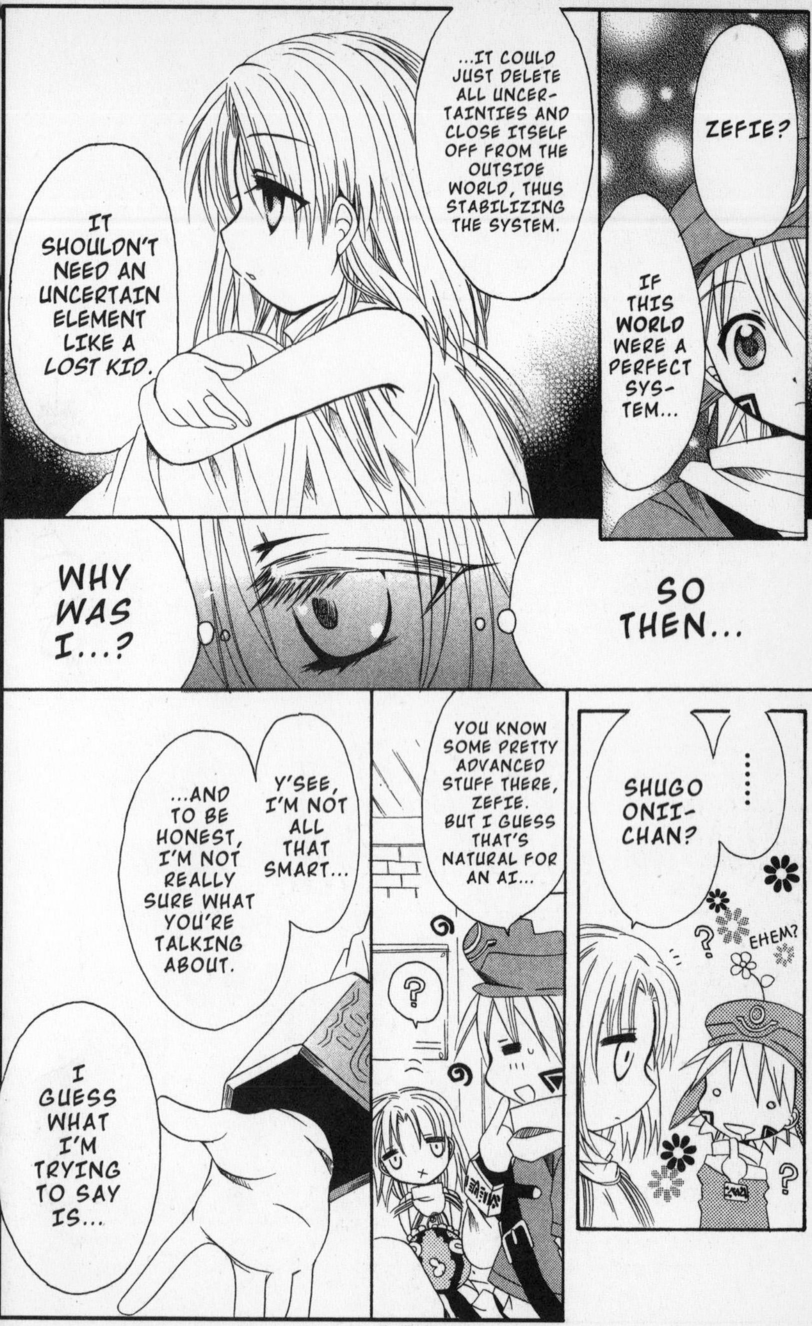
ZEFIE?
IF THIS WORLD WERE A PERFECT SYSTEM...
...IT COULD JUST DELETE ALL UNCERTAINTIES AND CLOSE ITSELF OFF FROM THE OUTSIDE WORLD, THUS STABILIZING THE SYSTEM.
IT SHOULDN'T NEED AN UNCERTAIN ELEMENT LIKE A LOST KID.
SO THEN...
WHY WAS I...?
......
SHUGO ONII-CHAN?
EHEM?
YOU KNOW SOME PRETTY ADVANCED STUFF THERE, ZEFIE. BUT I GUESS THAT'S NATURAL FOR AN AI...
?
Y'SEE, I'M NOT ALL THAT SMART...
...AND TO BE HONEST, I'M NOT REALLY SURE WHAT YOU'RE TALKING ABOUT.
I GUESS WHAT I'M TRYING TO SAY IS...

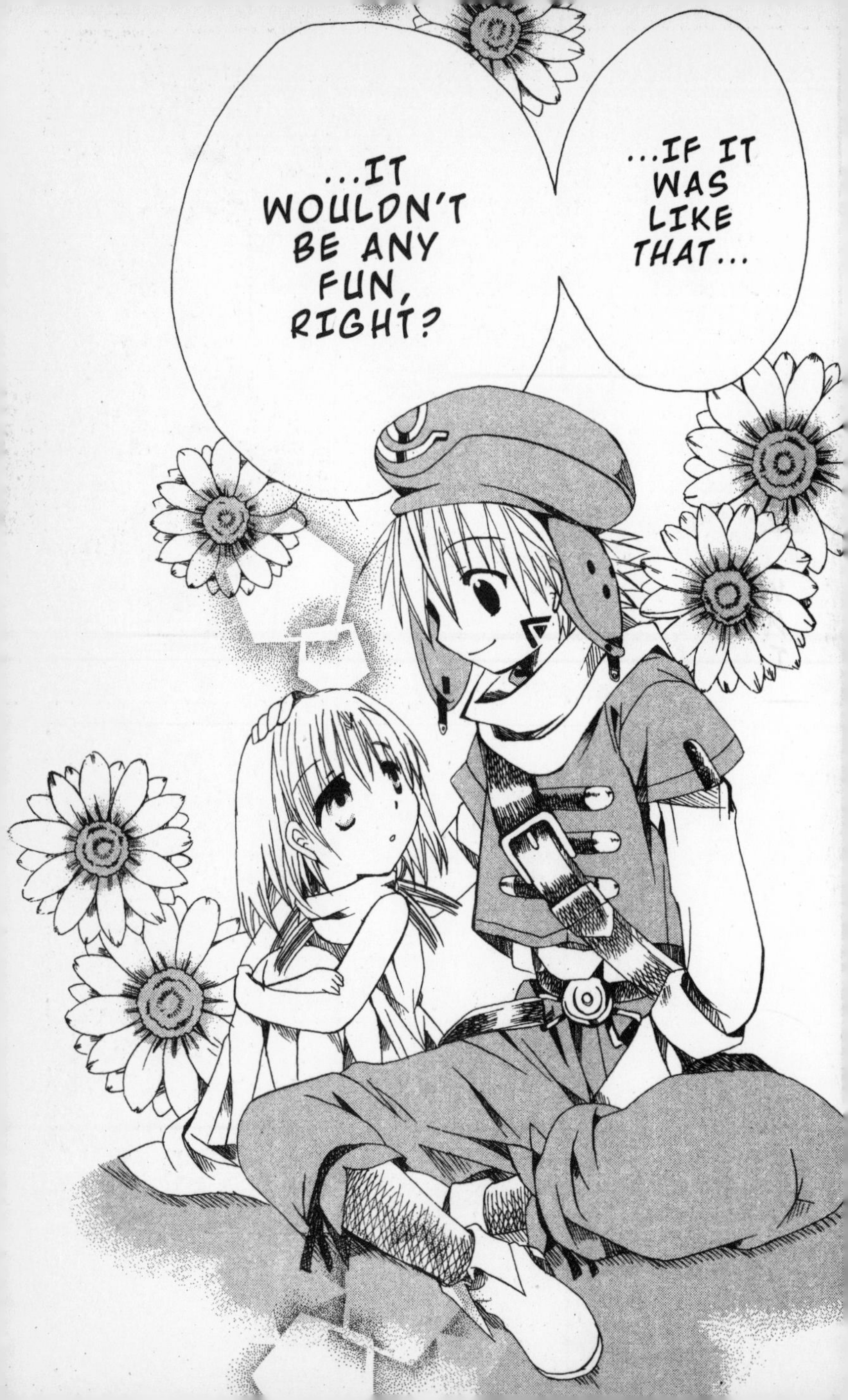
...IF IT WAS LIKE THAT...
...IT WOULDN'T BE ANY FUN, RIGHT?

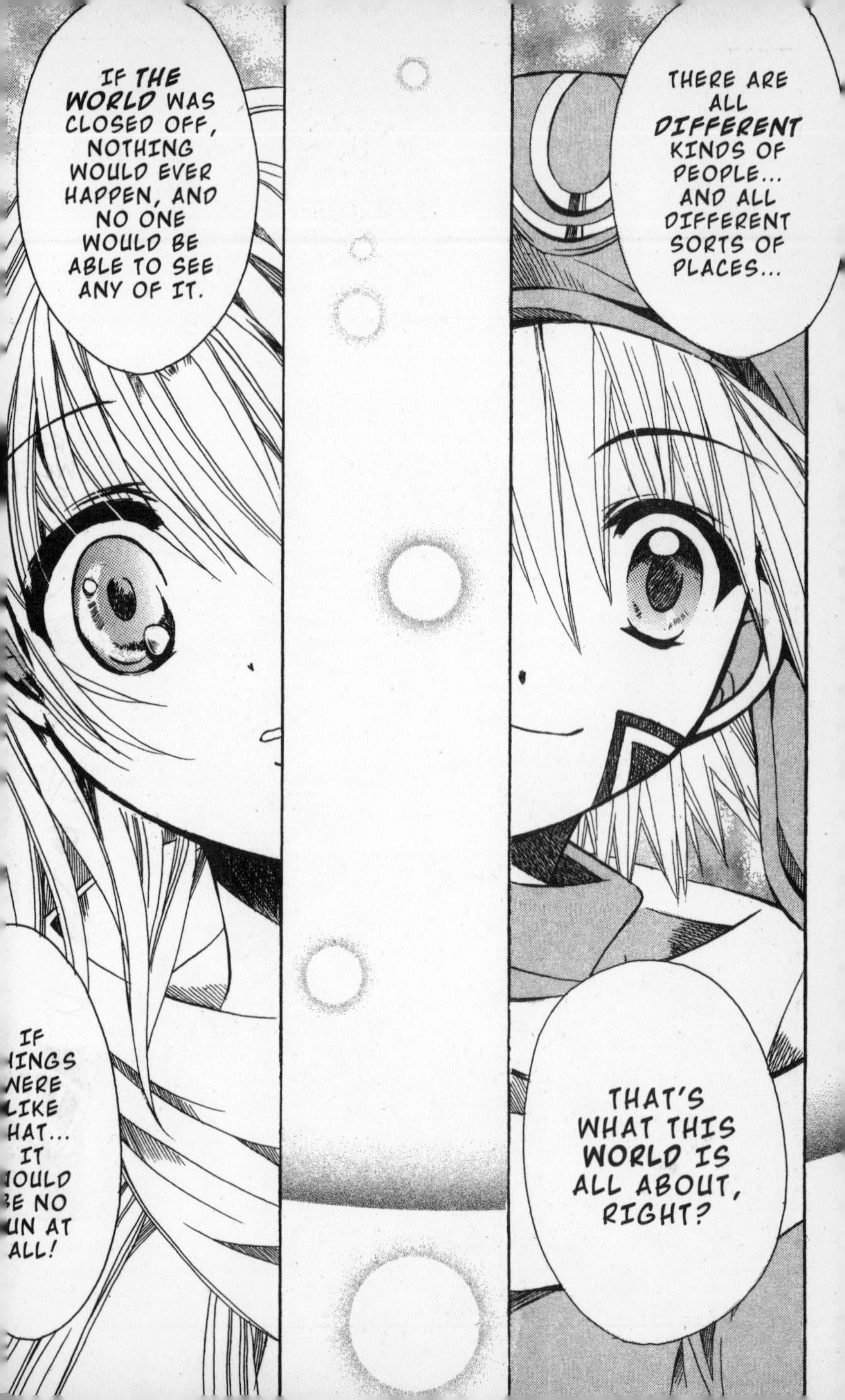
THERE ARE ALL DIFFERENT KINDS OF PEOPLE... AND ALL DIFFERENT SORTS OF PLACES...
THAT'S WHAT THIS WORLD IS ALL ABOUT, RIGHT?
IF THE WORLD WAS CLOSED OFF, NOTHING WOULD EVER HAPPEN, AND NO ONE WOULD BE ABLE TO SEE ANY OF IT.
IF INGS NERE LIKE HAT... IT IOULD E NO UN AT ALL!

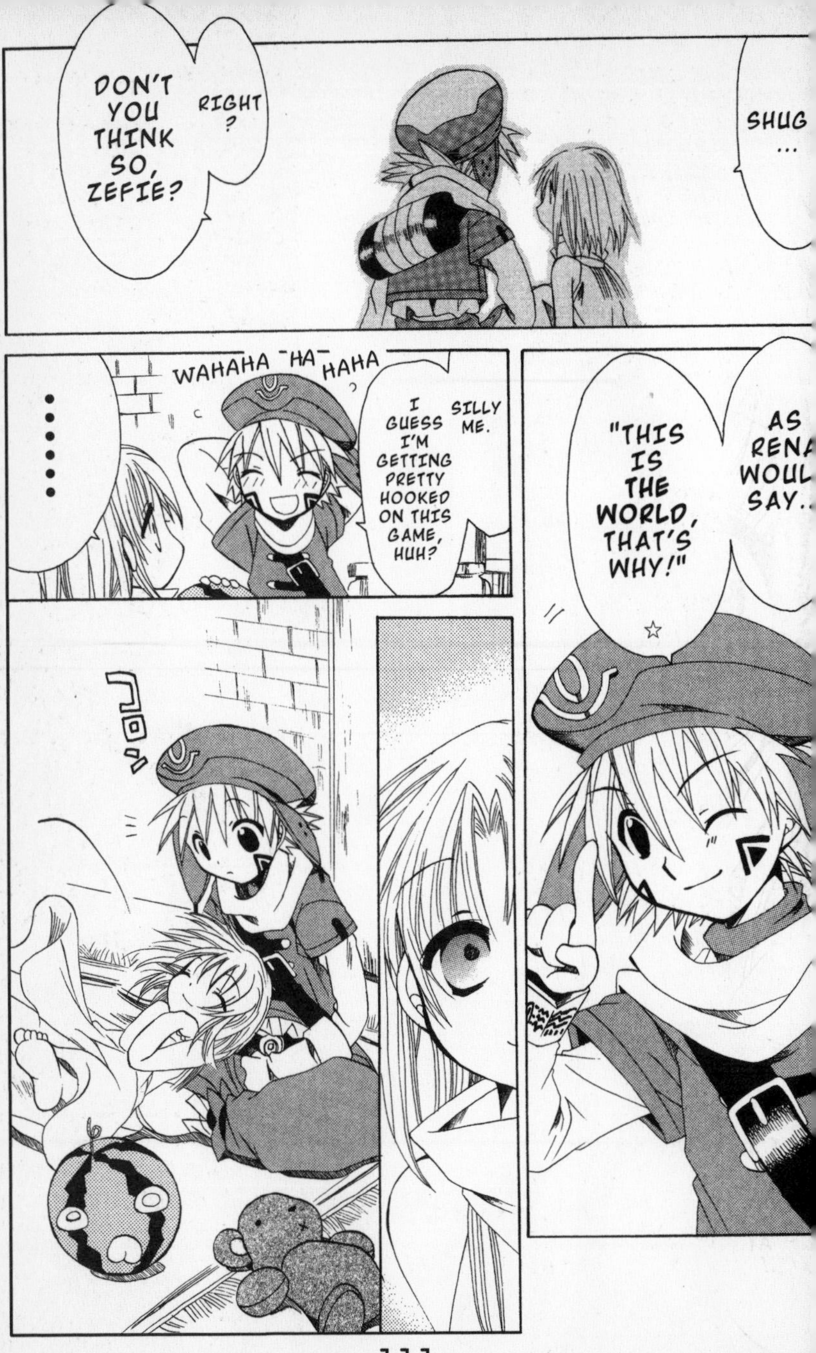
SHUG ...
DON'T YOU THINK SO, ZEFIE? RIGHT?
AS RENA WOUL SAY..
"THIS IS THE WORLD, THAT'S WHY!" ☆
WAHAHA HA HAHA
SILLY ME.
I GUESS I'M GETTING PRETTY HOOKED ON THIS GAME, HUH?
......
コロッ

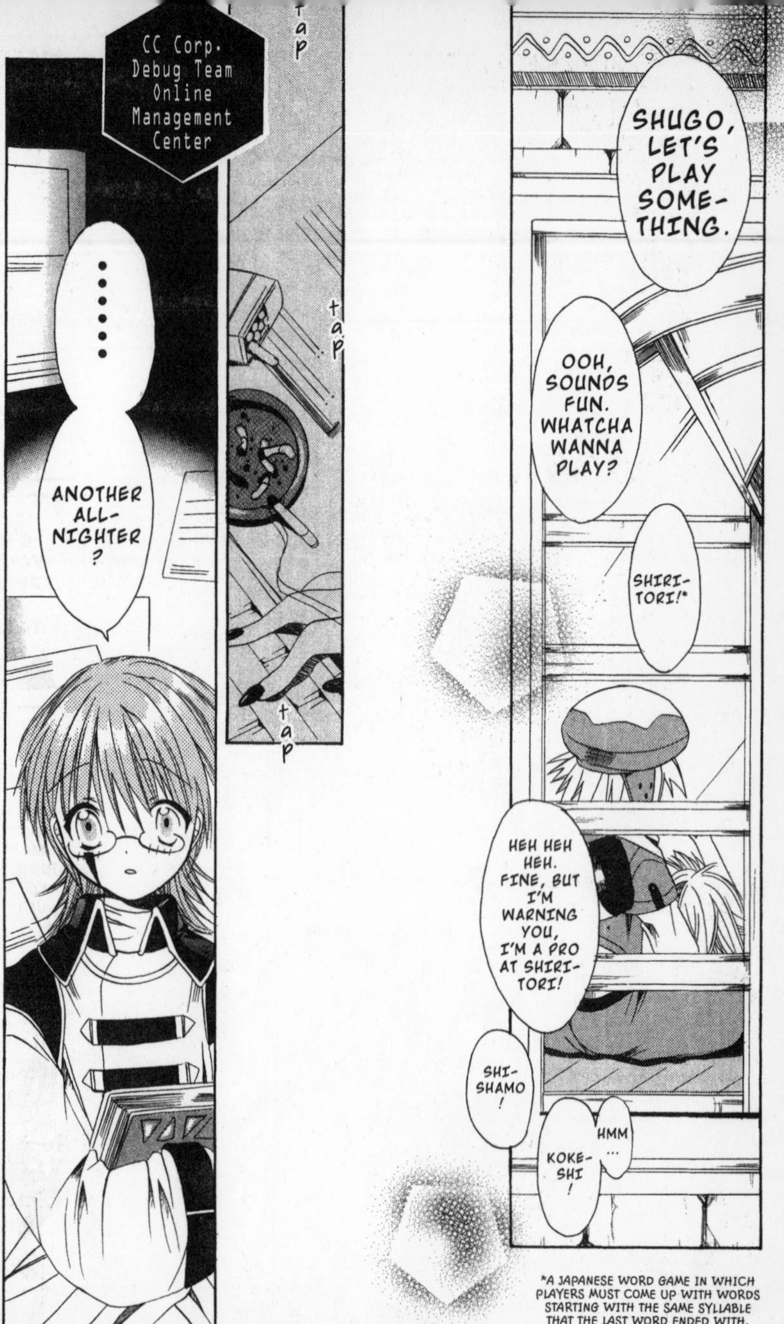
SHUGO, LET'S PLAY SOME-THING.
OOH, SOUNDS FUN. WHATCHA WANNA PLAY?
SHIRI-TORI!*
HEH HEH HEH. FINE, BUT I'M WARNING YOU, I'M A PRO AT SHIRI-TORI!
SHI-SHAMO!
HMM...
KOKE-SHI!
tap
tap
tap
CC Corp. Debug Team Online Management Center
......
ANOTHER ALL-NIGHTER?

*A JAPANESE WORD GAME IN WHICH PLAYERS MUST COME UP WITH WORDS STARTING WITH THE SAME SYLLABLE THAT THE LAST WORD ENDED WITH.

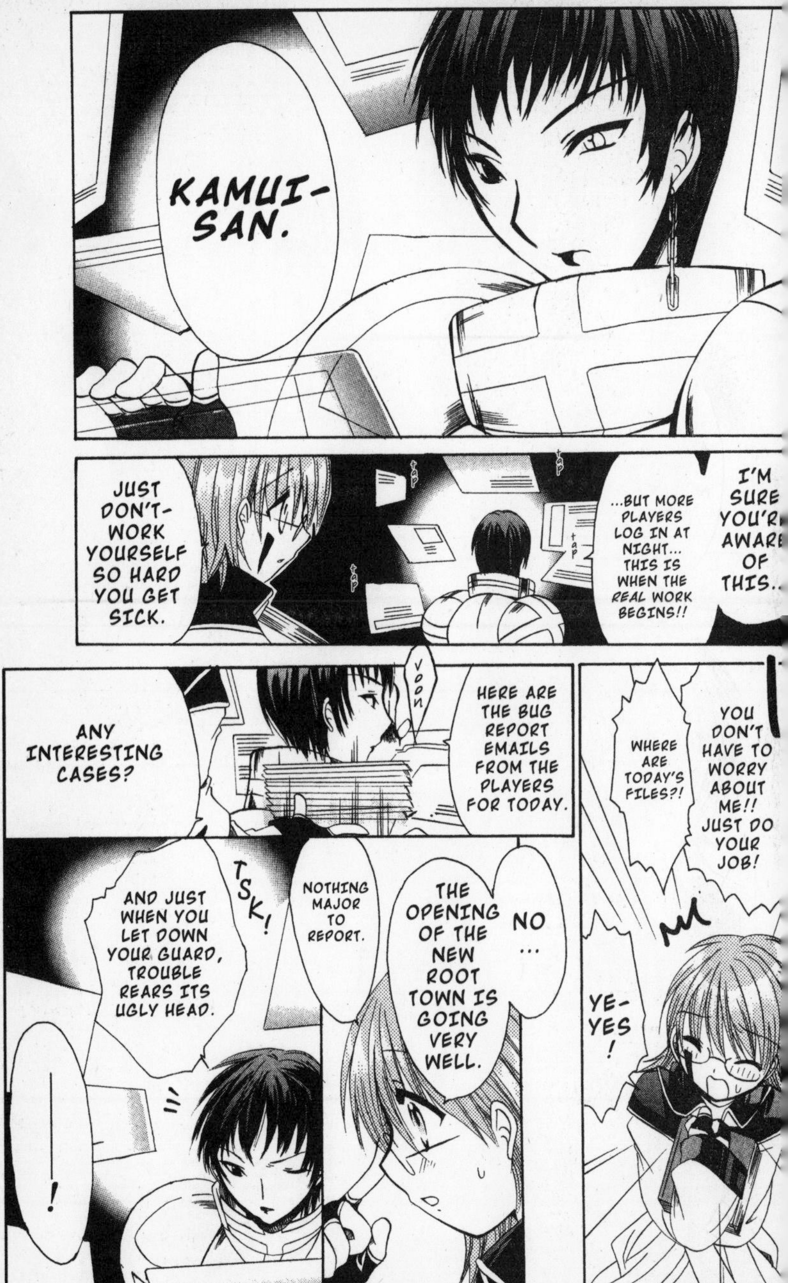
KAMUI-SAN.
I'M SURE YOU'R AWARE OF THIS..
...BUT MORE PLAYERS LOG IN AT NIGHT... THIS IS WHEN THE REAL WORK BEGINS!!
tap
tap
tap
tap
JUST DON'T-WORK YOURSELF SO HARD YOU GET SICK.
YOU DON'T HAVE TO WORRY ABOUT ME!! JUST DO YOUR JOB!
WHERE ARE TODAY'S FILES?!
YE-YES!
HERE ARE THE BUG REPORT EMAILS FROM THE PLAYERS FOR TODAY.
voon
ANY INTERESTING CASES?
NO ...
THE OPENING OF THE NEW ROOT TOWN IS GOING VERY WELL.
NOTHING MAJOR TO REPORT.
TSK!
AND JUST WHEN YOU LET DOWN YOUR GUARD, TROUBLE REARS ITS UGLY HEAD.
--!

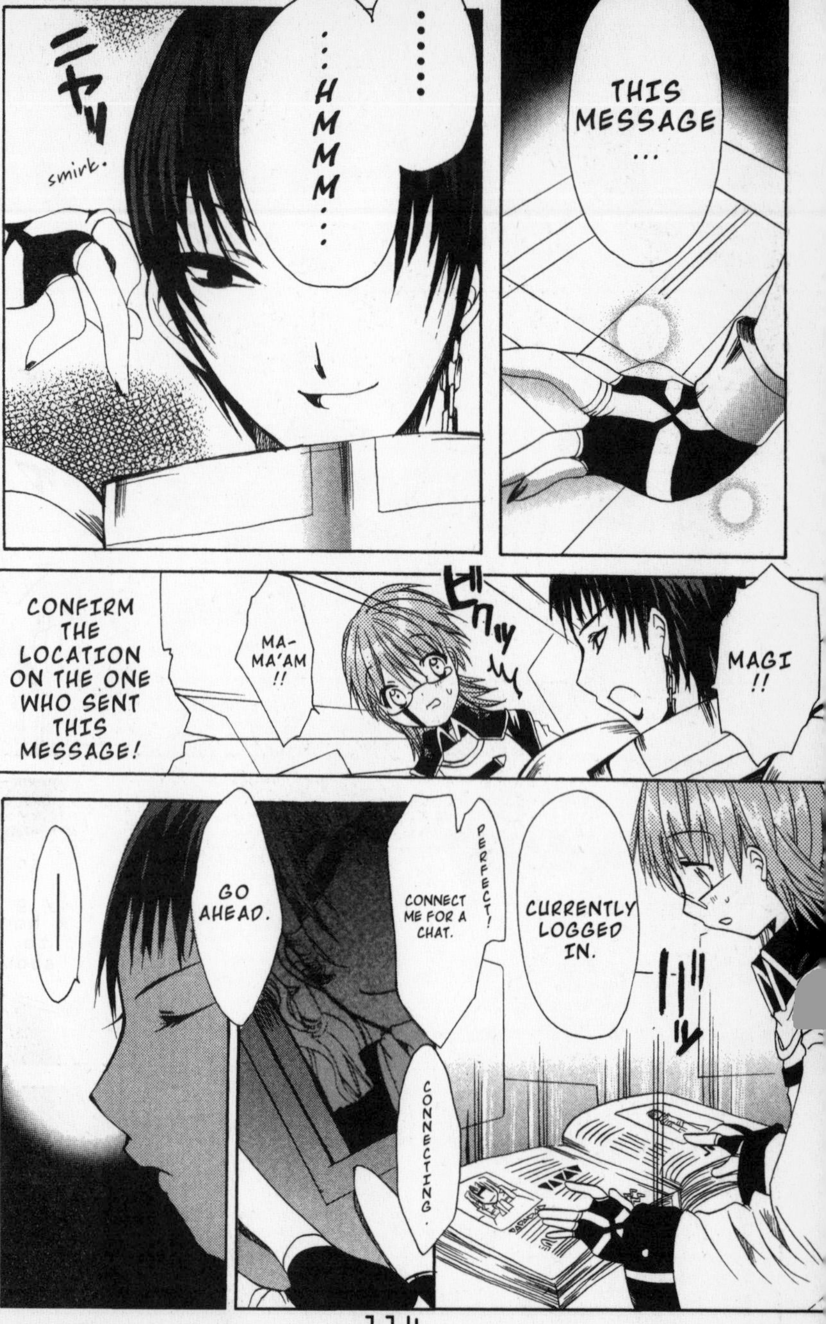
THIS MESSAGE ...
......HMMMM...
ニヤリ
smirk.
MAGI !!
ビクッ
MA-MA'AM !!
CONFIRM THE LOCATION ON THE ONE WHO SENT THIS MESSAGE!
CURRENTLY LOGGED IN.
PERFECT!
CONNECT ME FOR A CHAT.
GO AHEAD.
CONNECTING.
—

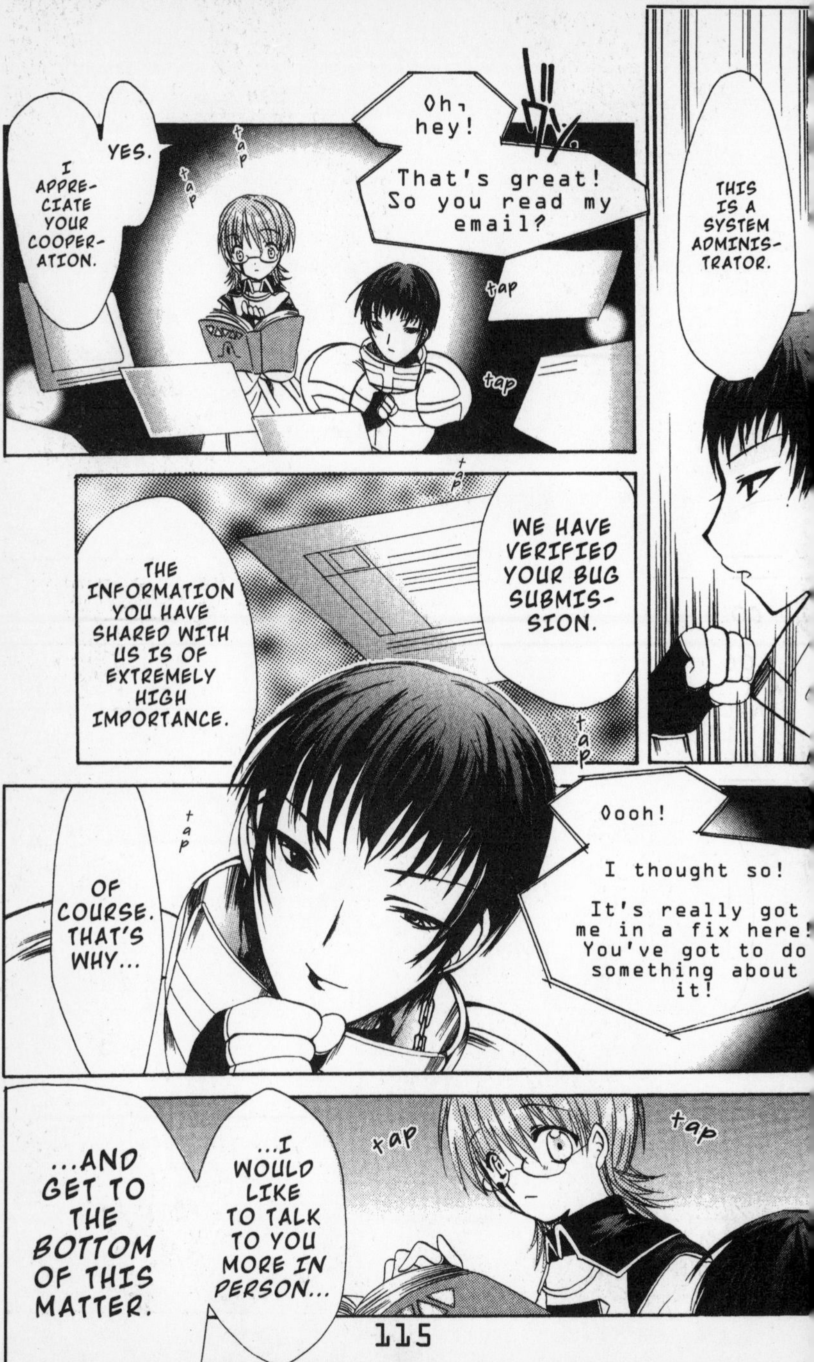
THIS IS A SYSTEM ADMINISTRATOR.
Oh, hey!
That's great! So you read my email?
tap
tap
YES.
I APPRECIATE YOUR COOPERATION.
tap
tap
tap
WE HAVE VERIFIED YOUR BUG SUBMISSION.
THE INFORMATION YOU HAVE SHARED WITH US IS OF EXTREMELY HIGH IMPORTANCE.
tap
Oooh!
I thought so!
It's really got me in a fix here! You've got to do something about it!
tap
OF COURSE. THAT'S WHY...
tap
tap
...I WOULD LIKE TO TALK TO YOU MORE IN PERSON...
...AND GET TO THE BOTTOM OF THIS MATTER.

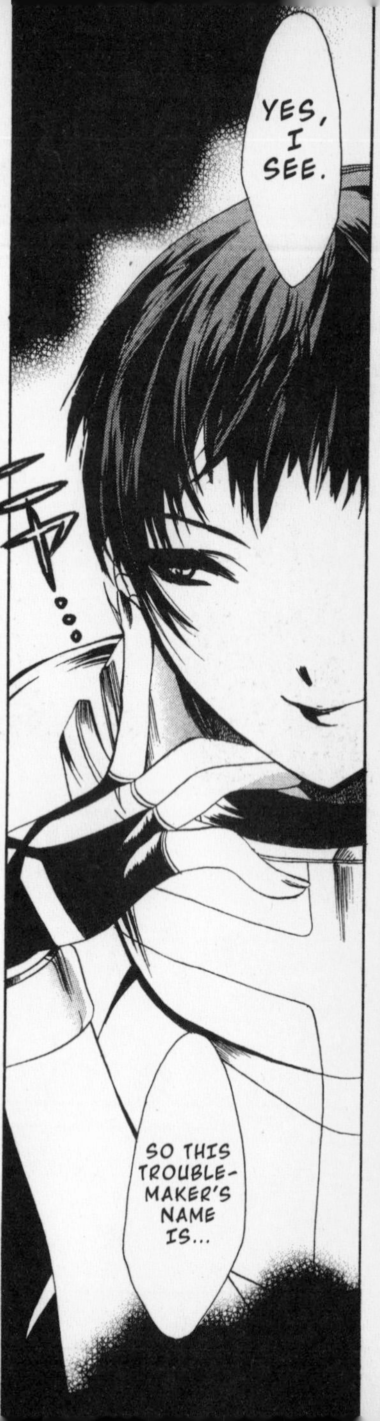
YES, I SEE.
ニヤ…
SO THIS TROUBLE-MAKER'S NAME IS...

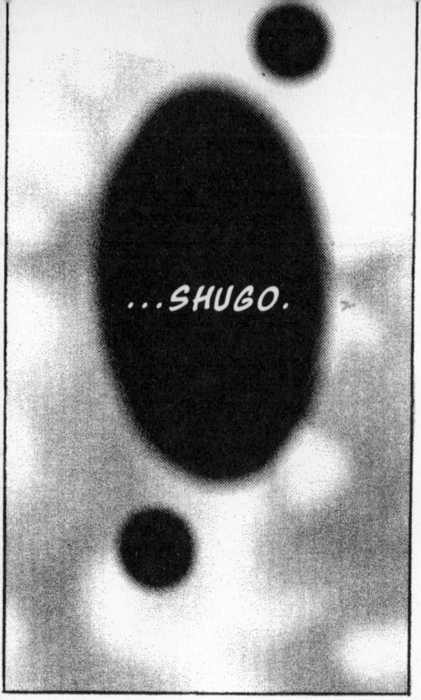
...SHUGO.

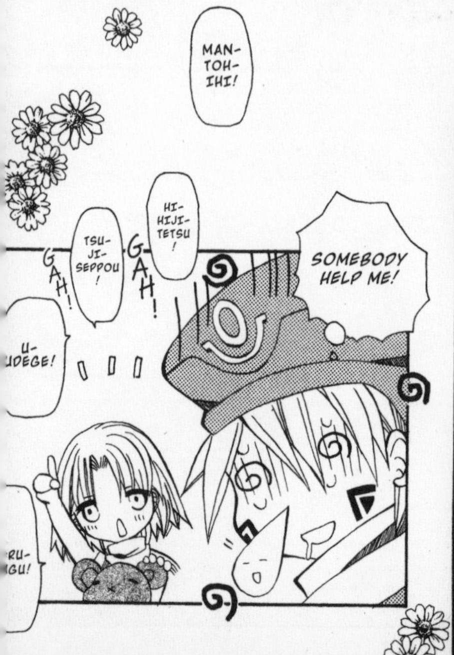
MAN-TOH-IHI!
SOMEBODY HELP ME!
HI-HIJI-TETSU!
GAH!
TSUJI-SEPPOU!
GAH!
U-UDEGE!
RU-GU!

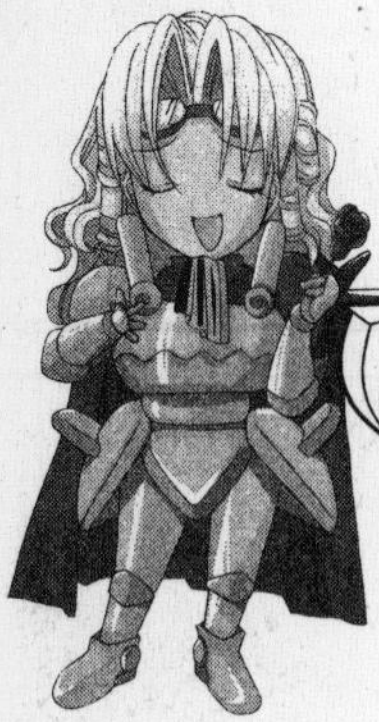

NEW GENERATION ONLINE

THE WORLD

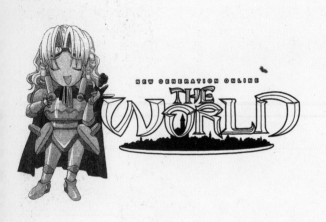

**SUBJECT: GOOD WORK TODAY**  **SENDER: MIREILLE**

WHIMPEEEER (PUPPY DOG EYES)
MIREILLE IS ALL TUCKERED OUT......Z Z Z

THE OCEAN, THAT HAUNTED HOUSE, VAGRANT AIS, NEW ROOT TOWNS...
TODAY WAS JUST CHOCK FULL OF ADVENTURE, WASN'T IT! (^_^)
IT'S OVERLOADING MY CIRCUITS.
KEEP CLOSING IN ON THE LAST MYSTERY OF THE DOT HACKERS! D(>_<)

I LOVE SUMMER VACATION 'CUZ I GET TO HANG OUT WITH YOU THE
WHOLE TIME, SHUGO.

FROM MIREILLE-CHAN

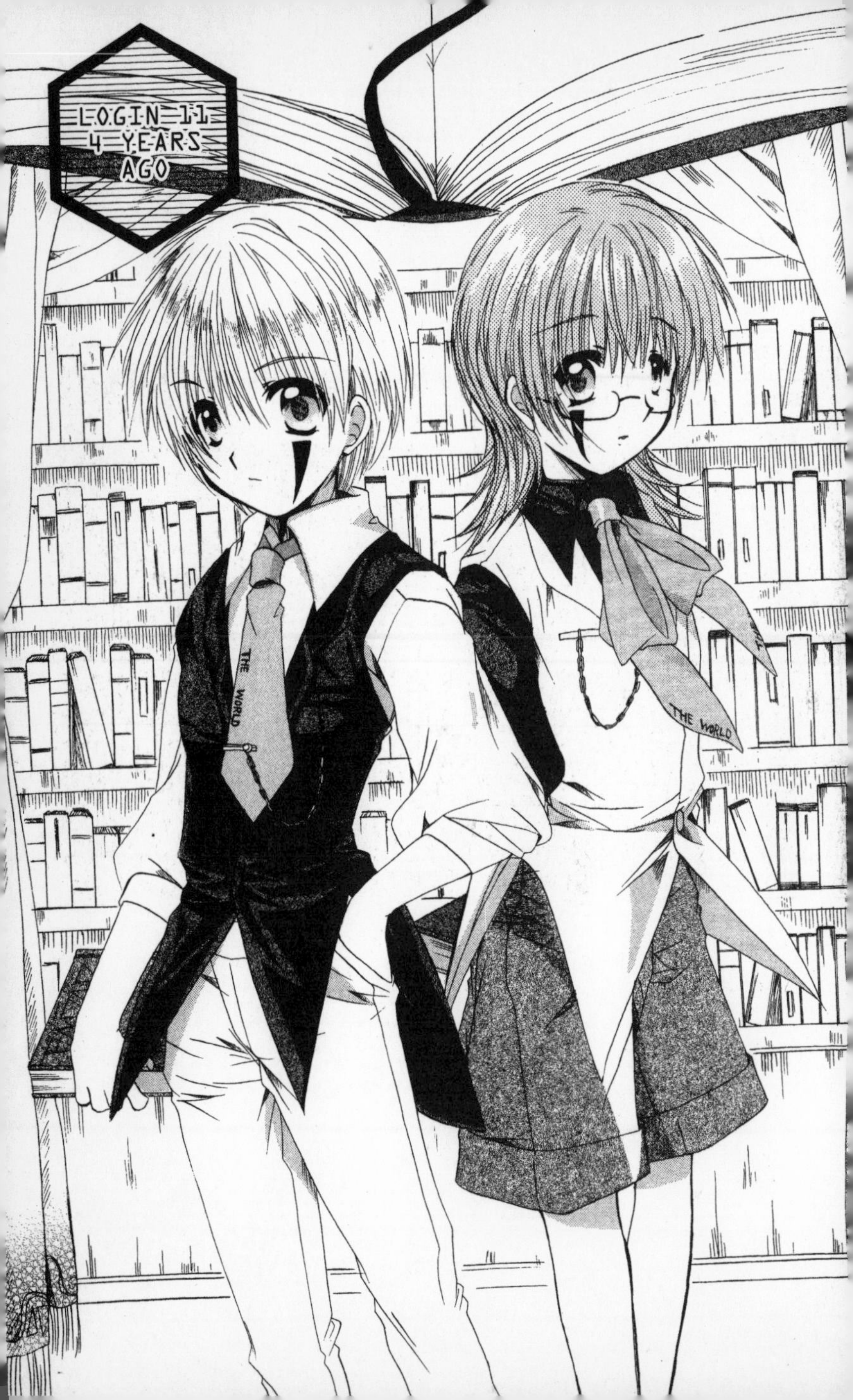
LOGIN 11
4 YEARS AGO
THE WORLD
THE WORLD

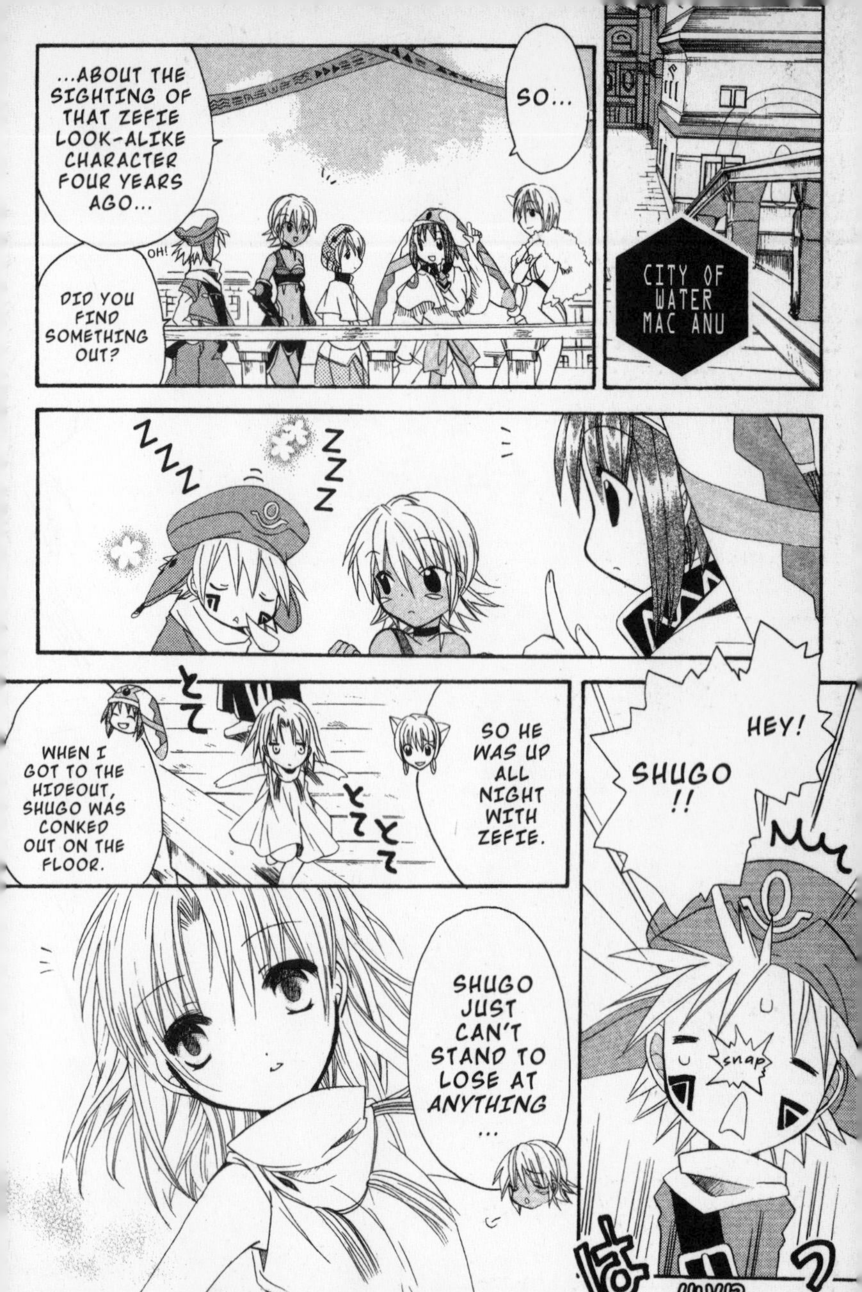
CITY OF WATER MAC ANU
SO...
...ABOUT THE SIGHTING OF THAT ZEFIE LOOK-ALIKE CHARACTER FOUR YEARS AGO...
OH!
DID YOU FIND SOMETHING OUT?
ZZZ
ZZZ
HEY!
SHUGO!!
snap
HUH?
SO HE WAS UP ALL NIGHT WITH ZEFIE.
WHEN I GOT TO THE HIDEOUT, SHUGO WAS CONKED OUT ON THE FLOOR.
SHUGO JUST CAN'T STAND TO LOSE AT ANYTHING...

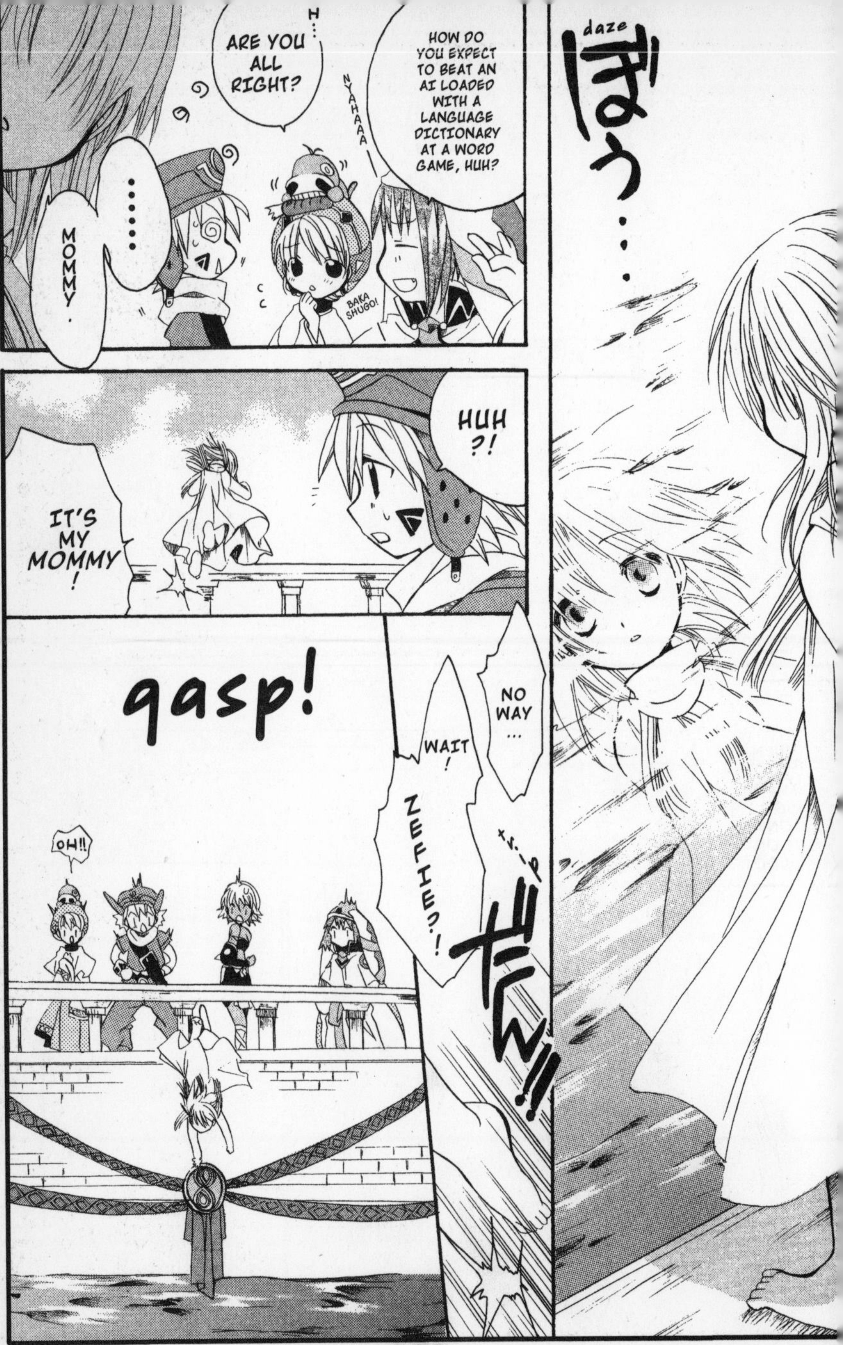
daze
ぼう…
HOW DO YOU EXPECT TO BEAT AN AI LOADED WITH A LANGUAGE DICTIONARY AT A WORD GAME, HUH?
NYAHAAA
BAKA SHUGO!
H... ARE YOU ALL RIGHT?
......
MOMMY.
HUH?!
IT'S MY MOMMY!
NO WAY...
WAIT!
ZEFIE?!
t.s.i.p
gasp!
OH!!

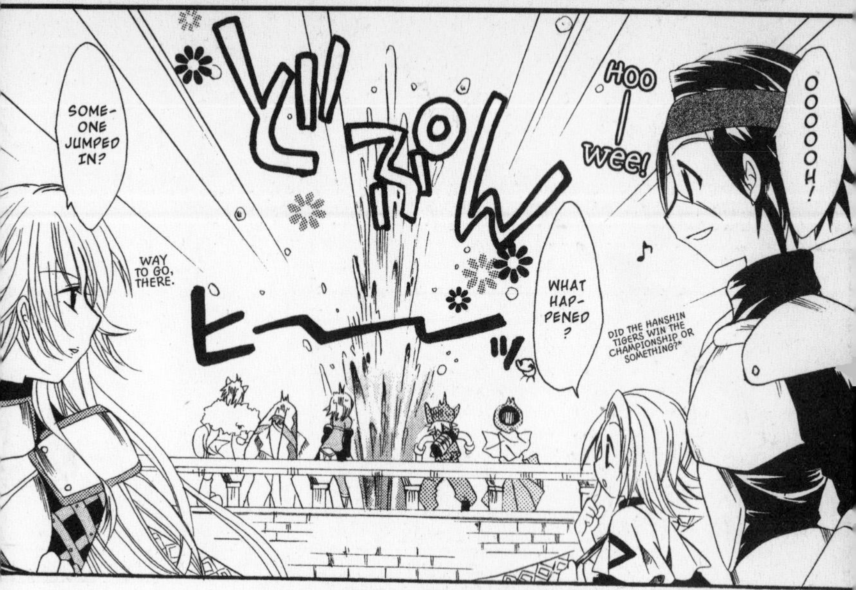
OOOOOOH!
HOO — wee!
どぷん
WHAT HAP-PENED?
DID THE HANSHIN TIGERS WIN THE CHAMPIONSHIP OR SOMETHING?*
SOME-ONE JUMPED IN?
WAY TO GO, THERE.
ヒ〜〜〜ッ

*Hanshin Tigers- The Osaka based professional baseball team. After they won the '85 series, fans jumped into the nearby river.

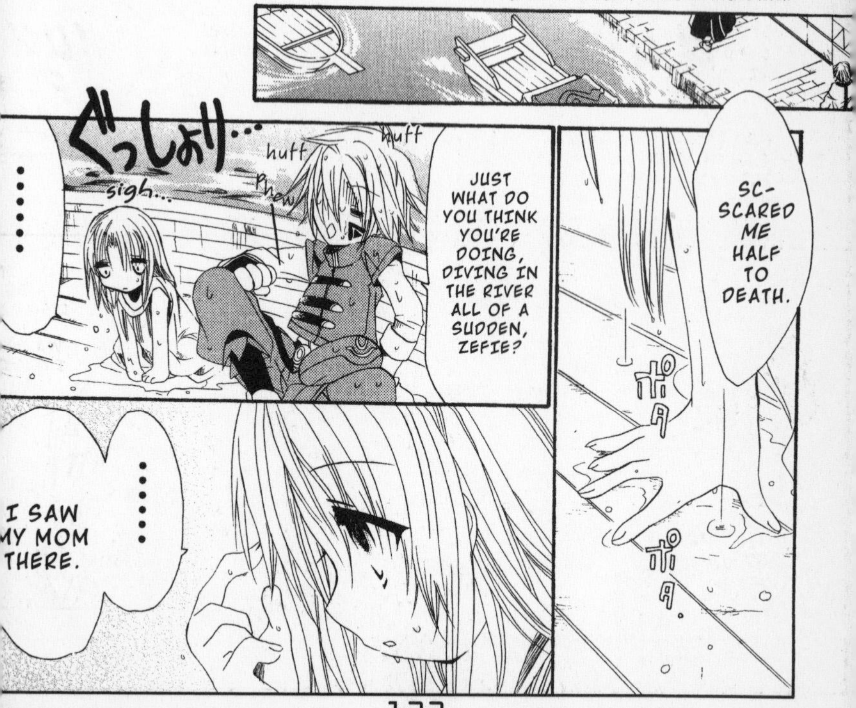
SC-SCARED ME HALF TO DEATH.
ポタ
ポタ
huff
huff
Phew
JUST WHAT DO YOU THINK YOU'RE DOING, DIVING IN THE RIVER ALL OF A SUDDEN, ZEFIE?
ぐっしょり…
sigh...
......
......
I SAW MY MOM THERE.

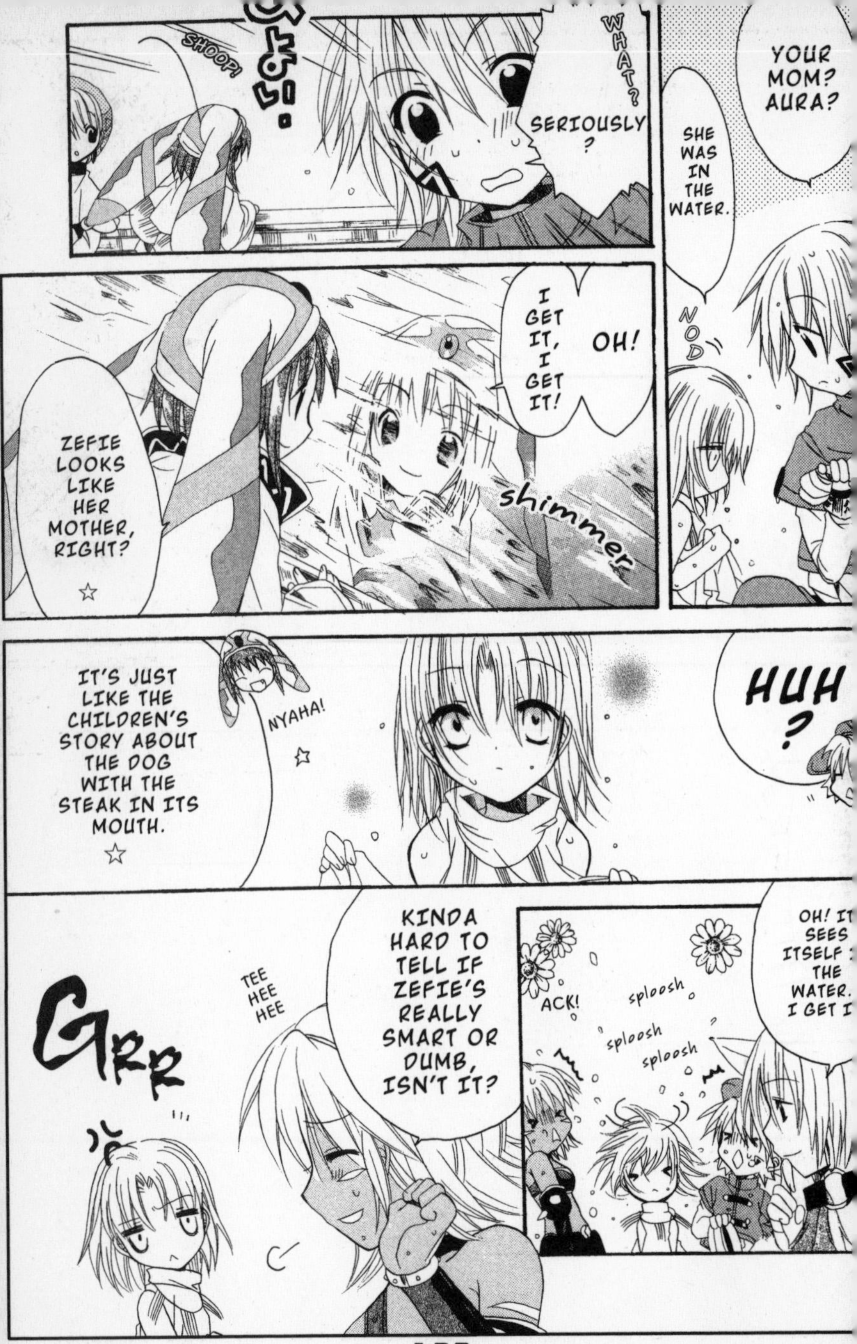
YOUR MOM? AURA?
SHE WAS IN THE WATER.
NOD
WHAT?
SERIOUSLY?
SHOOP!
OH!
I GET IT, I GET IT!
shimmer
ZEFIE LOOKS LIKE HER MOTHER, RIGHT? ☆
HUH?
IT'S JUST LIKE THE CHILDREN'S STORY ABOUT THE DOG WITH THE STEAK IN ITS MOUTH. ☆
NYAHA! ☆
OH! IT SEES ITSELF I THE WATER. I GET I
ACK!
sploosh
sploosh
sploosh
KINDA HARD TO TELL IF ZEFIE'S REALLY SMART OR DUMB, ISN'T IT?
TEE HEE HEE
GRR

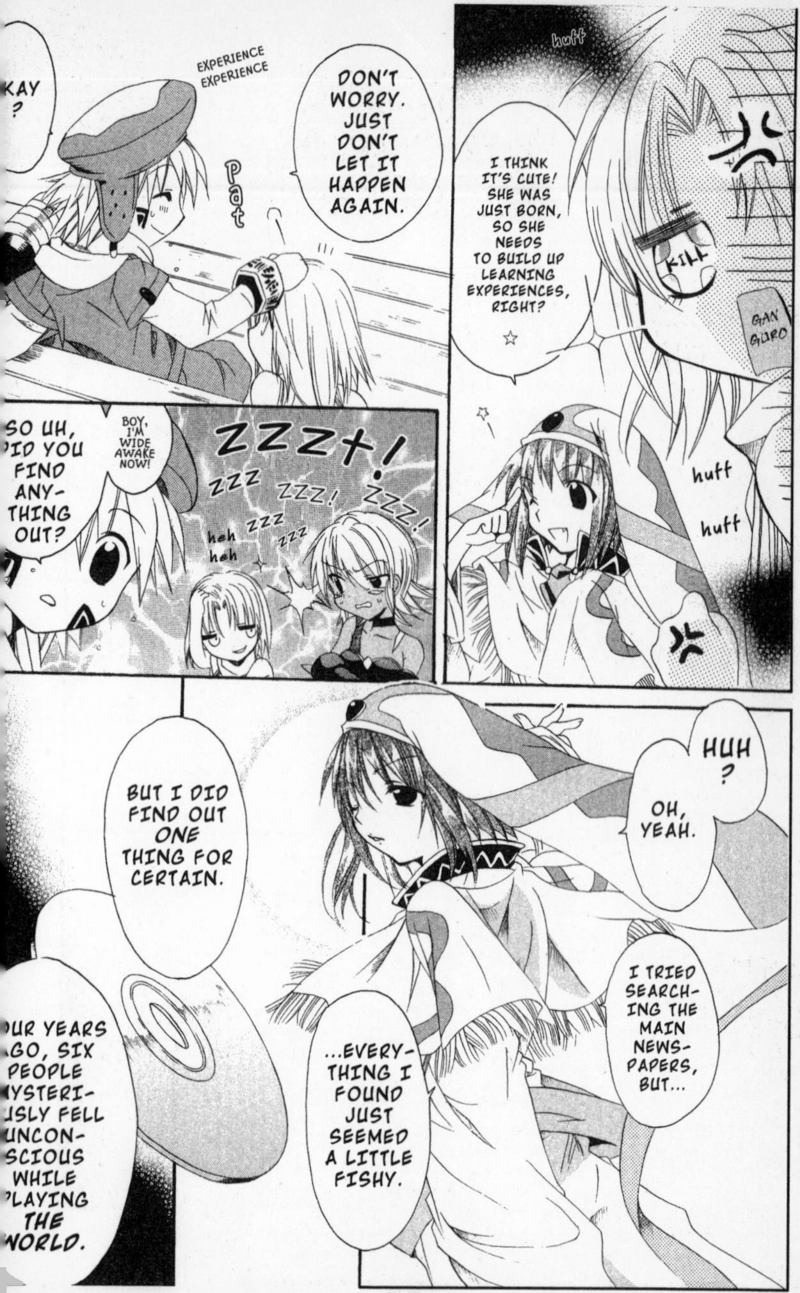
huff
I THINK IT'S CUTE! SHE WAS JUST BORN, SO SHE NEEDS TO BUILD UP LEARNING EXPERIENCES, RIGHT?
KILL
GAN GURO
huff
huff
DON'T WORRY. JUST DON'T LET IT HAPPEN AGAIN.
Pat
EXPERIENCE EXPERIENCE
KAY ?
ZZZT!
BOY, I'M WIDE AWAKE NOW!
ZZZ ZZZ! ZZZ! ZZZ ZZZ
heh heh
SO UH, ID YOU FIND ANYTHING OUT?
HUH ? OH, YEAH.
I TRIED SEARCHING THE MAIN NEWSPAPERS, BUT...
...EVERYTHING I FOUND JUST SEEMED A LITTLE FISHY.
BUT I DID FIND OUT ONE THING FOR CERTAIN.
UR YEARS GO, SIX PEOPLE YSTERI- USLY FELL UNCON- SCIOUS WHILE LAYING THE WORLD.

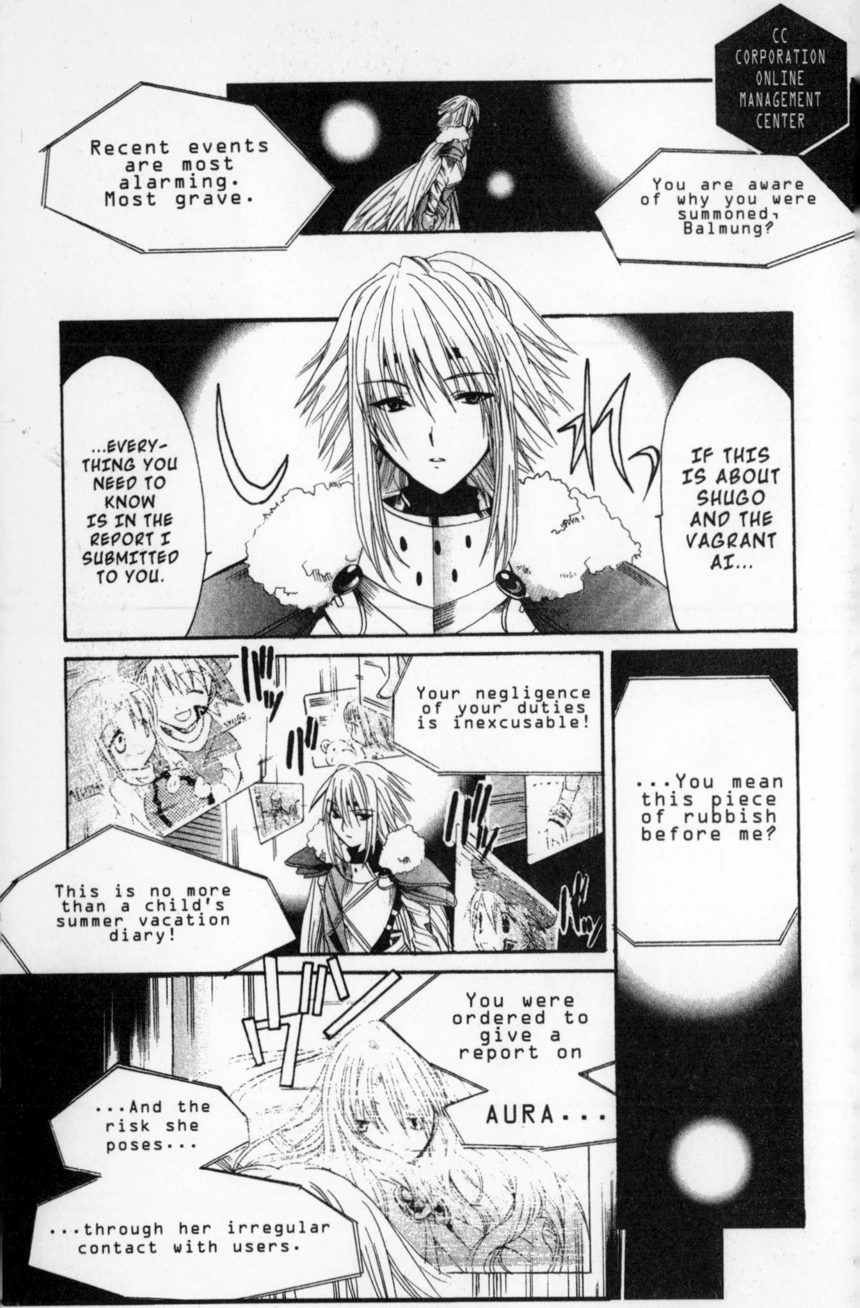
CC CORPORATION ONLINE MANAGEMENT CENTER
Recent events are most alarming. Most grave.
You are aware of why you were summoned, Balmung?
IF THIS IS ABOUT SHUGO AND THE VAGRANT AI...
...EVERYTHING YOU NEED TO KNOW IS IN THE REPORT I SUBMITTED TO YOU.
...You mean this piece of rubbish before me?
Your negligence of your duties is inexcusable!
This is no more than a child's summer vacation diary!
You were ordered to give a report on
AURA...
...And the risk she poses...
...through her irregular contact with users.

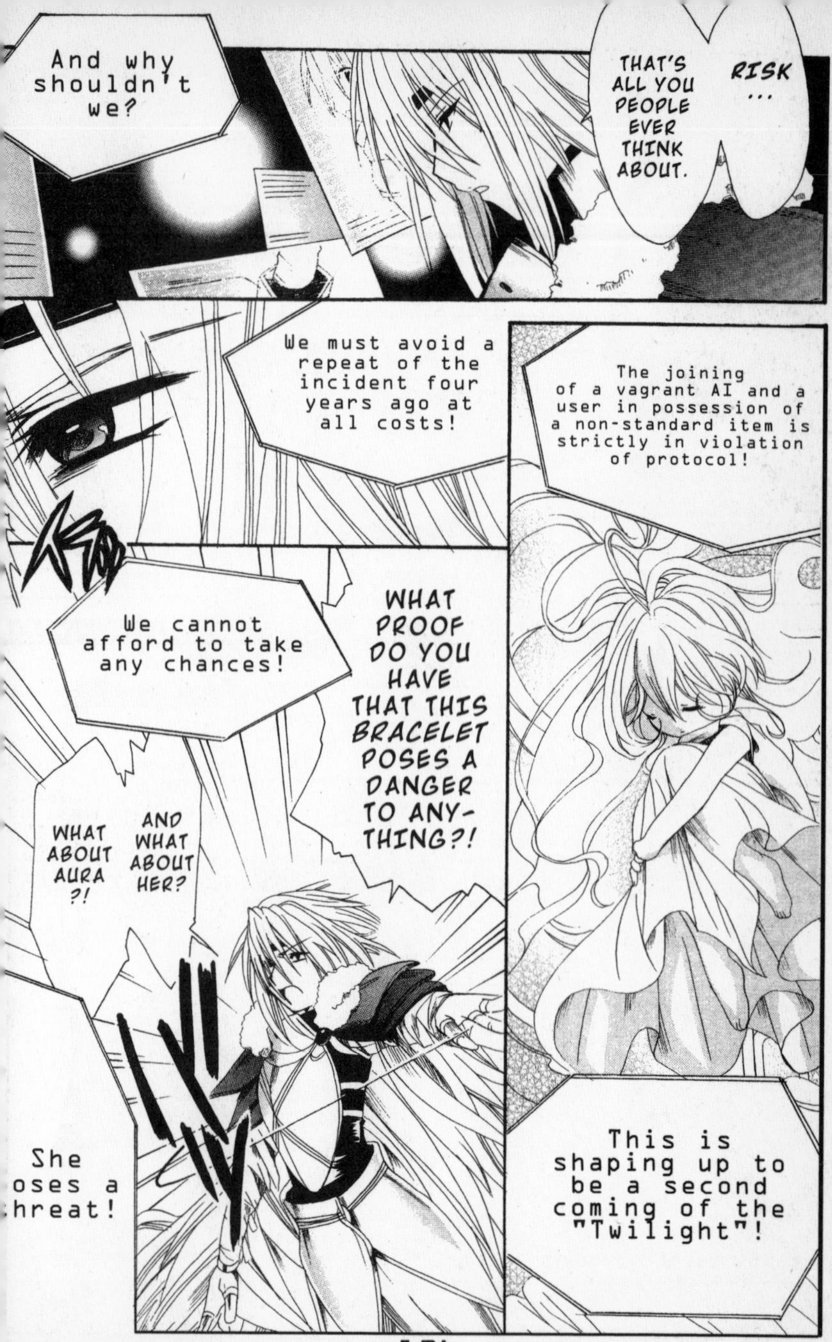

RISK...
THAT'S ALL YOU PEOPLE EVER THINK ABOUT.
And why shouldn't we?
The joining of a vagrant AI and a user in possession of a non-standard item is strictly in violation of protocol!
This is shaping up to be a second coming of the "Twilight"!
We must avoid a repeat of the incident four years ago at all costs!
WHAT PROOF DO YOU HAVE THAT THIS BRACELET POSES A DANGER TO ANY-THING?!
We cannot afford to take any chances!
AND WHAT ABOUT HER?
WHAT ABOUT AURA?!
She oses a hreat!

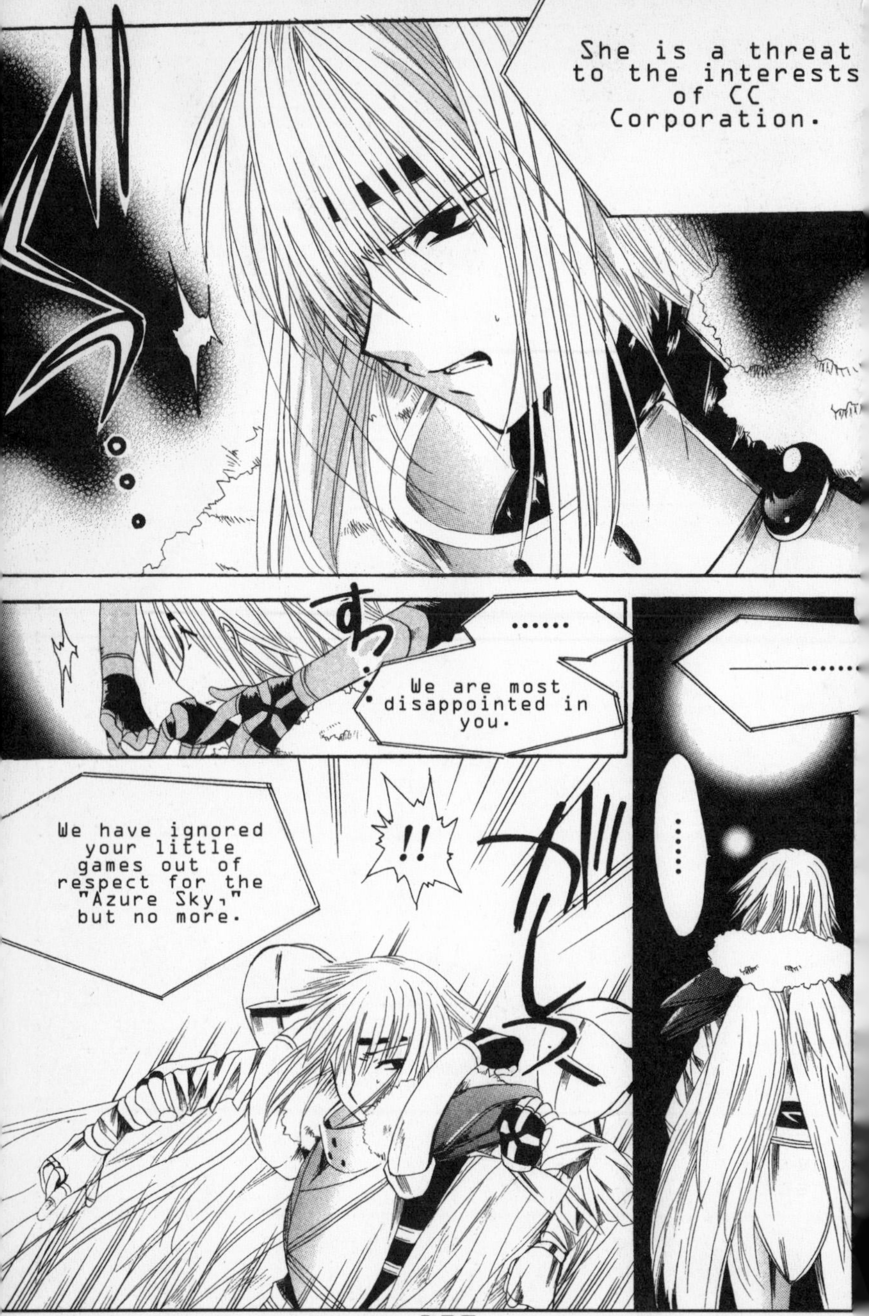

She is a threat to the interests of CC Corporation.
——......
......
......
We are most disappointed in you.
!!
We have ignored your little games out of respect for the "Azure Sky," but no more.

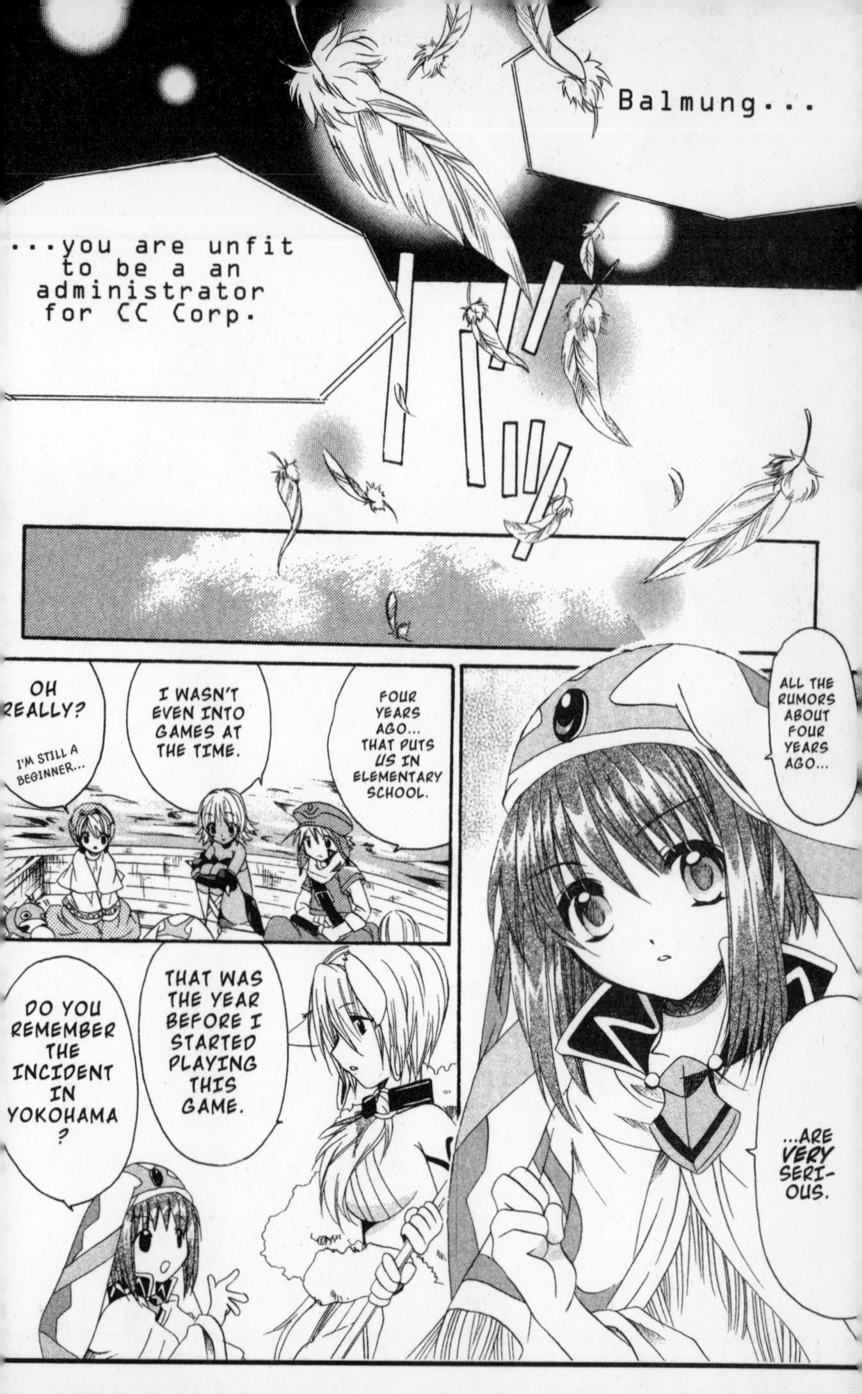
Balmung...
...you are unfit to be a an administrator for CC Corp.
ALL THE RUMORS ABOUT FOUR YEARS AGO...
...ARE VERY SERIOUS.
FOUR YEARS AGO... THAT PUTS US IN ELEMENTARY SCHOOL.
I WASN'T EVEN INTO GAMES AT THE TIME.
OH REALLY?
I'M STILL A BEGINNER...
THAT WAS THE YEAR BEFORE I STARTED PLAYING THIS GAME.
DO YOU REMEMBER THE INCIDENT IN YOKOHAMA?

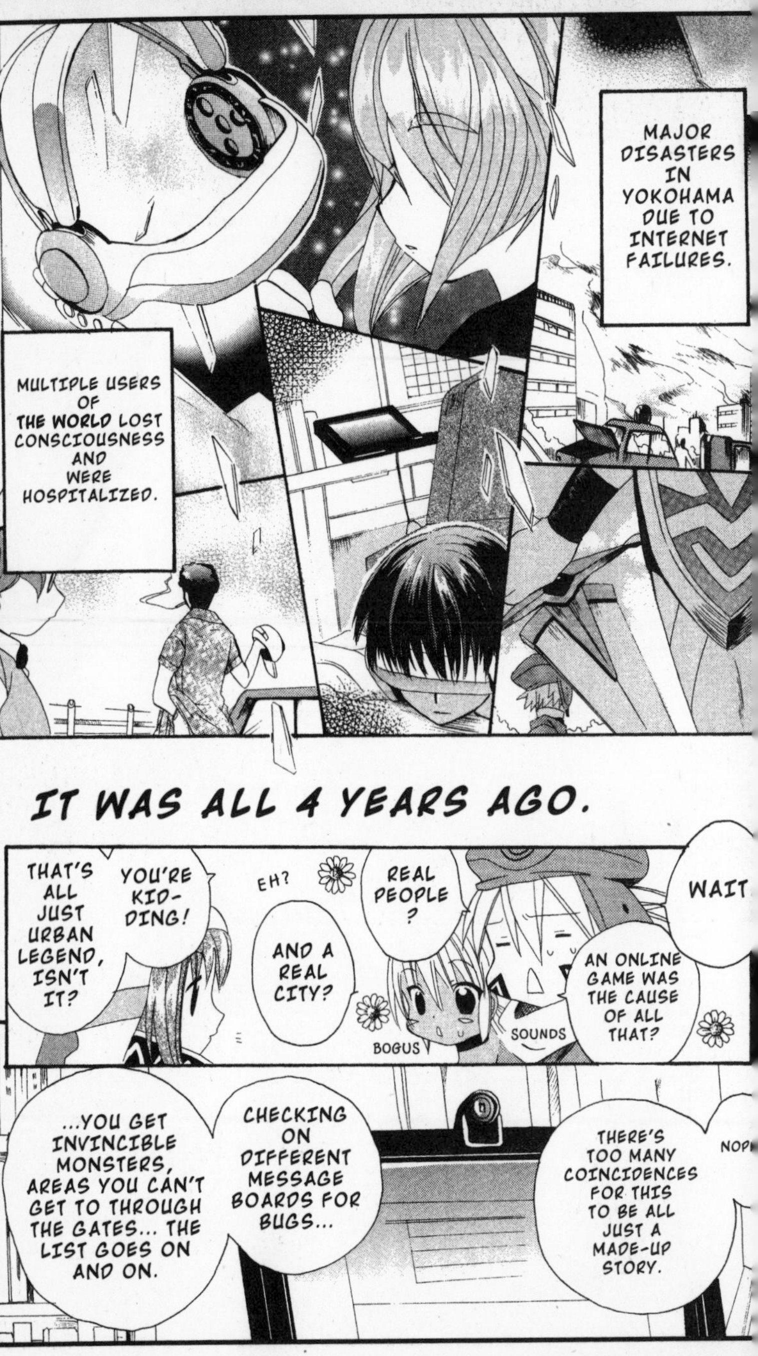
MAJOR DISASTERS IN YOKOHAMA DUE TO INTERNET FAILURES.
MULTIPLE USERS OF THE WORLD LOST CONSCIOUSNESS AND WERE HOSPITALIZED.
IT WAS ALL 4 YEARS AGO.
WAIT
AN ONLINE GAME WAS THE CAUSE OF ALL THAT?
SOUNDS
REAL PEOPLE?
EH?
AND A REAL CITY?
BOGUS
YOU'RE KID-DING!
THAT'S ALL JUST URBAN LEGEND, ISN'T IT?
NOP
THERE'S TOO MANY COINCIDENCES FOR THIS TO BE ALL JUST A MADE-UP STORY.
CHECKING ON DIFFERENT MESSAGE BOARDS FOR BUGS...
...YOU GET INVINCIBLE MONSTERS, AREAS YOU CAN'T GET TO THROUGH THE GATES... THE LIST GOES ON AND ON.

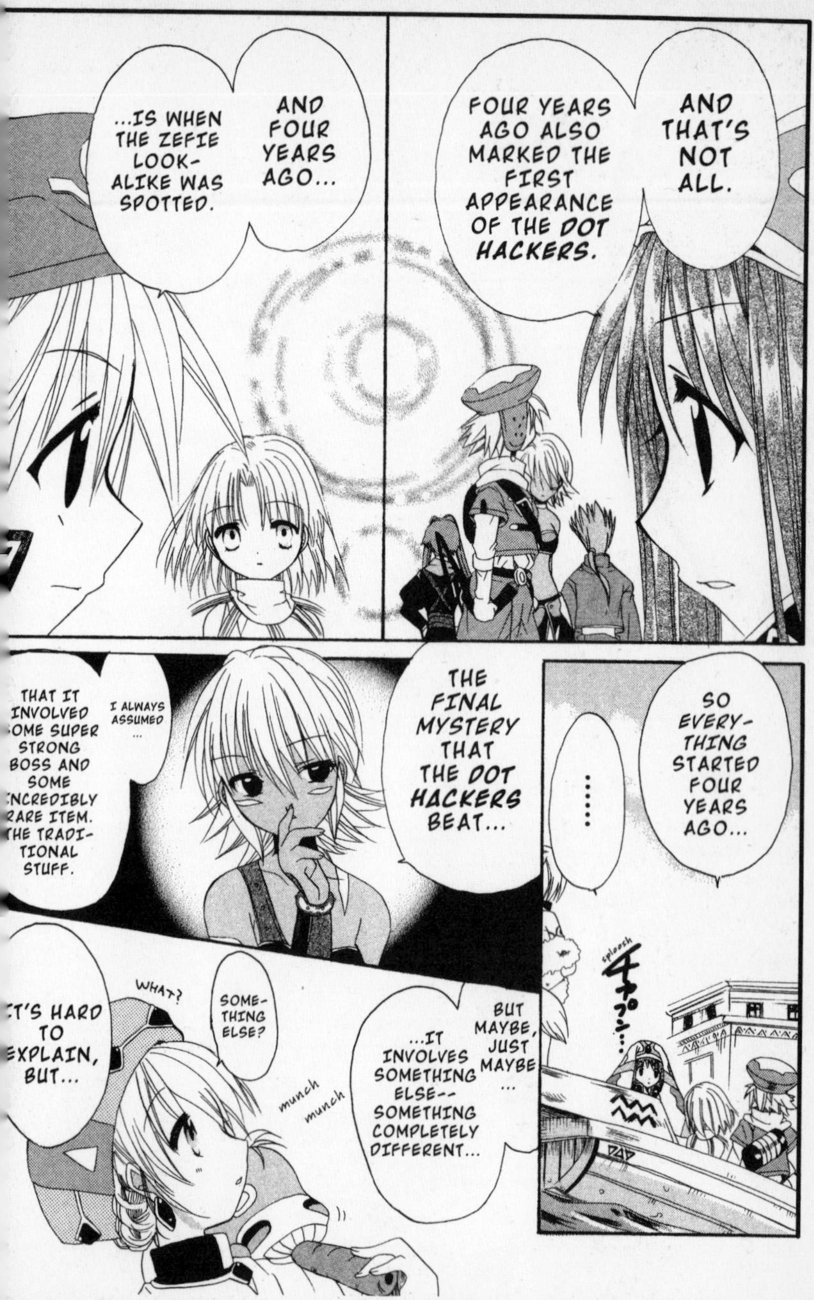
AND THAT'S NOT ALL.
FOUR YEARS AGO ALSO MARKED THE FIRST APPEARANCE OF THE DOT HACKERS.
AND FOUR YEARS AGO...
...IS WHEN THE ZEFIE LOOK-ALIKE WAS SPOTTED.
SO EVERY-THING STARTED FOUR YEARS AGO...
......
sploosh
チャプン...
THE FINAL MYSTERY THAT THE DOT HACKERS BEAT...
I ALWAYS ASSUMED...
THAT IT INVOLVED OME SUPER STRONG BOSS AND SOME NCREDIBLY ARE ITEM. HE TRADI-TIONAL STUFF.
BUT MAYBE, JUST MAYBE...
...IT INVOLVES SOMETHING ELSE--SOMETHING COMPLETELY DIFFERENT...
SOME-THING ELSE?
WHAT?
munch munch
T'S HARD TO XPLAIN, BUT...

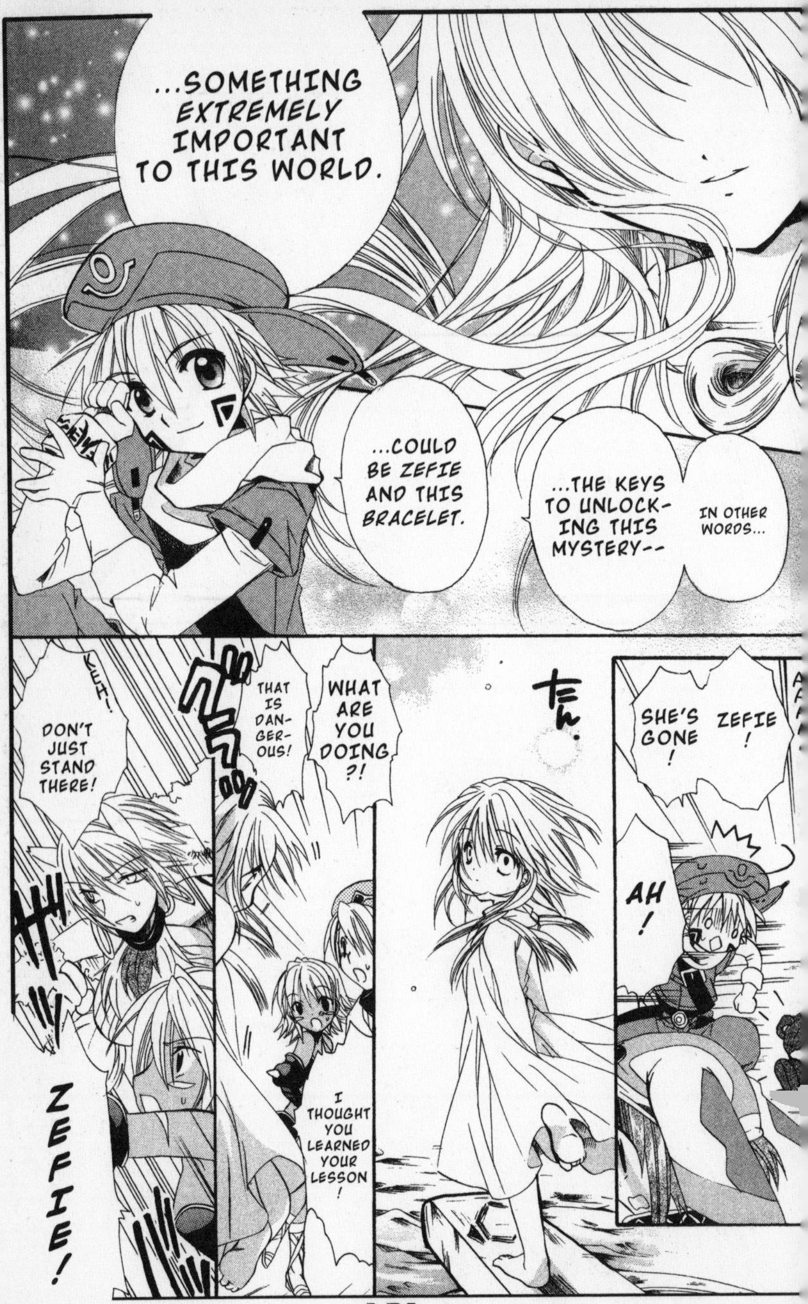
IN OTHER WORDS...
...THE KEYS TO UNLOCKING THIS MYSTERY--
...COULD BE ZEFIE AND THIS BRACELET.
...SOMETHING EXTREMELY IMPORTANT TO THIS WORLD.
ZEFIE!
SHE'S GONE!
AH!
WHAT ARE YOU DOING?!
THAT IS DANGEROUS!
I THOUGHT YOU LEARNED YOUR LESSON!
KEH!
DON'T JUST STAND THERE!
ZEFIE!

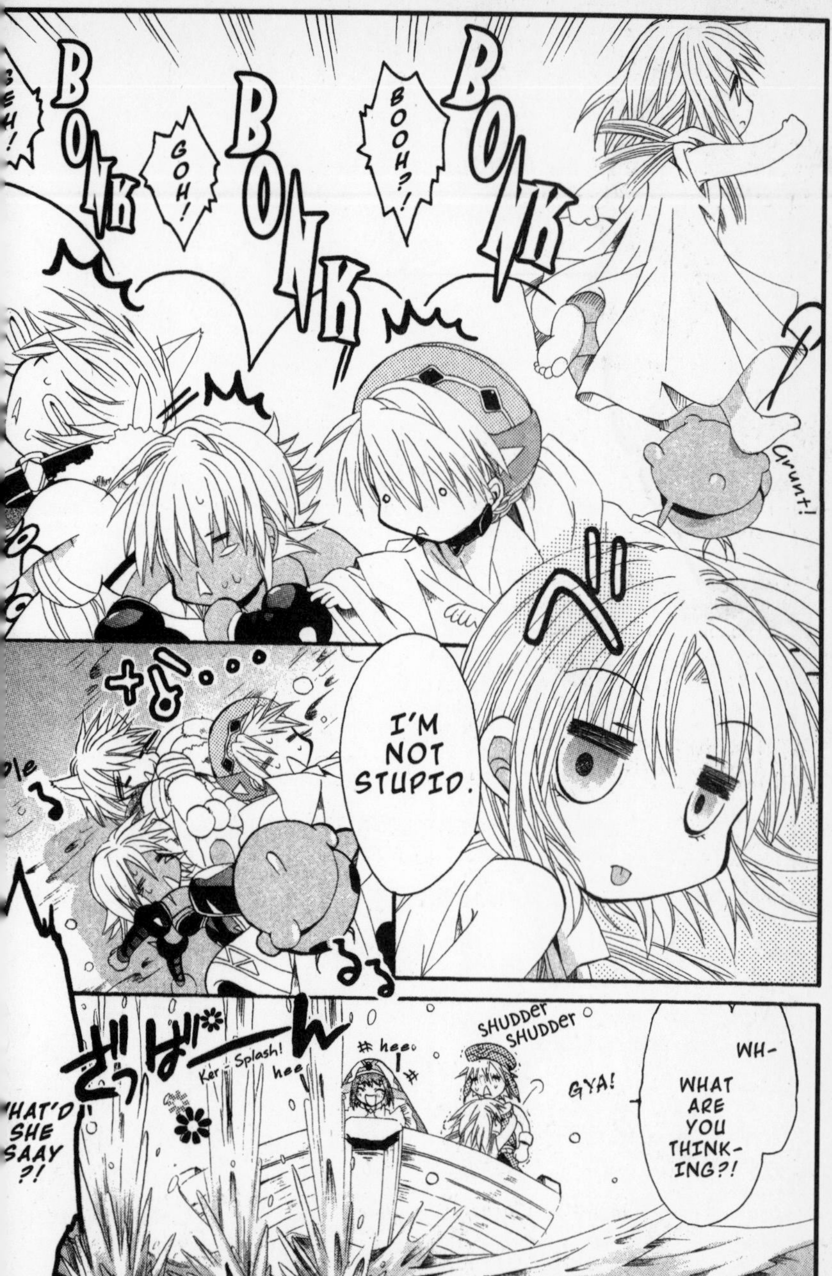
BONK
Grunt!
BOOH?!
BONK
GOH!
BONK
BEH!
I'M NOT STUPID.
WH- WHAT ARE YOU THINKING?!
GYA!
SHUDDER SHUDDER
hee hee
Ker-Splash!
HAT'D SHE SAAY?!

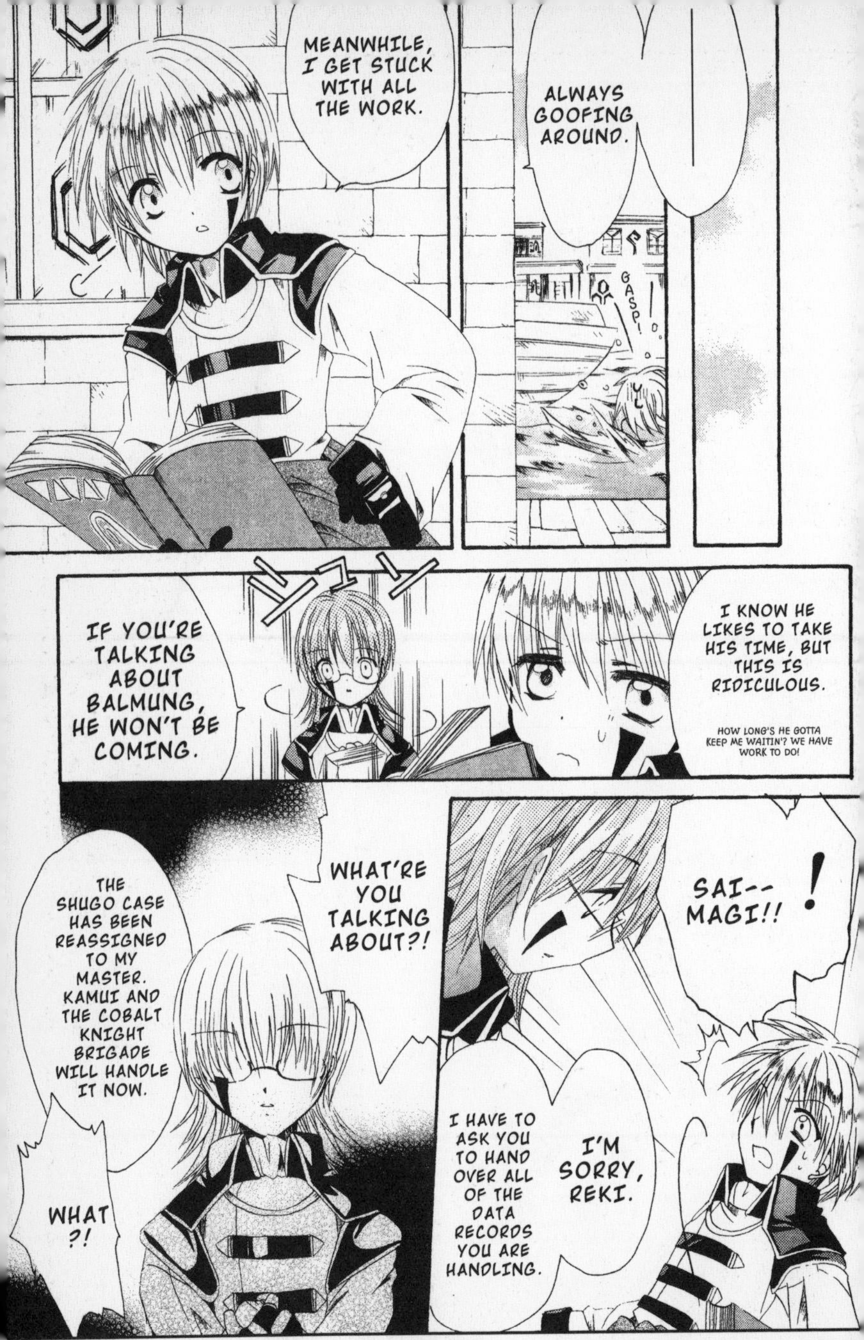
ALWAYS GOOFING AROUND.
GASP!
MEANWHILE, I GET STUCK WITH ALL THE WORK.
I KNOW HE LIKES TO TAKE HIS TIME, BUT THIS IS RIDICULOUS.
HOW LONG'S HE GOTTA KEEP ME WAITIN'? WE HAVE WORK TO DO!
IF YOU'RE TALKING ABOUT BALMUNG, HE WON'T BE COMING.
SAI-- MAGI!!
I'M SORRY, REKI.
I HAVE TO ASK YOU TO HAND OVER ALL OF THE DATA RECORDS YOU ARE HANDLING.
WHAT'RE YOU TALKING ABOUT?!
THE SHUGO CASE HAS BEEN REASSIGNED TO MY MASTER. KAMUI AND THE COBALT KNIGHT BRIGADE WILL HANDLE IT NOW.
WHAT?!

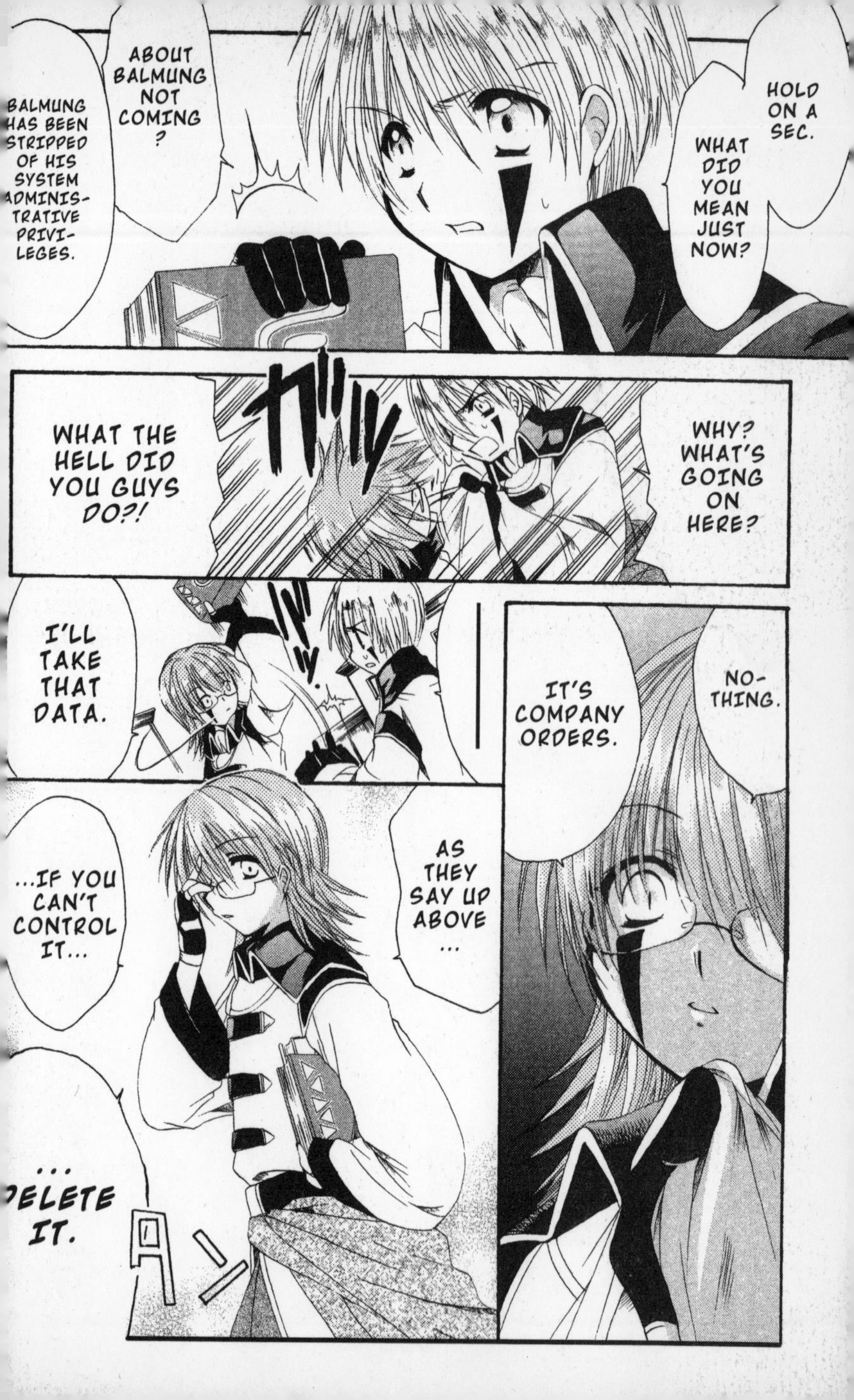
HOLD ON A SEC.
WHAT DID YOU MEAN JUST NOW?
ABOUT BALMUNG NOT COMING?
BALMUNG HAS BEEN STRIPPED OF HIS SYSTEM ADMINIS-TRATIVE PRIVI-LEGES.
WHY? WHAT'S GOING ON HERE?
WHAT THE HELL DID YOU GUYS DO?!
NO-THING.
IT'S COMPANY ORDERS.
I'LL TAKE THAT DATA.
AS THEY SAY UP ABOVE...
...IF YOU CAN'T CONTROL IT...
...DELETE IT.

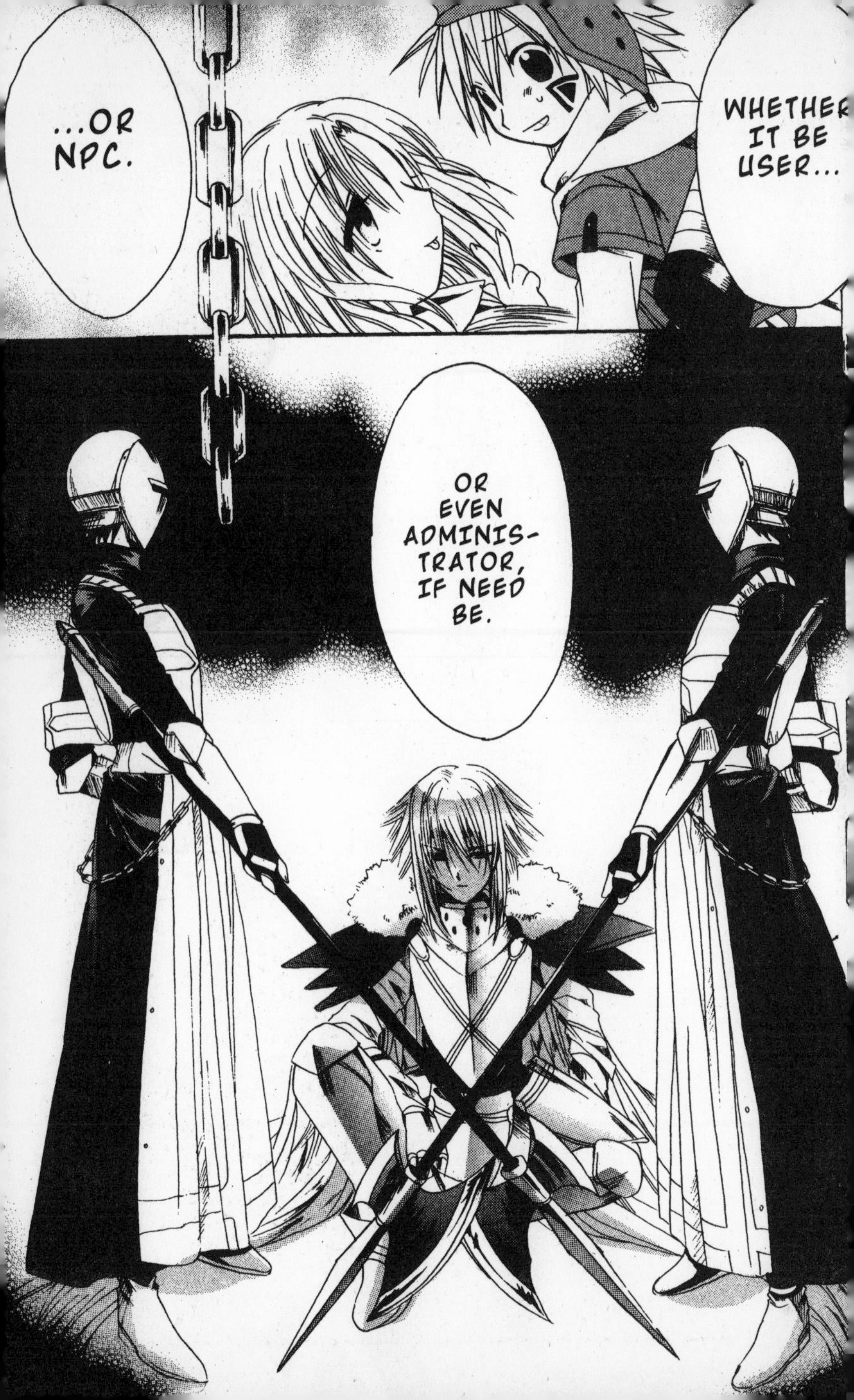
WHETHER IT BE USER...
...OR NPC.
OR EVEN ADMINIS-TRATOR, IF NEED BE.

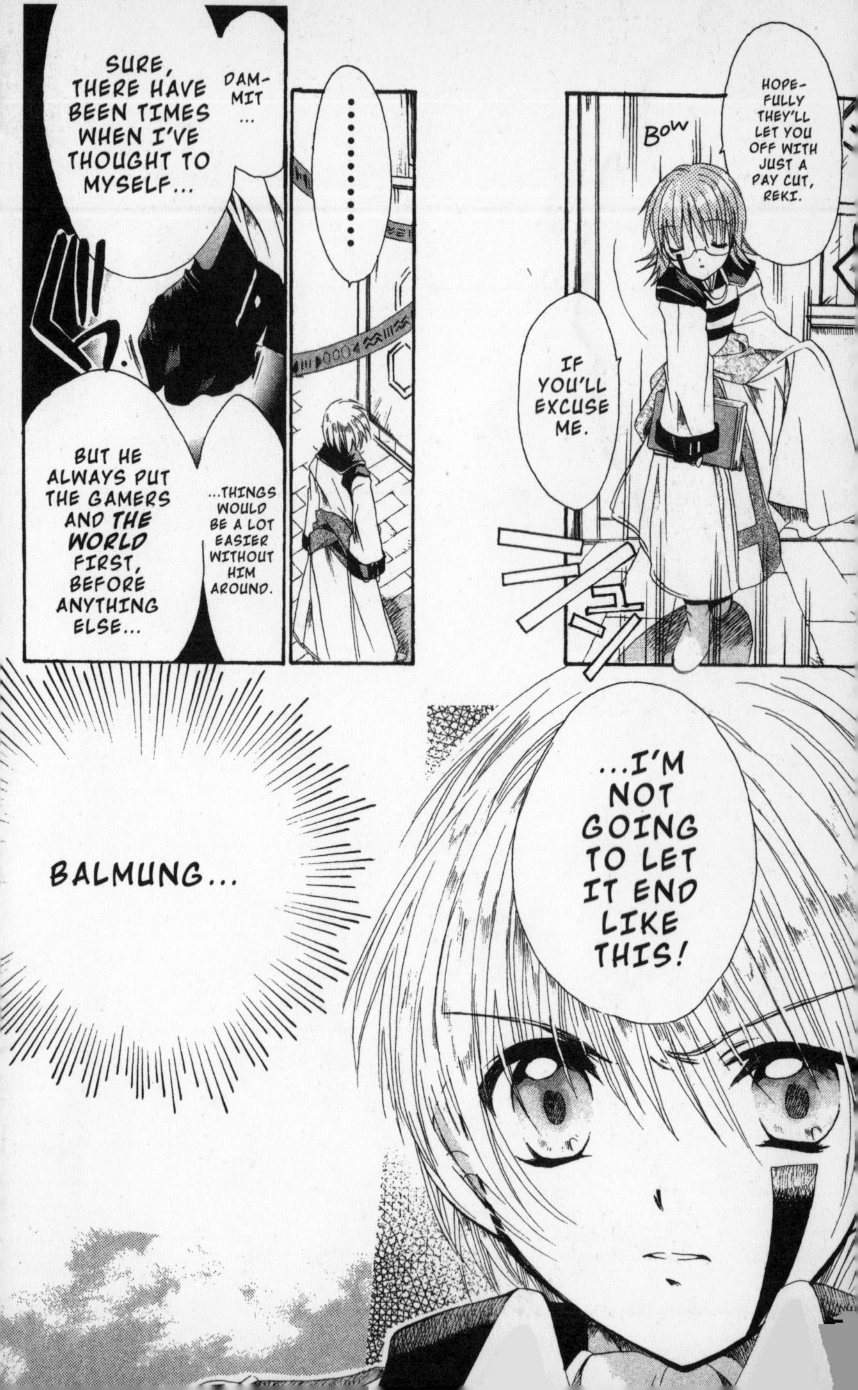
HOPE-FULLY THEY'LL LET YOU OFF WITH JUST A PAY CUT, REKI.
BOW
IF YOU'LL EXCUSE ME.
........
SURE, THERE HAVE BEEN TIMES WHEN I'VE THOUGHT TO MYSELF...
DAM-MIT...
...THINGS WOULD BE A LOT EASIER WITHOUT HIM AROUND.
BUT HE ALWAYS PUT THE GAMERS AND *THE WORLD* FIRST, BEFORE ANYTHING ELSE...
...I'M NOT GOING TO LET IT END LIKE THIS!
BALMUNG...

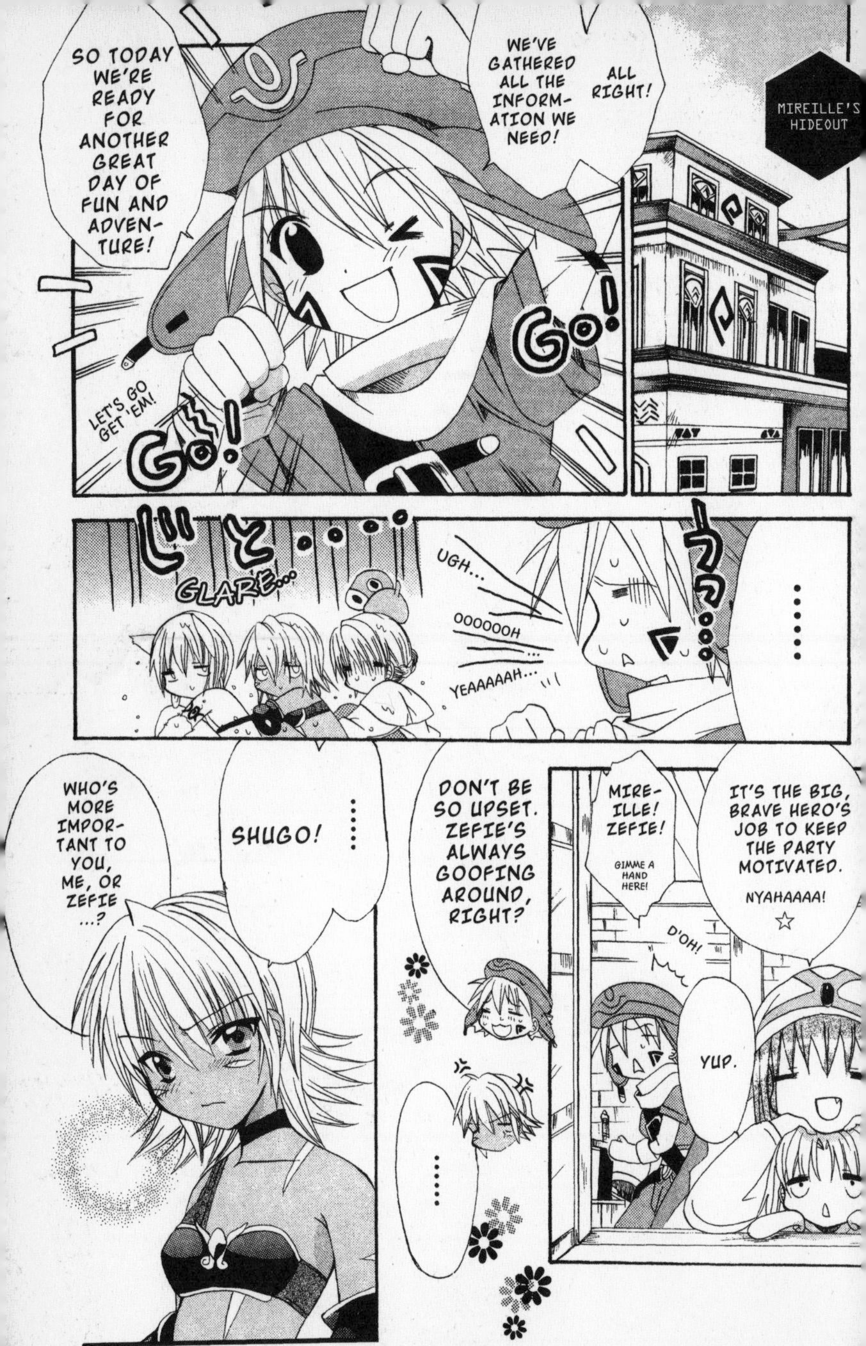
MIREILLE'S HIDEOUT
ALL RIGHT!
WE'VE GATHERED ALL THE INFORMATION WE NEED!
SO TODAY WE'RE READY FOR ANOTHER GREAT DAY OF FUN AND ADVENTURE!
GO!
LET'S GO GET 'EM!
GO!
......
UGH... OOOOOOH... YEAAAAAH...
GLARE...
IT'S THE BIG, BRAVE HERO'S JOB TO KEEP THE PARTY MOTIVATED.
NYAHAAAA! ☆
MIREILLE! ZEFIE!
GIMME A HAND HERE!
D'OH!
YUP.
DON'T BE SO UPSET. ZEFIE'S ALWAYS GOOFING AROUND, RIGHT?
......
......
SHUGO!
WHO'S MORE IMPORTANT TO YOU, ME, OR ZEFIE ...?

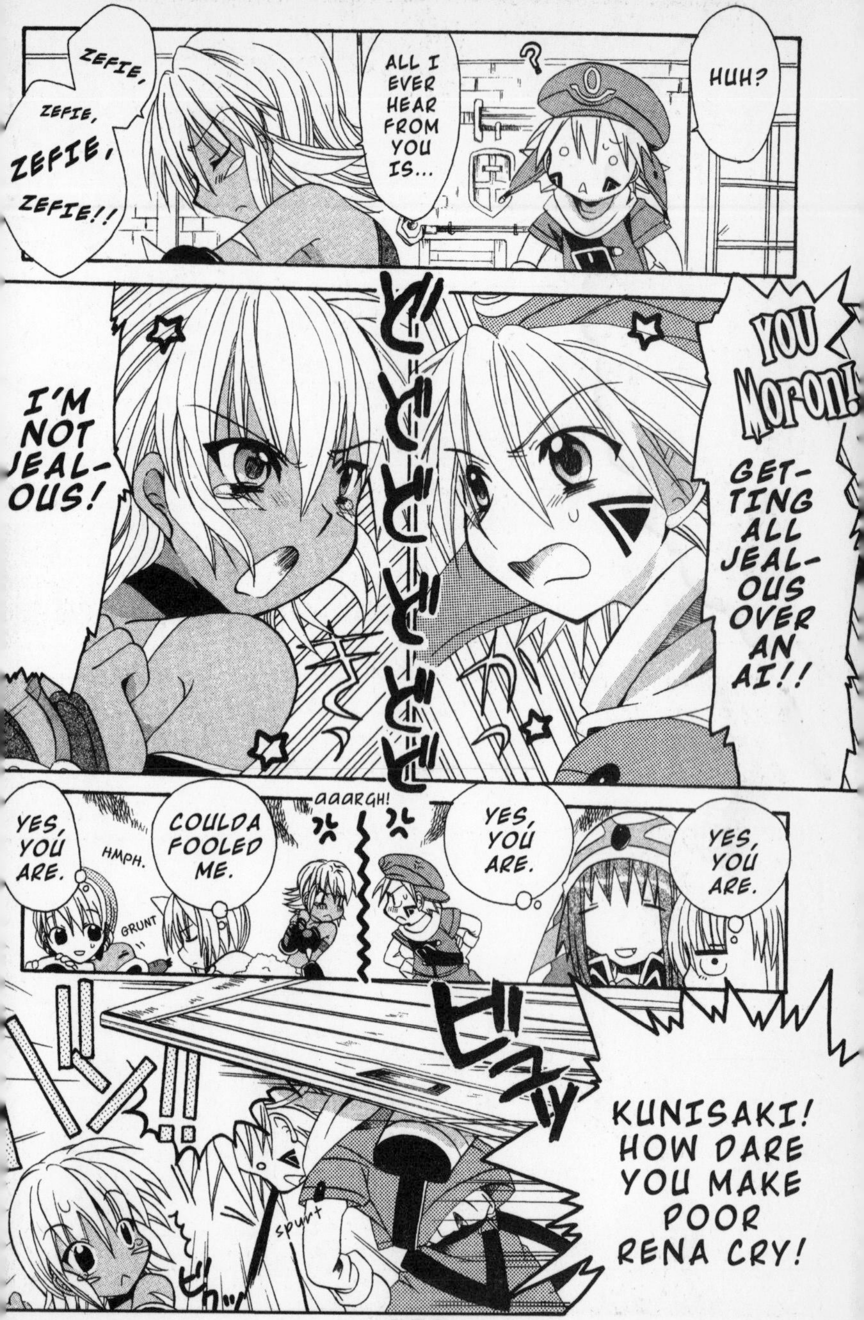
HUH?
ALL I EVER HEAR FROM YOU IS...
ZEFIE, ZEFIE, ZEFIE, ZEFIE!!
YOU MORON!
GETTING ALL JEALOUS OVER AN AI!!
I'M NOT JEALOUS!
YES, YOU ARE.
YES, YOU ARE.
aaargh!
COULDA FOOLED ME.
HMPH.
YES, YOU ARE.
GRUNT
KUNISAKI! HOW DARE YOU MAKE POOR RENA CRY!
spurt

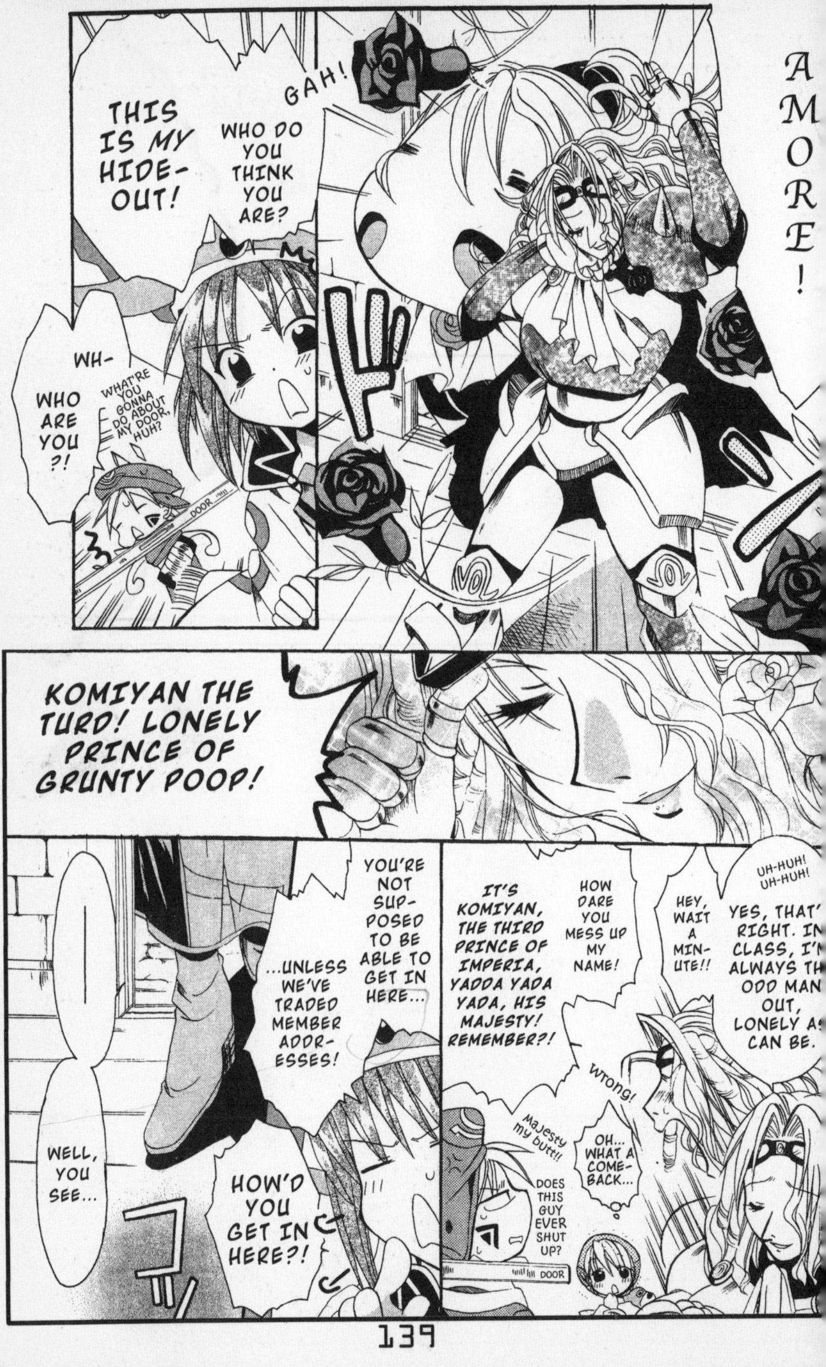
AMORE!
GAH!
WHO DO YOU THINK YOU ARE?
THIS IS MY HIDE-OUT!
WH-
WHO ARE YOU?!
WHAT'RE YOU GONNA DO ABOUT MY DOOR, HUH?
DOOR
KOMIYAN THE TURD! LONELY PRINCE OF GRUNTY POOP!
UH-HUH! UH-HUH!
YES, THAT' RIGHT. IN CLASS, I'M ALWAYS TH ODD MAN OUT, LONELY A CAN BE.
HEY, WAIT A MIN-UTE!!
HOW DARE YOU MESS UP MY NAME!
IT'S KOMIYAN, THE THIRD PRINCE OF IMPERIA, YADDA YADA YADA, HIS MAJESTY! REMEMBER?!
wrong!
OH... WHAT A COME-BACK...
Majesty my butt!!
DOES THIS GUY EVER SHUT UP?
DOOR
YOU'RE NOT SUP-POSED TO BE ABLE TO GET IN HERE...
...UNLESS WE'VE TRADED MEMBER ADDR-ESSES!
HOW'D YOU GET IN HERE?!
WELL, YOU SEE...

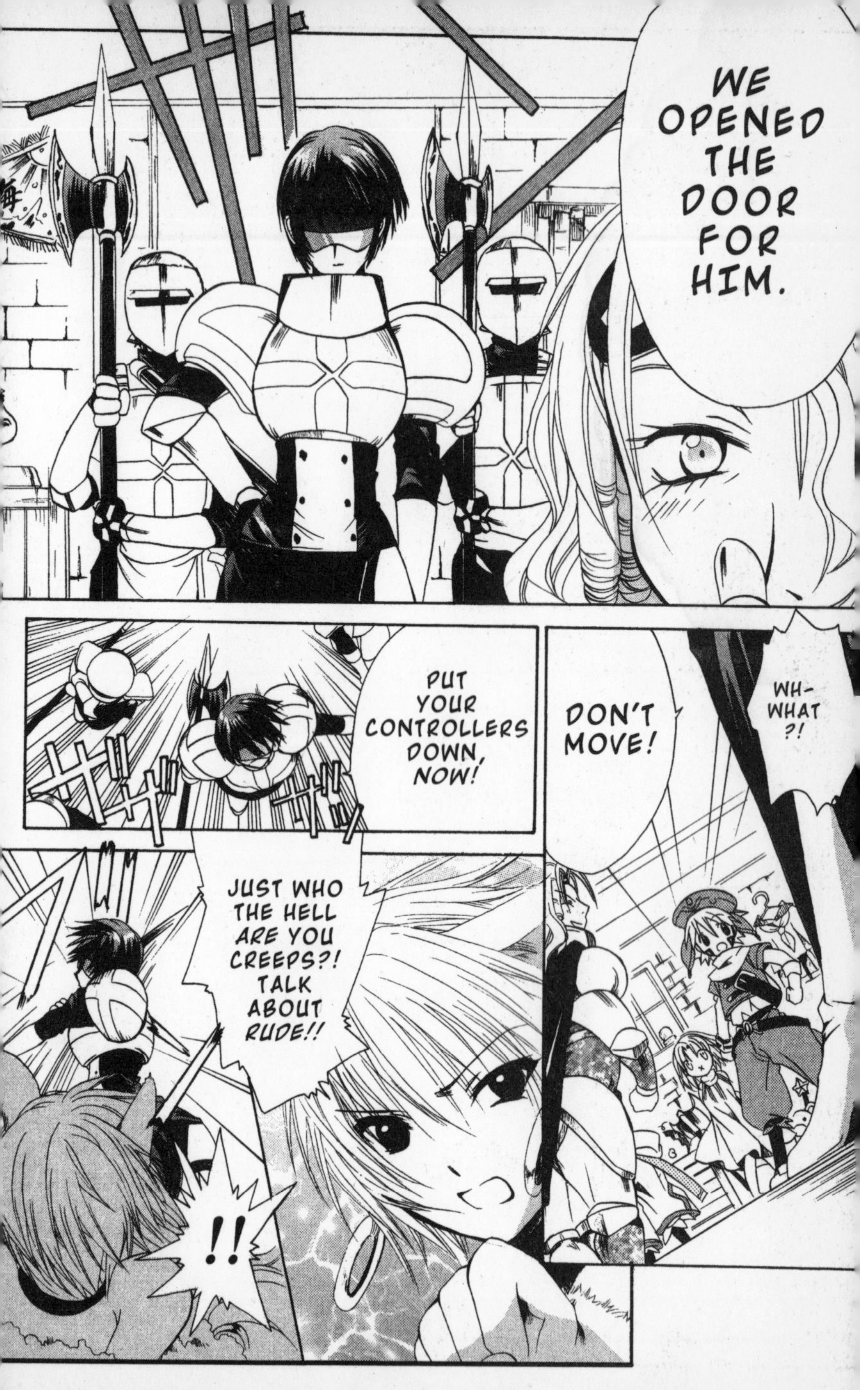
WE OPENED THE DOOR FOR HIM.
WH- WHAT ?!
DON'T MOVE!
PUT YOUR CONTROLLERS DOWN, NOW!
JUST WHO THE HELL ARE YOU CREEPS?! TALK ABOUT RUDE!!
!!

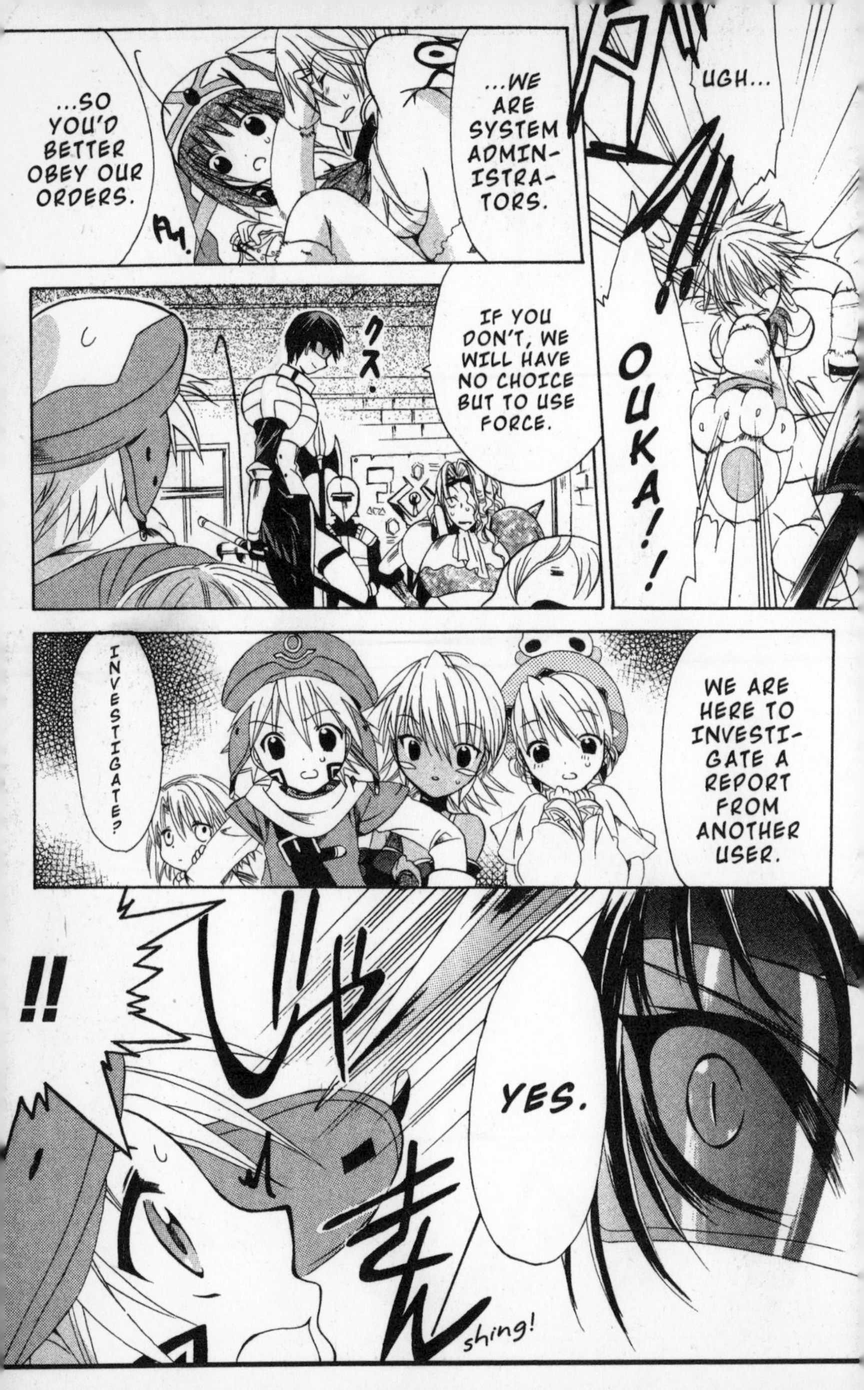
UGH...
OUKA!!
...WE ARE SYSTEM ADMINISTRATORS.
...SO YOU'D BETTER OBEY OUR ORDERS.
FM.
IF YOU DON'T, WE WILL HAVE NO CHOICE BUT TO USE FORCE.
クス.
WE ARE HERE TO INVESTIGATE A REPORT FROM ANOTHER USER.
INVESTIGATE?
YES.
じゃきん
shing!
!!

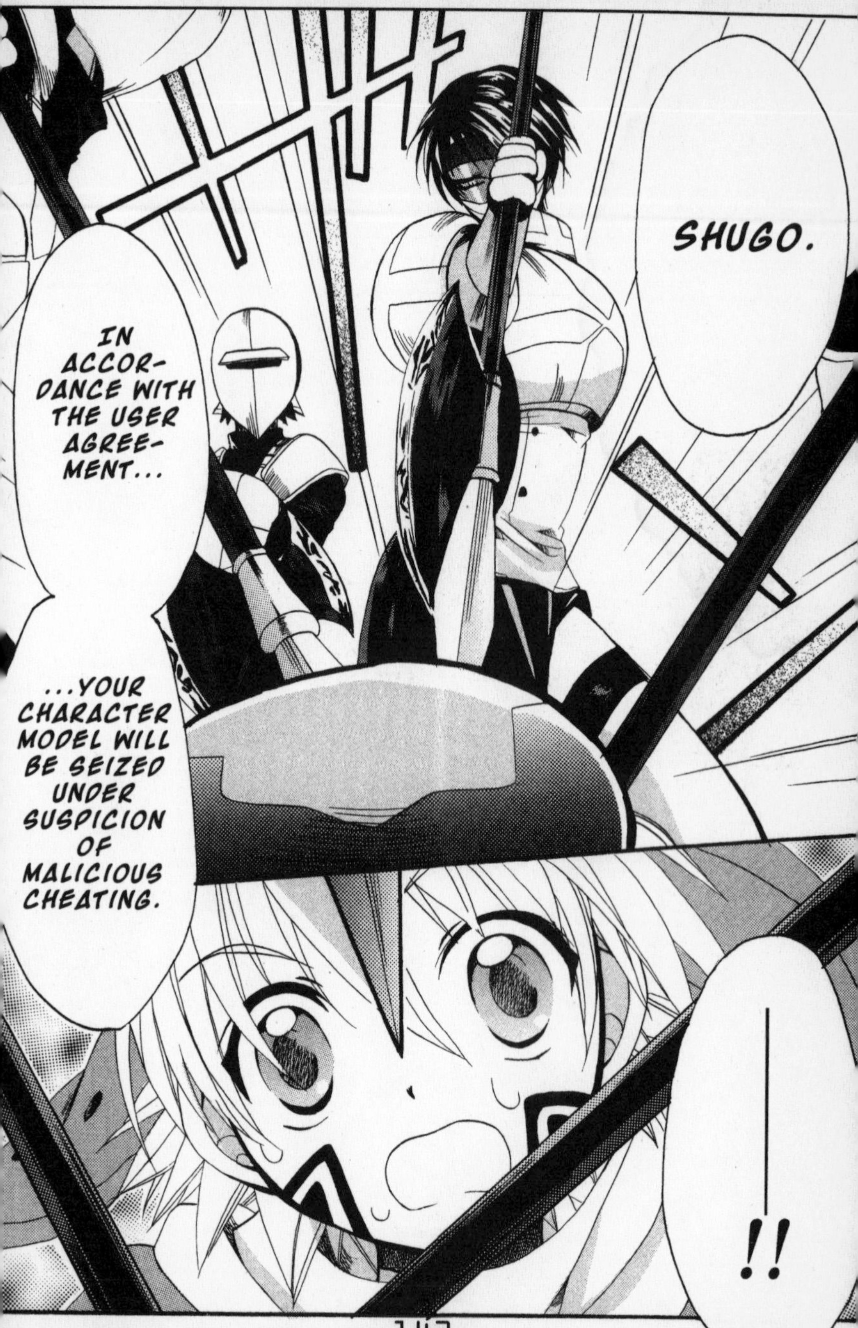
SHUGO.
IN ACCORDANCE WITH THE USER AGREEMENT...
...YOUR CHARACTER MODEL WILL BE SEIZED UNDER SUSPICION OF MALICIOUS CHEATING.
——!!

NEW GENERATION ONLINE

THE WORLD

 SUBJECT: FOUL PLAY  SENDER: KAMIYAN III

Dear The World User Support Director, CC Corp.

First of all, I am one of the biggest fans of The World.
Please listen.
My precious character data has been ruined by
another user.
If you take a look at the attached screen shot, you will see
what I mean.

The user that did this to me is named Shugo. I just know he's
been cheating.
He also has a weird bracelet that's not listed in the
strategy guide. He shouldn't be allowed to get away with
this! Please shut down this criminal's account at once!

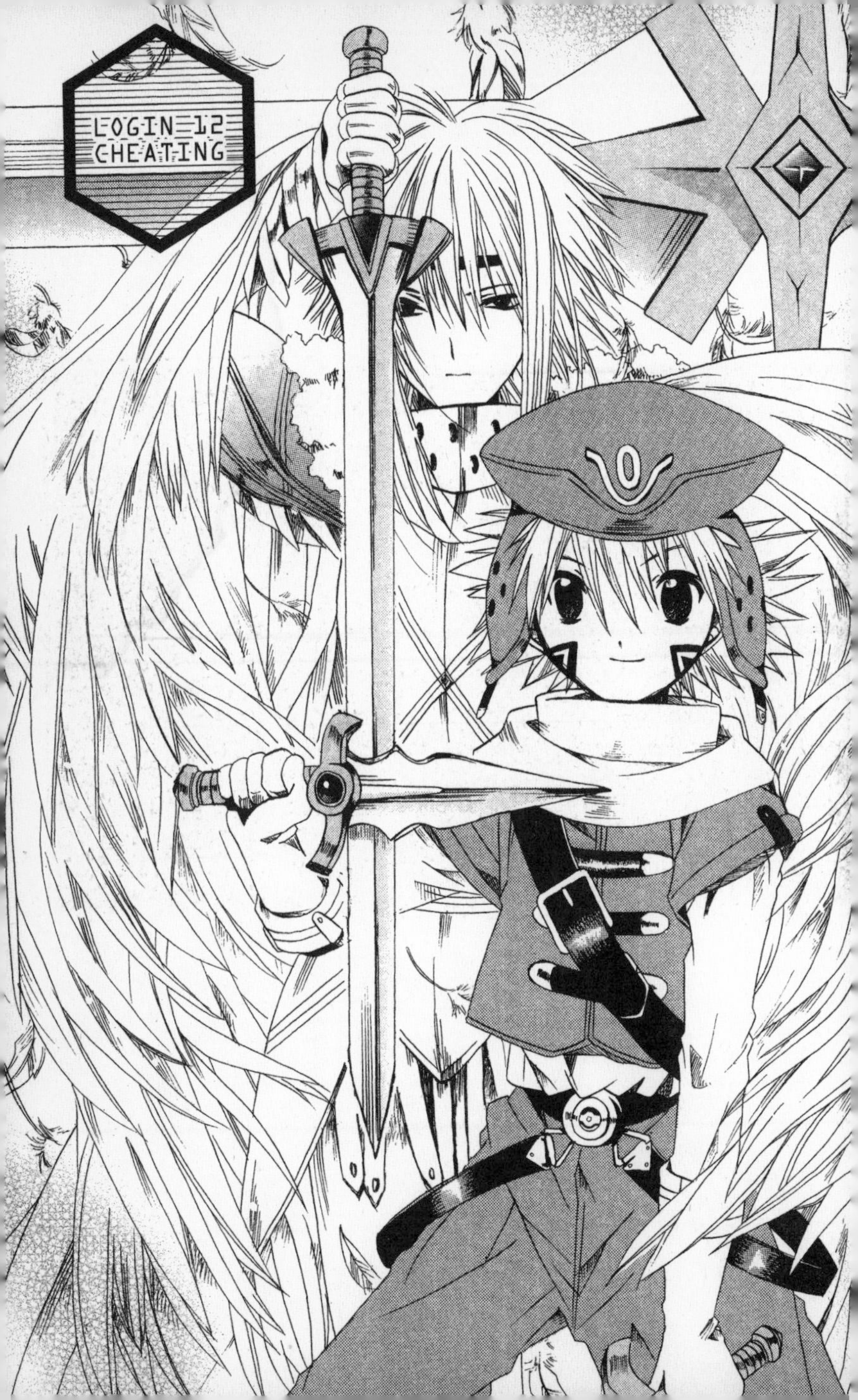
LOGIN 12
CHEATING

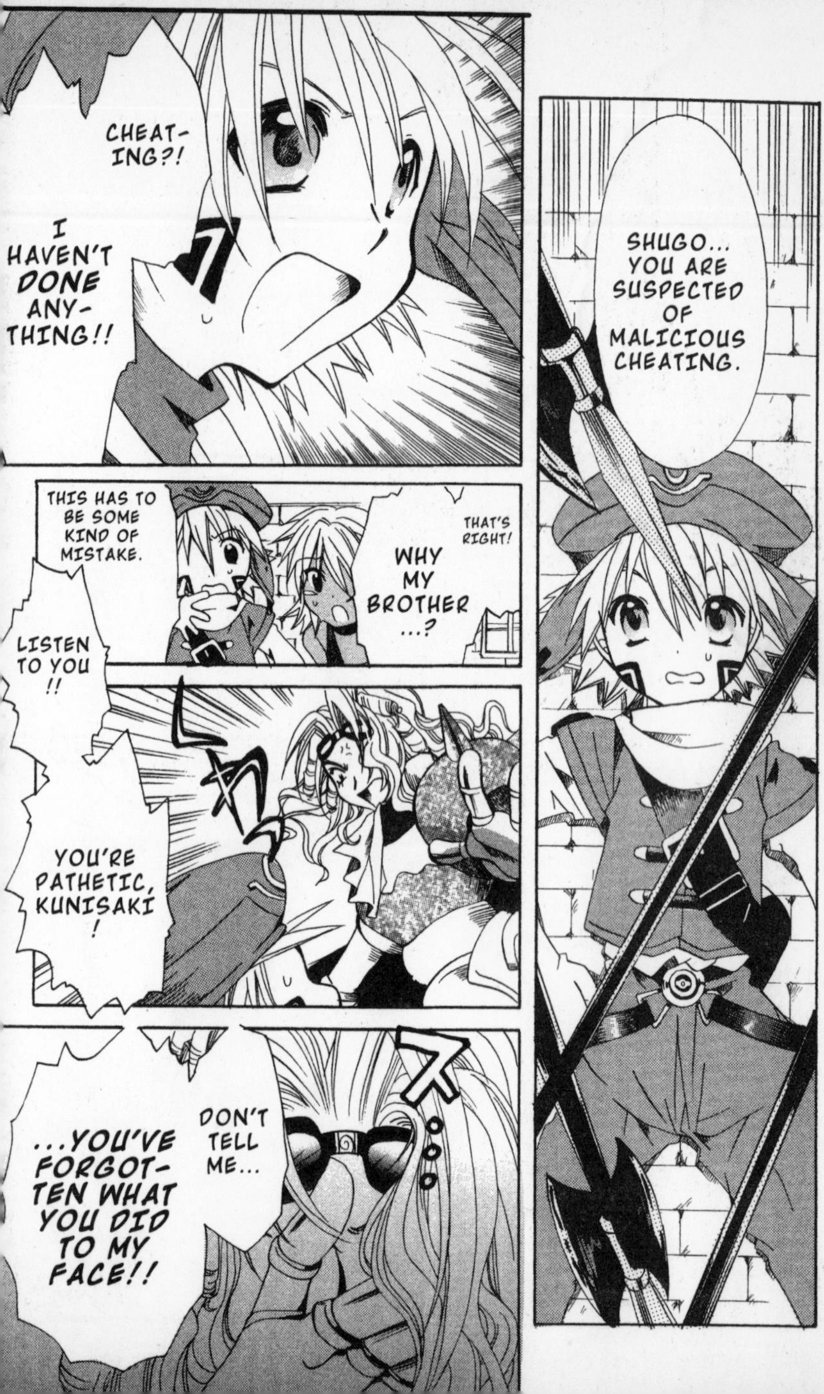
SHUGO... YOU ARE SUSPECTED OF MALICIOUS CHEATING.
CHEAT-ING?!
I HAVEN'T DONE ANY-THING!!
THAT'S RIGHT!
WHY MY BROTHER ...?
THIS HAS TO BE SOME KIND OF MISTAKE.
LISTEN TO YOU !!
YOU'RE PATHETIC, KUNISAKI !
DON'T TELL ME...
...YOU'VE FORGOT-TEN WHAT YOU DID TO MY FACE!!

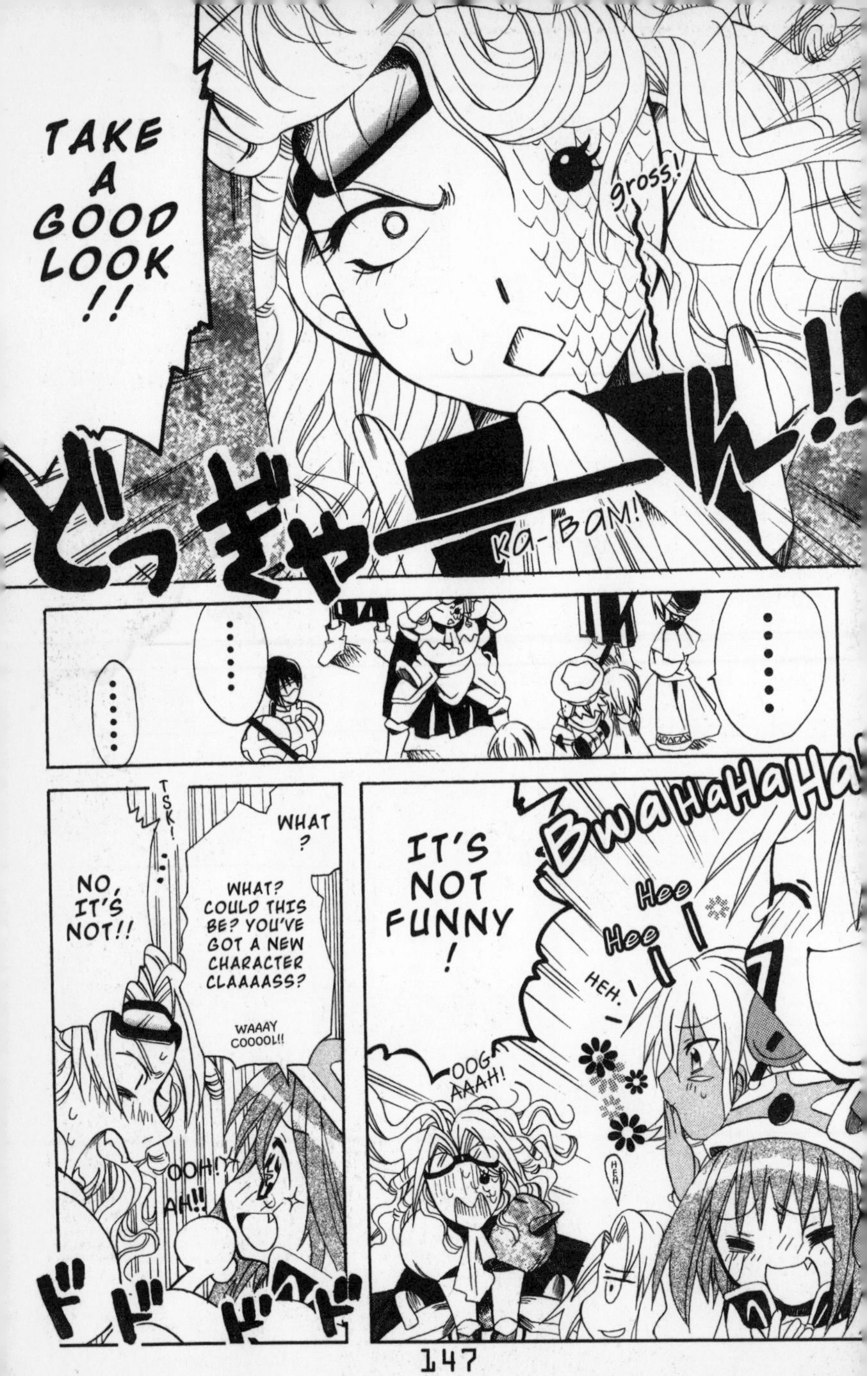

TAKE A GOOD LOOK!!
gross!
どっぎゃーーん!!
KA-BAM!
......
......
......
BwaHaHaHaHa
IT'S NOT FUNNY!
Hee Hee
HEH.
OOG AAAH!
HEH.
WHAT?
TSK!
WHAT? COULD THIS BE? YOU'VE GOT A NEW CHARACTER CLAAAASS?
NO, IT'S NOT!!
WAAAY COOOOL!!
OOH!
AH!!
ドドドド

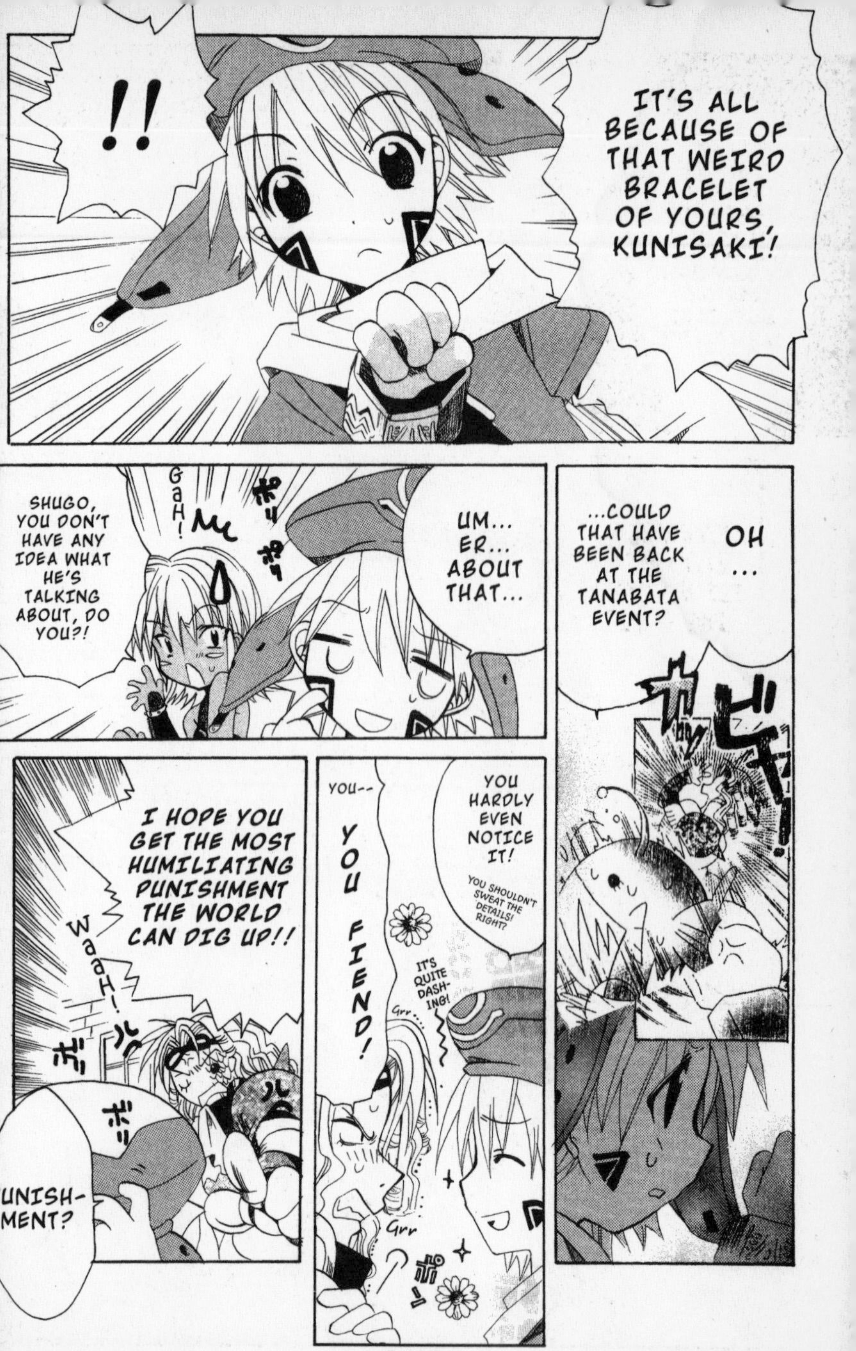
IT'S ALL BECAUSE OF THAT WEIRD BRACELET OF YOURS, KUNISAKI!
!!
OH ...
...COULD THAT HAVE BEEN BACK AT THE TANABATA EVENT?
UM... ER... ABOUT THAT...
GaH!
SHUGO, YOU DON'T HAVE ANY IDEA WHAT HE'S TALKING ABOUT, DO YOU?!
YOU HARDLY EVEN NOTICE IT!
YOU SHOULDN'T SWEAT THE DETAILS! RIGHT?
YOU--
YOU FIEND!
IT'S QUITE DASHING!
Grr....
Grr
I HOPE YOU GET THE MOST HUMILIATING PUNISHMENT THE WORLD CAN DIG UP!!
WaaH!
PUNISH-MENT?

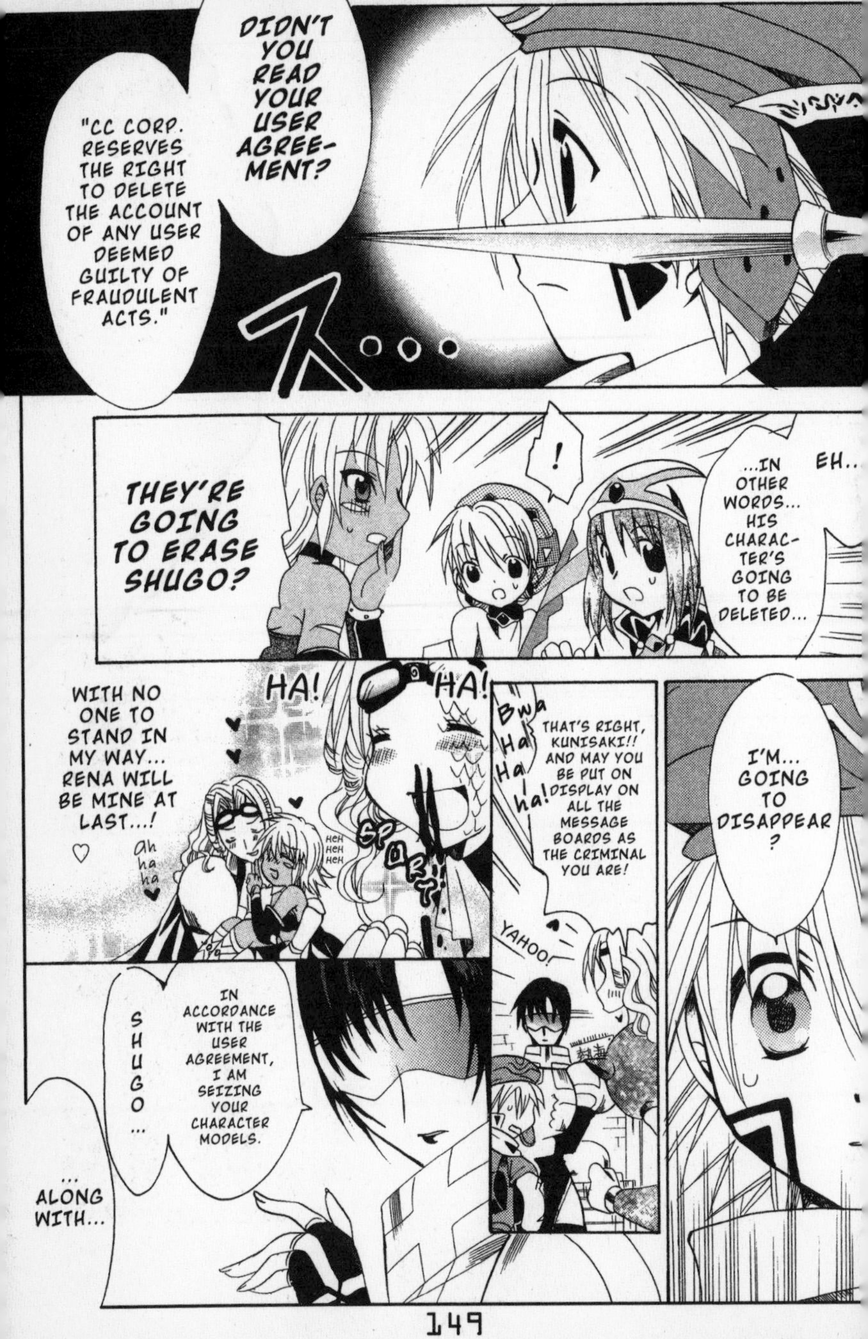
DIDN'T YOU READ YOUR USER AGREEMENT?
"CC CORP. RESERVES THE RIGHT TO DELETE THE ACCOUNT OF ANY USER DEEMED GUILTY OF FRAUDULENT ACTS."
EH...
...IN OTHER WORDS... HIS CHARACTER'S GOING TO BE DELETED...
!
THEY'RE GOING TO ERASE SHUGO?
I'M... GOING TO DISAPPEAR?
Bwa Ha Ha ha!
THAT'S RIGHT, KUNISAKI!! AND MAY YOU BE PUT ON DISPLAY ON ALL THE MESSAGE BOARDS AS THE CRIMINAL YOU ARE!
YAHOO!
HA! HA!
SPORT!!
HEH HEH HEH
WITH NO ONE TO STAND IN MY WAY... RENA WILL BE MINE AT LAST...!
Ah ha ha
SHUGO...
IN ACCORDANCE WITH THE USER AGREEMENT, I AM SEIZING YOUR CHARACTER MODELS.
...ALONG WITH...

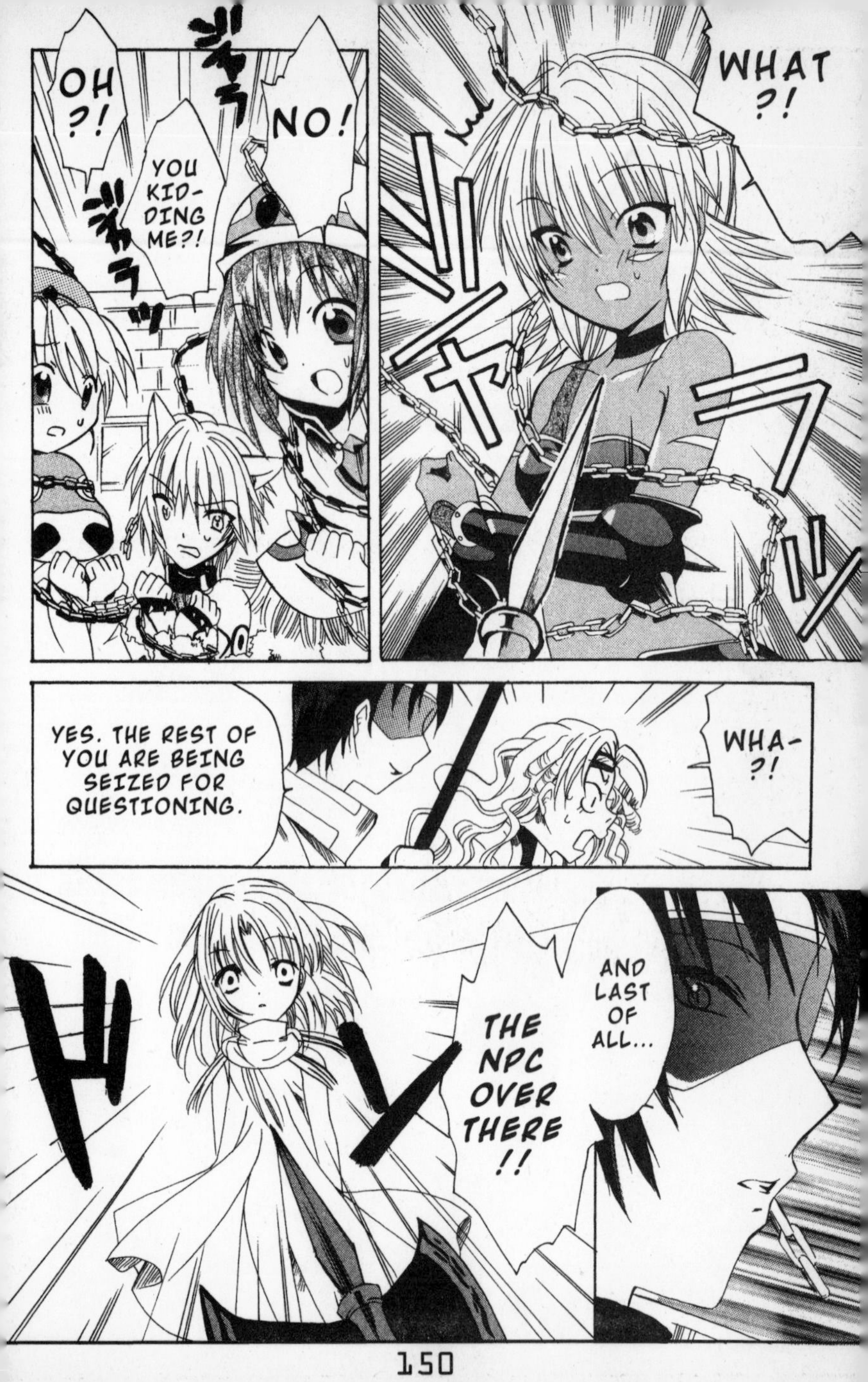
WHAT?!
NO!
OH?!
YOU KIDDING ME?!
WHA-?!
YES. THE REST OF YOU ARE BEING SEIZED FOR QUESTIONING.
AND LAST OF ALL...
THE NPC OVER THERE!!

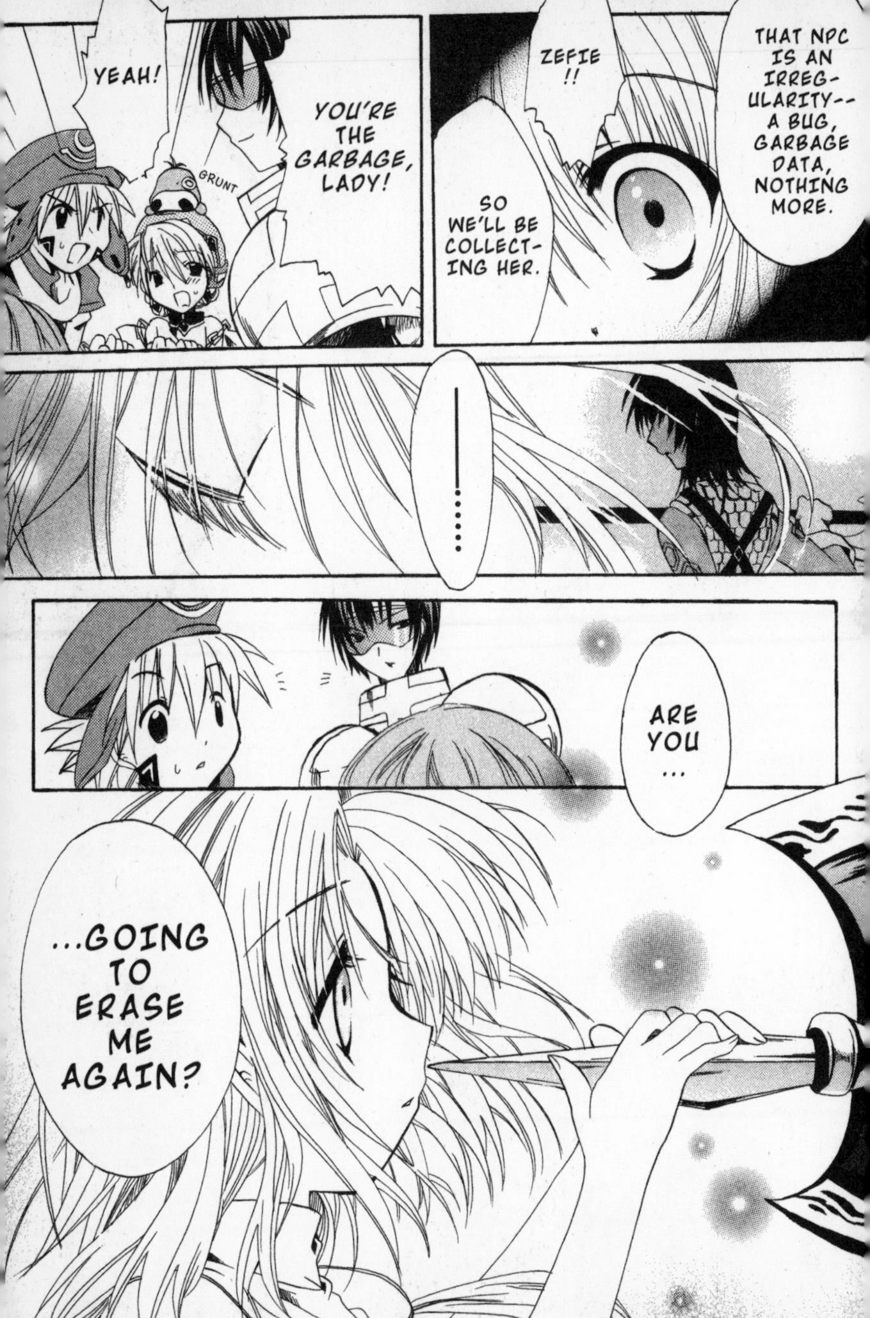
THAT NPC IS AN IRREGULARITY-- A BUG, GARBAGE DATA, NOTHING MORE.
ZEFIE !!
SO WE'LL BE COLLECTING HER.
YOU'RE THE GARBAGE, LADY!
YEAH!
GRUNT
—......
ARE YOU ...
...GOING TO ERASE ME AGAIN?

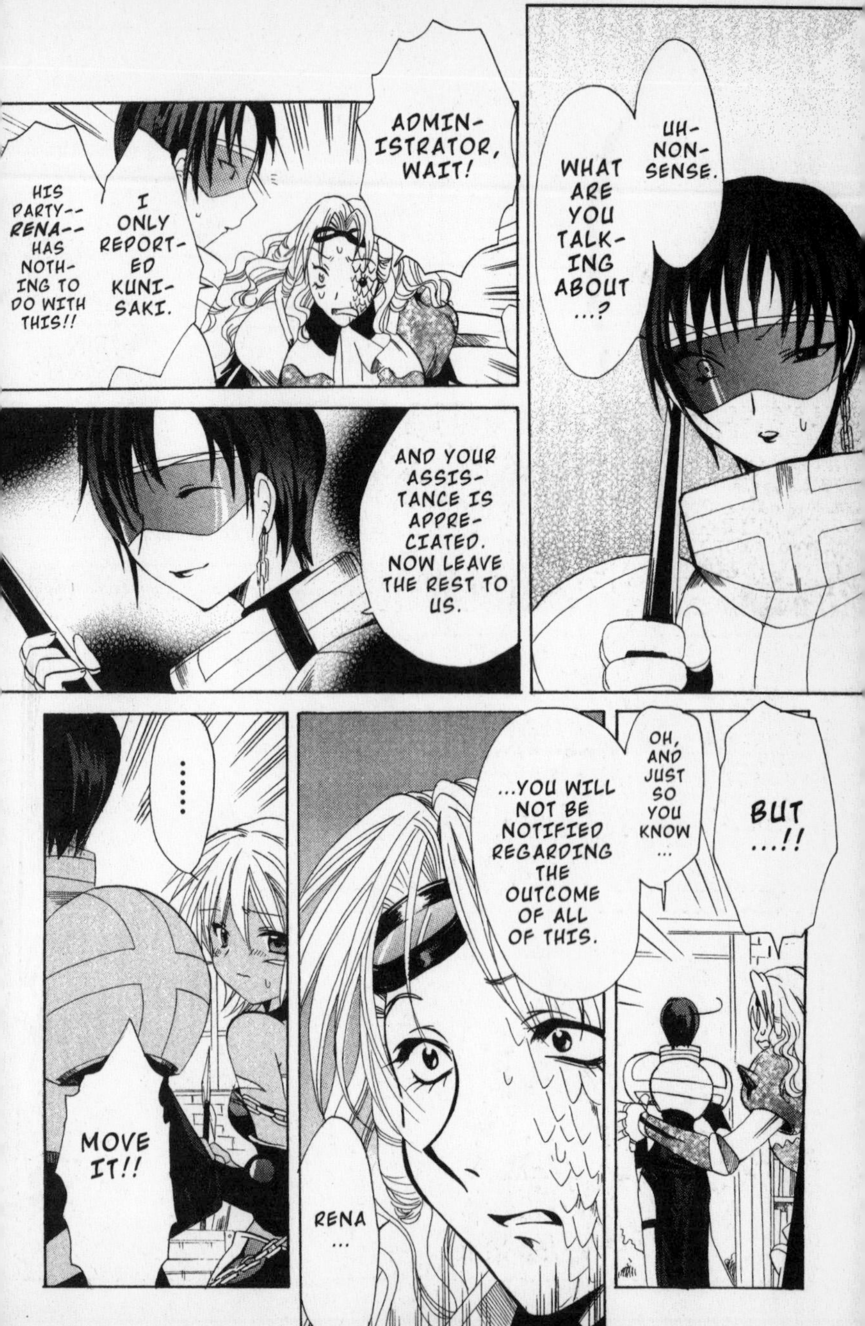
UH-NONSENSE.
WHAT ARE YOU TALKING ABOUT...?
ADMINISTRATOR, WAIT!
I ONLY REPORTED KUNISAKI.
HIS PARTY--RENA--HAS NOTHING TO DO WITH THIS!!
AND YOUR ASSISTANCE IS APPRECIATED. NOW LEAVE THE REST TO US.
BUT...!!
OH, AND JUST SO YOU KNOW...
...YOU WILL NOT BE NOTIFIED REGARDING THE OUTCOME OF ALL OF THIS.
RENA...
......
MOVE IT!!

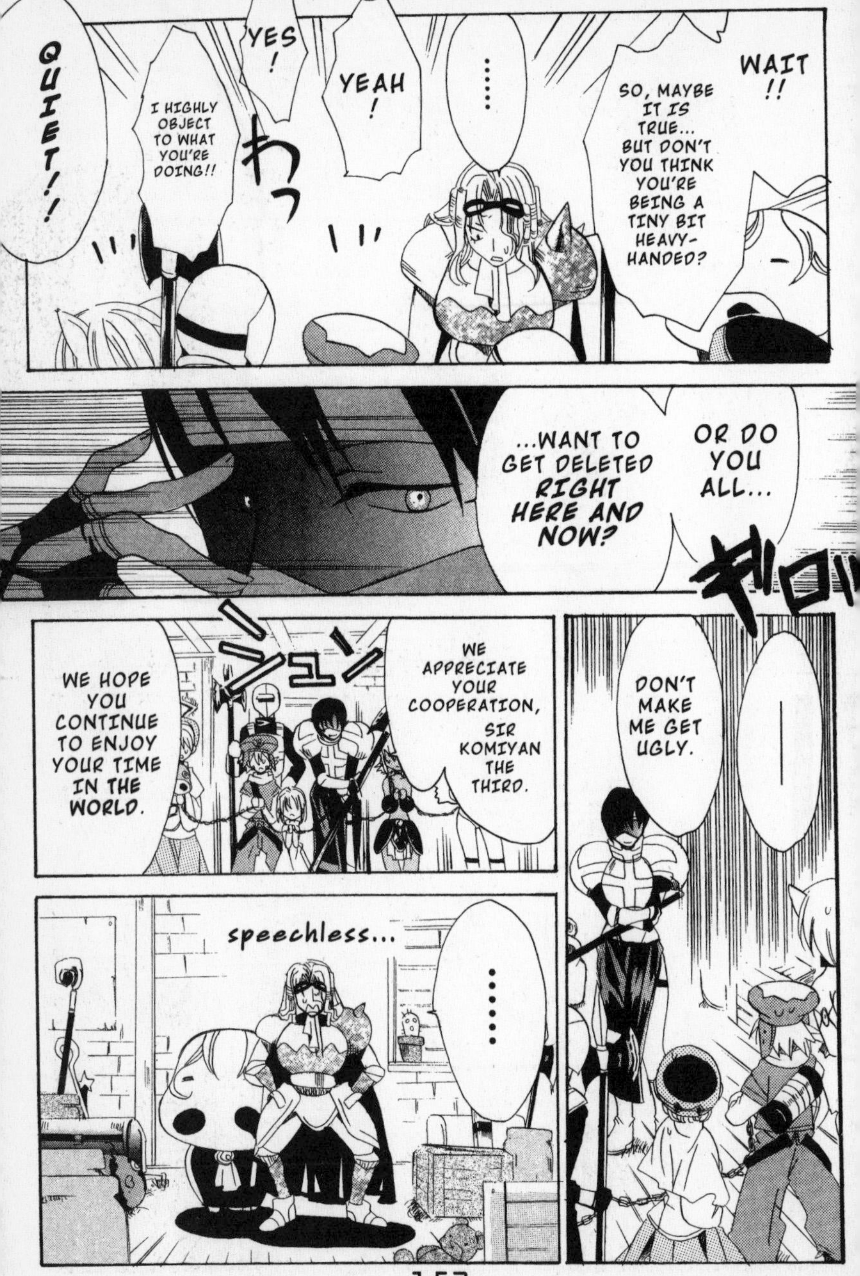
WAIT!!
SO, MAYBE IT IS TRUE... BUT DON'T YOU THINK YOU'RE BEING A TINY BIT HEAVY-HANDED?
......
YEAH!
YES!
わっ
I HIGHLY OBJECT TO WHAT YOU'RE DOING!!
QUIET!!
OR DO YOU ALL...
...WANT TO GET DELETED RIGHT HERE AND NOW?
—
DON'T MAKE ME GET UGLY.
WE APPRECIATE YOUR COOPERATION, SIR KOMIYAN THE THIRD.
WE HOPE YOU CONTINUE TO ENJOY YOUR TIME IN THE WORLD.
......
speechless...

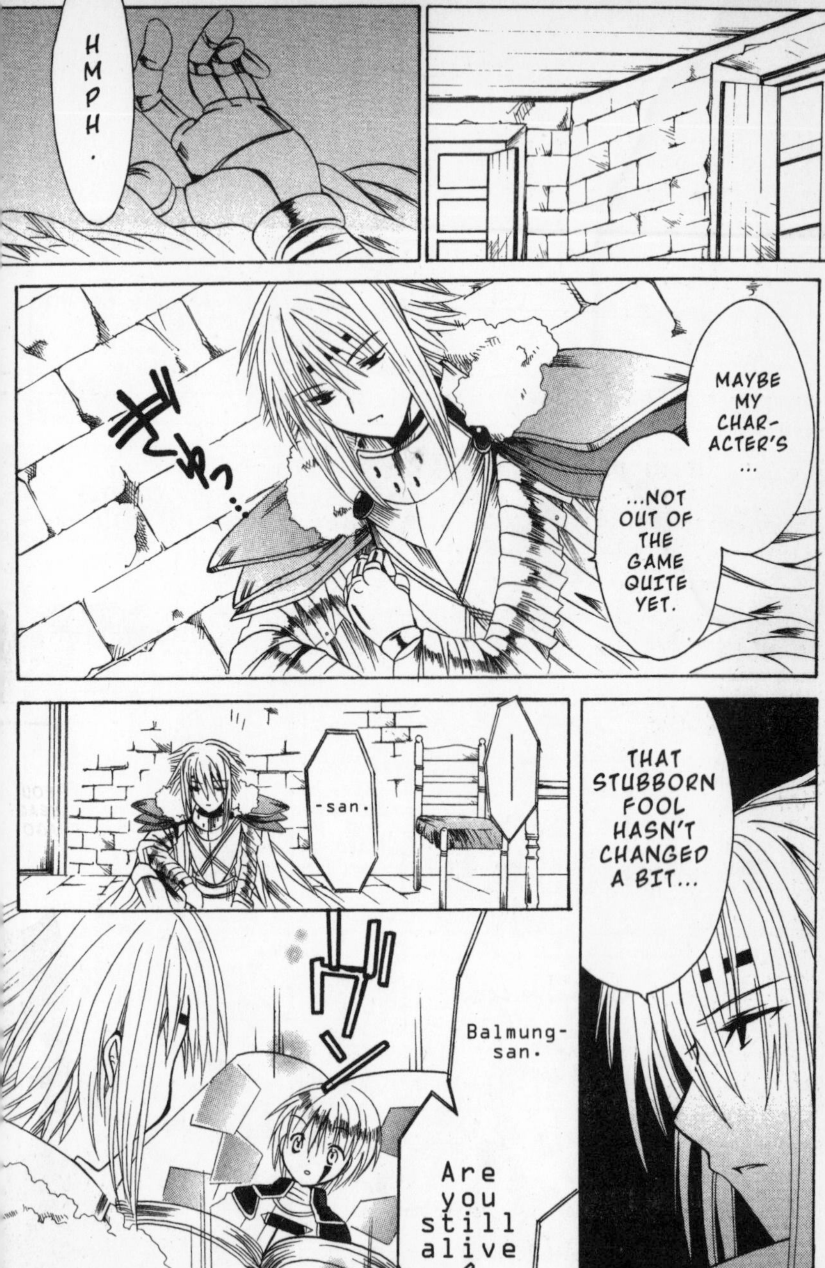
HMPH.
MAYBE MY CHAR-ACTER'S ...
...NOT OUT OF THE GAME QUITE YET.
THAT STUBBORN FOOL HASN'T CHANGED A BIT...
!
-san.
Balmung-san.
Are you still alive?

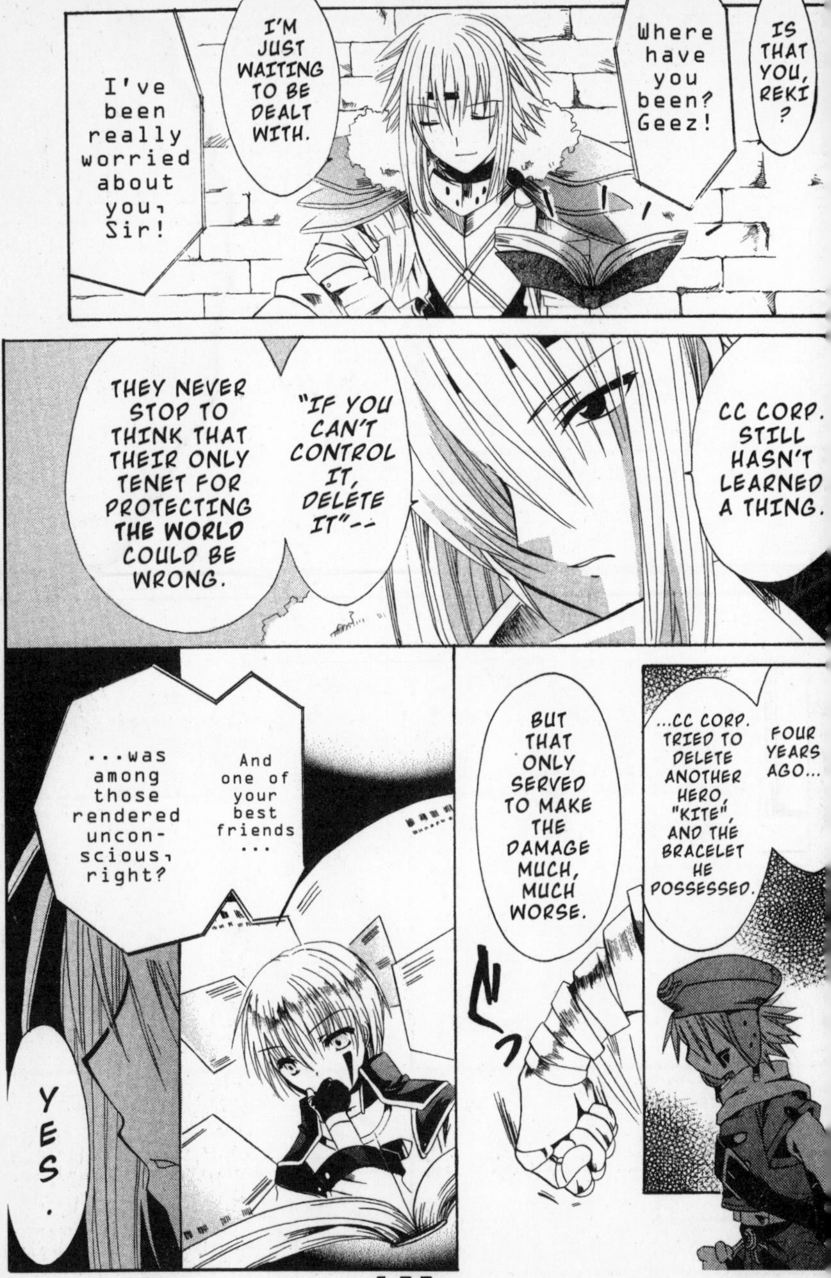
IS THAT YOU, REKI?
Where have you been? Geez!
I'M JUST WAITING TO BE DEALT WITH.
I've been really worried about you, Sir!
CC CORP. STILL HASN'T LEARNED A THING.
"IF YOU CAN'T CONTROL IT, DELETE IT"--
THEY NEVER STOP TO THINK THAT THEIR ONLY TENET FOR PROTECTING THE WORLD COULD BE WRONG.
FOUR YEARS AGO...
...CC CORP. TRIED TO DELETE ANOTHER HERO, "KITE", AND THE BRACELET HE POSSESSED.
BUT THAT ONLY SERVED TO MAKE THE DAMAGE MUCH, MUCH WORSE.
And one of your best friends...
...was among those rendered uncon-scious, right?
YES.

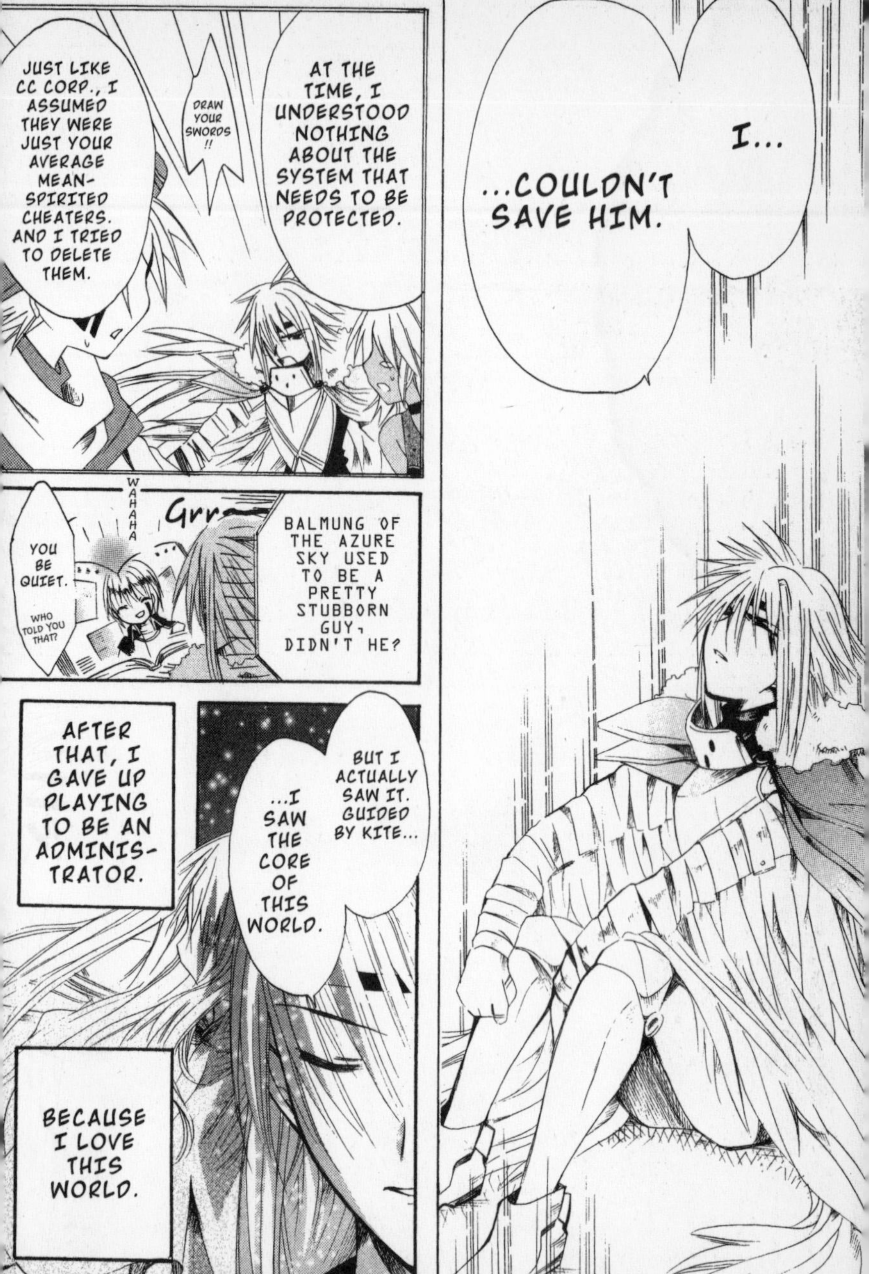
I...
...COULDN'T SAVE HIM.
AT THE TIME, I UNDERSTOOD NOTHING ABOUT THE SYSTEM THAT NEEDS TO BE PROTECTED.
DRAW YOUR SWORDS!!
JUST LIKE CC CORP., I ASSUMED THEY WERE JUST YOUR AVERAGE MEAN-SPIRITED CHEATERS. AND I TRIED TO DELETE THEM.
BALMUNG OF THE AZURE SKY USED TO BE A PRETTY STUBBORN GUY, DIDN'T HE?
Grr
WAHAHA
YOU BE QUIET.
WHO TOLD YOU THAT?
BUT I ACTUALLY SAW IT. GUIDED BY KITE...
...I SAW THE CORE OF THIS WORLD.
AFTER THAT, I GAVE UP PLAYING TO BE AN ADMINISTRATOR.
BECAUSE I LOVE THIS WORLD.

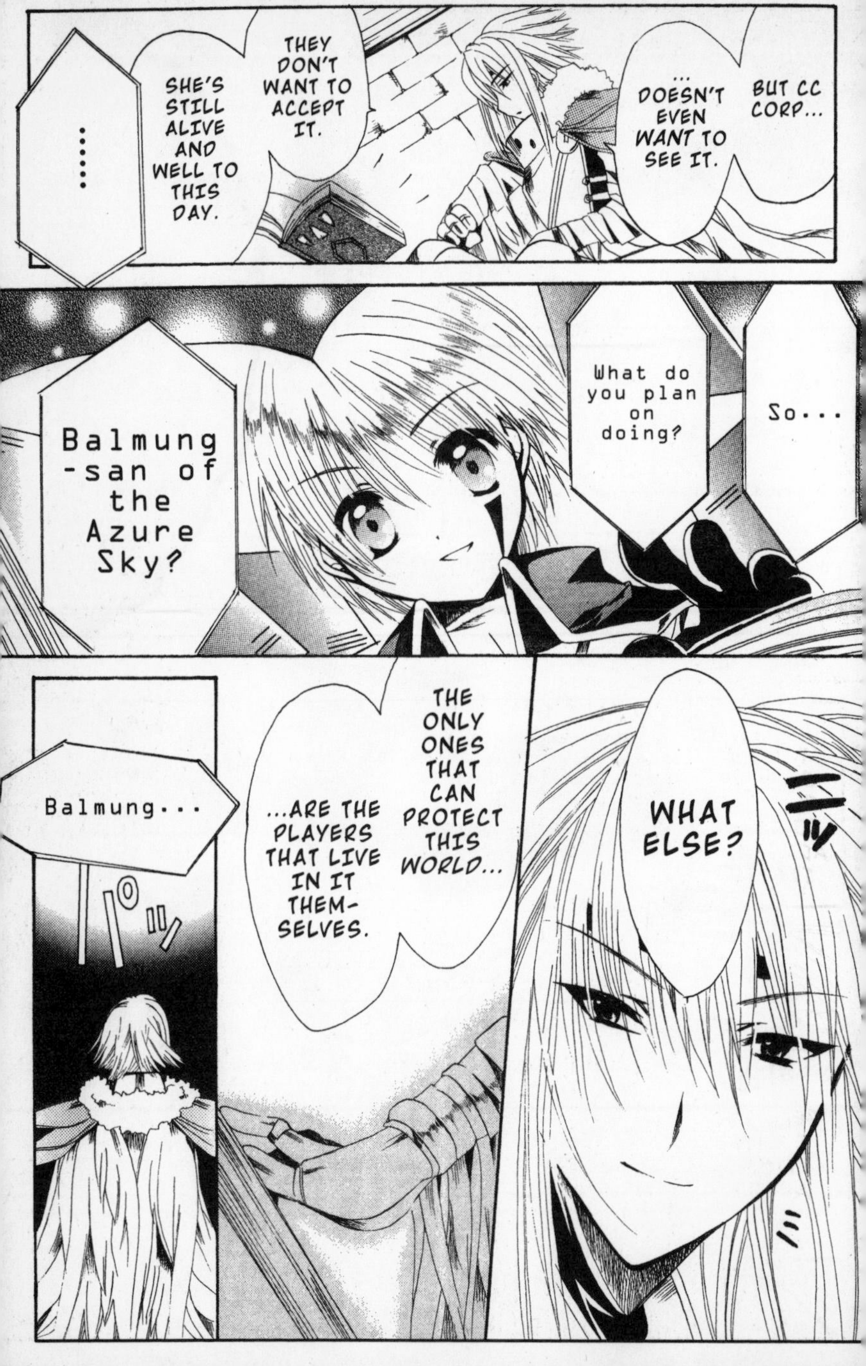
BUT CC CORP...
...DOESN'T EVEN WANT TO SEE IT.
THEY DON'T WANT TO ACCEPT IT.
SHE'S STILL ALIVE AND WELL TO THIS DAY.
......
So....
What do you plan on doing?
Balmung-san of the Azure Sky?
WHAT ELSE?
THE ONLY ONES THAT CAN PROTECT THIS WORLD...
...ARE THE PLAYERS THAT LIVE IN IT THEMSELVES.
Balmung...

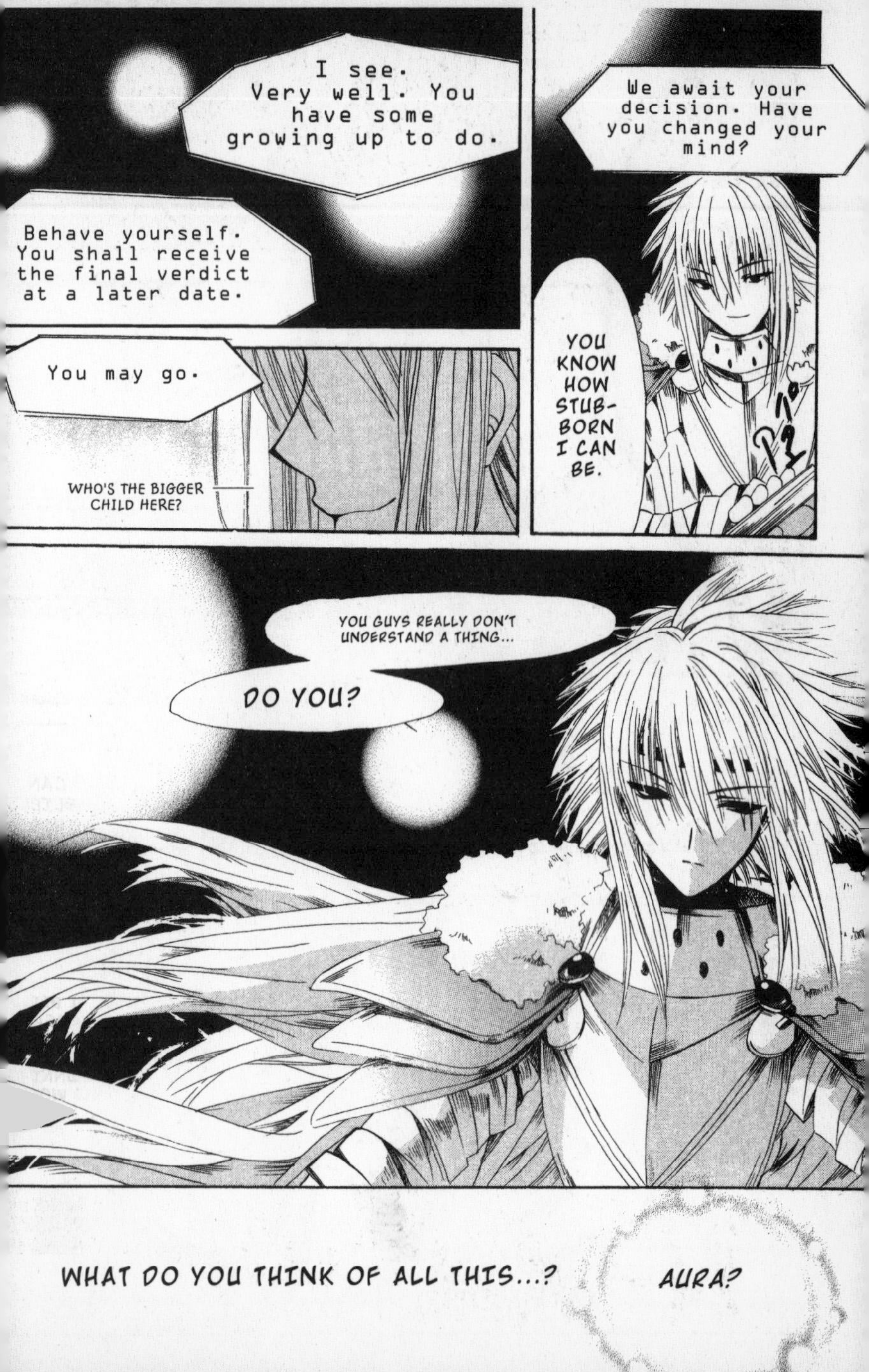
We await your decision. Have you changed your mind?
YOU KNOW HOW STUBBORN I CAN BE.
I see. Very well. You have some growing up to do.
Behave yourself. You shall receive the final verdict at a later date.
You may go.
WHO'S THE BIGGER CHILD HERE?
YOU GUYS REALLY DON'T UNDERSTAND A THING...
DO YOU?
WHAT DO YOU THINK OF ALL THIS...?
AURA?

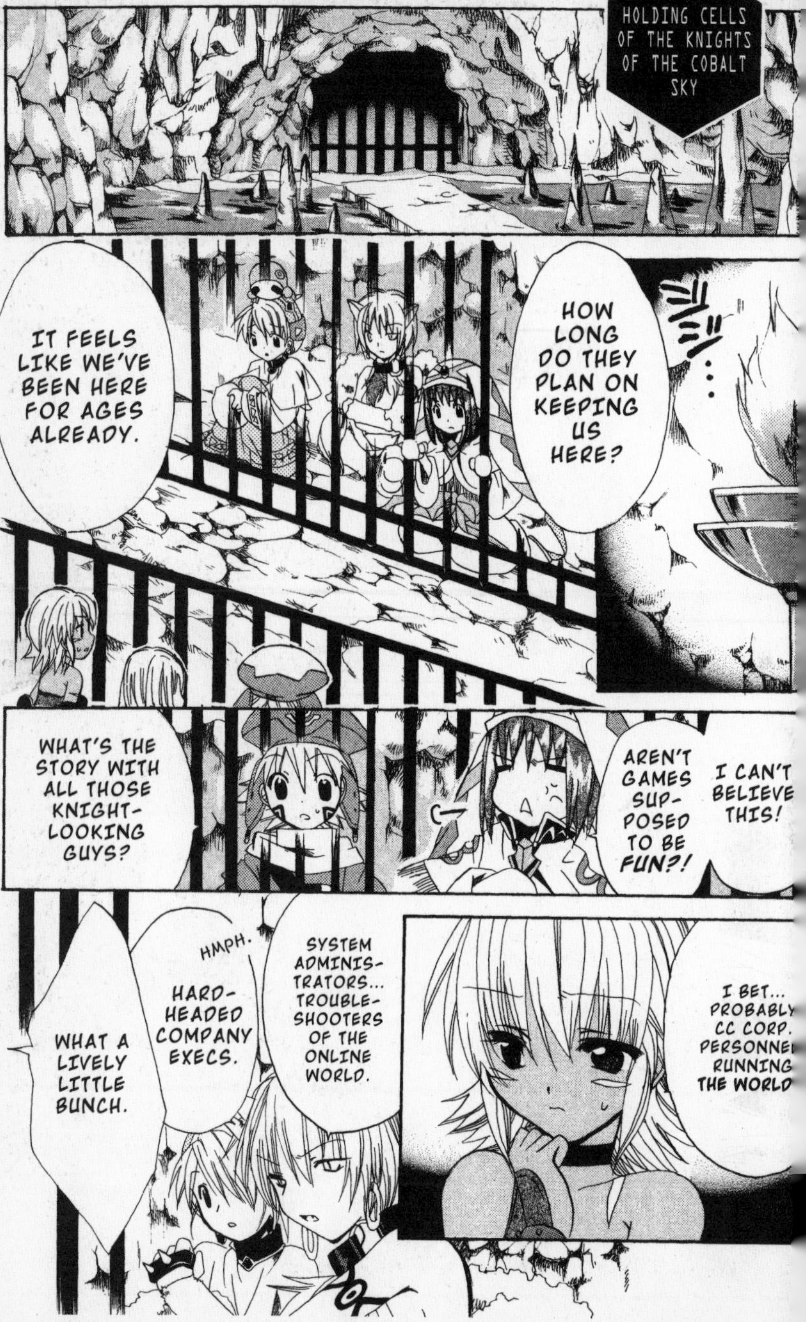
HOLDING CELLS OF THE KNIGHTS OF THE COBALT SKY
...
HOW LONG DO THEY PLAN ON KEEPING US HERE?
IT FEELS LIKE WE'VE BEEN HERE FOR AGES ALREADY.
I CAN'T BELIEVE THIS!
AREN'T GAMES SUP-POSED TO BE FUN?!
WHAT'S THE STORY WITH ALL THOSE KNIGHT-LOOKING GUYS?
I BET... PROBABLY CC CORP. PERSONNE RUNNING THE WORLD
SYSTEM ADMINIS-TRATORS... TROUBLE-SHOOTERS OF THE ONLINE WORLD.
HMPH.
HARD-HEADED COMPANY EXECS.
WHAT A LIVELY LITTLE BUNCH.

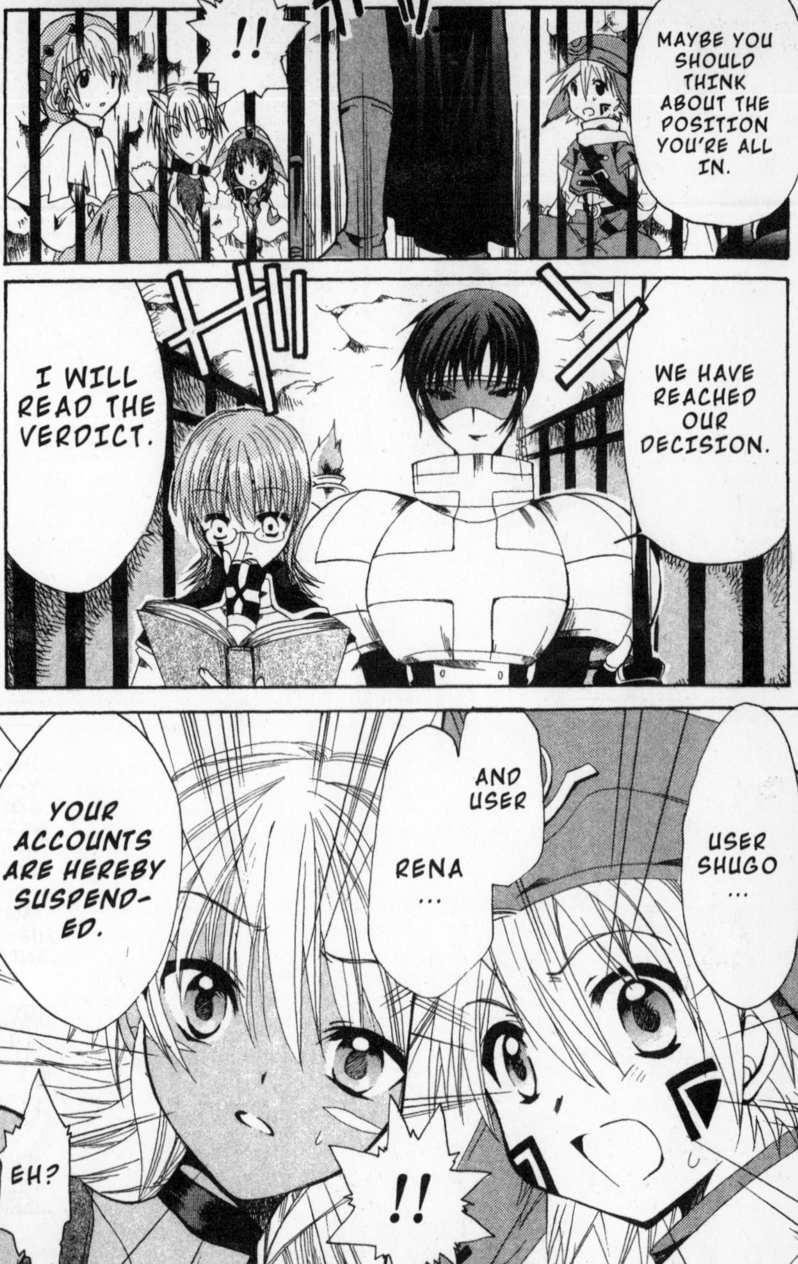
MAYBE YOU SHOULD THINK ABOUT THE POSITION YOU'RE ALL IN.
!!
WE HAVE REACHED OUR DECISION.
I WILL READ THE VERDICT.
USER SHUGO ...
AND USER RENA ...
YOUR ACCOUNTS ARE HEREBY SUSPEND-ED.
!!
EH?

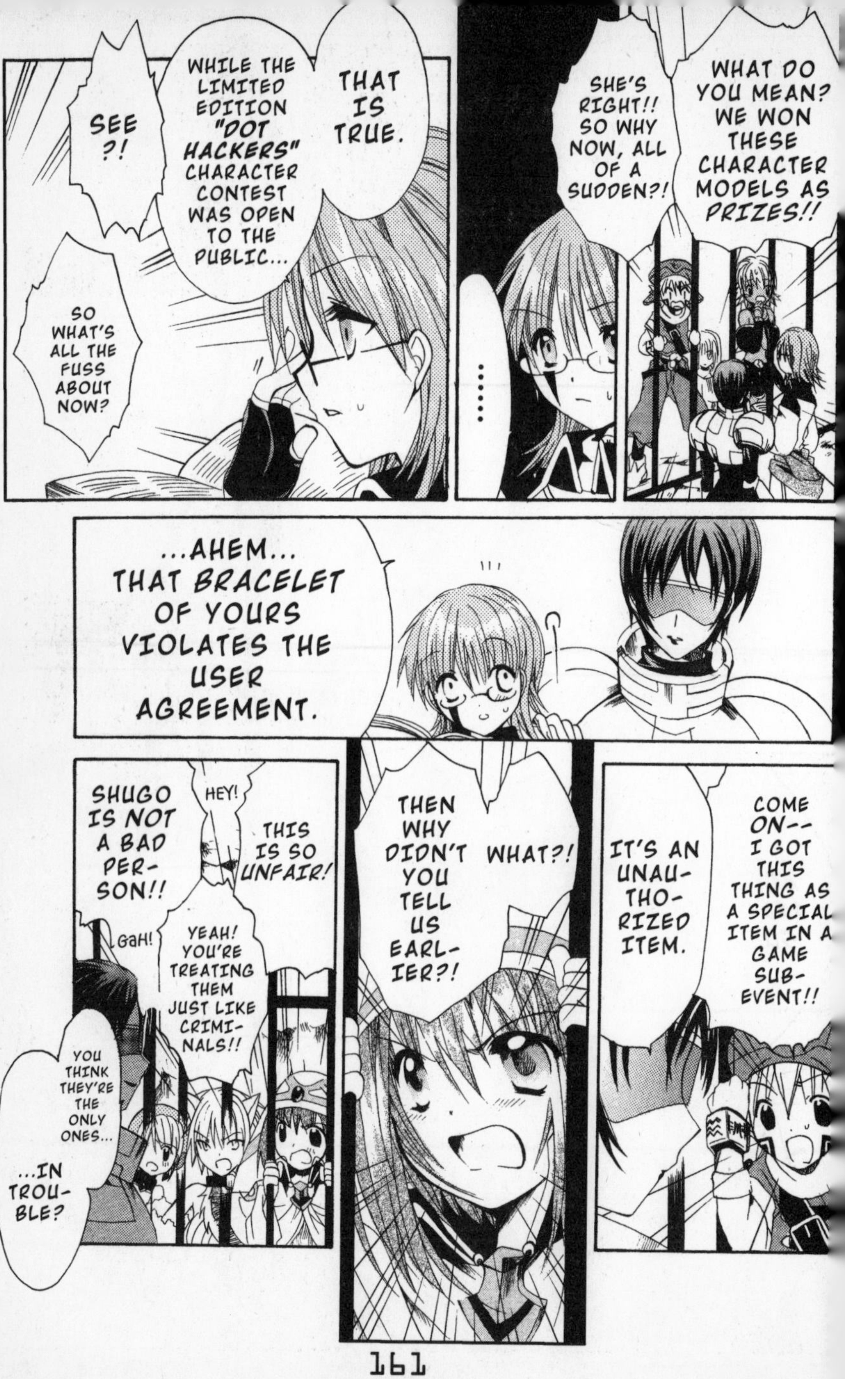
WHAT DO YOU MEAN? WE WON THESE CHARACTER MODELS AS *PRIZES!!*
SHE'S RIGHT!! SO WHY NOW, ALL OF A SUDDEN?!
......
THAT IS TRUE.
WHILE THE LIMITED EDITION *"DOT HACKERS"* CHARACTER CONTEST WAS OPEN TO THE PUBLIC...
SEE?!
SO WHAT'S ALL THE FUSS ABOUT NOW?
...AHEM... THAT *BRACELET* OF YOURS VIOLATES THE USER AGREEMENT.
COME ON-- I GOT THIS THING AS A SPECIAL ITEM IN A GAME SUB-EVENT!!
IT'S AN UNAU-THO-RIZED ITEM.
WHAT?!
THEN WHY DIDN'T YOU TELL US EARL-IER?!
THIS IS SO *UNFAIR!*
HEY!
SHUGO IS *NOT* A BAD PER-SON!!
YEAH! YOU'RE TREATING THEM JUST LIKE CRIMI-NALS!!
GAH!
YOU THINK THEY'RE THE ONLY ONES...
...IN TROU-BLE?

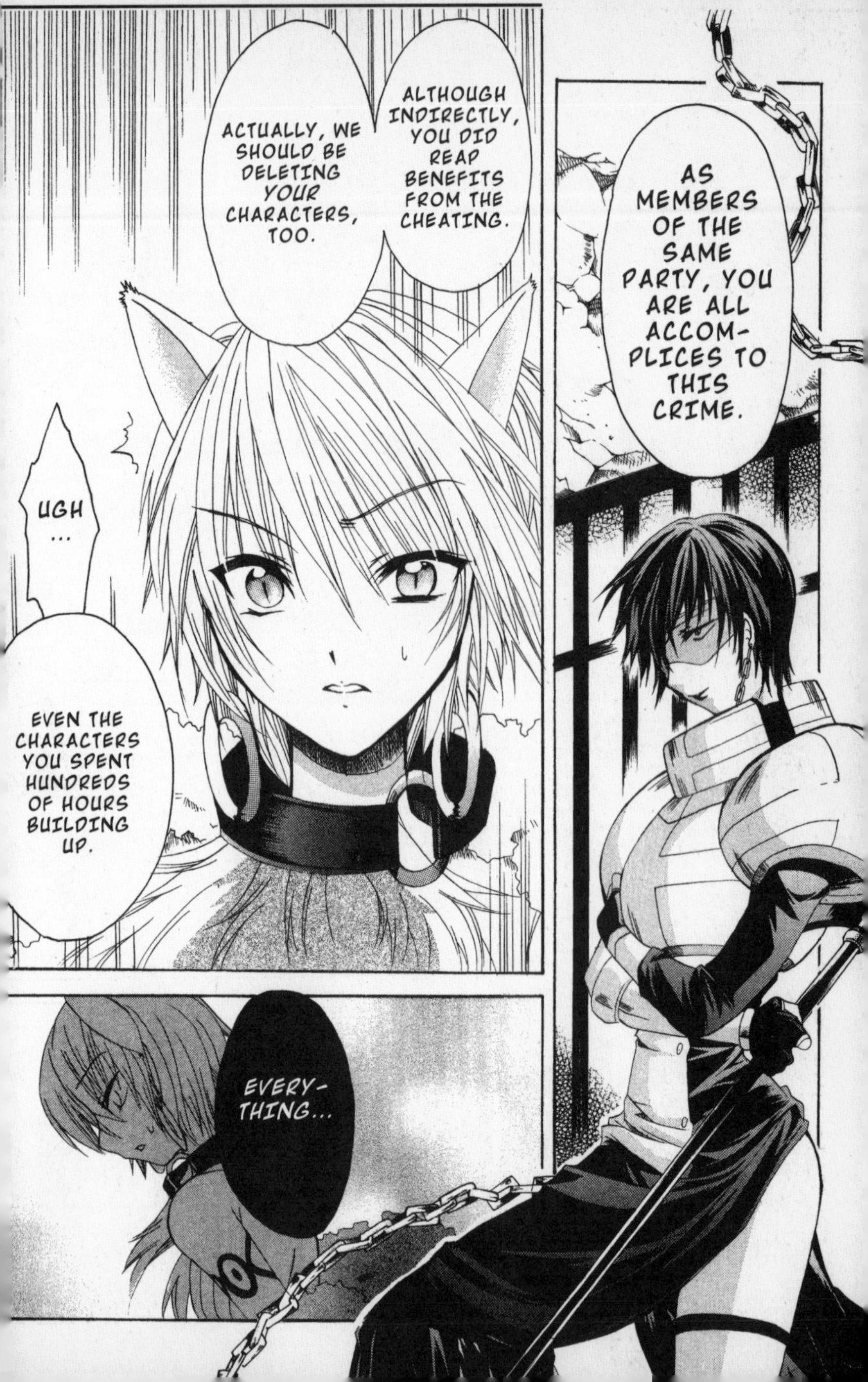
AS MEMBERS OF THE SAME PARTY, YOU ARE ALL ACCOMPLICES TO THIS CRIME.
ALTHOUGH INDIRECTLY, YOU DID REAP BENEFITS FROM THE CHEATING.
ACTUALLY, WE SHOULD BE DELETING *YOUR* CHARACTERS, TOO.
UGH ...
EVEN THE CHARACTERS YOU SPENT HUNDREDS OF HOURS BUILDING UP.
*EVERYTHING...*

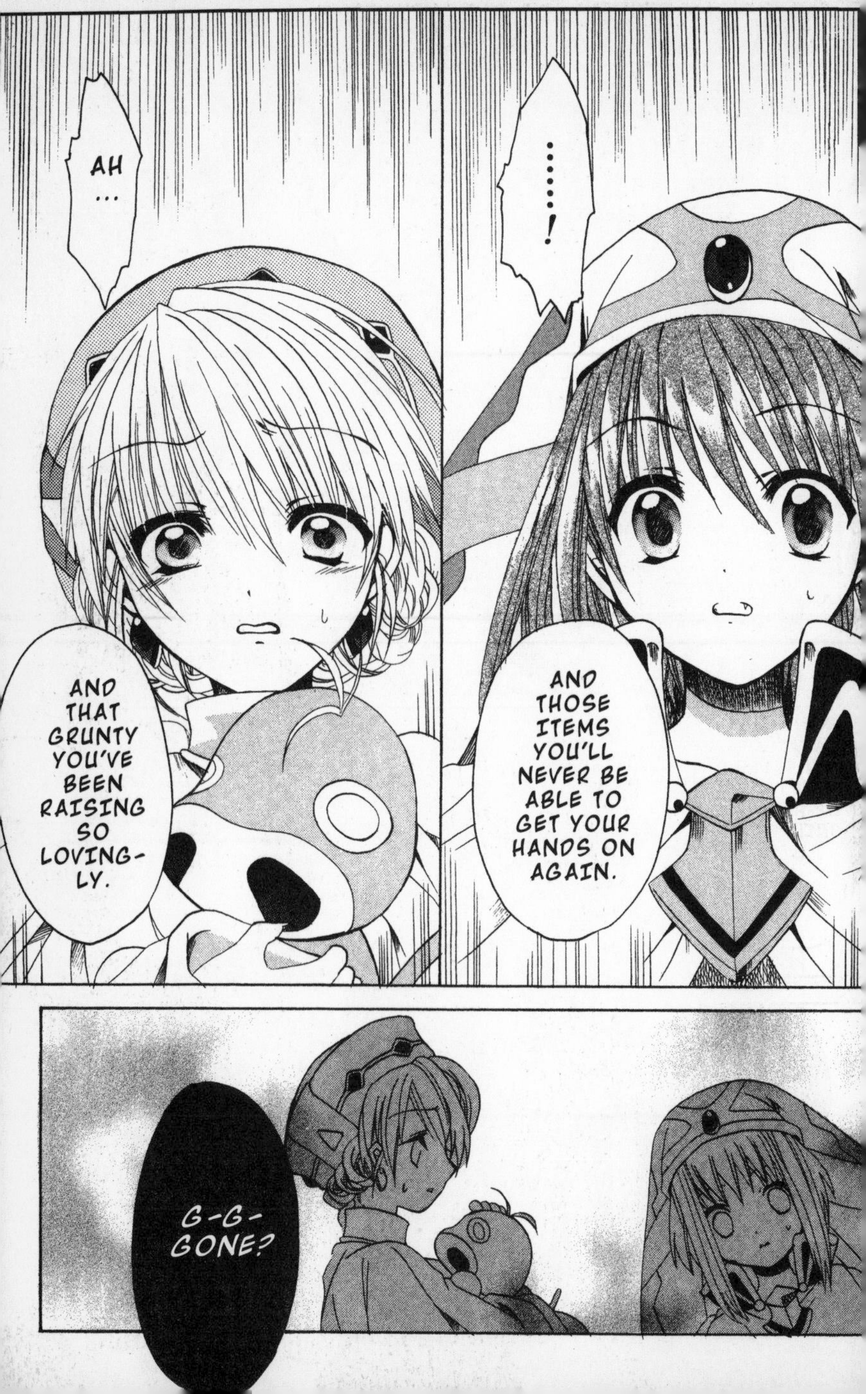
......!
AND THOSE ITEMS YOU'LL NEVER BE ABLE TO GET YOUR HANDS ON AGAIN.
AH ...
AND THAT GRUNTY YOU'VE BEEN RAISING SO LOVING-LY.
G-G-GONE?

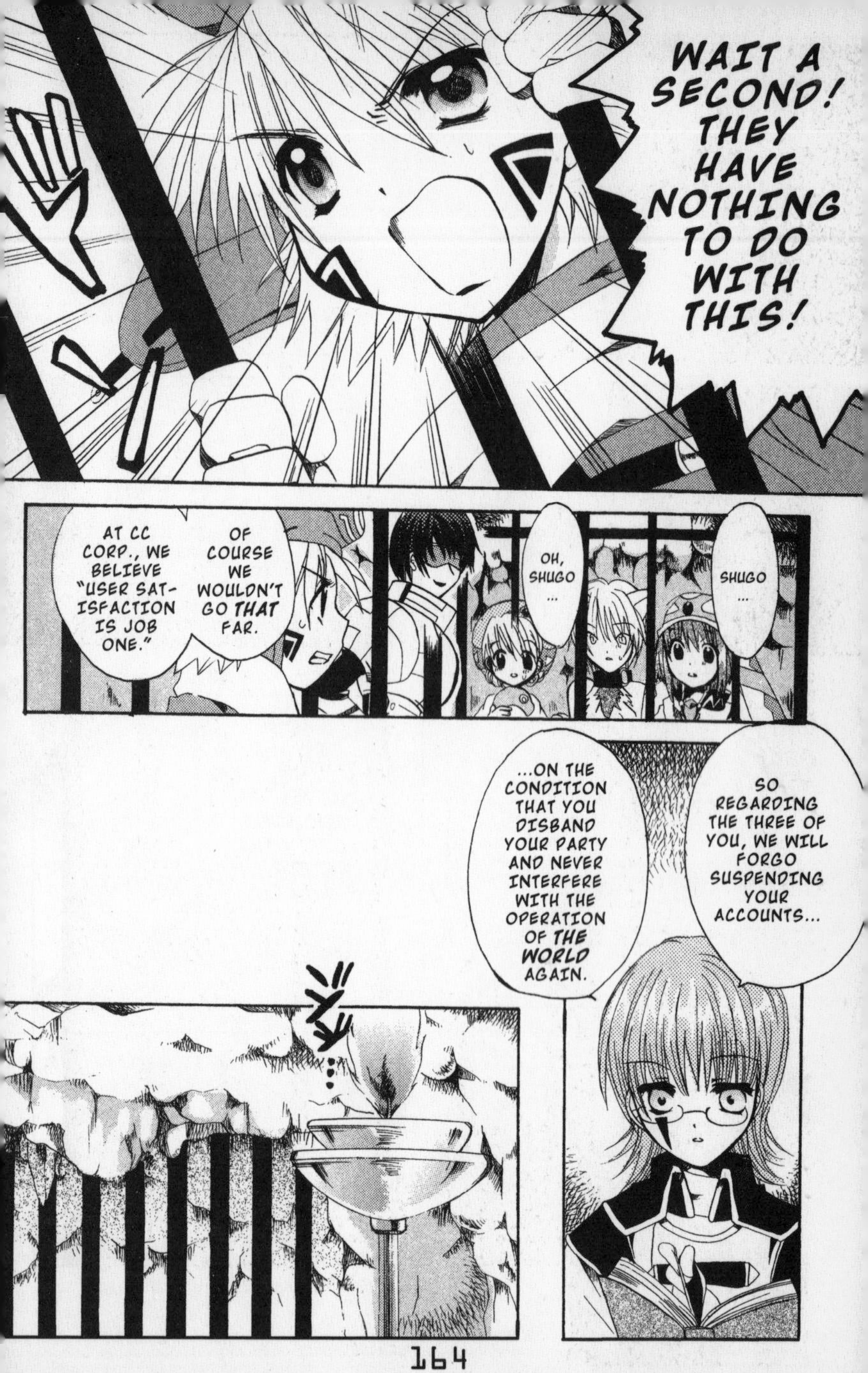
WAIT A SECOND! THEY HAVE NOTHING TO DO WITH THIS!
SHUGO ...
OH, SHUGO ...
OF COURSE WE WOULDN'T GO THAT FAR.
AT CC CORP., WE BELIEVE "USER SATISFACTION IS JOB ONE."
SO REGARDING THE THREE OF YOU, WE WILL FORGO SUSPENDING YOUR ACCOUNTS...
...ON THE CONDITION THAT YOU DISBAND YOUR PARTY AND NEVER INTERFERE WITH THE OPERATION OF THE WORLD AGAIN.

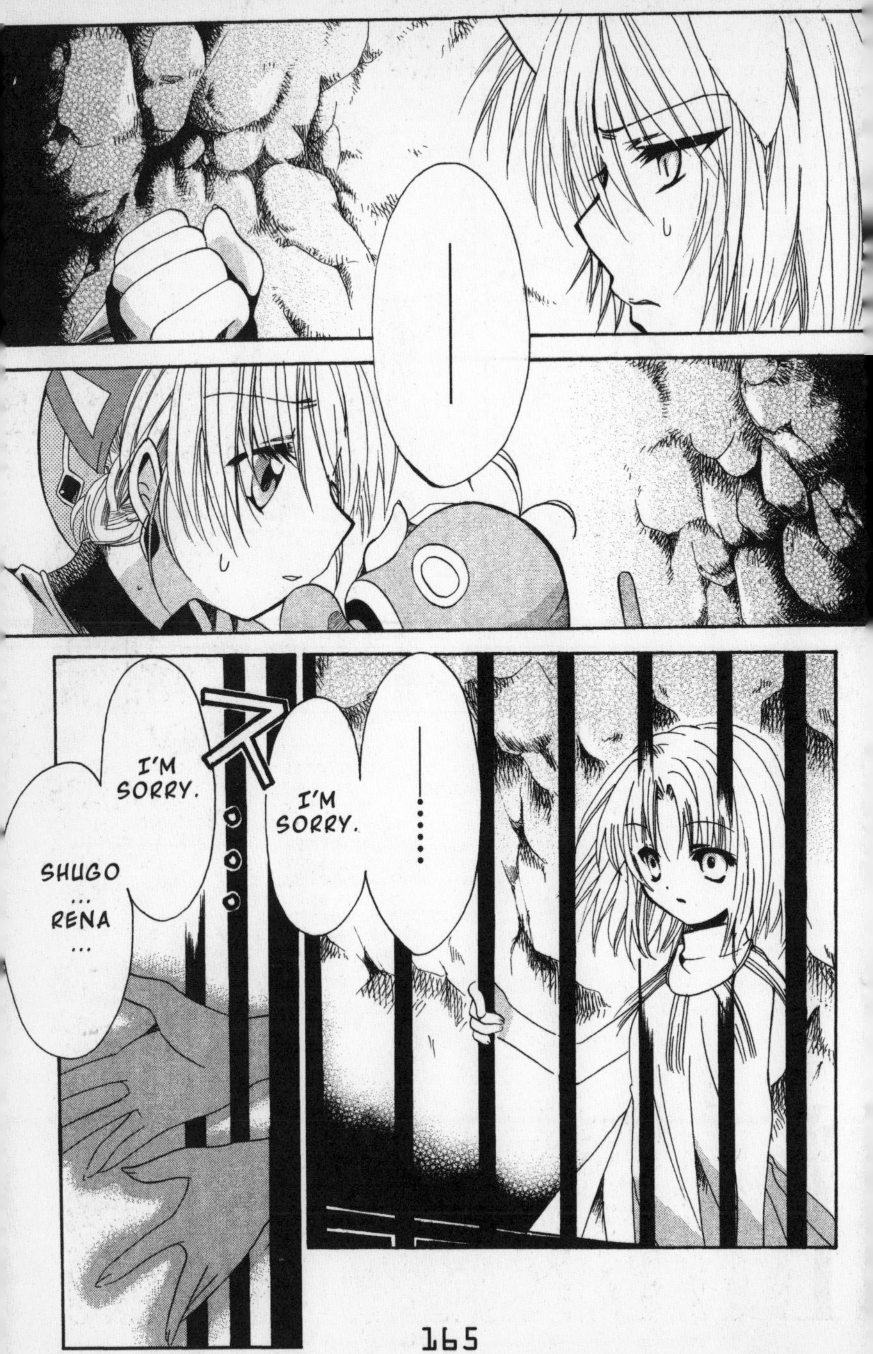
—
—......
I'M SORRY.
I'M SORRY.
SHUGO ... RENA ...

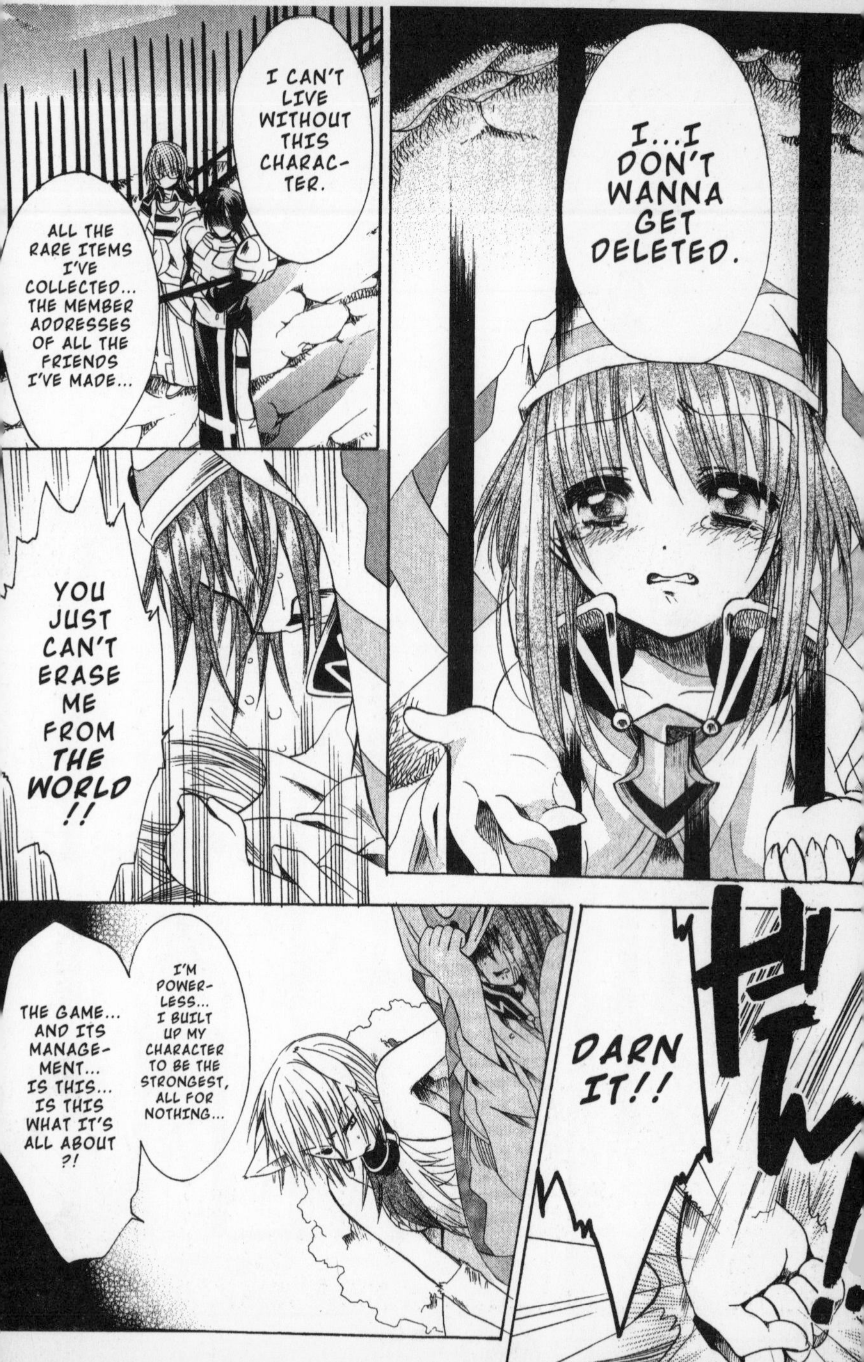
I...I DON'T WANNA GET DELETED.
I CAN'T LIVE WITHOUT THIS CHARACTER.
ALL THE RARE ITEMS I'VE COLLECTED... THE MEMBER ADDRESSES OF ALL THE FRIENDS I'VE MADE...
YOU JUST CAN'T ERASE ME FROM THE WORLD!!
DARN IT!!
I'M POWERLESS... I BUILT UP MY CHARACTER TO BE THE STRONGEST, ALL FOR NOTHING...
THE GAME... AND ITS MANAGEMENT... IS THIS... IS THIS WHAT IT'S ALL ABOUT?!

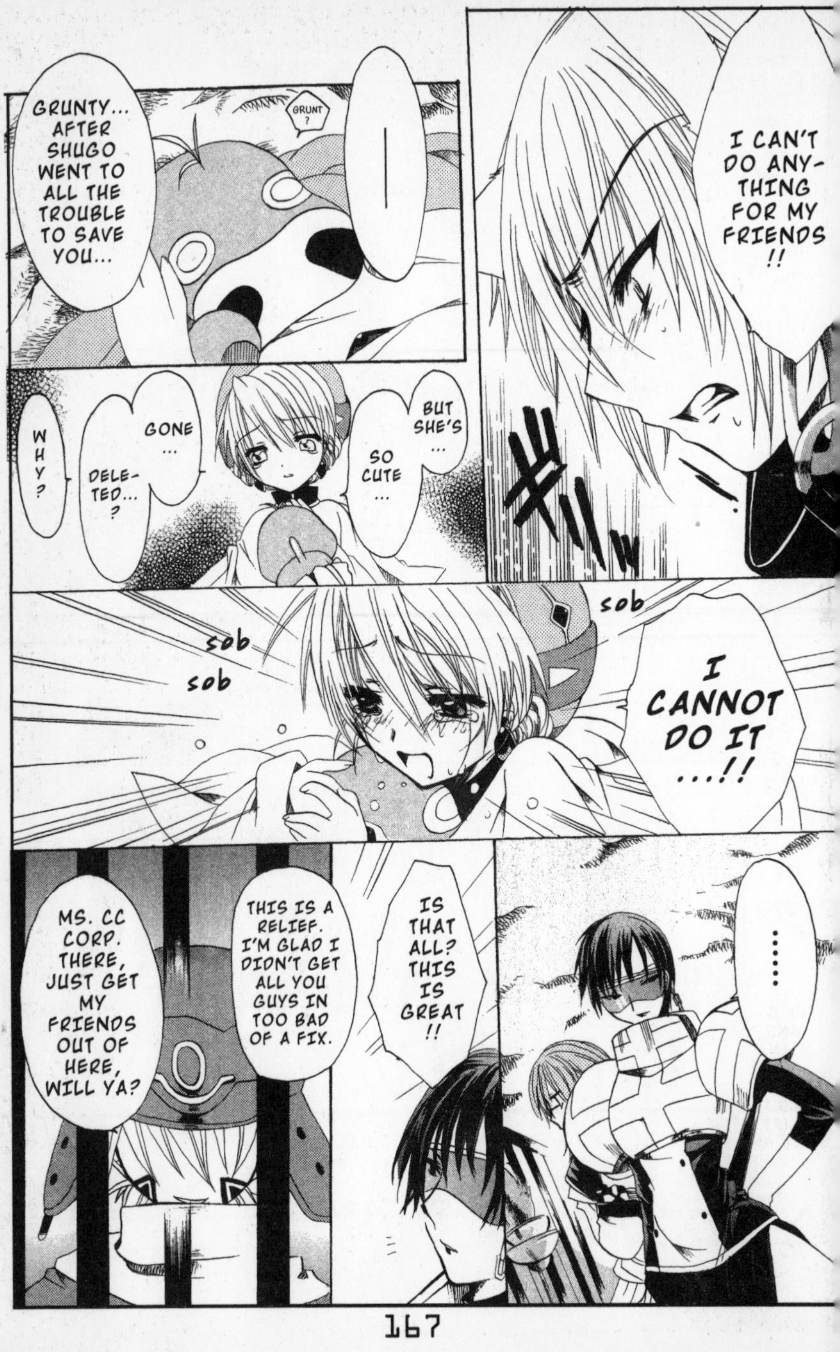
I CAN'T DO ANY-THING FOR MY FRIENDS!!
—
GRUNT?
GRUNTY... AFTER SHUGO WENT TO ALL THE TROUBLE TO SAVE YOU...
BUT SHE'S... SO CUTE...
GONE... DELETED...?
WHY?
sob
I CANNOT DO IT...!!
sob
sob
......
IS THAT ALL? THIS IS GREAT!!
THIS IS A RELIEF. I'M GLAD I DIDN'T GET ALL YOU GUYS IN TOO BAD OF A FIX.
MS. CC CORP. THERE, JUST GET MY FRIENDS OUT OF HERE, WILL YA?

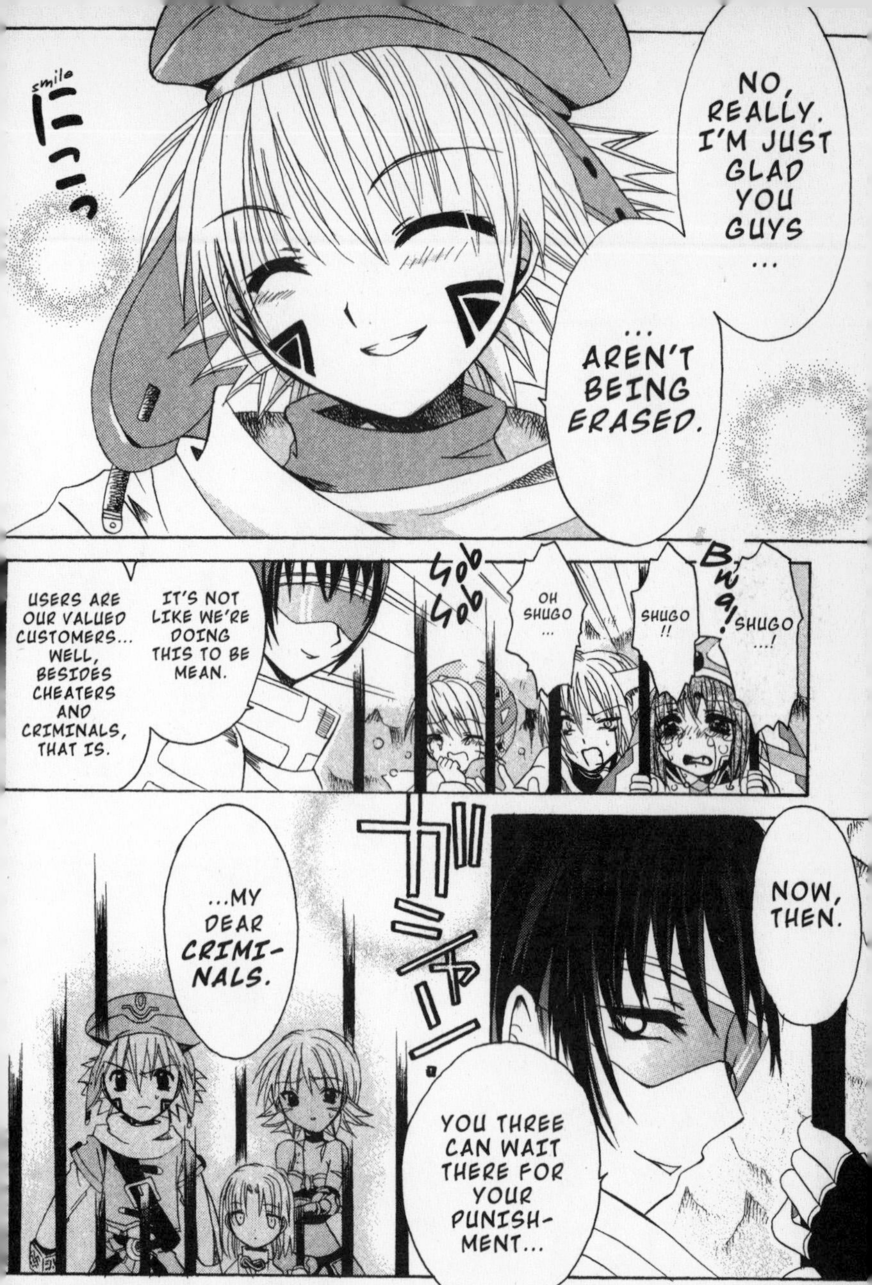
NO, REALLY. I'M JUST GLAD YOU GUYS ...
... AREN'T BEING ERASED.
smile
ニコっ
SHUGO ...!
Bwa!
SHUGO !!
OH SHUGO ...
Sob Sob
IT'S NOT LIKE WE'RE DOING THIS TO BE MEAN.
USERS ARE OUR VALUED CUSTOMERS... WELL, BESIDES CHEATERS AND CRIMINALS, THAT IS.
NOW, THEN.
YOU THREE CAN WAIT THERE FOR YOUR PUNISHMENT...
ガシャーン
...MY DEAR CRIMINALS.

NEW GENERATION ONLINE

THE WORLD

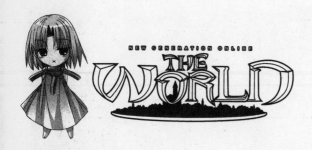

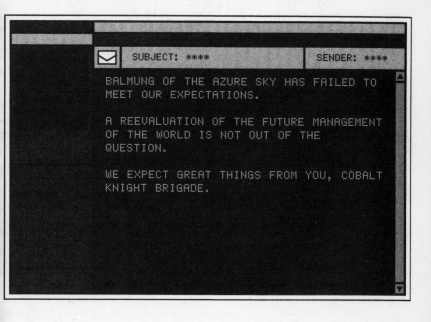

SUBJECT: ****     SENDER: ****

BALMUNG OF THE AZURE SKY HAS FAILED TO MEET OUR EXPECTATIONS.

A REEVALUATION OF THE FUTURE MANAGEMENT OF THE WORLD IS NOT OUT OF THE QUESTION.

WE EXPECT GREAT THINGS FROM YOU, COBALT KNIGHT BRIGADE.

# .hack //omake gallery

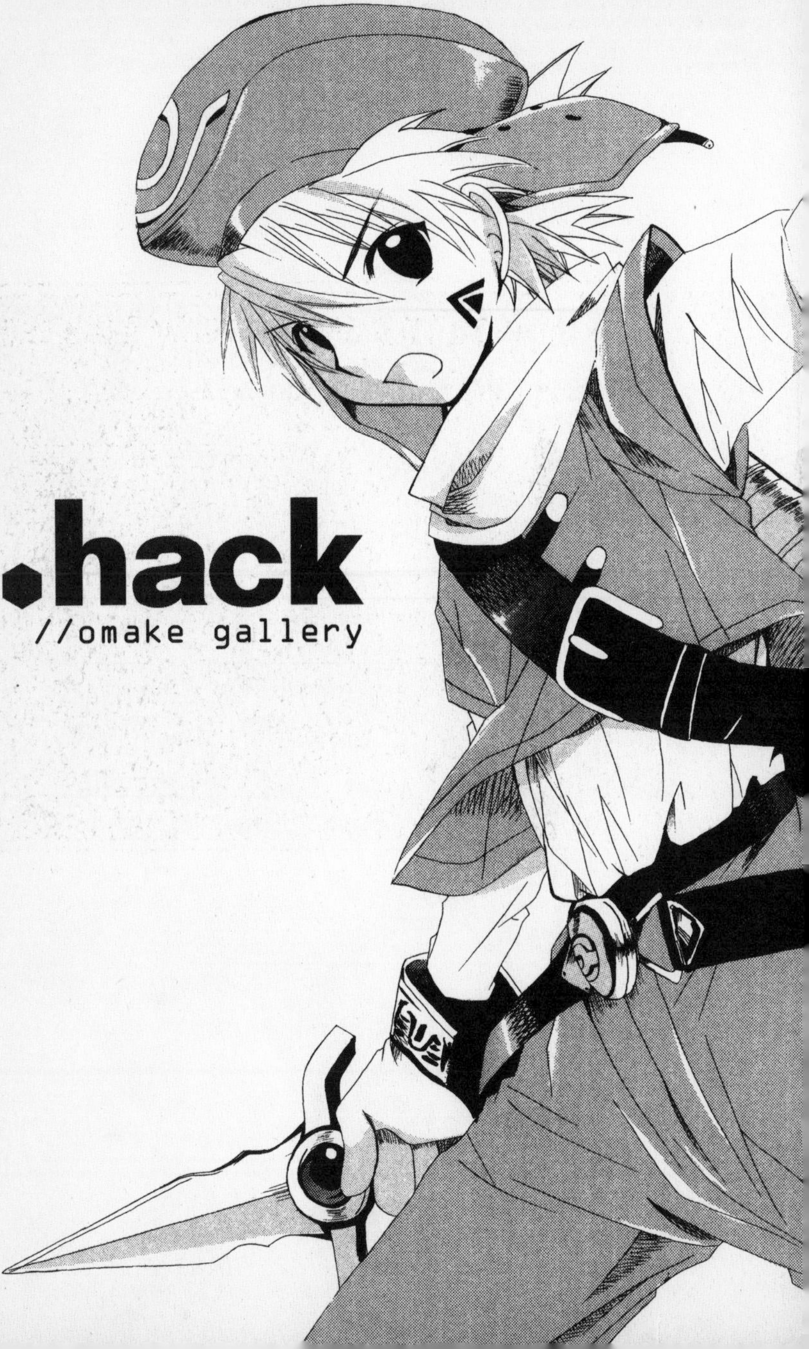

This has been such a joy to work on, having so many more people supporting me than during my work on the first volume... Plus having this made into a cartoon! I'm so glad I've had the chance to come into contact with such a great work as .hack, such great people to work with, and such great readers and fans. It makes me glad I've come this far in my career.

I hope you stick with me till the end!
See you again in Volume 3!

Volume 2 Staff
Mune Marino
Seiko Toda
Yuki Tanaka
saa
Akihiko Higuchi
Hirona
Yuki Kodama
Imai

Rei IZUMI

Thank you very much!

I'm sooo looking forward to Piroshi's serialization. I'm so happy. I love you!
Thank you, everyone who gave us comments for this volume!
Hamazaki, you're always there for me.
I love you!!

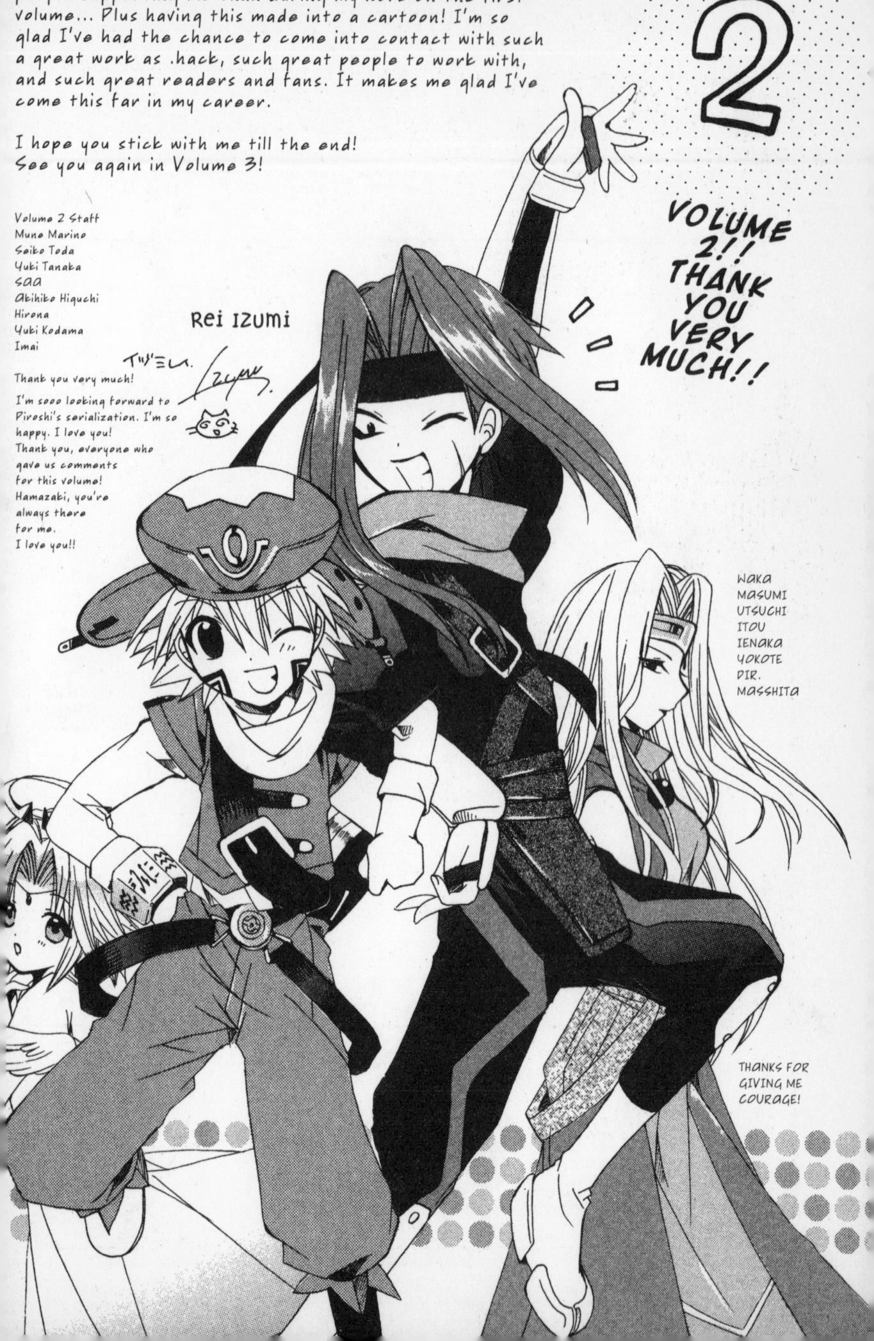
2
VOLUME 2!! THANK YOU VERY MUCH!!

Waka
Masumi
Utsuchi
Itou
Ienaka
Yokote
Dir. Masshita

THANKS FOR GIVING ME COURAGE!

# どっと吐く@コミック版
# DEEP SIGH @ COMIX

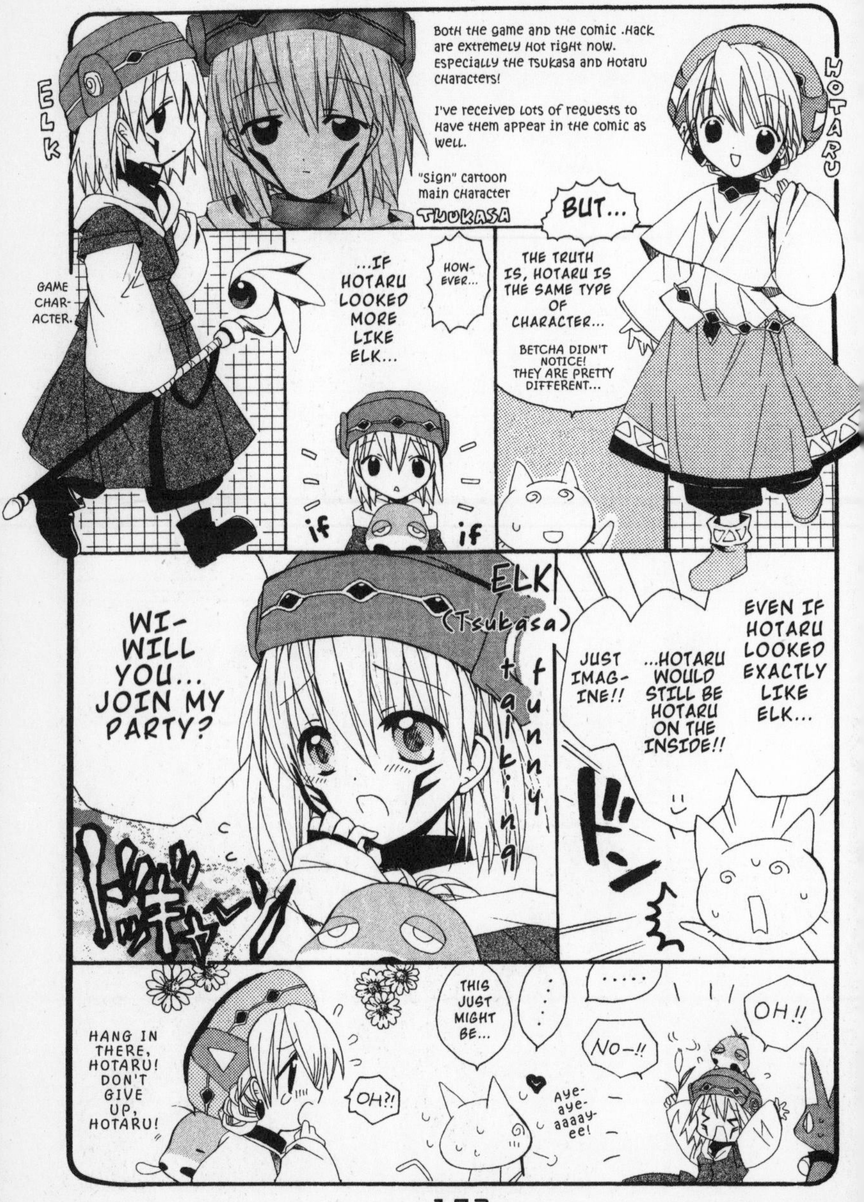
HOTARU
Both the game and the comic .Hack are extremely hot right now. Especially the Tsukasa and Hotaru characters!
I've received lots of requests to have them appear in the comic as well.
"sign" cartoon main character
TSUKASA
ELK
GAME CHARACTER.
BUT...
THE TRUTH IS, HOTARU IS THE SAME TYPE OF CHARACTER...
BETCHA DIDN'T NOTICE! THEY ARE PRETTY DIFFERENT...
HOW-EVER...
...IF HOTARU LOOKED MORE LIKE ELK...
if
if
EVEN IF HOTARU LOOKED EXACTLY LIKE ELK...
...HOTARU WOULD STILL BE HOTARU ON THE INSIDE!!
JUST IMAG-INE!!
ELK (Tsukasa)
talking funny
WI-WILL YOU... JOIN MY PARTY?
OH!!
No-!!
.....
...
THIS JUST MIGHT BE...
Aye-aye-aaaay-ee!
OH?!
HANG IN THERE, HOTARU! DON'T GIVE UP, HOTARU!

.hack//OUTTAKE

(WHEN MEDIAS COLLIDE!)

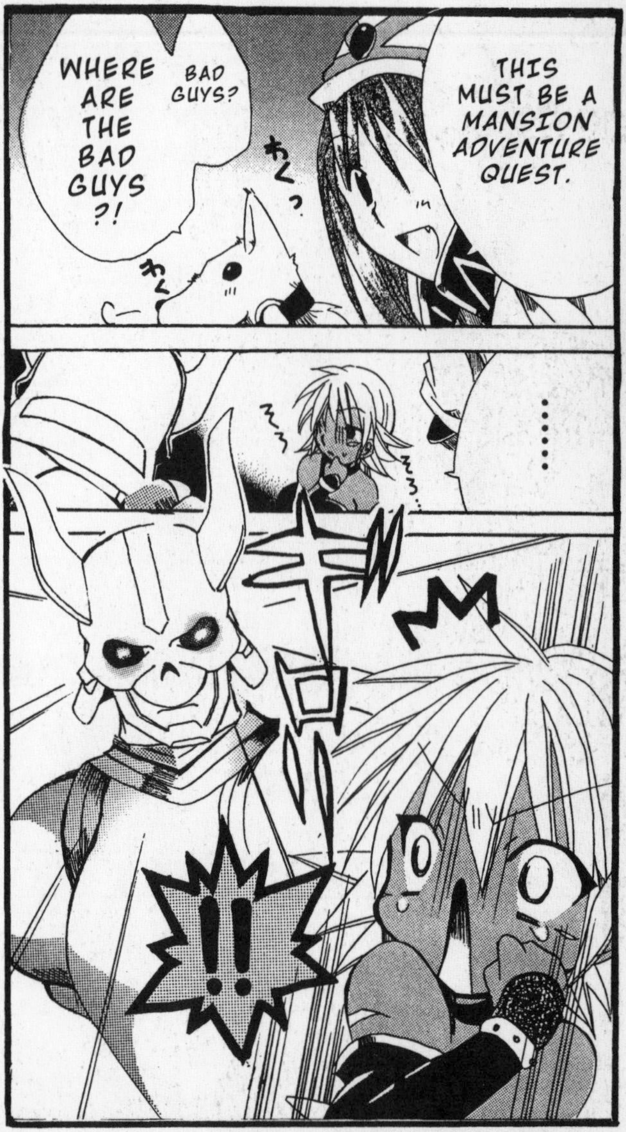
THIS MUST BE A MANSION ADVENTURE QUEST.
WHERE ARE THE BAD GUYS?!
BAD GUYS?
......
!!

Super-hot game version, .hack Volume 2 Cyber Connect 2
(Piroshi Matsuyama)

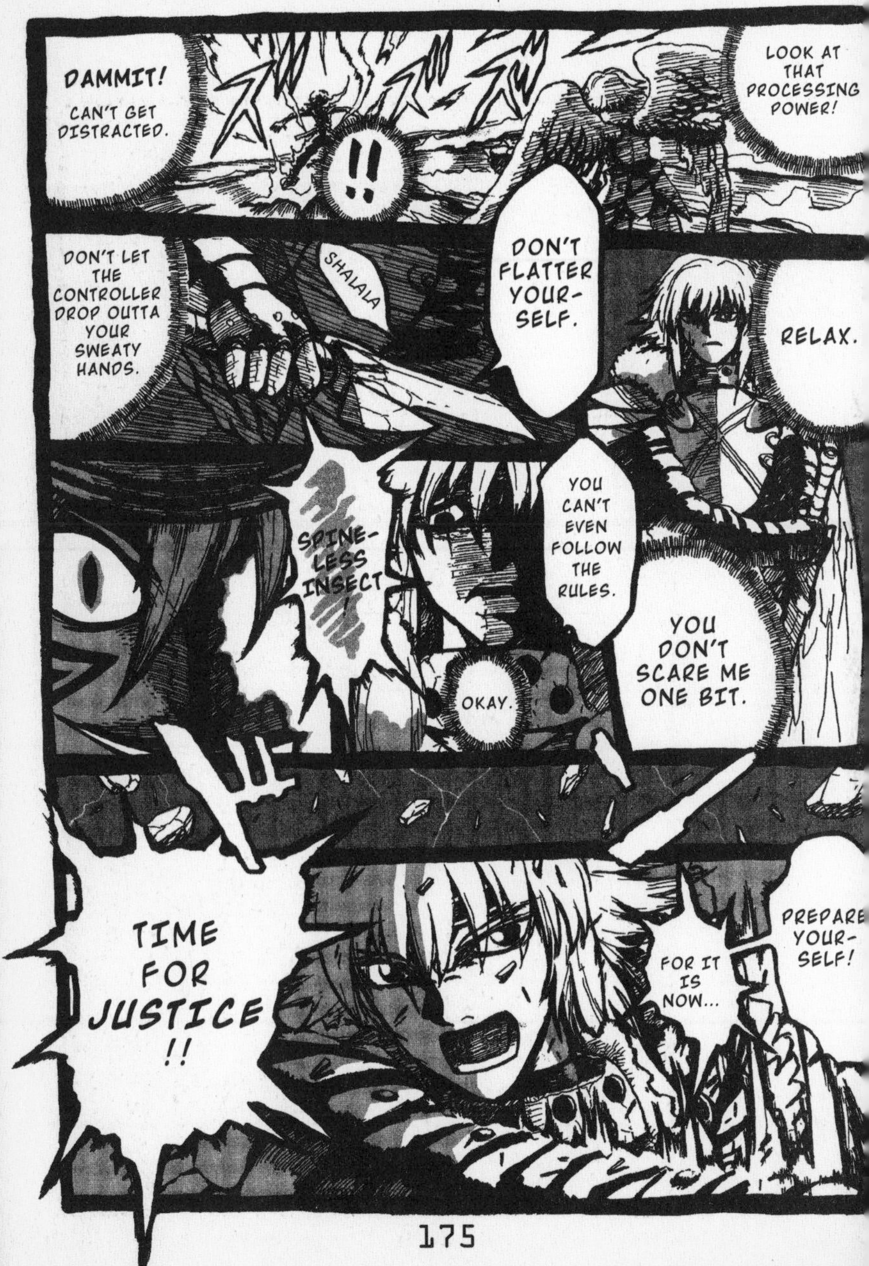
LOOK AT THAT PROCESSING POWER!
!!
DAMMIT!
CAN'T GET DISTRACTED.
RELAX.
DON'T FLATTER YOURSELF.
SHALALA
DON'T LET THE CONTROLLER DROP OUTTA YOUR SWEATY HANDS.
YOU CAN'T EVEN FOLLOW THE RULES.
YOU DON'T SCARE ME ONE BIT.
OKAY.
SPINELESS INSECT!
PREPARE YOURSELF!
FOR IT IS NOW...
TIME FOR JUSTICE!!

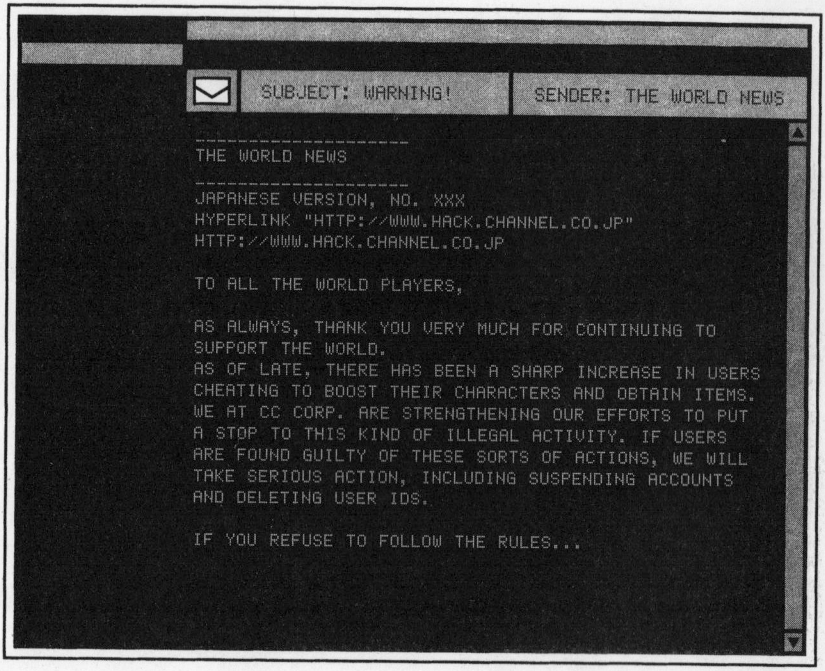
SUBJECT: WARNING!
SENDER: THE WORLD NEWS
--------------------
THE WORLD NEWS
--------------------
JAPANESE VERSION, NO. XXX
HYPERLINK "HTTP://WWW.HACK.CHANNEL.CO.JP"
HTTP://WWW.HACK.CHANNEL.CO.JP
TO ALL THE WORLD PLAYERS,
AS ALWAYS, THANK YOU VERY MUCH FOR CONTINUING TO SUPPORT THE WORLD.
AS OF LATE, THERE HAS BEEN A SHARP INCREASE IN USERS CHEATING TO BOOST THEIR CHARACTERS AND OBTAIN ITEMS. WE AT CC CORP. ARE STRENGTHENING OUR EFFORTS TO PUT A STOP TO THIS KIND OF ILLEGAL ACTIVITY. IF USERS ARE FOUND GUILTY OF THESE SORTS OF ACTIONS, WE WILL TAKE SERIOUS ACTION, INCLUDING SUSPENDING ACCOUNTS AND DELETING USER IDS.
IF YOU REFUSE TO FOLLOW THE RULES...

Kadokawa Comics A

# .hack
ドットハック//たそがれのうでわでんせつ
# //黄昏の腕輪伝説

2

漫画
IZUMI REI
依澄れい

原作
HAMAZAKI TATSUYA
浜崎達也

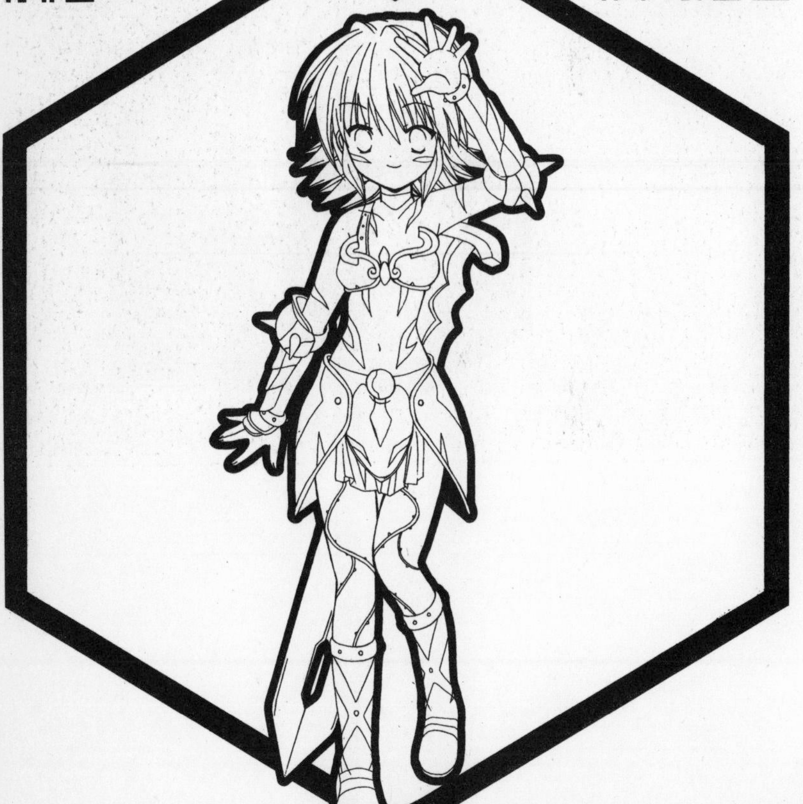

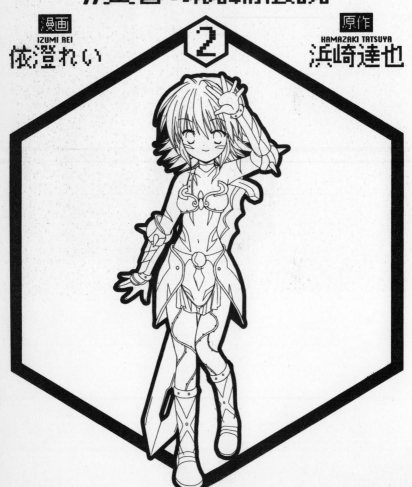

.hack
//黄昏の腕輪伝説
2

NEW GENERATION ONLINE

THE WORLD

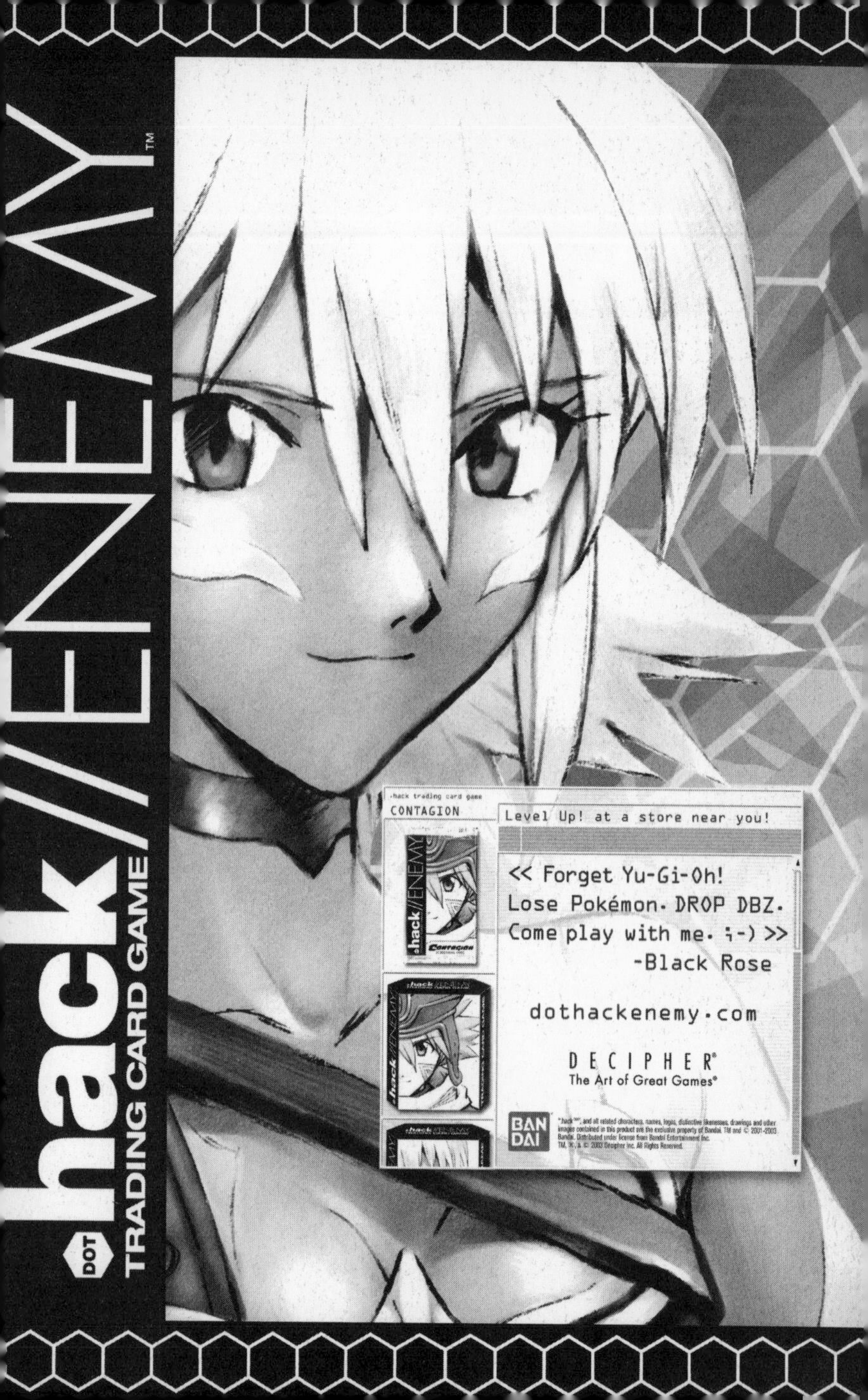

.hack//ENEMY™
TRADING CARD GAME
.hack trading card game
CONTAGION
Level Up! at a store near you!
<< Forget Yu-Gi-Oh!
Lose Pokémon. DROP DBZ.
Come play with me. ;-) >>
-Black Rose
dothackenemy.com
DECIPHER®
The Art of Great Games®
BANDAI
".hack", and all related characters, names, logos, distinctive likenesses, drawings and other images contained in this product are the exclusive property of Bandai. TM and © 2001-2003 Bandai. Distributed under license from Bandai Entertainment Inc.
TM, ®, & © 2003 Decipher Inc. All Rights Reserved.

Sgt. Frog © 2003 Mine Yoshizaki

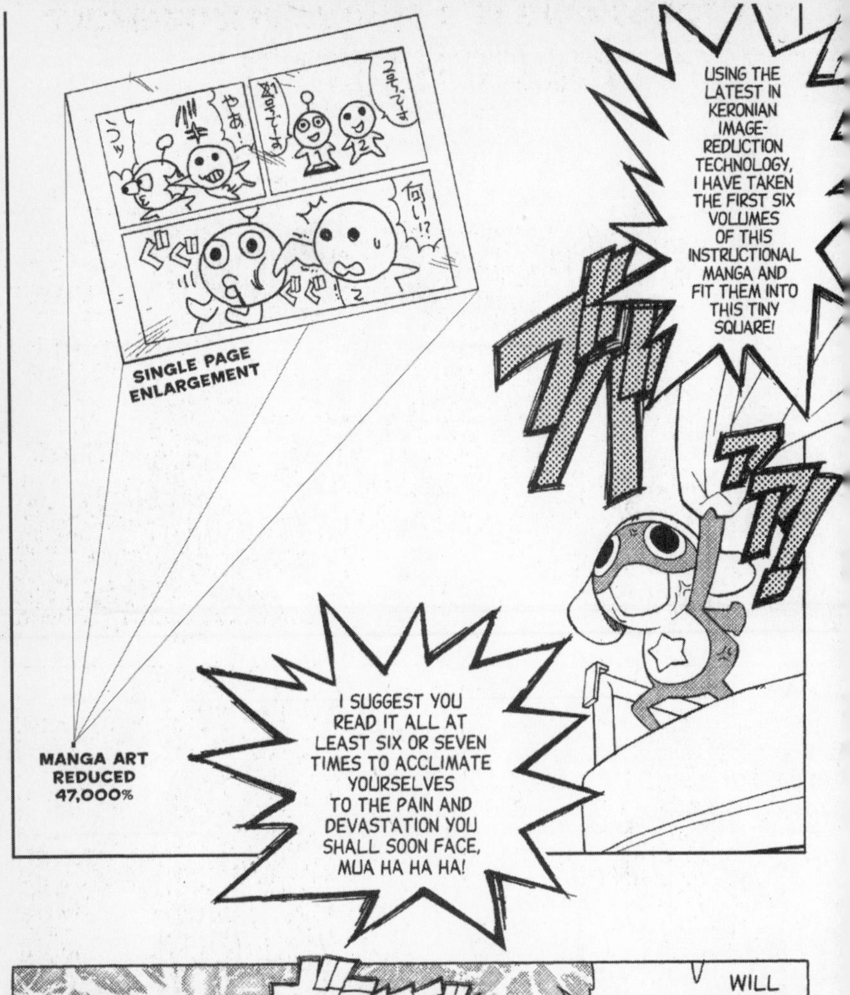
USING THE LATEST IN KERONIAN IMAGE-REDUCTION TECHNOLOGY, I HAVE TAKEN THE FIRST SIX VOLUMES OF THIS INSTRUCTIONAL MANGA AND FIT THEM INTO THIS TINY SQUARE!
SINGLE PAGE ENLARGEMENT
MANGA ART REDUCED 47,000%
I SUGGEST YOU READ IT ALL AT LEAST SIX OR SEVEN TIMES TO ACCLIMATE YOURSELVES TO THE PAIN AND DEVASTATION YOU SHALL SOON FACE, MUA HA HA HA!

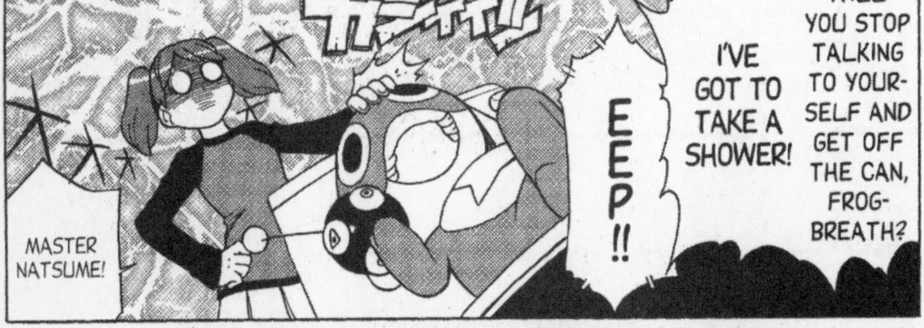
WILL YOU STOP TALKING TO YOURSELF AND GET OFF THE CAN, FROG-BREATH?
I'VE GOT TO TAKE A SHOWER!
EEP!!
MASTER NATSUME!

**COMING TO EARTH MARCH 2004**

# 白 姫 抄
## SHIRAHIME-SYO

*When It Snows, Anything Is Possible!*

*Five Magical Tales In One Manga from CLAMP.*

**Special Hardcover Edition**

**SRP $19.99**

**100% AUTHENTIC MANGA**

**Coming December 2003 To Your Favorite Book & Comic Stores.**

STEALING IS EASY - DECIDING
WHAT TO TAKE IS HARD.

AVAILABLE NOW AT YOUR FAVORITE
BOOK AND COMIC STORES

TEEN
AGE 13+

www.TOKYOPOP.com

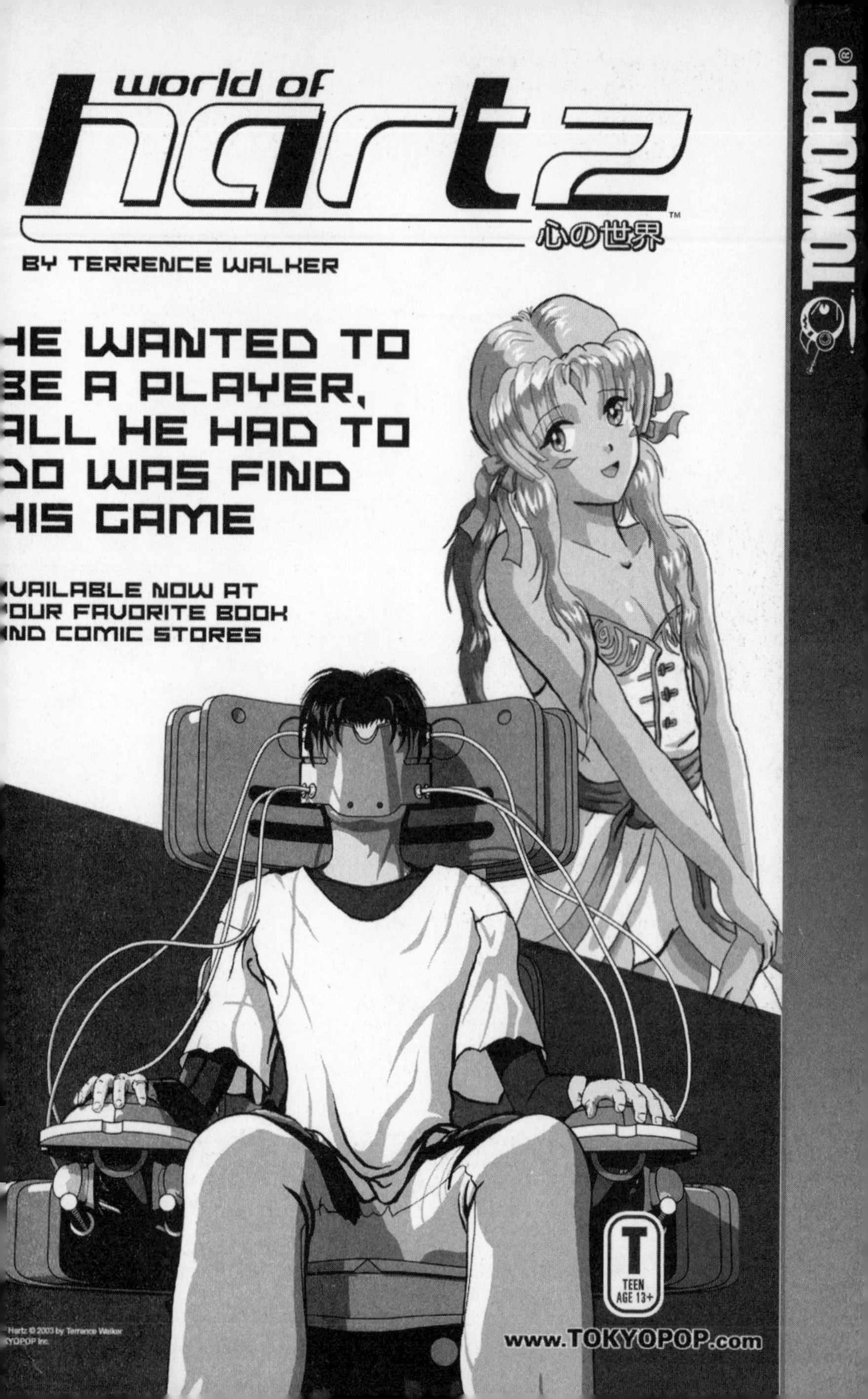

world of
hartz
心の世界™
BY TERRENCE WALKER
HE WANTED TO
BE A PLAYER,
ALL HE HAD TO
DO WAS FIND
HIS GAME
AVAILABLE NOW AT
YOUR FAVORITE BOOK
AND COMIC STORES
TOKYOPOP
T
TEEN
AGE 13+
Hartz © 2003 by Terrence Walker
KYOPOP Inc.
www.TOKYOPOP.com

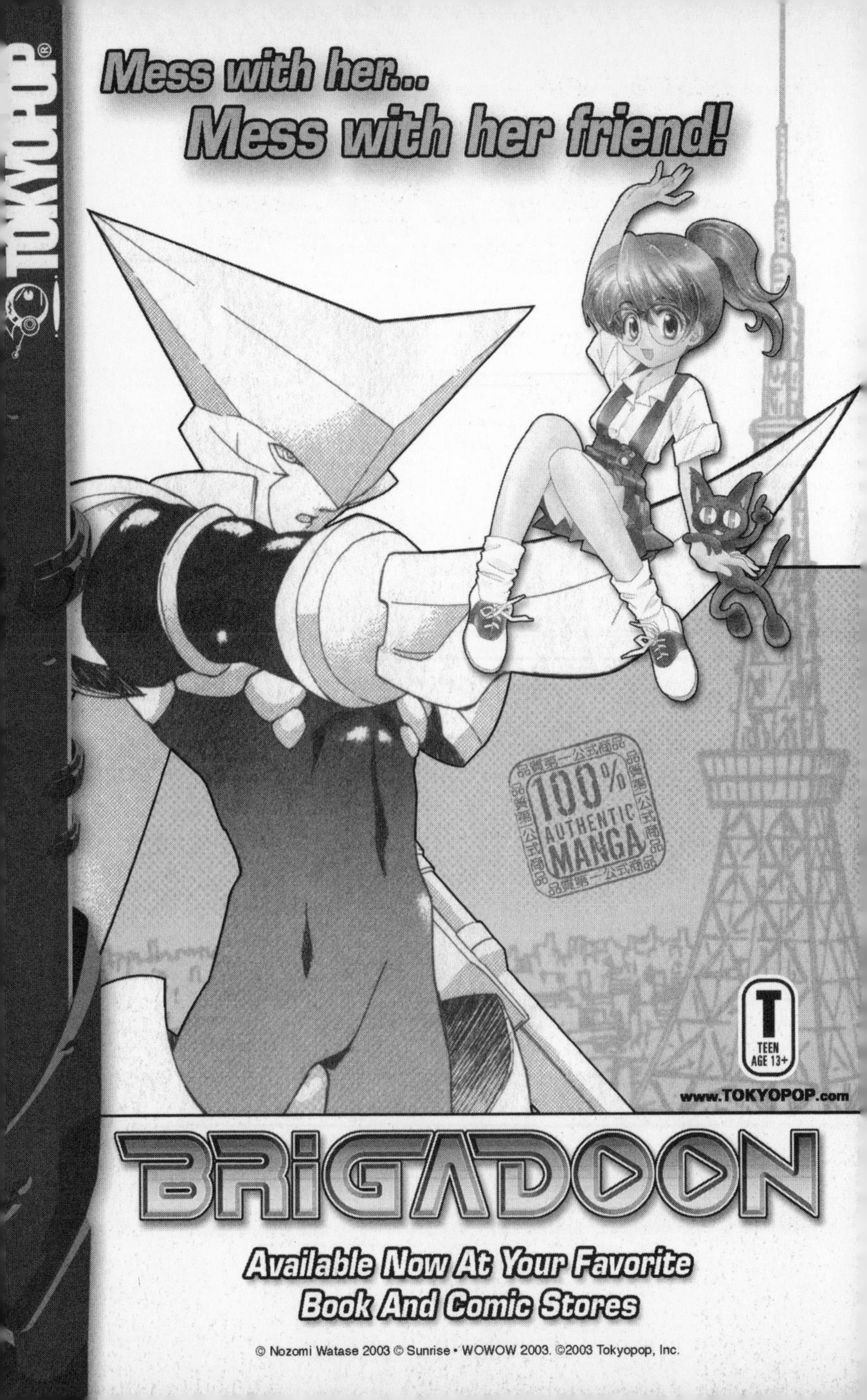
TOKYOPOP®
Mess with her...
Mess with her friend!
100% AUTHENTIC MANGA
T
TEEN
AGE 13+
www.TOKYOPOP.com
BRIGADOON
Available Now At Your Favorite
Book And Comic Stores
© Nozomi Watase 2003 © Sunrise • WOWOW 2003. ©2003 Tokyopop, Inc.

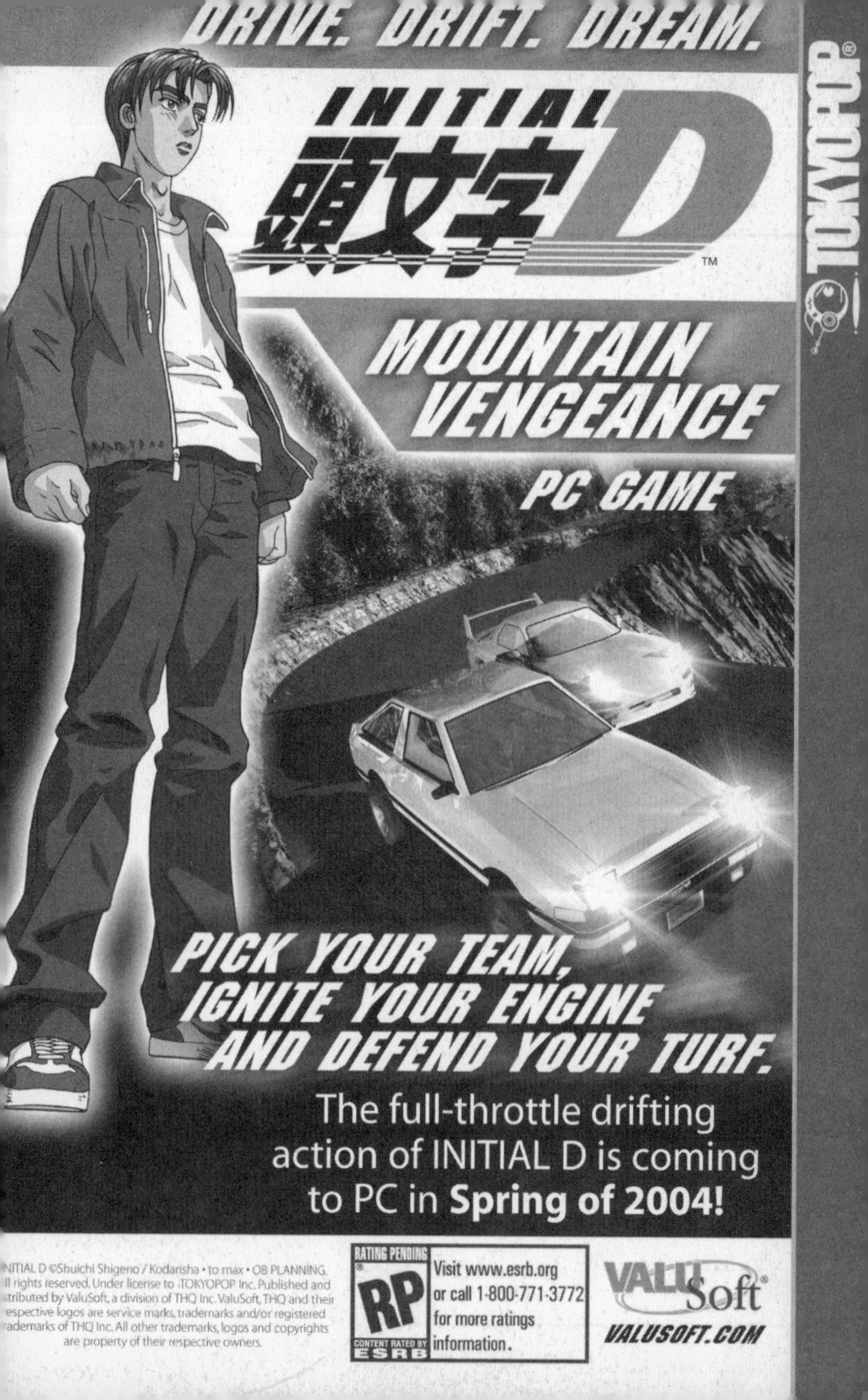
DRIVE. DRIFT. DREAM.
INITIAL 頭文字 D™
TOKYOPOP®
MOUNTAIN VENGEANCE
PC GAME
PICK YOUR TEAM, IGNITE YOUR ENGINE AND DEFEND YOUR TURF.
The full-throttle drifting action of INITIAL D is coming to PC in Spring of 2004!
NITIAL D ©Shuichi Shigeno / Kodansha • to max • OB PLANNING. ll rights reserved. Under license to TOKYOPOP Inc. Published and stributed by ValuSoft, a division of THQ Inc. ValuSoft, THQ and their espective logos are service marks, trademarks and/or registered ademarks of THQ Inc. All other trademarks, logos and copyrights are property of their respective owners.
RATING PENDING
RP
CONTENT RATED BY ESRB
Visit www.esrb.org or call 1-800-771-3772 for more ratings information.
VALUSoft®
VALUSOFT.COM

# PLANETES

By Makoto Yukimura

## Hachi Needed Time...
## What He Found Was Space

**100% AUTHENTIC MANGA**

品質第一公式商品

## A Sci-Fi Saga About
## Personal Conquest

## Coming Soon to Your Favorite
## Book and Comic Stores.

**T** TEEN AGE 13+

**www.TOKYOPOP.c**

TOKYOPOP

# CHRONICLES OF THE
# CURSED SWORD

## BY YUY BEOP-RYONG

A living sword forged in darkness
A hero born outside the light
One can destroy the other
But both can save the world

**Available Now At Your Favorite
Book And Comic Stores.**

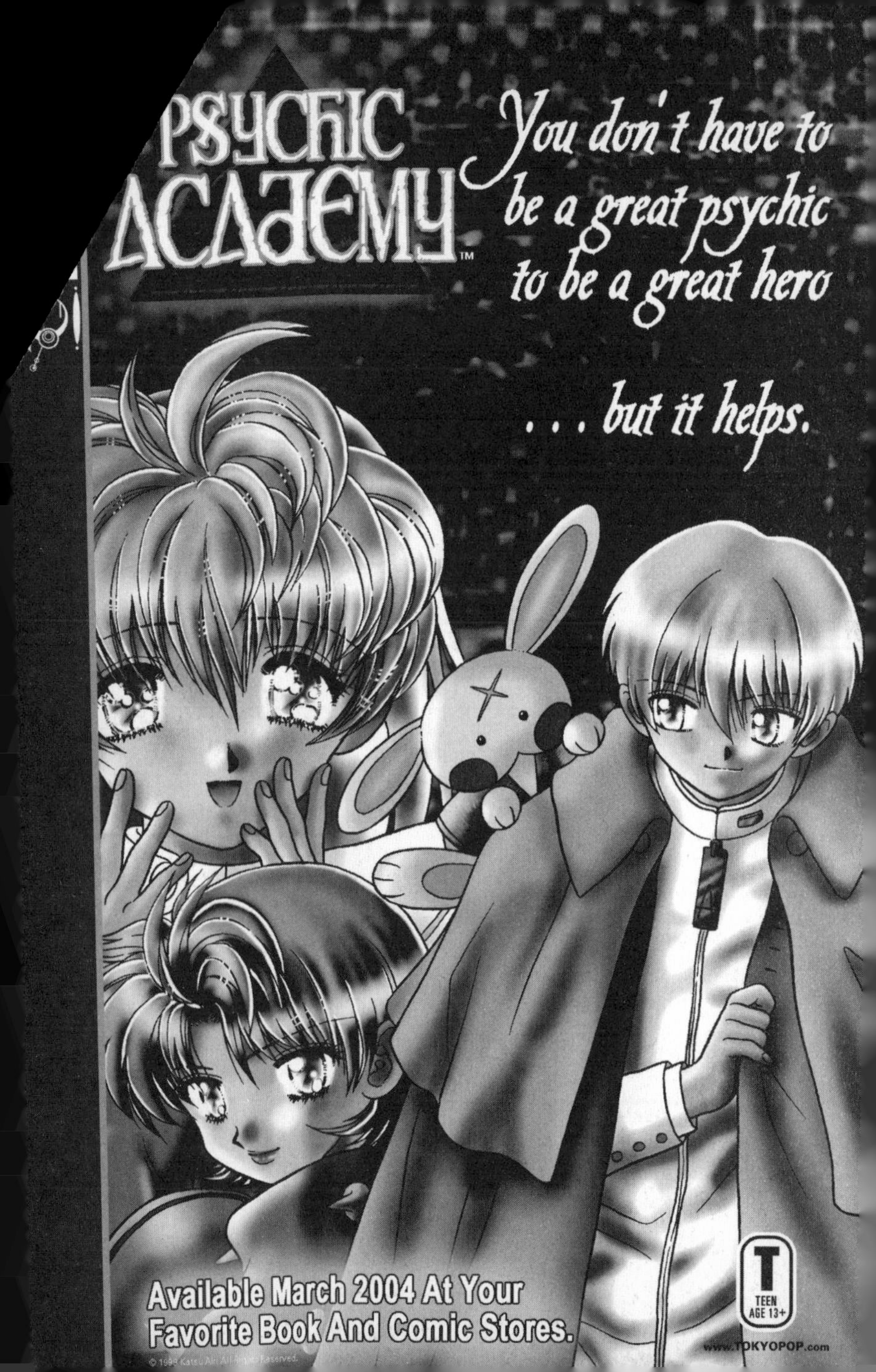
PSYCHIC ACADEMY™
You don't have to be a great psychic to be a great hero
. . . but it helps.
Available March 2004 At Your Favorite Book And Comic Stores.
T TEEN AGE 13+
www.TOKYOPOP.com

# ALSO AVAILABLE FROM ☜TOKYOPOP®

REALITY CHECK
REBIRTH
REBOUND
REMOTE June 2004
RISING STARS OF MANGA December 2003
SABER MARIONETTE J
SAILOR MOON
SAINT TAIL
SAIYUKI
SAMURAI DEEPER KYO
SAMURAI GIRL REAL BOUT HIGH SCHOOL
SCRYED
SGT. FROG March 2004
SHAOLIN SISTERS
SHIRAHIME-SYO: SNOW GODDESS TALES December 2004
SHUTTERBOX
SNOW DROP January 2004
SOKORA REFUGEES  May 2004
SORCEROR HUNTERS
SUIKODEN May 2004
SUKI February 2004
THE CANDIDATE FOR GODDESS April 2004
THE DEMON ORORON  April 2004
THE LEGEND OF CHUN HYANG
THE SKULL MAN
THE VISION OF ESCAFLOWNE
TOKYO MEW MEW
TREASURE CHESS  March 2004
UNDER THE GLASS MOON
VAMPIRE GAME
WILD ACT
WISH
WORLD OF HARTZ
X-DAY
ZODIAC P.I.

## NOVELS

KARMA CLUB APRIL 2004
SAILOR MOON

## ART BOOKS

CARDCAPTOR SAKURA
MAGIC KNIGHT RAYEARTH
PEACH GIRL ART BOOK January 2004

## ANIME GUIDES

COWBOY BEBOP ANIME GUIDES
GUNDAM TECHNICAL MANUALS
SAILOR MOON SCOUT GUIDES

## CINE-MANGA™

CARDCAPTORS
FAIRLY ODD PARENTS MARCH 2004
FINDING NEMO
G.I. JOE SPY TROOPS
JACKIE CHAN ADVENTURES
KIM POSSIBLE
LIZZIE MCGUIRE
POWER RANGERS: NINJA STORM
SPONGEBOB SQUAREPANTS
SPY KIDS
SPY KIDS 3-D March 2004
THE ADVENTURES OF JIMMY NEUTRON: BOY GENIUS
TRANSFORMERS: ARMADA
TRANSFORMERS: ENERGON May 2004

## TOKYOPOP KIDS

STRAY SHEEP

# For more
# information visit
# www.TOKYOPOP.com

# ALSO AVAILABLE FROM TOKYOPOP®

## MANGA

.HACK//LEGEND OF THE TWILIGHT
@LARGE
A.I. LOVE YOU February 2004
AI YORI AOSHI January 2004
ANGELIC LAYER
BABY BIRTH
BATTLE ROYALE
BATTLE VIXENS April 2004
BIRTH May 2004
BRAIN POWERED
BRIGADOON
B'TX January 2004
CARDCAPTOR SAKURA
CARDCAPTOR SAKURA - MASTER OF THE CLOW
CARDCAPTOR SAKURA: BOXED SET COLLECTION 1
CARDCAPTOR SAKURA: BOXED SET COLLECTION 2
    March 2004
CHOBITS
CHRONICLES OF THE CURSED SWORD
CLAMP SCHOOL DETECTIVES
CLOVER
COMIC PARTY June 2004
CONFIDENTIAL CONFESSIONS
CORRECTOR YUI
COWBOY BEBOP: BOXED SET THE COMPLETE
    COLLECTION
CRESCENT MOON May 2004
CREST OF THE STARS June 2004
CYBORG 009
DEMON DIARY
DIGIMON
DIGIMON SERIES 3 April 2004
DIGIMON ZERO TWO February 2004
DNANGEL April 2004
DOLL May 2004
DRAGON HUNTER
DRAGON KNIGHTS
DUKLYON: CLAMP SCHOOL DEFENDERS:
DV June 2004
ERICA SAKURAZAWA
FAERIES' LANDING January 2004
FAKE
FLCL
FORBIDDEN DANCE
FRUITS BASKET February 2004
G GUNDAM
GATEKEEPERS
GETBACKERS February 2004
GHOST! March 2004
GIRL GOT GAME January 2004
GRAVITATION
GTO

GUNDAM WING
GUNDAM WING: BATTLEFIELD OF PACIFISTS
GUNDAM WING: ENDLESS WALTZ
GUNDAM WING: THE LAST OUTPOST
HAPPY MANIA
HARLEM BEAT
I.N.V.U.
INITIAL D
ISLAND
JING: KING OF BANDITS
JULINE
JUROR 13 March 2004
KARE KANO
KILL ME, KISS ME February 2004
KINDAICHI CASE FILES, THE
KING OF HELL
KODOCHA: SANA'S STAGE
LAMENT OF THE LAMB May 2004
LES BIJOUX February 2004
LIZZIE MCGUIRE
LOVE HINA
LUPIN III
LUPIN III SERIES 2
MAGIC KNIGHT RAYEARTH I
MAGIC KNIGHT RAYEARTH II February 2004
MAHOROMATIC: AUTOMATIC MAIDEN May 2004
MAN OF MANY FACES
MARMALADE BOY
MARS
METEOR METHUSELA June 2004
METROID June 2004
MINK April 2004
MIRACLE GIRLS
MIYUKI-CHAN IN WONDERLAND
MODEL May 2004
NELLY MUSIC MANGA April 2004
ONE April 2004
PARADISE KISS
PARASYTE
PEACH GIRL
PEACH GIRL CHANGE OF HEART
PEACH GIRL RELAUNCH BOX SET
PET SHOP OF HORRORS
PITA-TEN January 2004
PLANET LADDER February 2004
PLANETES
PRIEST
PRINCESS AI April 2004
PSYCHIC ACADEMY March 2004
RAGNAROK
RAGNAROK: BOXED SET COLLECTION 1
RAVE MASTER
RAVE MASTER: BOXED SET March 2004

10103

# STOP!

## This is the back of the book.
## You wouldn't want to spoil a great ending!

This book is printed "manga-style," in the authentic Japanese right-to-left format. Since none of the artwork has been flipped or altered, readers get to experience the story just as the creator intended. You've been asking for it, so TOKYOPOP® delivered: authentic, hot-off-the-press, and far more fun!

# DIRECTIONS

If this is your first time reading manga-style, here's a quick guide to help you understand how it works.

It's easy... just start in the top right panel and follow the numbers. Have fun, and look for more 100% authentic manga from TOKYOPOP®!